D0212296

entrepreneurship

THE ART, SCIENCE, AND PROCESS FOR SUCCESS

second edition

Charles E. Bamford
University of Notre Dame

Garry D. Bruton
Texas Christian University

USED BOOKS
College Store
Sacramento City College
Sell your books on campus
during finals

McGraw Hill Education

ENTREPRENEURSHIP: THE ART, SCIENCE, AND PROCESS FOR SUCCESS, SECOND EDITION

Published by McGraw-Hill Education, 2 Penn Plaza, New York, NY 10121. Copyright ©2016 by McGraw-Hill Education. All rights reserved. Printed in the United States of America. Previous editions ©2011. No part of this publication may be reproduced or distributed in any form or by any means, or stored in a database or retrieval system, without the prior written consent of McGraw-Hill Education, including, but not limited to, in any network or other electronic storage or transmission, or broadcast for distance learning.

Some ancillaries, including electronic and print components, may not be available to customers outside the United States.

This book is printed on acid-free paper.

3 4 5 6 7 8 9 LMN 21 20 19 18 17 16

ISBN 978-0-07-802318-7
MHID 0-07-802318-1

Senior Vice President, Products & Markets: *Kurt L. Strand*
Vice President, General Manager, Products & Markets: *Michael Ryan*
Vice President, Content Design & Delivery: *Kimberly Meriwether David*
Managing Director: *Susan Gouijnstook*
Senior Brand Manager: *Anke Weekes*
Director, Product Development: *Meghan Campbell*
Senior Product Developer: *Laura Griffin*
Marketing Manager: *Michael Gedatus*
Marketing Specialist: *Liz Steiner*
Digital Product Analyst: *Kerry Shanahan*
Director, Content Design & Delivery: *Terri Schiesl*
Executive Program Manager: *Mary Conzachi*
Content Project Managers: *Danielle Clement, Judi David*
Buyer: *Carol A. Bielski*
Senior Designer: *Srdjan Savanovic*
Lead Content Licensing Specialists: *Keri Johnson*
Cover Image: Background: © Alexander Chernyakov/Getty Images, Coaster: © seewhatmitchsee/Getty Images; Glass: © Lauri Patterson/Getty Images
Compositor: *Lumina Datamatics, Inc.*
Printer: LSC Communications

All credits appearing on page or at the end of the book are considered to be an extension of the copyright page.

Library of Congress Cataloging-in-Publication Data

Bamford, Charles E.
Entrepreneurship: The art, science, and process for success / Charles E. Bamford, Garry D. Bruton. —Second edition.
pages cm
Revised edition of the authors' Entrepreneurship: A small business approach, 1st ed., published in 2011.
Includes bibliographical references and index.
ISBN 978-0-07-802318-7
1. New business enterprises. 2. Small business. 3. Success in business. I. Bruton, Garry D. II. Title.
HD62.5.B36 2016
658.1'1—dc23

2014040557

The Internet addresses listed in the text were accurate at the time of publication. The inclusion of a website does not indicate an endorsement by the authors or McGraw-Hill Education, and McGraw-Hill Education does not guarantee the accuracy of the information presented at these sites.

www.mhhe.com

dedication

To my family for all the support and fun we have together: my wife, Yvonne; sons, Rob and Sean; daughter, Ada; daughter-in-law, Jane; son-in-law, Andrew; and our grandson, Silas.

Charles E. Bamford

To my parents, John C. and Ruth W. Bruton, who empowered me with their love, encouragement, and support throughout their lives.

Garry D. Bruton

about the authors

© Charles E. Bamford

CHARLES ("CHUCK") E. BAMFORD is the managing partner of Bamford Associates, LLC., a firm focused on the development of implementable strategic plans and an entrepreneurial orientation to growth.

He is an adjunct professor of strategy and entrepreneurship at the University of Notre Dame where he has won the EMBA Professor of the Year Award three times.

Dr. Bamford worked in M&A / Business Analysis for twelve years prior to pursuing his PhD. A regular speaker at conferences trade shows and conventions, he is the author of five textbooks used by businesses and universities throughout the globe.

His writings include regular contributions to news organizations and his first fiction novel *Some Things Are Never Forgiven* (Penguin Press).

Chuck's research has been published in the *Strategic Management Journal, Journal of Business Venturing, Entrepreneurship Theory & Practice, Journal of Business Research, Journal of Business Strategies, Journal of Managerial Issues, Journal of Technology Transfer,* and *Journal of Small Business Management,* among others.

Chuck has taught courses in strategy and entrepreneurship at the undergraduate, graduate, and executive levels. His teaching experience includes courses taught at universities in Scotland, Hungary, and the Czech Republic. He has been a professor at the University of Notre Dame, Queens University of Charlotte, University of Richmond, Texas Christian University, and Tulane University. He has won eighteen teaching excellence awards including nine Executive MBA Professor of the Year Awards. He is a Noble Foundation Fellow in Teaching Excellence.

Chuck earned his B.S. degree at the University of Virginia (McIntire School of Commerce), an MBA at Virginia Tech, and a PhD in strategy and entrepreneurship at the University of Tennessee.

© Texas Christian University
Neeley School of Business

GARRY D. BRUTON is a professor of entrepreneurship and strategy at the M. J. Neeley School of Business at Texas Christian University in Fort Worth, Texas. He received his BA with Honors from the University of Oklahoma, an MBA from George Washington University, and a PhD from Oklahoma State University in 1989. Garry worked as a bank economist for one of the leading commercial banks in the southwest United States prior to pursuing his doctorate.

Dr. Bruton has published or has forthcoming over 100 academic articles in some of the leading academic publications for small business and entrepreneurship, including the *Academy of Management Journal, Strategic Management Journal, Journal of International Business, Journal of Business Venturing,* and *Entrepreneurship Theory & Practice.* Garry currently serves as a senior editor for the *Journal of Management Studies* and as an associate editor of the *Strategic Entrepreneurship Journal.* He is also the past president of the Asia Academy of Management and serves on five additional editorial boards. His research interests focus on entrepreneurship in emerging economies.

Garry's publications have been used in some of the leading MBA programs around the world, and his writings have appeared in the *Wall Street Journal.* He was selected as the first holder of the Kathryn and Craig Hall Distinguished Chair in Entrepreneurship in 2005, sponsored by the Fulbright Program.

Garry has taught around the world, including courses in Russia, Vienna, Austria, in multiple locations in China and in Hong Kong, Korea, France, and Poland. The courses he has taught at the graduate and undergraduate levels have included small business management, entrepreneurship, venture capital, international strategy, strategy, and international management. Currently he is an honorary professor at Sun Yat-sen University – China, Jilin University – China, and the South China University of Technology.

He has won a variety of teaching and research awards at each of the schools with which he has been associated. In addition, he has advised a number of MBA teams that have participated and placed in regional and national competitions for business plans and case analysis.

brief table of contents

Preface vii

PART 1 Laying the Groundwork for Small Business

Chapter 1 THE TWENTY-FIRST-CENTURY ENTREPRENEUR 2

Chapter 2 INDIVIDUAL LEADERSHIP AND ENTREPRENEURIAL START-UPS 18

Chapter 3 BUSINESS IDEA GENERATION AND INITIAL EVALUATION 36

PART 2 Due Diligence on the Business Idea

Chapter 4 EXTERNAL ANALYSIS 56

Chapter 5 BUSINESS MISSION AND STRATEGY 76

Chapter 6 ANALYZING CASH FLOW AND OTHER FINANCIAL INFORMATION 96

PART 3 Establishing the Business

Chapter 7 FINANCING AND ACCOUNTING 118

Chapter 8 FINANCIAL ANALYSIS 136

Chapter 9 ESTABLISHING THE LEGAL FOUNDATION 156

PART 4 Building the Business

Chapter 10 HUMAN RESOURCES MANAGEMENT 176

Chapter 11 MARKETING 196

Chapter 12 ESTABLISHING OPERATIONS 214

PART 5 Important Issues for Entrpreneurs

Chapter 13 EXIT/HARVEST/TURNAROUND 234

Chapter 14 FRANCHISING AND PURCHASING AN EXISTING BUSINESS 254

PART 6 MiniCases

Appendix 300
Glossary 315
Case Index 319
Subject Index 320

preface

Crafting the second edition of this book was both a pleasure and a challenge. The overwhelming goal of the book is to emphasize three core tenets to starting an entrepreneurial venture:

1. *Science* of practice as the heart of starting and running a successful entrepreneurial venture.
2. *Art* of turning an entrepreneurial venture into a success.
3. *Processes* that tie these two areas together into a coherent and organized business.

The first tenet is that the *science* of practice is central to your success as an entrepreneur. There is an inherent belief by many potential entrepreneurs that they know what needs to be done. However, extensive research suggests that one of the biggest causes of entrepreneurial failure is a lack of knowledge about how to design and build a business. The business that seems so clear to the entrepreneur turns out quite differently. The result is that a lack of knowledge leads to the entrepreneurial venture running out of cash and time.

This book presents a systematic and thorough means for students and potential entrepreneurs to think through their venture and the rich range of concerns around it. Extensive research has been going on in this area for decades, and we know a lot more about what works and what does not work. One of the significant goals of this text is to provide you with information about what really works. Without trying to overwhelm the reader with research citations, but also ensuring that the student has well-researched information, this text is grounded in the academic research with a practitioner view to everything that is done.

The second tenet is that there is a lot of *art* to the concept, design, and implementation effort required to start a new business. To teach the art we present what other entrepreneurs have done in the past, so students can consider what they would like to have as their own approach. In this text we provide a great variety of real-world examples.

To fulfill this real worldview of entrepreneurship as an art, you will find that each chapter starts with a story about a successful entrepreneur and how he or she grew their business. Additionally, you will find throughout the text two running cases that provide direct, applicable context to the chapter contents. The first running case is that of **Friends' Home Health Care**. Friends' Home Health Care was created by two friends to provide better, more sophisticated, and more reliable home health care in their community. The second running case is a family business called **Flow Right Brewery & Bar: A Family Affair**. This running case follows the development, design, troubles, and start-up of a family business. Finally, we have included fourteen MiniCases at the end of the book where we personally interviewed entrepreneurs about their story. Each MiniCase finishes with advice from the entrepreneur and questions to consider about applying the MiniCase learning to the development of your own business.

The third tenet of our approach involves the *processes* of conceptualizing, designing, starting, and running a new business. Hundreds of things must be considered, analyzed, and completed to take an idea to a successful business. We firmly believe that these processes are crucial steps along the way and have built this book in a manner that allows the reader to build upon each concept by developing a process that results in a fully crafted plan by the time you finish the book.

The ability to apply the science, art, and process of entrepreneurship developed here, we argue, will lay the foundation for succeeding in entrepreneurship. We say proudly that the overarching desire of this book, *Entrepreneurship: The Art, Science, and Process for Success,* is that students establish highly successful and very profitable businesses. We believe that following and acting on the issues we lay out here will establish the foundation for that success.

Entrepreneurship Is Not a Scary Word

If you are taking this course you have at least some level of desire to be your own boss one day by establishing an entrepreneurial venture. You have a plan to start (and succeed) at your own business venture, and you see this course as groundwork for that plan. Beyond a personal desire to be an entrepreneur, there are real, applicable reasons to take this course. Today, 50 percent of all U.S. employees work for entrepreneurial businesses. Even if you do not ultimately start an entrepreneurial venture, the odds are at some point in your career you will work for one. Entrepreneurial businesses are everywhere. They include a wide range of visible firms on the Internet. These firms are the makers and sellers of a myriad of other goods plus providers of services that impact our daily lives. Understanding the components of success and failure for your future employer makes you a better employee.

Book Outline

To develop the understanding necessary to design, start, and manage an entrepreneurial business, we have organized the book into fourteen chapters that are, in turn, organized into five major sections. The first section lays the groundwork needed prior to developing a new business idea. Many individuals have considered starting a new business when an opportunity was presented to them or when they were frustrated by their current positions. However, prior to this step there are several areas that demand examination. Chapter 1 introduces the students to the text with a fun and engaging look at the twenty-first-century entrepreneur. Chapter 2 examines the potential entrepreneur's personal propensities or willingness to take on risk, a core aspect of entrepreneurship. Chapter 3 focuses on how to generate ideas and perform an initial evaluation for a new business.

The second section of the text is entitled "Due Diligence on the Business Idea." In the last chapter of section one, the potential entrepreneur has generated a business idea. In this section there is due diligence on that idea. Due diligence is a process of examining the environment around the new business to establish the opportunity for the new business and then using that knowledge to craft the approach. Chapter 4 launches the first step in the due diligence process by developing a set of methods for examining the external environment in which the new business might operate to understand if there is an opportunity for such a business. Chapter 5 develops the crucial steps necessary for the development of a strategy, including the firm's mission.

A key element in the success of the entrepreneurial venture is the financial foundation of the venture; no matter how good the idea, without a solid financial foundation the business will likely fail. Accordingly, Section 3 is titled "Establishing a Financial Foundation." The chapters in this section include Chapter 6, which establishes how to analyze the cash flow of the firm. Chapter 7 discusses methods that the entrepreneur can use to analyze the financial health of the new business.

The fourth section of the text is titled "Building the Business" and focuses on putting the new venture in operation. Chapter 9 discusses marketing the business. Chapter 10 reviews the legal frameworks for a new business, including the many approaches that are available to protect the business. Chapter 11 details human resource management. Chapter 12 rounds out this important section of the book by discussing the business operations design.

The last section of the book is titled "Important Issues for Entrepreneurs" and examines two other issues critical for an entrepreneur to consider as the entrepreneur starts a business. Chapter 13 examines both exiting the business and the need to turn the firm around if performance is not as great as desired. Chapter 14 examines two means to buy into a business rather than starting it from scratch. They are buying an existing business and franchising.

Features New to This Second Edition

- The entire book has been reorganized to present the material in a manner that is more aligned with the entrepreneur's efforts to develop a business. We moved the three chapters that relate to financing, accounting, and financial analysis forward into the third section of the book.
- The opening vignettes to each chapter have been changed from the prior edition to include cutting-edge entrepreneurial companies including Uber, Zane's Cycles, Numi Organic Tea, Weedmaps, Ploom, Philly Pretzel, and AeroPress, among others.
- Two new running cases are in each chapter in the revised text. Each chapter follows Friends' Home Health Care and Flow Right Brewery & Bar: A Family Affair as they moved from idea to successful businesses. Each running case is tied to the chapter material.
- In addition to Review Questions in the end-of-chapter material, every chapter now also includes a new section called Business Plan Development Questions. The goal of these questions is to turn the material in the chapter into actions for the business plans being developed by the students. Also, both Individual and Group Exercise sections have been added to help students develop their entrepreneurial skills individually as well as within a group.
- Fourteen MiniCases are now included at the end of the text. Each case is based on interviews by the authors and provides context and entrepreneurial advice simply not available in any other text. These include: The Varsity Shop, The ClearCollar, Hannington Massage, OCJ Apparel, Alton's Kitchen & Cocktails, and RavioliOli.
- A new Business Plan (The Fraudian Slip) that has been annotated by the authors is provided as an example of how this is all pulled together by students in a course.

Additional Changes by Chapter

Chapter 1 The Twenty-First-Century Entrepreneur

- New Opening Vignette: Oren's Daily Roast Coffee and Tea.
- Completely rewritten to provide a more engaging and fun introduction to the text.
- Every statistic brought forward to 2014.
- Redesigned how the Business Plan is developed.
- Addition of a one-page pitch sheet example.

Chapter 2 Individual Leadership and Entrepreneurial Start-Ups

- New Opening Vignette: Philly Pretzel and Dan DiZio.
- Introduce what is meant by a family business. Family business issues are then addressed in each chapter particularly as we discuss the running case about the brewery and bar noted below.
- Friends' Home Health Care running case is introduced. This case develops in each chapter through the rest of the text. It follows the design, start-up, and running of a business with friends as business partners.
- Flow Right Brewery & Bar: A Family Affair running case is introduced. This case develops in each chapter through the rest of the text. It follows the design, start-up, and running of a family business.

Chapter 3 Business Idea Generation and Initial Evaluation

- New Opening Vignette: Uber Changes the Business (the wildly fast-growing ride-sharing business)

Chapter 4 External Analysis

- Updated and carried forward one of our favorite vignettes: Guayakí Sustainable Rainforest Products, Inc.
- Introduced the concepts of "Normal" and "Unusual" capabilities to address developing a competitive advantage.

Chapter 5 Business Mission and Strategy

- New Opening Vignette: Zane's Cycles.

Chapter 6 Analyzing Cash Flow and Other Financial Information

- New Opening Vignette: Numi Organic Tea

Chapter 7 Financing and Accounting

- This was previously Chapter 9. We brought forward this chapter and others to tie together all the financial statements and analysis into the same section.
- New Opening Vignette: AeroPress.
- Added a section on crowd funding, which has become a popular entrepreneurial finance mechanism.

Chapter 8 Financial Analysis

- This was previously Chapter 12. The Pro Forma Cash Flow Statements, Chart of Accounts, P&L, Income Statement, and Balance Sheet have been recrafted.
- We updated and carried forward one of our favorite vignettes: VaVaVroomonline.com.

Chapter 9 Establishing the Legal Foundation

- This was previously Chapter 7. This move was suggested by our students and the professors using this text, who indicated that it worked better after all the financials were developed and analyzed.
- New Opening Vignette: Weedmaps: The Yelp of Marijuana Buying.
- Everything was updated to reflect changes in the law.

Chapter 10 Human Resource Management

- New Opening Vignette: USA Gypsum (a recycling story).
- The chapter has been updated to reflect the dramatic changes in recruiting methods that have occurred in the past few years.

Chapter 11 Marketing

- New Opening Vignette: James Monsees and Adam Bowen: Ploom (high-end electronic cigarette).
- Updated all the delivery mechanisms to include the vast array of new approaches to marketing, especially social media.

Chapter 12 Establishing Operations

- This was formerly Chapter 8. We thought that it would work better as the next step in the process of starting a new business. While the potential entrepreneur has to consider operations early on, the details might be best developed after much of the business has been vetted.
- New Opening Vignette: Indigo IT (an IT support company).

Chapter 13 Exit/Harvest/Turnaround

- With all the changes in tea consumption and availability, we decided to update and carry forward one of our favorite vignettes: Tealuxe.

Chapter 14 Franchising and Purchasing an Existing Business

- New Opening Vignette: La Madeleine and Patrick Leon Esquerré (one of the truly exceptional restaurant entrepreneurs).

Outcomes

Our ultimate goal is that students will leave this class not only with a much greater appreciation for what it takes to start a business, but with the foundations necessary to actually start that business. The entrepreneurial businesses that surround you every day did not come into operation or stay in operation by chance. Instead, it took tremendous effort and work for these businesses to exist and succeed.

We expect that students will be able to take what we present here as a foundation for your own business. Entrepreneurs are the economic backbone of this nation and the central hope for its future.

acknowledgments

We would like to acknowledge the dedicated instructors who have graciously provided their insights for this second edition. Their input has been extremely helpful in pointing out corrections to be made, suggesting areas that needed further development, or topics that needed to be included or covered earlier in the text.

George Bernard
Seminole State College of Florida

Nancy Brown
Lakeland Community College

Carlene Cassidy
Anne Arundel Community College

Raven Davenport
Houston Community College

Kimberly Ann Goudy
Central Ohio Technical College

Kurt Heppard
United States Air Force Academy

R. Michael Holmes
Florida State University

Andreea N. Kiss
Iowa State University

Jonathan Krabill
Columbus State Community College

Ted W. Legatski
Texas Christian University

David Lucero
Greenville Technical College

Tim McCabe
Tompkins Cortland Community College

Jeffrey E. McGee
The University of Texas at Arlington

Michelle Neujahr
Southern Maine Community College

Diane R. Sabato
Springfield Technical Community College

Leo Trudel
University of Maine at Fort Kent

Cassmer Ward
Queens University of Charlotte

Mark Zarycki
Hillsborough Community College

Key Text Features

Each chapter includes key features that help illuminate important ideas in interesting and applied ways.

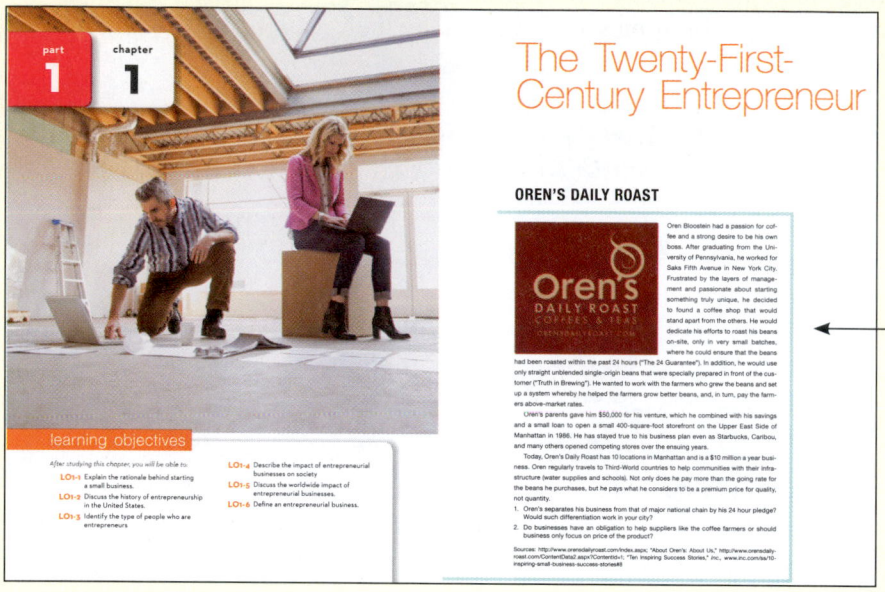

part 1 chapter 1

The Twenty-First-Century Entrepreneur

OREN'S DAILY ROAST

Oren Bloostein had a passion for coffee and a strong desire to be his own boss. After graduating from the University of Pennsylvania, he worked for Saks Fifth Avenue in New York City. Frustrated by the layers of management and passionate about starting something truly unique, he decided to found a coffee shop that would stand apart from the others. He would dedicate his efforts to roast his beans on-site, only in very small batches, where he could ensure that the beans had been roasted within the past 24 hours ("The 24 Guarantee"). In addition, he would use only straight unblended single-origin beans that were specially prepared in front of the customer ("Truth in Brewing"). He wanted to work with the farmers who grew the beans and set up a system whereby he helped the farmers grow better beans, and, in turn, pay the farmers above-market rates.

Oren's parents gave him $50,000 for his venture, which he combined with his savings and a small loan to open a small 400-square-foot storefront on the Upper East Side of Manhattan in 1986. He has stayed true to his business plan even as Starbucks, Caribou, and many others opened competing stores over the ensuing years.

Today, Oren's Daily Roast has 10 locations in Manhattan and is a $10 million a year business. Oren regularly travels to Third-World countries to help communities with their infrastructure (water supplies and schools). Not only does he pay more than the going rate for the beans he purchases, but he pays what he considers to be a premium price for quality, not quantity.

1. Oren's separates his business from that of major national chain by his 24 hour pledge? Would such differentiation work in your city?
2. Do businesses have an obligation to help suppliers like the coffee farmers or should business only focus on price of the product?

Sources: http://www.orensdailyroast.com/index.aspx; "About Oren's: About Us," http://www.orensdailyroast.com/ContentData2.aspx?Contentid=1; "Ten Inspiring Success Stories," *Inc.*, www.inc.com/slo/10-inspiring-small-business-success-stories#8

learning objectives

After studying this chapter, you will be able to:

- LO1-1 Explain the rationale behind starting a small business.
- LO1-2 Discuss the history of entrepreneurship in the United States.
- LO1-3 Identify the type of people who are entrepreneurs.
- LO1-4 Describe the impact of entrepreneurial businesses on society.
- LO1-5 Discuss the worldwide impact of entrepreneurial businesses.
- LO1-6 Define an entrepreneurial business.

Chapter-Opening Vignettes

Every chapter begins with a profile of a real entrepreneurial business. These portraits provide an overview of both the everyday successes and the failures associated with business ownership. Each of these vignettes end with thought-provoking questions for discussion.

Running Cases

Friends' Home Health

Beginning with Chapter 2 and running throughout the rest of the book, this case looks at chapter topics within the context of a new entrepreneurial business in the home health industry. Each chapter provides a new aspect of this business to consider, ultimately giving you a fully realized look at how a business must work through a series of issues as it moves from idea to reality. Each chapter's case concludes with questions designed to help the students think through issues related to the business they wish to start.

FRIENDS' HOME HEALTH

In 2012 three friends who worked in the same nursing facility started talking about starting a business together. The three friends had known each other for a number of years. The friends include one registered nurse (RN) (Betty), and two licensed practical nurses (LPNs) (Joan and Bob). The RN typically is the supervising nurse on the ward and the LPNs do more of the direct care of individual patients. The friends observed the increasing numbers of elderly people in the hospital. As they talked with the family members of these patients they realized there was a need for a reliable home health firm in the area. Despite the existence of several operations in the area (one a national chain), the patients' families were constantly talking about problems with the current group of home health firms. The families told stories about caregivers who did not show up, were not willing to do distasteful jobs, had poor training, and some who outright stole from the home.

Home health workers go to the homes of clients to help the individuals bathe and eat, and generally assist the elderly or otherwise physically impaired individuals in their homes. Often a family member provides this assistance but needs support to adequately care for the individual or to be able to take a break from their caregiving. Home health workers typically undergo far less training than do LPNs, and some operators provide very little oversight of the in-home workers.

The three friends (Betty, Joan, and Bob) wanted more control over their lives and the opportunity to be paid more for their efforts. Working in the health care facility involved long and odd hours where they might work all night and never see their families. They felt that in their current positions, they were working very hard but were receiving only limited direct rewards for that effort. These issues pushed the three to talk about starting a business. The discussions initially were little more than talk; however, in the past few months these discussions had become more serious. They were not sure how to make a home health business unique, but they knew they wanted to start one.

Joan's uncle had founded several businesses and appeared to understand what it took to be successful in business. The three potential entrepreneurs had a conversation with the uncle; he advised them to spend a little more time investigating their motivations and personal risk orientation before they actually considered going into business together. He related the story of his first business, which he had started with his best friend. The two had been lifelong friends and thought they knew all there was to know about each other. Not only had they been friends since childhood, each had been the best man in the others' wedding, and each was the godfather for the other's oldest child. Although they thought they knew each other well, when it came to money and the level of risk they were capable of handling, they were substantially different people. Whereas the uncle was very frugal, his partner believed that money needed to be enjoyed today. Ultimately their business partnership fell apart. Although the financial loss was significant, even more devastating was the loss of the friendship between the two men and their families. He has always felt the experience was a significant failure and not one he wanted to repeat.

Joan's uncle has had other businesses and partnerships since that initial failure. He now believes that although he needs to like a person in order to work closely with him or her, it is much more important that they agree on such key issues as money and risk.

Therefore, the uncle suggested the three friends prepare with some simple tasks:

QUESTIONS

1. Compare how each of them prepared his or her monthly family budget.
2. Discuss how much debt each was willing to take on credit cards.
3. Discuss whether each was willing to lend family members money, and the reasons for their answer.
4. Have each person answer this question: If you inherited $250,000, what would you do with it?

The outcome of this exercise for our three potential business owners will be discussed after Exercise 1.

Flow Right Brewery & Bar: A Family Affair

A second running case throughout the book focuses on a family business. Family businesses must deal with the same issues that all new businesses must address. However, everything is complicated by the family interactions and interests. The case also ends with questions designed to help the students to think through issues related to the business.

FLOW RIGHT BREWERY & BAR: A FAMILY AFFAIR*

Chris Flow had long wanted to be his own boss. Working for one of the bigger banks in the area, he sat in a cubicle processing mortgage applications. Although there was always something different in each application, he had the process down to a science. He was so good at his work that his boss gave him the unenviable task of handling mortgage workouts for people who had fallen behind in their payments. By 2014 he could see the writing on the wall. Virtually anyone involved in the mortgage processing business was eligible to be laid off as the mortgage crisis had subsided. Several of the nation's largest banks had rounds of layoffs in their mortgage divisions that amounted to thousands of employees.

Since graduating from college, Chris had a fascination with brewing beer. He worked at a microbrewery in Boulder, Colorado, during his college years and had taken a number of classes on making beer. He was a member of the local brewing club and regularly won the club awards for the beer he brewed at home. What's more is that Chris's passion to brew beer had taken over his two-car garage much to the consternation of his wife. He regularly worked with new club members to learn what he considered a craft.

On his way home from work one day he was shocked to see that one of his favorite restaurants had closed. The location was very good, but there was never much of a crowd. Chris personally knew the owner, although he was only peripherally aware that the owner had been in the heat of a divorce. Once the divorce was final the owner planned to move from the area, but there was not sufficient cash flow generated in the business to entice anyone to buy it. Thus, he had decided simply to close the business.

That night Chris and his wife talked at length about Chris taking over that location and turning it into a brew pub where aficionados of brewing could gather and enjoy locally brewed beers. He and his wife had saved up over $100,000, which they were willing to commit to the venture, and he was confident that he could bring in a set of partners who would also invest in the business. There were a lot of things to do over the next few weeks if this was going to be a reality, but Chris was truly excited about business for the first time in years.

The next day Chris contacted a real estate agent and found out that the previous owner of the restaurant had broken a 10-year lease that still had 6 years left on it but no personal guarantee. The owner of the property was anxious to get the property leased again and was willing to throw in everything inside the restaurant for no extra monthly charge if Chris would sign a new 10-year lease that Chris would personally guarantee. Even though the lease payments seemed quite reasonable—especially given that all of the kitchen equipment, tables, chairs, counters were his for free—it was nevertheless a big financial commitment as Chris would have to still pay for the lease even if the business was not a success. Chris and his wife decided to take the plunge and FLOW RIGHT BREWERY & BAR was born.

*The names and small details have been changed in this running case. We will use this case throughout the text to illustrate concepts raised in each chapter and how this particular firm addressed them as they built the business.

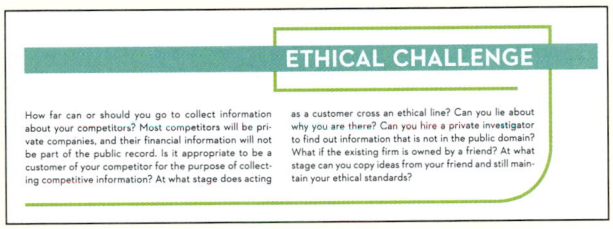
ETHICAL CHALLENGE

How far can or should you go to collect information about your competitors? Most competitors will be private companies, and their financial information will not be part of the public record. Is it appropriate to be a customer of your competitor for the purpose of collecting competitive information? At what stage does acting as a customer cross an ethical line? Can you lie about why you are there? Can you hire a private investigator to find out information that is not in the public domain? What if the existing firm is owned by a friend? At what stage can you copy ideas from your friend and still maintain your ethical standards?

Ethical Challenge Boxes

These dilemma-based scenarios and questions look at ethical realities within the successful creation of a business, and challenge students to examine the moral complexities of starting a business. Each challenge ends with questions designed to encourage the students to think how such ethical challenges will apply to their potential business.

Exercises

Extensive exercises in every chapter include open-ended questions for students to ask themselves as potential entrepreneurs. These exercises not only provide general exercises for discussion in class but also help guide the student so that by the last chapter the students will have developed a full business plan that can be used to launch a new business.

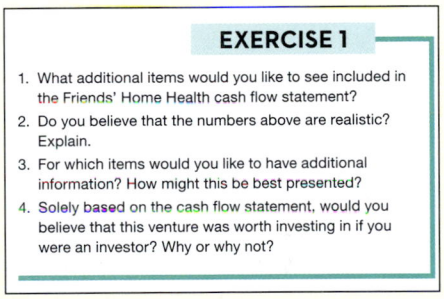
EXERCISE 1

1. What additional items would you like to see included in the Friends' Home Health cash flow statement?
2. Do you believe that the numbers above are realistic? Explain.
3. For which items would you like to have additional information? How might this be best presented?
4. Solely based on the cash flow statement, would you believe that this venture was worth investing in if you were an investor? Why or why not?

End-of-Chapter Material

Each chapter concludes with the following:

- Summary
- Key Terms
- Review Questions
- Business Plan Development Questions
- Individual Exercises
- Group Exercises

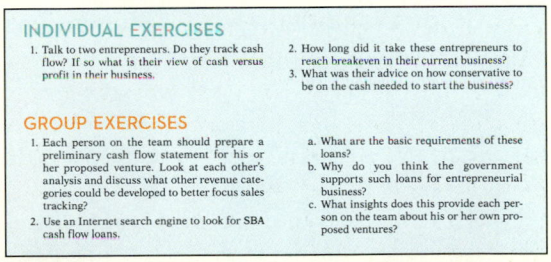
INDIVIDUAL EXERCISES

1. Talk to two entrepreneurs. Do they track cash flow? If so what is their view of cash versus profit in their business.
2. How long did it take these entrepreneurs to reach breakeven in their current business?
3. What was their advice on how conservative to be on the cash needed to start the business?

GROUP EXERCISES

1. Each person on the team should prepare a preliminary cash flow statement for his or her proposed venture. Look at each other's analysis and discuss what other revenue categories could be developed to better focus sales tracking?
2. Use an Internet search engine to look for SBA cash flow loans.
   a. What are the basic requirements of these loans?
   b. Why do you think the government supports such loans for entrepreneurial business?
   c. What insights does this provide each person on the team about his or her own proposed ventures?

MiniCases

MiniCases are now included at the end of the text. These longer cases look at real businesses. They examine a real entrepreneur and how that owner approached the business and the struggles associated with success. They offer practical, real-world examples of core concepts within the entrepreneurial framework discussed in the book.

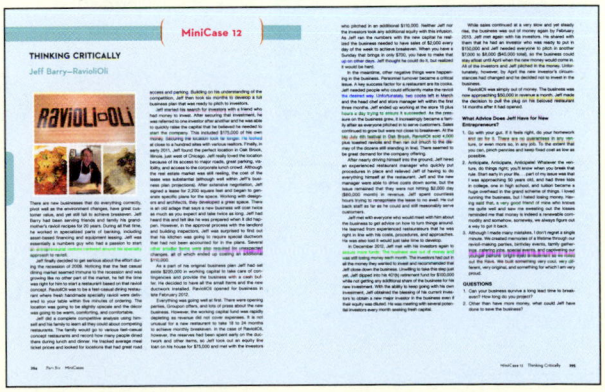
MiniCase 12

THINKING CRITICALLY

Jeff Barry—RavioliOli

Results-Driven Technology

Across the country, instructors and students continue to raise an important question: How can entrepreneurship courses further support students throughout the learning process to shape future business leaders? While there is no one solution, we see the impact of new learning technologies and innovative study tools that not only fully engage students in course material but also inform instructors of the students' skill and comprehension levels.

Interactive learning tools, including those offered through McGraw-Hill *Connect*, are being implemented to increase teaching effectiveness and learning efficiency in thousands of colleges and universities. By facilitating a stronger connection with the course and incorporating the latest technologies—such as McGraw-Hill LearnSmart, an adaptive learning program—these tools enable students to succeed in their college careers, which will ultimately increase the percentage of students completing their postsecondary degrees and create the business leaders of the future.

connect MANAGEMENT

McGraw-Hill Connect

Connect is an all-digital teaching and learning environment designed from the ground up to work with the way instructors and students think, teach, and learn. As a digital teaching, assignment, and assessment platform, *Connect* strengthens the link among faculty, students, and coursework, helping everyone accomplish more in less time.

LearnSmart

The smartest way to get from B to A

LearnSmart is the most widely used and intelligent adaptive learning resource. It is proven to strengthen memory recall, improve course retention, and boost grades by distinguishing between what students know and what they don't know and honing in on the concepts that they are most likely to forget. LearnSmart continuously adapts to each student's needs by building an individual learning path. As a result, students study smarter and retain more knowledge.

Grade Distribution

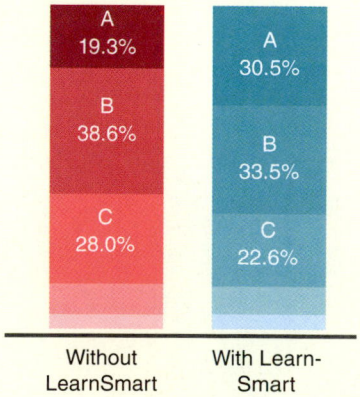

58% more As with LearnSmart

Student Pass Rate

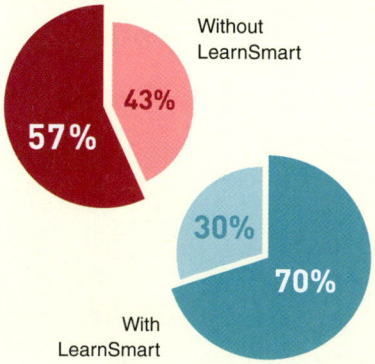

25% more students passed with LearnSmart

SmartBook

A Revolution in Reading

Fueled by LearnSmart, SmartBook is the first and only adaptive reading experience available today. SmartBook personalizes content for each student in a continuously adapting reading experience. Reading is no longer a passive and linear experience, but an engaging and dynamic one where students are more likely to master and retain important concepts, coming to class better prepared.

Media Rich eBook

Connect, provides students with a cost-saving alternative to the traditional textbook. A seamless integration of a media rich eBook features the following:

- A web-optimized eBook, allowing for anytime, anywhere online access to the textbook.
- Powerful search function to pinpoint and connect key concepts in a snap.
- Highlighting and note-taking capabilities as well as access to shared instructors' notations.

McGraw-Hill strengthens the link between faculty, students, and coursework, helping everyone accomplish more in less time.

connect® | MANAGEMENT

Efficient Administrative Capabilities

Connect offers you, the instructor, auto-gradable material in an effort to facilitate teaching and learning.

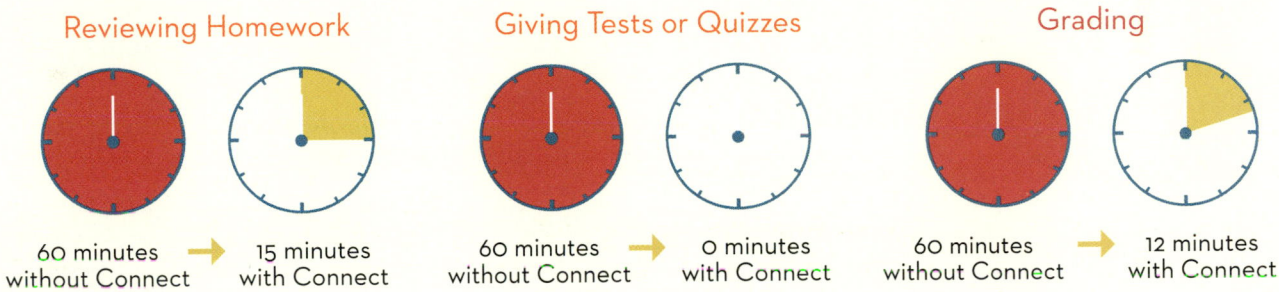

Student Progress Tracking

Connect keeps instructors informed about how each student, section, and class is performing, allowing for more productive use of lecture and office hours. The progress tracking function enables instructors to:

- View scored work immediately and track individual or group performance with assignment and grade reports.
- Access an instant view of student or class performance relative to learning objectives.
- Collect data and generate reports required by many accreditation organizations, such as AACSB.

> *Connect* and LearnSmart allow instructors to present course material to students in more ways than just the explanations they hear from me directly. Because of this, students are processing the material in new ways, requiring them to think. I now have more students asking questions in class because the more we think, the more we question.
>
> *Instructor at Hinds Community College*

Actionable Data

Connect Insight is a powerful data analytics tool that allows instructors to leverage aggregated information about their courses and students to provide a more personalized teaching and learning experience.

Connect Instructor Library

Connect's instructor library serves as a one-stop, secure site for essential course materials, allowing you to save prep time before class. The instructor resources found in the library include:

Test Bank: Every chapter provides a series of true/false, multiple choice, and short answer test questions, available in our Test Bank. Questions can be organized by Learning Objective, topic, level of difficulty, Bloom's Taxonomy, and AACSB.

Instructor's Manual: The IM outlines course materials, additional in-class activities, and support for classroom use of the text. It has been organized by Learning Objective to both give instructors a basic outline of the chapter and assist in all facets of instruction. For every question posed in the text, the IM provides a viable answer. Ultimately, this will be to an instructor's greatest advantage in using all materials to reach all learners.

PowerPoint Slides: PowerPoint slides include important chapter content and teaching notes tied directly to Learning Objectives. They are designed to engage students in classroom discussions about the text.

Asset Map: We know that instructors' time is valuable. To help you prepare, we have revised the Asset Map. The Asset Map identifies the chapter, Learning Objective, page number, and exactly which supplements are available for you to use.

Course Design and Delivery

Blackboard® Partnership

McGraw-Hill Education and Blackboard have teamed up to simplify your life. Now you and your students can access *Connect* and Create right from within your Blackboard course—all with one single sign-on. The grade books are seamless, so when a student completes an integrated *Connect* assignment, the grade for that assignment automatically (and instantly) feeds your Blackboard grade center. Learn more at **www.domorenow.com**.

McGraw-Hill Campus™

McGraw-Hill Campus is a new one-stop teaching and learning experience available to users of any learning management system. This institutional service allows faculty and students to enjoy single sign-on (SSO) access to all McGraw-Hill Higher Education materials, including the award-winning McGraw-Hill *Connect* platform, from directly within the institution's website. With McGraw-Hill Campus, faculty receive instant access to teaching materials (e.g., eTextbooks, test banks, PowerPoint slides, animations, learning objects, etc.), allowing them to browse, search, and use any instructor ancillary content in our vast library at no additional cost to instructor or students.

In addition, students enjoy SSO access to a variety of free content (e.g., quizzes, flash cards, narrated presentations, etc.) and subscription-based products (e.g., McGraw-Hill *Connect*). With McGraw-Hill Campus enabled, faculty and students will never need to create another account to access McGraw-Hill products and services. Learn more at **www.mhcampus.com**.

Create

Instructors can now tailor their teaching resources to match the way they teach! With McGraw-Hill Create, **www.mcgrawhillcreate.com**, instructors can easily rearrange chapters, combine material from other content sources, and quickly upload and integrate their own content, like course syllabi or teaching notes. Find the right content in Create by searching through thousands of leading McGraw-Hill textbooks. Arrange the material to fit your teaching style. Order a Create book and receive a complimentary print review copy in three to five business days or a complimentary electronic review copy via e-mail within one hour. Go to **www.mcgrawhillcreate.com** today and register.

Tegrity Campus

Tegrity makes class time available 24/7 by automatically capturing every lecture in a searchable format for students to review when they study and complete assignments. With a simple one-click start-and-stop process, you capture all computer screens and corresponding audio. Students can replay any part of any class with easy-to-use browser-based viewing on a PC or Mac. Educators know that the more students can see, hear, and experience class resources, the better they learn. In fact, studies prove it. With patented Tegrity "search anything" technology, students instantly recall key class moments for replay online or on iPods and mobile devices. Instructors can

help turn all their students' study time into learning moments immediately supported by their lecture. To learn more about Tegrity, watch a two-minute Flash demo at **http://tegritycampus.mhhe.com**.

Assurance of Learning Ready

Many educational institutions today focus on the notion of *assurance of learning,* an important element of some accreditation standards. *Entrepreneurship* is designed specifically to support instructors' assurance of learning initiatives with a simple yet powerful solution. Each test bank question for *Entrepreneurship* maps to a specific chapter learning objective listed in the text. Instructors can use our test bank software, EZ Test and EZ Test Online, to easily query for learning objectives that directly relate to the learning outcomes for their course. Instructors can then use the reporting features of EZ Test to aggregate student results in similar fashion, making the collection and presentation of assurance of learning data simple and easy.

AACSB Tagging

AACSB INTERNATIONAL

McGraw-Hill Education is a proud corporate member of AACSB International. Understanding the importance and value of AACSB accreditation, *Entrepreneurship* recognizes the curricula guidelines detailed in the AACSB standards for business accreditation by connecting selected questions in the text and the test bank to the six general knowledge and skill guidelines in the AACSB standards. The statements contained in *Entrepreneurship* are provided only as a guide for the users of this textbook. The AACSB leaves content coverage and assessment within the purview of individual schools, the mission of the school, and the faculty. While the *Entrepreneurship* teaching package makes no claim of any specific AACSB qualification or evaluation, we have within *Entrepreneurship* labeled selected questions according to the six general knowledge and skills areas.

McGraw-Hill Customer Experience Group Contact Information

At McGraw-Hill Education, we understand that getting the most from new technology can be challenging. That's why our services don't stop after you purchase our products. You can e-mail our Product Specialists 24 hours a day to get product training online. Or you can search our knowledge bank of Frequently Asked Questions on our support website. For Customer Support, call **800-331-5094** or visit **www.mhhe.com/support**. One of our Technical Support Analysts will be able to assist you in a timely fashion.

table of contents

Preface vii

PART 1 Laying the Groundwork for Small Business

chapter 1
THE TWENTY-FIRST-CENTURY ENTREPRENEUR 2

Why Start a Business? 4
A Brief History of Entrepreneurial Businesses in the United States 6
Who Are Entrepreneurial Business Owners Today? 8
How Does Society Benefit? 8
Entrepreneurship Around the World 11
What Is an Entrepreneurial Business? 11
- Summary 16
- Key Terms 16
- Review Questions 16
- Individual Exercises 16
- Group Exercises 16
- Endnotes 16
- Credits 17

chapter 2
INDIVIDUAL LEADERSHIP AND ENTREPRENEURIAL START-UPS 18

Founders Are the Reason Why Entrepreneurial Businesses Work So Well 22
Evaluating Your Entrepreneurial Orientation 23
Triggers for Starting a Business 27
Supports 29
Form a Business Doing What You Like 33
- Summary 34
- Key Terms 34
- Review Questions 34
- Business Plan Development Questions 34
- Individual Exercises 35
- Group Exercises 35
- Endnotes 35
- Credits 35

chapter 3
BUSINESS IDEA GENERATION AND INITIAL EVALUATION 36

Generating Business Ideas 39
Opportunity Identification 44
Choosing a Business 46
- Summary 54
- Key Terms 54
- Review Questions 54
- Business Plan Development Questions 54
- Individual Exercises 54
- Group Exercises 55
- Endnotes 55
- Credits 55

PART 2 Due Diligence on the Business Idea

chapter 4
EXTERNAL ANALYSIS 56

Defining Your Industry 58
Defining Your Customers 60
Developing the Information for the External Analysis of Competitors 62
Developing a Competitive Map 65
Additional Issues for External Analysis 68
Competitive Advantage 70
- Summary 73
- Key Terms 73
- Review Questions 74
- Business Plan Development Questions 74
- Individual Exercises 74
- Group Exercises 74
- Endnotes 74
- Credits 75

chapter 5
BUSINESS MISSION AND STRATEGY 76

Mission Statements 78
Sustainable Competitive Advantage 84
Step 1: Develop a List of Your Business's Assets and Capabilities 85
Step 2: Split the List into Standard and Unique Assets 85
Step 3: Evaluate Competitiveness of Unique Resources or Capabilities 87
Strategy 89
- Summary 93
- Key Terms 94
- Review Questions 94
- Business Plan Development Questions 94
- Individual Exercises 94
- Group Exercises 94
- Endnotes 95
- Credits 95

PART 3 Establishing a Financial Foundation

chapter 6
ANALYZING CASH FLOW AND OTHER FINANCIAL INFORMATION 96

Importance of Cash Flow Analysis 98
Developing Cash Flow Statements and Budgets 106
Other Financial Tools 111
- Summary 116
- Key Terms 116
- Review Questions 116
- Business Plan Development Questions 117
- Individual Exercises 117
- Group Exercises 117
- Endnotes 117
- Credits 117

chapter 7
FINANCING AND ACCOUNTING 118

Key Financial Issues Involved with Starting a Business 120
Basics of Funding a Business 122
Importance of Proper Accounting When Starting a Business 129
- Summary 134
- Key Terms 134
- Review Questions 134
- Business Plan Development Questions 134
- Individual Exercises 135
- Group Exercises 135
- Endnotes 135
- Credits 135

chapter 8
FINANCIAL ANALYSIS 136

Importance of a Solid Financial Foundation in an Entrepreneurial Business 138
Techniques for Measuring Performance 138
Ratio Analysis 141
Deviation Analysis 148
Sensitivity Analysis 149
Use of Short Surveys in Business 150
Importance of Having a Measurement Focus 153
- Summary 154
- Key Terms 154
- Review Questions 154
- Business Plan Development Questions 155
- Individual Exercises 155
- Group Exercises 155
- Endnotes 155
- Credits 155

PART 4 Building the Business

chapter 9
ESTABLISHING THE LEGAL FOUNDATION 156

Various Legal Forms of Business to Determine the Best Design for a Proposed New Business 160
Basics of Contracts 166
Role of Leases in the Legal Formation of the New Business 167
How Laws, Rules, and Regulations Benefit New Businesses 169
Importance of Copyrights, Trademarks, and Patents to a New Business 171
Role That Insurance Plays in the Risk Portfolio of the New Business 172
How to Develop an Effective Board of Advisors and Board of Directors 173

Summary 174
Key Terms 174
Review Questions 174
Business Plan Development Questions 175
Individual Exercises 175
Group Exercises 175
Endnotes 175
Credits 175

chapter 10
HUMAN RESOURCES MANAGEMENT 176

The Elements of Human Resources 179
The Process of Hiring Employees 179
The Means for Retaining Employees 185
The Pertinent Aspects of Employee Probation and Firing 190
Broad Coverage Regulations and Laws 190
The Unique Aspects of Human Resources Within a Family Business 192
Summary 193
Key Terms 194
Review Questions 194
Business Plan Development Questions 194
Individual Exercises 194
Group Exercises 194
Endnotes 195
Credits 195

chapter 11
MARKETING 196

Basics of a Marketing Plan 198
How to Develop a Pricing Model 202
The Various Types of Promotion Available to a New Business 204
The Methods for Sales Management 207
Summary 212
Key Terms 212
Review Questions 212
Business Plan Development Questions 212
Individual Exercises 213
Group Exercises 213
Endnotes 213
Credits 213

chapter 12
ESTABLISHING OPERATIONS 214

The Use of a Critical Path Chart 218
How Location Can Be Used as a Competitive Advantage 221
The Important Issues in the Financing Considerations of New Firms 223
The Various Methods with Which a New Firm Establishes Legitimacy in the Market 224
The Importance of Production Management in Start-Up Ventures 226
How Production Charting Is Accomplished 226
The Importance of Quality as a Competitive Tool 228
The Type and Condition of Equipment Needed at Start-Up 229
How Timing Is a Competitive Advantage 231
The Issues Related to Time Management in the Starting of a New Business 231
Summary 232
Key Terms 232
Review Questions 232
Business Plan Development Questions 233
Individual Exercises 233
Group Exercises 233
Endnotes 233
Credits 233

PART 5 Important Issues for Entrepreneurs

chapter 13
EXIT/HARVEST/TURNAROUND 234

Need for Developing an Exit or Harvest Plan and Ideal Timing for That Plan 236
Steps for Selling a Business 238
Turnaround and Business in Decline 249
Implications and Issues Involved in Closing a Business 251
Summary 252
Key Terms 252
Review Questions 253
Business Plan Development Questions 253
Individual Exercises 253
Group Exercises 253
Endnotes 253
Credits 253

chapter 14
FRANCHISING AND PURCHASING AN EXISTING BUSINESS 254
The Elements of Franchising 257
The Process of Buying a Franchise 259
The Process for Buying an Existing Business 265
Summary 268
Key Terms 268
Review Questions 269
Individual Exercises 269
Group Exercises 269
Endnotes 269
Credits 269

PART 6 MiniCases

Appendix 300
Glossary 315
Case Index 319
Subject Index 320

entrepreneurship

THE ART, SCIENCE, AND PROCESS FOR SUCCESS

second edition

part 1

chapter 1

learning objectives

After studying this chapter, you will be able to:

LO1-1 Explain the rationale behind starting an entrepreneurial business.

LO1-2 Discuss the history of entrepreneurship in the United States.

LO1-3 Identify the type of people who are entrepreneurs.

LO1-4 Describe the impact of entrepreneurial businesses on society.

LO1-5 Discuss the worldwide impact of entrepreneurial businesses.

LO1-6 Define an entrepreneurial business.

The Twenty-First-Century Entrepreneur

OREN'S DAILY ROAST

Oren Bloostein had a passion for coffee and a strong desire to be his own boss. After graduating from the University of Pennsylvania, he worked for Saks Fifth Avenue in New York City. Frustrated by the layers of management and passionate about starting something truly unique, he decided to found a coffee shop that would stand apart from the others. He would dedicate his efforts to roast his beans on-site, only in very small batches, where he could ensure that the beans had been roasted within the past 24 hours ("Freshness 24 Guarantee"). In addition, he would use only straight unblended single-origin beans that were specially prepared in front of the customer ("Truth in Brewing"). He wanted to work with the farmers who grew the beans and set up a system whereby he helped the farmers grow better beans, and, in turn, pay the farmers above-market rates.

Oren's parents gave him $50,000 for his venture, which he combined with his savings and a small loan to open a small 400-square-foot storefront on the Upper East Side of Manhattan in 1986. He has stayed true to his business plan even as Starbucks, Caribou, and many others opened competing stores over the ensuing years.

Today, Oren's Daily Roast has 10 locations in Manhattan and is a $10 million a year business. Oren regularly travels to Third-World countries to help communities with their infrastructure (water supplies and schools). Not only does he pay more than the going rate for the beans he purchases, but he pays what he considers to be a premium price for quality, not quantity.

Questions

1. Oren separates his business from that of major national chains by his 24-hour pledge? Would such differentiation work in your city?
2. Do businesses have an obligation to help suppliers like the coffee farmers or should business only focus on price of the product?

Sources: http://www.orensdailyroast.com/index.aspx; "About Oren's: About Us," http://www.orensdailyroast.com/ContentData2.aspx?Contentid=1; "Ten Inspiring Success Stories," *Inc.*, www.inc.com/ss/10-inspiring-small-business-success-stories#8

LO1-1

Explain the rationale behind starting an entrepreneurial business.

Why Start a Business?

There are many reasons that individuals decide to start a new business. A lifelong dream, a desire to make a difference in the lives of other people, a realization that you can solve a nagging problem for yourself and others, your sudden unemployment, a desire to be your own boss, a response to an opportunity brought to you, and many more. These reasons have been shared with us by many people who are part of the tremendous pent-up desire by many people to be an entrepreneur. Although people are regularly bombarded with stories about the new businesses that explode into massive companies (Amazon, Facebook, Five Guys, Starbucks, Apple, etc.), most new companies stay well under the press radar. Yet many of these firms you never hear of are very successful and are an essential element in any economy.

United States Small Business Administration (SBA)

The SBA is the agency officially organized in 1953 as a part of the Small Business Act of July 30, 1953, to "aid, counsel, assist and protect, insofar as is possible, the interests of small business concerns." The agency provides a wealth of information and assistance at all levels of organizational development and management for new entrepreneurial businesses. See www.sba.gov.

The evidence of entrepreneurial businesses' importance to the economy can be seen in the following 2014 statistics from the **United States Small Business Administration (SBA)**[1]**:**

- The 23 million small entrepreneurial businesses in America accounted for 54 percent of all U.S. sales.
- Small businesses provided 55 percent of all jobs and 66 percent of all net new jobs since the 1970s.
- The 600,000 plus franchised businesses in the United States accounted for 40 percent of all retail sales and provided jobs for some 8 million people.
- The small-business sector in America occupied 30 to 50 percent of all commercial space, an estimated 20 to 34 billion square feet.

Furthermore, these entrepreneurial businesses are growing rapidly. Whereas corporate America has been downsizing, the rate of start-ups has grown, and the rate for small-business failures has declined.

- The number of small businesses in the United States has increased 49 percent since 1982.
- Since 1990, as big business eliminated 4 million jobs, new entrepreneurial businesses added 8 million new jobs.

Fortune 500

The Fortune 500 is published annually by *Fortune* magazine and documents the 500 largest corporations (by sales) in the United States.

Beyond the statistics, there are also countless stories of successful entrepreneurial new ventures in every community around the world. Every business in the **Fortune 500** started out as a new venture. Each one was the brainchild of a single individual or a small group of people. Recall from history that entrepreneurs such as Henry Ford (Ford Motor Company), Steve Jobs (Apple computers), Ron Brilland and Pat Farrah (Home Depot), Thomas Edison and Charles Coffin (General Electric), Barney Kroger (Kroger), Ralph Lauren (fashion), Sam Walton (Walmart), Estee Lauder (cosmetics), Oprah Winfrey (media), and Richard Branson (Virgin) all started out as small-business owners.

To illustrate how entrepreneurial businesses can grow to be on the Fortune 500 list consider how in 1966 Richard M. Schulze started a new business with a store called Sound of Music in St. Paul, Minnesota. Capitalizing on the new interest in everything electronic, his sales allowed him to earn a first-year salary of $17,000. He never expected to grow the business much beyond the St. Paul market, but a tornado in 1981 took the retail store, yet spared the stockroom. To clean out the stock that was left he held a "tornado sale,"which was a huge success. Schulze realized from the tornado sale that a combination of heavy advertising, a large selection of goods in one location, and low prices would bring people out in droves. Schulze next put up everything he owned as collateral to finance a new 18,000-square-foot superstore and changed the name of the store to Best

Buy. The company went public in 1987 and Schulze stepped down as the CEO in 2002.[2]

We do not mean to suggest that every new venture will ultimately grow to dominate some aspect of world business. What it does mean is that new ventures are the foundation for all businesses. Some grow large; some do not. Regardless, they all initially go through a process much like the one you will study in this book, and that process of business development from scratch is quite different from the processes followed by established businesses. The process of developing, initiating, and running a new business is so unique that it has developed into one of the most sought-out areas of study at colleges and universities around the globe.

Frank Perdue is an excellent example of a small-business owner with a vision that exceeded expectations. In his case, he took a commodity and turned it into a unique, sought-after product.

The success of entrepreneurial businesses occur partially because they are simply more focused than their large corporate counterparts. Without the burden of policies, procedures, corporate layers of management, and public stockholders, new businesses are free to put all their energy into satisfying the needs of their customers. A customer calling on a big jewelry chain to get a battery changed in his or her watch will find that the chain either does not perform those services or treats the effort to change the battery as a burden. The same customer calling on a locally owned jewelry store, however, will most likely get immediate assistance and gratitude for the business. The local business has the advantage of an owner whose fortunes are directly tied to the success of the firm. The average manager of a large firm, although interested in the success of the company, does not have any personal capital at risk. If the firm does not do well, the manager moves to another firm, whereas an owner may lose everything.

Large firms can obtain **economies of scale** in some industries. In other words, large firms can sometimes do things more efficiently because of their ability to operate on a larger scale than can a small firm.[3] For example, advertising is typically much cheaper per unit if purchased in large volume. Thus, a large firm such as Walmart can buy its advertising much cheaper on a per-unit basis than can a small retailer. Similarly, in manufacturing it is often much cheaper on a per-unit basis to produce large volumes of a product than to produce small volumes. This is the reason that small car manufacturers must charge an extraordinarily high price to cover their costs. Tesla Motors, which produces an all-electric car, has taken the battery car concept and crafted it into a high-performance car. The support structure to roll out and support a new automobile such as this is challenging and very expensive. The development of the firm's support structure is such that in January 2014, a Tesla owner was able to drive a battery-powered Tesla from New York City to Los Angeles as there are now enough charging stations to charge the cars spread throughout the nation.[4] But the building of such a support structure is expensive. This expense in part explains why a Tesla automobile in 2014 was priced between $50,000 and $100,000. In 2013, approximately 22,000 Teslas were sold. If the expected increase in sales continues, this price is expected to drop significantly owing to economies of scale.

economies of scale
A condition that allows the long-run average cost to continue downward as production increases. It leads (in its most extreme case) to a condition where a single firm making 100 percent of the product is the most efficient. In reality, this condition is moderated by the ability of management to control the size.

Many years ago the apparent efficiencies of very large businesses led some economists to predict that small entrepreneurial businesses would be largely replaced by a much smaller number of large businesses. The exact opposite has happened. The ability of entrepreneurs to respond more quickly and to operate more effectively (more focused on the specific needs of customers) has led to a growth in the raw number of entrepreneurial businesses rather than a decline.

This text develops the methods, applications, and processes that lead to the idea generation, investigation, start-up, and successful management of a new entrepreneurial business. How you grow your new business is a function of how you start your business. We firmly believe that the development and implementation of a new business is part art and part science. This field has been studied for a long time and there is a well-developed body of knowledge that should be the foundation of all your efforts. This text lays out a process for the "science" of forming and managing a new entrepreneurial business in a clear, sequential manner that is rich in its practical application as well as well-grounded in research. The "art" is a matter of practice, example, and the skill of the founder or founders of the new business. The text encourages you as you go through the process of developing your ideas and work to develop your own business plan. Although we will not be with you as you actually found your business, the goal of this text is to provide you with the fundamentals of starting the business and help you to develop your business into a functioning entity. Beyond all the statistics about how many new businesses fail (and many of them do fail), research (including our own studies) has found that there are three critical elements that an entrepreneur must solve for success:

1. An effective sales generation model. You are only as good as your pipeline. You must develop the ability to generate consistent and growing sales.
2. Sustainable operating profit margins. Profit margins are a key to successful businesses.
3. Being properly financed. It is crucial that you have sufficient resources (either yourself or by raising funds) to get the business to the point where it is self-funding.[5]

We believe that the principal way to be a part of the group that survives and thrives is to thoroughly plan and lay a solid basis for the business.

LO1-2

Discuss the history of entrepreneurship in the United States.

A Brief History of Entrepreneurial Businesses in the United States

Before we start looking at entrepreneurial businesses today, it is important to note that entrepreneurs have always been a critical part of the country's success. Alexis de Tocqueville was a Frenchman who toured the United States in the early 1830s and wrote a famous analysis of the country. One of his observations was that the United States was not so much a nation with ventures that were marvelous in their grandeur, but instead, a nation of innumerable small ventures. The history of the United States has always been intimately tied to entrepreneurial businesses. In fact, until the mid-1880s, almost all U.S. businesses were still relatively small.

The 1880s saw the initial development of the nation's large industrial base. It was from these beginnings that the robber barons developed. We associate their names today not only with great success but also with great abuses in business. They took advantage of the economies of scale that were suddenly possible with the industrial age and quickly came to dominate new sectors of the economy (e.g., Andrew Carnegie's domination of the steel industry). However, the robber barons were coming to dominate industrial sectors that had not existed historically, so they generally did not put smaller operations out of business. In fact, smaller entrepreneurial businesses continued to thrive during these times as new businesses grew up to serve the needs of these new industrial sectors.[6]

The Great Depression of the 1930s was harder on entrepreneurial businesses than on larger more mature businesses, and as a result it encouraged industrial concentration. The outcome was that following World War II, entrepreneurial business as a percentage of the U.S. economic output began to decline. It was during this time that Charles Wilson, Secretary of Defense for President Eisenhower, made the famous statement that "what is good for General Motors is good for the nation." The implication was that what was good for big business would be good for all of the people in the country.

In the late 1970s and early 1980s, the nation was in economic turmoil as many of the large firms that had grown to dominate the U.S. economy were having difficulty, owing to global competition. Entire industries, such as steel and automobile manufacturing, were in decline. It was during this time that President Jimmy Carter described the country as in a "malaise." The Japanese were in the dominant economic position in the world, and the widely discussed fear was that the United States was in decline much as Britain had been 100 years earlier. However, the decline of the large multinational firms in the United States opened new opportunities that entrepreneurial businesses rose to fill. The economic growth and success that the nation experiences today is due primarily to the entrepreneurial firms that found an economic footing and grew very rapidly. The vast number of businesses that start up each year are responsible for much of the innovation that pushes established companies to new levels.

Therefore, as you begin your study of entrepreneurial businesses you should recognize that you are examining a domain that has historically been the backbone of the economic success of the nation. Entrepreneurial businesses today continue to play a dominant role in the ability of the nation to adapt quickly and to make economic progress. The time line of business in the United States (Figure 1.1) highlights the central role of new business development.

Figure 1.1
Business Time Line
The time line of business provides both constants and natural evolution.

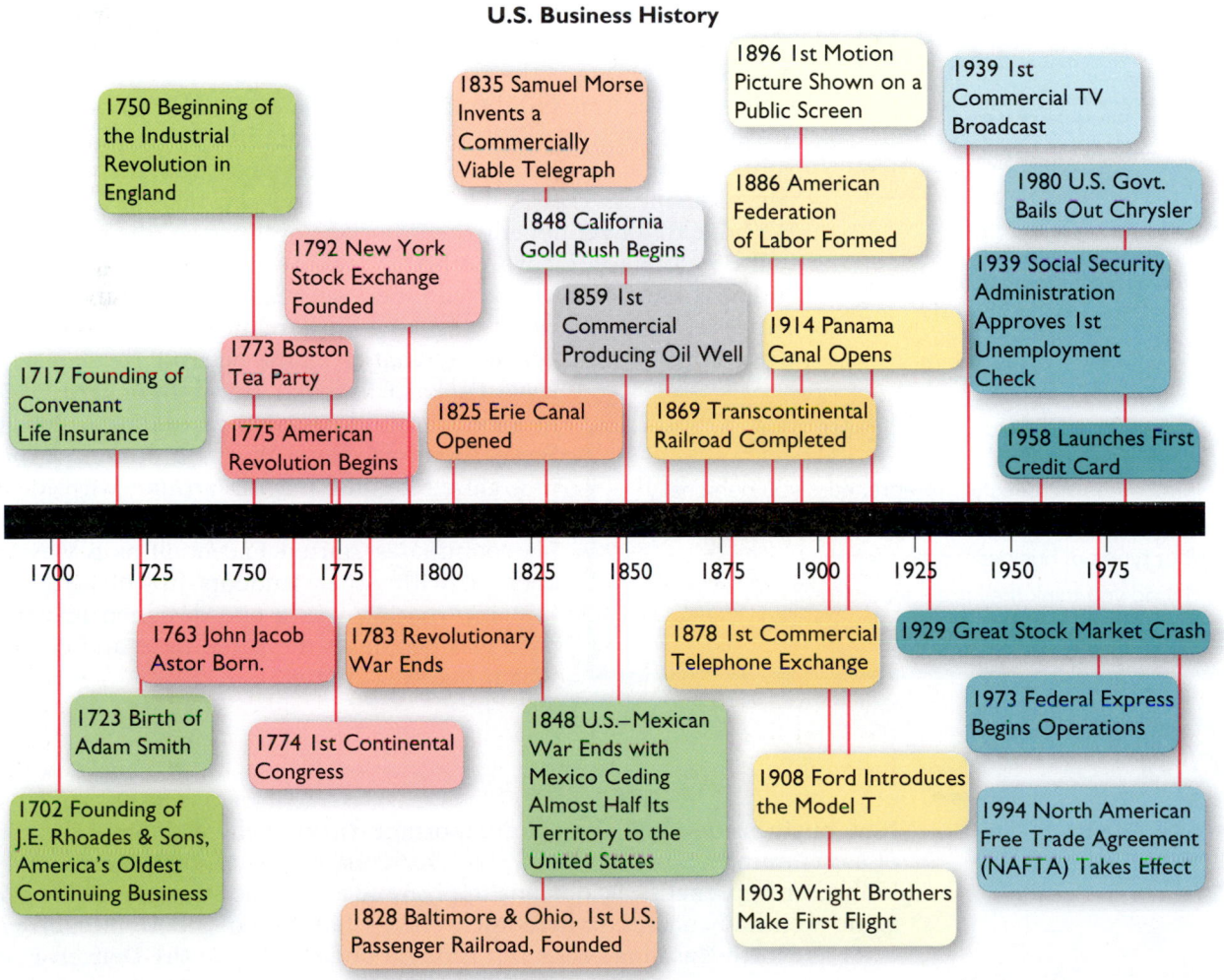

LO1-3

Identify the type of people who are entrepreneurs.

Who Are Entrepreneurial Business Owners Today?

stakeholders
Individuals or other organizations that impact the success of a business.

One of the huge advantages of starting one's own business is that it provides the setting where the business owner can be the boss. As we will discuss in Chapter 2, the owners of a new business are the most important single factor in the business's success. The new business owners have both the opportunity and the responsibility to lead. However, although many new business owners want this independence, they also need to recognize they are not alone in the business; there are other important **stakeholders** of their entrepreneurial business. These are individuals or other organizations that may impact the success of the business and depend on the success of the business for their own livelihood. Stakeholders include key suppliers, customers, and employees—all of whom are critical to the success of the new business.

The Millionaire Next Door *is a fascinating study of success stories associated with entrepreneurial business ventures. What would you consider to be a successful new business venture?*

It is true that the rewards of owning a business extend far beyond the financial. That said, the financial rewards to entrepreneurs can be stunning. In their book entitled *The Millionaire Next Door,* Thomas Stanley and William Danko highlight statistics that demonstrate the potential for financial rewards from starting a business.[7] For example, they point out that almost two-thirds of U.S. millionaires are self-employed, despite the fact that self-employed people make up fewer than 20 percent of the workers in America. They go on to state that 75 percent of these self-employed millionaires are entrepreneurs; the other 25 percent are self-employed professionals, such as doctors and accountants. So, close to 50 percent of the millionaires in this country are entrepreneurs. These are the individuals who start a business, run it well, and over time build their financial success. Most millionaires are individuals you know in your community. These individuals achieved their success by taking the bold step to actually start and run a business. This is the same step you can take at any time. We hope that by following the processes outlined in this book, you will be more confident and better prepared to succeed.

The financial rewards can be overwhelming for successful entrepreneurs who often start with little or no thought of where the company could grow or what it might be. Bill Hewlett and Dave Packard founded Hewlett-Packard (HP) in a garage building using an audio oscillator. Steve Jobs and Steve Wozniak started Apple in a garage by just playing around with ideas related to computers. Mark Zuckerberg and his roommates started Facebook as a way to connect with other students at Harvard (its first incarnation was a site designed to compare two people at the same time and decide which one was "hotter").

EXERCISE 1

1. Name some successful entrepreneurs you personally know.
2. What types of businesses do they run?
3. Why do you think they are successful?
4. How would they define success?

LO1-4

Describe the impact of entrepreneurial businesses on society.

How Does Society Benefit?

New business development is an important driver of the economic success of a community, a region, and a state. As a result, civic leaders increasingly look to entrepreneurs as a means to promote economic strength. There are some well-known areas where such efforts have been widely publicized, such as North Carolina's research triangle; Austin, Texas; the Denver–Fort

Collins Innovation Corridor; Silicon Valley; and Boston's 128 corridor. These areas are well known for generating new employment with entrepreneurial ventures, providing a growing tax revenue base, and providing a basis for significant improvements to the area's economic vitality.[8] The success of these areas has encouraged others to seek to promote entrepreneurship to a much greater degree. A program called Economic Gardening is growing across the United States to help start new entrepreneurial businesses in an area. The support provided includes financing for the venture, tax incentives, support classes, and more. Memphis, Tennessee, has used the program as a way to revitalize key elements in the city's economy.[9]

Entrepreneurial businesses act as a catalyst for societal change in other ways as well. They have the ability to garner profits in markets that have been ignored by large corporations. Large organizations will regularly ignore business opportunities if they do not believe the results will generate high profits, whereas entrepreneurial businesses are more flexible and willing to pursue a wider range of opportunities. The owners and employees of the entrepreneurial businesses have an understanding of the local community not easily obtained by a large conglomerate. For example, after a large military base or factory closes, there is obvious economic damage to that region, as the businesses that catered to the base or factory must either reset their target market or close their doors. Examinations of these areas suggest that a crisis such as a military base closing can lead to the formation of a much higher level of new business formations. Those individuals who have lost their jobs generally don't wish to leave the area (or cannot afford to leave the area). These individuals may have been satisfied with their location and while they dreamed of starting a business it was only when faced with the challenge of unemployment that they took the risk to start their dream. Studies have found that people facing a crisis from closure of an existing business often form new businesses which, in many cases, can turn the economic fortunes of the area around.

In 2001, the federal General Accounting Office did an analysis of the impact of the closure of military bases. They found that in cities with base closings including Salt Lake City, Kansas City, and San Jose, the areas around the bases had unemployment rates lower than the national average and income growth higher than the national average. There had been large initial job losses in these communities; however, the state and community leaders had responded to the closing of the bases with tax breaks and programs to support the development of new businesses. The result was that numerous new businesses rose up to fill the economic gap that had resulted from the closing of the bases.[10]

In Aurora, Colorado, the Fitzsimons Life Science District was developed on the site of the former Fitzsimons Army Medical Center, which was closed in 1999. Within two years of its opening the area had 17 start-up or early-stage bioscience businesses housed there.[11] Today it is a thriving center of research, employment, and new business growth.

Entrepreneurial businesses provide more than just jobs; they also provide a means to meet the varied demands that individuals face in a society. Individuals can become frustrated with large corporations over the lack of promotion opportunities or the inflexibility of the corporations in dealing with the needs of family and children. Starting a new business may allow individuals to meet these demands in their lives in a way that large corporations are simply unwilling to do.

Memphis, TN, is currently going through an economic revitalization.

ETHICAL CHALLENGE

What is the goal of business? Milton Friedman (among others) has argued that the only goal of business should be to make a profit. Following this line of thinking, a business owner who pursues anything other than a singular focus on profit is diverting money from the investors who rightfully own that money. On the other hand, a wide variety of people have argued that all businesses are part of a larger society and, as a result, should seek not only to make a profit, but also to try to better society by providing employment, making wise use of resources, giving back to the community, and supporting the efforts of the community to provide a better place to live for all people.

So, where do you fall on this debate? Does a business have an ethical obligation to do more than observe the laws of a society? Although the absolute minimum requirement may be that a businessperson must observe the laws, ethical decision-making is the conscious examination of a wide variety of issues, including the purpose of the business. All business owners need to at least consider these issues.

QUESTIONS

1. How do you weigh the importance in business of making a profit versus providing broader benefits to society?
2. Do you believe that obeying the laws is sufficient for making an ethical choice?

The number of women starting new businesses has increased to the point where they are now the largest single group of new business founders. In part, this growth has come from the fact that women are often frustrated by what is referred to as the "glass ceiling." This refers to the fact that women, like minorities, may be hired by large firms but experience limits placed on their advancement. As a result, these women leave the large firms and start their own businesses. Women entrepreneurs also start businesses to allow them to have greater control over their lives so they can better balance their family's and children's needs. A new business provides a valuable safety valve so that the citizens of a society can address the demands and needs in their lives.

Heather Schuck (left) worked in investments and then in a psychiatric treatment home before her frustration with work–life balance helped push her to start her own business, Glamajama, which makes trendy baby clothes. Founded in 2003, the firm's products today can be found at national retailers such as Bed Bath & Beyond, Nordstrom, Target, and J.C. Penney. Using her experience, Schuck wanted to encourage women to achieve business success while also being allowed to stay focused on family, so she later started the very popular GlamaLIFE.com online community, which connects women interested in business. This community is built around the ideas in Schuck's 2013 book entitled *The Working Mom Manifesto: How to Stop Hoping for Happiness and Start Creating It*. The central argument is that women can create successful businesses around family rather than forcing the family to be centered around the business. Ms. Schuck has appeared on every significant talk show and is a classic example of how one can achieve in many facets of life.[12]

Entrepreneurship Around the World

LO1-5

Discuss the worldwide impact of entrepreneurial businesses.

New and growing businesses are critically important around the world. The World Bank estimates that one of the strongest factors in the growth in any nation's GNP is the presence of entrepreneurial small- and medium-sized enterprises (SMEs). Today there are widespread efforts in almost all nations to encourage the development of small and medium enterprises. These governmental efforts range from tiny contributions of capital or time to large, multidimensional programs that cross the boundaries of multiple nations.

Some of the efforts to encourage SMEs around the world are quite small, but still have a big impact. For example, microloan programs have been in existence for years to encourage self-development. These loans are often for only a few dollars each and are made directly to entrepreneurs, often women. The businesses founded through such loans can be as simple as delivering lunches, weaving baskets, or washing clothes. However, the success of such loans has been substantial, with great strides being made in many desperately poor nations. It is interesting that the repayment rate on such loans is typically 99 to 100 percent, a much higher repayment rate than on most types of loans. The success of these loans has resulted in an increasing dedication of the U.S. aid budget to microloans for developing nations.[13]

At the other extreme are nations that have prepared a full range of programs to encourage new venture start-ups. A program in Singapore is aimed at encouraging high-technology ventures among highly educated individuals. The government is providing a range of services and facilities to assist in the development of these ventures and encourage the founding of firms that might result. Although these two examples are at different extremes, they both demonstrate a high level of interest and investment by governments in small-business initiation. The result of these efforts is that the pace of small-business start-ups is increasing around the world.

EXERCISE 2

1. What motivates your interest in entrepreneurship?
2. What opportunities do you see in your community?
3. Have these opportunities attracted other businesses, large or small? Why or why not?

What Is an Entrepreneurial Business?

LO1-6

Define an entrepreneurial business.

It is clear from the previous discussion that new businesses have benefits for individuals and society within the United States and around the world. Individuals typically associate small and entrepreneurial businesses together. For classification purposes, the U.S. government considers any business with fewer than 500 employees to be a small business while the European Union caps that number at 50. We would suggest that a business with almost 500 employees is actually a large firm requiring formal personnel policies, specialized groups, and an administrative structure that is in no way close to the reality of most small businesses. For the vast majority of people, the businesses formed will have far fewer than 500 employees.

We suggest that there is a further level of definition that is needed for clarity. Multiple terms can be used to refer to the same types of businesses including *entrepreneurial businesses, small businesses*, sometimes as *small- to-medium-sized businesses or enterprises* (SMBs or SMEs), and *family businesses*. These terms are roughly equivalent and do not specify the differences between the two main types of new business. We see two main categories of start-up businesses.

The first category of start-up businesses are those formed as high-growth, often high-tech ventures that have several unique characteristics and are generally referred to as venture capital–backed firms. Venture capital start-ups can be characterized by the following descriptions:

1. The businesses are well-funded by venture capital or angel investment. In fact, without such capital it is virtually impossible to begin this particular type of venture.* Venture capitalists are a specialized type of investor; they typically do not invest less than $2 million and in return they expect extraordinary returns.
2. These businesses are formed with a **harvest plan** in place; this is a plan to exit the business that allows the investors to take advantage of growth. A harvest plan may include selling the business to another firm, selling it to a group of investors, or even participating in an IPO (a public offering of stock). Size is the deciding metric in a potential public offering or sale to a larger organization.
3. As a result of the harvest plan, these firms are organized to grow as quickly as possible and are generally heavily laden with debt. Many are harvested before they can achieve positive net cash flow.
4. They have a developed organizational structure.
5. They often hire an experienced president to grow the company.
6. They tend to develop operations in multiple locations very shortly after the initial investment.
7. They are inherently risky operations whose growth is dependent on the exploitation of unknowns in the market (a new invention, unique patents, etc.).
8. These businesses either start or grow quickly to employ a relatively large number of employees.

harvest plan

A plan to exit a business. Typically, the owners have the intention to sell the business to another firm or take it to an IPO.

The second category of business is a more common type of business and is the focus of this book. These firms are most often referred to as entrepreneurial firms and are defined by these characteristics:

1. The start-up is self-funded or closely funded.
2. The development plan is oriented around positive cash flow.
3. The management structure is designed to take advantage of the skills of the founder or founders.
4. The operation is designed in the image of the founder(s).
5. The business is oriented toward the personal goals of the founder(s).
6. The number of employees may be zero or as few as one, and typically would not be expected to grow to more than 50 to 100.

When we discuss *entrepreneurial businesses* throughout this text, it is this second category of firms to which we refer. Such entrepreneurial businesses are the type you are much more likely to found than are venture capital–backed firms. This is not to suggest that a business founded as an

*The concepts of venture capital and angel investors will be dealt with in greater detail in later chapters. For reference here, both are investors who provide capital to the start-up firm in exchange for ownership in the new firm. This ownership level can be and often is at over 50 percent of the firm.

entrepreneurial business does not sometimes become a capital-backed business. Although Facebook or even LinkedIn was founded as an entrepreneurial business, we would more accurately describe either of them as a venture capital–backed business, since both quickly required millions of dollars of investment from venture capitalists to grow. In contrast, the businesses of the majority of millionaires discussed in the book *The Millionaire Next Door* almost always started as entrepreneurial businesses. These individuals made their fortunes in areas such as lawn care, plumbing, and electrical work, and their businesses were almost all founded in a manner consistent with the second category of business.

Mark Zuckerberg is a great example of massive entrepreneurial business success. His story is more the exception than the rule. What lessons can we learn from Zuckerberg's success that might apply to businesses on a smaller scale?

Although some of the concepts discussed in this text are applicable to venture capital–backed firms, the focus in this text is on the systematic designing of a successful entrepreneurial business start-up. The U.S. Census tracks employment by number of employees (among many other statistics) and the latest census reports indicate that firms with fewer than 99 employees represent the majority of all firms in the United States, and also represent approximately 35 percent of all full-time employees in the United States.[14]

Business Plans—Another Difference in Types of Firms

Another critical difference between an entrepreneurial business and a venture capital–backed firm is in the size and detail required in their initial business plans. An entrepreneurial business's resources are significantly more constrained than those of venture capital–backed business. Whereas the entrepreneurial firm generally develops a business plan as a promotional tool to be sent to venture capitalists and other potential investors, the entrepreneurial business develops a business plan as a guide for the running of the business. Many entrepreneurial ventures hire professional consultants to assist them in the development of their business plans; in contrast, we strongly advise all entrepreneurial business owners to develop their own plans as a part of their process.

EXERCISE 3

1. Do you have any initial ideas for a new business? Write these ideas down. As we go through the course you will be asked to evaluate your business idea in light of the concepts presented in that chapter. Most ideas will undergo significant evolution as you begin to study the topic more.
2. How many employees would your initial business require?

A venture capital–backed business plan runs from 25 to 45 pages long, though we have seen many that are more than 100 pages (ugh). The business plan for a small business should be relatively short (15 to 25 pages) and should be developed in a manner that helps the small-business person understand the industry, the firm that he or she wishes to develop, and what will be needed to create success in that business. Thus, the business plan for a new entrepreneurial business is developed with three goals in mind:

1. To be a guide to managing the business in its early development.
2. To provide a self-evaluation: putting the information down in writing allows for evaluation and honest analysis.
3. To provide potential closely held investors with the critical information necessary to evaluate the key criteria of the business: its cash flow, management team, and competitive advantage.

The business planning process that we develop in this text is a very practical and logical guide for the establishment and initial management of a new business. We do not discuss the long, intricate business plans that are sometimes written to attract venture capital. Instead, you will develop a working document that is grounded in the needs of the new entrepreneurial business. A well-thought-out business plan has heightened importance for the new business as a tool for you to think through a wide range of issues, as most new businesses will not actually obtain financing from big-money investors. This type of business will either be self-funded or will obtain financing from friends and family. These types of investors are not looking for a slick five-year formal plan; instead, they are looking for a document that explains the value of the business and how it will succeed.

Therefore, you should note the following:

1. *No cookie-cutter business plan programs.* We will not use any of the cookie-cutter business plan programs that are available. If you google the term *business plan,* you will find any number of programs on the Internet that encourage you to plug in information and allow the program to "generate" a plan. We believe such programs really inhibit the process of designing a business. Each business plan, much like each business, should have its own voice, feel, and presentation. We suggest to you that a good business plan is best developed by the individual(s) contemplating the business, not by paid consultants who will have none of the enthusiasm of the founder(s). The fact that potential investors to an entrepreneurial business will be those closest to the founder makes it critical that the entrepreneur(s) seek to ensure the chances of success by doing thorough planning and thinking. It is one thing to lose money and close a business if the investment comes from investors you know casually. However, if the investors are your parents, in-laws, grandparents, or siblings and the business closes, it can be truly painful and may, in fact, cause ruptures in the relationships you hold most dear. A well-designed business plan has already helped the founder(s) consider every aspect of the new business and allows everyone else involved to have a true "feel" for where this opportunity is heading.
2. *You should plan to develop the elements of your plan as you finish each chapter.* This text is designed for you to have a full business plan crafted by the time you reach the end of the book. Crafting that section of your plan along the lines developed in the chapter leads to a more comprehensive and well-designed plan that is fresh in your mind as you write. The final section of the book has a fully developed entrepreneurial business plan and a full discussion about each section of that plan. The plan in the appendix is one developed by students as a class project. Our hope is that you will be able to produce an equally detailed plan in this class. The business plan you produce should ultimately be a good solid start on a plan you could use to begin your own business. You will want to refine the plan more after you leave the class, but the class will provide you with the tools to begin the process of forming your own business.
3. *Don't be intimidated by the effort needed to bring forth a business.* It is a daunting task to think about all the aspects of crafting a new business. It should be done in pieces with each piece fitting into a whole picture. At the end of every chapter, you should ask yourself whether the business you are designing still makes business sense. There is as much value in deciding not to pursue a particular business idea as there is in actually starting a business. It is a process, take it step-by-step.

4. *Craft a one-page pitch for your business.* We will discuss this several times in this text, but it is crucial that you develop an attractive, one-page pitch about your business. It clearly lays out the crucial information about the new business idea and provides an effective starting point for every potential supplier, employee, or investor. Although each one will be somewhat unique, a one-page pitch generally should look like the one in Figure 1.2.

Figure 1.2
One-Page Pitch Sheet
An example one-page pitch sheet provides a snapshot of the business at a point in time.

The Fraudian Slip

Course Name

Product Offering: The Fraudian Ship provides a total solution that helps insurance companies reduce the number of claims paid by reducing their risk through the real time tracking and monitoring of high-value items.

Customer Problem: Items sent via shipping companies and couriers are still at the mercy of the company's tracking systems. Scanning and RF trackers can be circumvented and fraud is possible. Fraudian Ship's service provides constant monitoring of packages for location and unauthorized opening. A total solution that helps insurance companies reduce the number of claims by reducing their risk through tracking the Fraudian Ship device, resulting in a reduction in financial payout due to a decrease in claims and lower fraud risk.

Target Market: The Fraudian Ship's initial target market is companies that sell shipping insurance (third-party shipping insurers, postal companies, and courier companies). $4.29 billion industry (Source: IBISWorld 2014).

Customers: Fraudian Ship's customers are (1) insurance companies; (2) shipping companies and companies or individuals shipping high-value items to reduce claims and risk fraud.

Sale/Marketing Strategy: Train insurance companies to sell this value-added service to all customers who ship insurable items. The strategy will be the ability of the shipper to offer "real-time" tracking to its customers.

Business Model: The Fraudian Ship's business model consists of a service relationship with insurance companies, which insure shipped goods. A GPS device is sent to the owner to embed in packages as part of their insurance policy. Shipments are tracked by The Fraudian Ship in exchange for a percentage of the policy.

Competitors: (1) Companies that target businesses (Agheera, Spark Nano, Global Tracking Group, self-insuring shipping cos.) (2) wholly owned subsidiaries (FED EX's SenseAware)

Competitive Advantage: Insurance companies spend huge amounts of time and money processing and paying claims for items lost or damaged during shipping. Current package-tracking software focuses on identifying where a package is in the shipping process and providing peace of mind to senders. The Fraudian Ship puts technology in the hands of insurance companies allowing them to identify where a package has been and what it's been through, allowing them to better identify fraud and reduce the cost of reviewing and paying claims.

SUMMARY

This chapter began by discussing the impact that new businesses have on the economy. A brief history of new ventures was discussed, with the observation that every business you can think of, regardless of size, was started by one person or a small group of people. Given that, there are still two very distinct types of businesses: (1) those that are funded by large amounts of outside venture capital with the intent of growing them as fast as possible, and (2) those that are primarily in business for the benefit of the founders and their families. The second group is far more prevalent around the globe and is the focus of this text. The remainder of the chapter set up three main principles we want you to remember: (1) No cookie-cutter business plan programs should be used,(2) build your own business plan along with the chapters in this book, and (3) this is a process, so take it in bite-sized pieces.

KEY TERMS

economies of scale 5
Fortune 500 4
harvest plan 12
stakeholders 8
United States Small Business Administration (SBA) 4

REVIEW QUESTIONS

1. How do entrepreneurial businesses impact the economy?
2. Name several entrepreneurs who have grown their businesses into major organizations.
3. Explain what is meant by the science and the art of starting and managing a business.
4. How have entrepreneurial businesses impacted the growth of the United States?
5. Why does "profit as a goal" present an ethical challenge to new business owners?
6. What differentiates an entrepreneurial business from one that is a venture-backed business?

INDIVIDUAL EXERCISES

1. What types of new businesses interest you most and why?
2. What aspects of those businesses are particularly appealing to you?
3. Do you see yourself as an entrepreneur in the next five years?

GROUP EXERCISES

Interview an Entrepreneur

Early in the semester, every person in the class should interview an entrepreneur. You have wide flexibility as to the types of entrepreneurs you select. However, each entrepreneur must be the original founder of the business or the current owner and should not be your close relative. Prepare a report on each entrepreneur interviewed. The report should be no more than three typed, double-spaced pages long, and cover three primary areas. First, discuss the background and characteristics of the entrepreneur, as well as the history and nature of the business. Second, discuss lessons learned by the entrepreneur as related to you by the entrepreneur. Third, include your evaluation of the entrepreneur, and state what you can personally take away from the experience. You should plan to make a short (5–7 minute) presentation on this individual to the rest of the class by midsemester.

ENDNOTES

1. http://www.sba.gov/content/small-business-trends
2. "Dick Schulze: The Houdini of Consumer Electronics," *BusinessWeek*, June 21, 1998. www.businessweek.com/stories/1998-06-21 /dick-schulze-the-houdini-of-consumer-electronics
3. R. Makaodok, "Interfirm Differences in Scale Economies and the Evolution of Market Share," *Strategic Management Journal* 20 (1999), pp. 935–52.
4. "Tesla Model S Owners Can Now Drive Across the Country for Free," *The Huffington Post*, January 28,

2014. www.huffingtonpost.com/2014/01/28/tesla-supercharger-network-model-s-country_n_4681027.html
5. K. H. Vesper, *New Venture Strategies* (Englewood Cliffs, NJ: Prentice Hall, 1990); C. E. Bamford and E. B. Douthett, "Venture Capital and Risk Management: Evidence from Initial Public Offerings" *Journal of Managerial Issues* 25, no. 3 (2013), pp. 220–40.
6. M. G. Blackford, *A History of Small Business in America* (New York: Twayne Publishers, 1991).
7. T. J. Stanley and W. D. Danko, *The Millionaire Next Door* (New York: Simon & Schuster, 1998).
8. Z. J. Acs, "Small Firms and Economic Growth," in *Small Business in the Modern Economy,* ed. P. H. Admiral (New York: Blackwell, 1996); A. Zacharakis, P. D. Reynolds, and W. D. Bygrave, "National Entrepreneurship Assessment: United States of America" (paper presented at Kauffman Center for Entrepreneurial Leadership. Kansas City, MO, 1999).
9. http://growth-engine.org/
10. General Accounting Office, "Military Base Closures: Overview of Economic Recovery, Property Transfer, and Environmental Cleanup." Statement by Barry H. Homan, Director, Defense Capabilities and Management, 2001. www.gao.gov/new.items/d011054t.pdf
11. http://fitzscience.com/; J. McCurry, "A Fighting Chance: Former U.S. Military Bases Are Now Home to Thriving Industry," *Site Selection Magazine*, November 2002. www.siteselection.com/issues/2002/nov/p803/
12. N. Fallon, "10 Female Entrepreneurs Who Inspired Us in 2013," *Business News Daily,* December 23, 2013. www.businessnewsdaily.com/5668-female-entrepreneurs-2013.html; http://workingmommanifesto.com/mom-entrepreneur/
13. P. Engardio, "Commentary: A Way for Africa to Help Itself," *BusinessWeek,* July 21, 2003. www.businessweek.com/magazine/content/03_29/b3842069_mz014.htm.
14. www.census.gov/econ/smallbus.html

CREDITS

Opener: Hero Images/Getty Images RF; p. 3: Courtesy of Oren's Daily Roast; p. 5: © Kevin Fleming/Corbis; p. 8: © Editorial Image, LLC/Alamy; p. 9: Ron Cogswell/Flickr/CC-BY-2.0; p. 10: http://glamajama.com; p. 13: Bloomberg via Getty Images.

chapter

2

Individual Leadership and Entrepreneurial Start-Ups

learning objectives

After studying this chapter, you will be able to:

LO2-1 Explain how entrepreneurial founders impact the business world as a whole.

LO2-2 Discuss the importance of an entrepreneurial orientation.

LO2-3 List the triggers that encourage new business formations.

LO2-4 Compare and contrast various types of new business supports.

LO2-5 Explain how you can evaluate those things that you enjoy the most and discover how they may lead to business opportunities.

PHILLY PRETZEL AND DAN DIZIO

At 11 years old Dan DiZio had the opportunity to sell pretzels for a man who had more than he could sell that particular day. Dan sold the pretzels on the street corner of his neighborhood and that one-day job turned into a money-making activity he would continue all the way through his college career. After graduating from college, he became a stockbroker. Relatively quickly Dan and his roommate (a psychological counselor) realized that they were not happy with their professions. Remarkably, the two decided to quit their jobs, gather as much capital as they could from their credit cards, and start a business as a soft pretzel wholesaler. Despite their intent to be a wholesaler, they were surprised to find that people would line up outside their business and buy pretzels individually. Taking their cue from their customers' actual behavior, Dan shifted the business from a wholesaler operation to a retail business. The demand for their pretzels was so strong that between 1998 and 2004 he and his partner were able to open eight retail stores. In 2005 they began to franchise their store concept and now there are more than 120 franchise and corporate locations of their pretzel business, employing 1,500 people.

DiZio clearly illustrates the risk taking that characterizes an entrepreneur. He quit his job and funded his venture initially with credit card debt. At different stages he illustrated leadership when he was willing to change first from a wholesaler to a retailer, and then to a franchiser. At each stage he has also been able to grow people to help him in the process. There are several pieces of advice that Dan offers to those who want to form a business:

- "Start-up money is valuable, so don't waste it. We wasted a lot at first and ultimately had to end up redoing a lot of the work. Really watch those dollars and know where the money is going."
- "As a business leader you have to understand your product and know the business. You need to be able to relay your thoughts and passion to others and train them."

Questions

1. What is your assessment of using credit cards to start a new business?
2. How much knowledge of an industry is enough for you to be willing to start a new business?
3. How would you maintain the "feeling" of a business as it spreads to hundreds of locations?

Sources: E. Cassano, "Plot Twist," *Smart Business Philadelphia* 7, no. 9 (May 2011), pp. 18–23; J. Bair, "Twisty Business," *Central Penn Business Journal* 24, no. 49 (November 28, 2008), pp. 3–8; D. DiZio, "The Accidental Entrepreneur," *Smart Business Philadelphia* 8, no. 2 (October 2011), p. 5.

In large, well-established organizations, no one person is crucial to the survival of the business, even the president of the company. The lack of dependence of large organizations on any one individual is due to the strong structures in the large firm such as extensive written procedures, clear lines of responsibility, and the presence of other individuals or units to step in when some failure occurs. Large organizations also have wide dispersion of knowledge throughout the business; in other words, there are multiple people who know about any given aspect of the business. As a result, if any single person leaves the organization, it has the ability to continue with minimal interruption. Finally, large organizations have greater excess resources, including financial resources, which allow them to hire outside experts to fill any critical need that arises. These excess resources are referred to as **organizational slack**; they allow large organizations flexibility that is not available to the typical entrepreneurial venture.

organizational slack
Excess resources in an organization that allow for redundancy and the quick deployment of personnel in crisis.

In contrast an entrepreneurial business is generally dependent on a single individual or a few individuals for the business to survive. A new entrepreneurial business starts as the brainchild of a single person or a small group of people, each of whom has an ownership stake in the business. The new business has few formal procedures, a concentration of knowledge in those individuals who start the business, and limited slack resources.[1] The absence of slack financial resources means the new firm has limited flexibility in responding to emergency issues such as the need to hire replacements if the company loses key individuals. As a result, the founders of an entrepreneurial business and the leadership they provide play a far more critical role in the business's success than does the senior leadership of the typical large organization. The importance of the individual in the founding and managing of a new business leads to the focus in this chapter on the individual who starts a business and his or her leadership.

Understanding and collaborating in small groups can be an essential part of new business success. What are some of the key characteristics you would look for in a partner?

This chapter includes a discussion of why individuals are so important to the success of a new business. It also provides ways for you to understand your own predisposition to start a business. The examination of your orientation includes an examination of your risk tolerance and the boundaries that may exist in your perception of events in the environment. It also includes an exercise to test your own entrepreneurial orientation.

Every individual brings a unique set of supports that can be used to help in the founding process; these supports are critical in the success of a new business. Therefore, we will examine those supports, the most important of which is the family. In some businesses the family is a more valuable support than in others as the family may all work in the firm. These businesses are referred to as **family businesses**. Family businesses have unique issues that extend beyond those of the normal new entrepreneurial business. We will address family businesses more at the end of this chapter.

family business
A business in which ownership and employment are centered around the family.

The authors of the text have had extensive experience working with entrepreneurs as they start and run their businesses. Throughout this text you will find that many of these firms are used as examples. In particular, we will follow two specific start-up businesses throughout the text. The first one we will see in this chapter is Friends' Home Health. This venture was the outcome of three friends' discussions after work and the effort to find new opportunities for themselves.

FRIENDS' HOME HEALTH

In 2012 three friends who worked in the same nursing facility started talking about starting a business together. The three friends had known each other for a number of years. The friends include one registered nurse (RN) (Betty), and two licensed practical nurses (LPNs) (Joan and Bob). The RN typically is the supervising nurse on the ward and the LPNs do more of the direct care of individual patients. The friends observed the increasing numbers of elderly people in the hospital. As they talked with the family members of these patients they realized there was a need for a reliable home health firm in the area. Despite the existence of several operations in the area (one a national chain), the patients' families were constantly talking about problems with the current group of home health firms. The families told stories about caregivers who did not show up, were not willing to do distasteful jobs, had poor training, and some who outright stole from the home.

Home health workers go to the homes of clients to help the individuals bathe and eat, and generally assist the elderly or otherwise physically impaired individuals in their homes. Often a family member provides this assistance but needs support to adequately care for the individual or to be able to take a break from their caregiving. Home health workers typically undergo far less training than do LPNs, and some operators provide very little oversight of the in-home workers.

The three friends (Betty, Joan, and Bob) wanted more control over their lives and the opportunity to be paid more for their efforts. Working in the health care facility involved long and odd hours where they might work all night and never see their families. They felt that in their current positions, they were working very hard but were receiving only limited direct rewards for that effort. These issues pushed the three to talk about starting a business. The discussions initially were little more than talk; however, in the past few months these discussions had become more serious. They were not sure how to make a home health business unique, but they knew they wanted to start one.

Joan's uncle had founded several businesses and appeared to understand what it took to be successful in business. The three potential entrepreneurs had a conversation with the uncle; he advised them to spend a little more time investigating their motivations and personal risk orientation before they actually considered going into business together. He related the story of his first business, which he had started with his best friend. The two had been lifelong friends and thought they knew all there was to know about each other. Not only had they been friends since childhood, each had been the best man in the others' wedding, and each was the godfather for the other's oldest child. Although they thought they knew each other well, when it came to money and the level of risk they were capable of handling, they were substantially different people. Whereas the uncle was very frugal, his partner believed that money needed to be enjoyed today. Ultimately their business partnership fell apart. Although the financial loss was significant, even more devastating was the loss of the friendship between the two men and their families. He has always felt the experience was a significant failure and not one he wanted to repeat.

Joan's uncle has had other businesses and partnerships since that initial failure. He now believes that although he needs to like a person in order to work closely with him or her, it is much more important that they agree on such key issues as money and risk.

Therefore, the uncle suggested the three friends prepare with some simple tasks:

QUESTIONS

1. Compare how each of them prepared his or her monthly family budget.
2. Discuss how much debt each was willing to take on credit cards.
3. Discuss whether each was willing to lend family members money, and the reasons for their answer.
4. Have each person answer this question: If you inherited $250,000, what would you do with it?

The outcome of this exercise for our three potential business owners will be discussed after Exercise 1.

EXERCISE 1

1. Evaluate your own views on the issues raised in Friends' Home Health. Discuss your results with others in your class. What is the range of answers that were given?
2. Have you ever lent money to a relative? Or have you heard stories from others who have? Would it be different if it were a close friend with whom you went into business?

The three potential entrepreneurs completed the exercise. Betty and Joan realized from the exercise they were far more frugal in their lives than Bob. From this insight Betty and Joan realized that they were more compatible as partners than either was with Bob. They realized that if they went into business with Bob they would soon have significant conflicts regarding both the approach to and the actual finances of the new business. The result would most likely be a loss of their friendship with him, and also the potential failure of the business. The discussions among the three friends also brought these issues home more clearly to Bob, who ultimately decided that a business was not for him. He realized that because of his current debt, if the business needed more money, he would not be able to put any more money into it; also, if the business failed, he had so few resources to fall back upon that he might have to file for bankruptcy.

LO2-1

Explain how entrepreneurial founders impact the business world as a whole.

Founders Are the Reason Why Entrepreneurial Businesses Work So Well

New businesses have some significant advantages over large businesses. For example, the very fact that entrepreneurial businesses start out small means that these firms have greater flexibility. Smaller firms can also respond quickly to changes around them, whereas a large firm tends to use many committees or project teams to approve the work of other committees or project teams. This feature alone allows the smaller firm led by the aware entrepreneur to respond quickly to opportunities or threats as they arise. Entrepreneurial firms also fill niches that large firms simply cannot afford to fill. Large firms do have an advantage in those situations where there are economies of scale; that is, the large firms have the ability to produce a service or product more cheaply because it is done on a large scale.[2] However, in small niches, the large firms' systems are not able to do small volumes of a particular activity profitably because of their large fixed costs and overhead. These niches are ideal for new businesses.

Even though these advantages can be substantial, the greatest advantage for an entrepreneurial business is that it is owned and run by the same person(s). Contrast this to most large corporations, where there is a division between owners and managers. The individuals who manage the operations of a large, established corporation do not typically have substantial ownership in the company. The managers (agents of the owners) may own some stock, but in a large business such as General Motors they own a very small percentage of the total stock.

agency theory
A managerial theory that believes individuals act to maximize their own benefit. Thus, in settings where there is a split between ownership and control (as in most publicly traded corporations), the agents (managers) must be monitored or they will act to maximize their own benefit, not necessarily the benefit of those who own the firm (the shareholders).

Agency theory suggests that individuals act to maximize their own individual benefit.[3] The result in a large corporation is that the manager of a business will tend to act to maximize his own benefit, not necessarily that of those who own the firm (typically the shareholders). This does not mean that the manager seeks to steal from the firm; instead, in subtle but pervasive ways, the manager will act for his or her own benefit. In contrast, the individual who owns the business will always act to maximize the value of the business, since the interest of the owner and that of the business itself are aligned: If the business makes money, the owner makes money.

To illustrate, the manager of a large firm can easily justify why it is important to fly nonstop, first class across the country for a meeting in New York City. That manager might argue the need to arrive fresh, with room to work, and rest on the flight. This trip may easily cost $6,000 if the ticket is bought on short notice. This comes out of the corporation's income, money that really belongs to the shareholders (the owners).

The cost of luxuries such as first-class airfare is an extravagance few entrepreneurial businesses can afford. How would you, as an entrepreneur, decide what constitutes a luxury and what is a necessity?

Compare this with the typical behavior of an entrepreneur. Just as it is for a corporation, the airline ticket is an expense; however, in this case, every dollar spent comes directly out of the pocket of the entrepreneur. The entrepreneur is more likely to go on the Internet and find the cheapest ticket possible. Although the entrepreneur would also like to arrive fresh and be able to work during the flight, he or she is more likely to fly economy class and fly through a hub airport to save the $4,000 or more. If the large, established business is doing poorly, the manager still collects a salary and benefits, although the shareholders (owners) are getting few rewards. The manager will move on to another firm if the business collapses, having no significant stake in the financial failure of the previous company. In contrast, if an entrepreneurial business is doing poorly, the owner may ultimately have to close the business and be responsible for any debts that have accumulated. As a result, the entrepreneur will treat the costs of the business very differently than will the manager of a firm. (When we deal with the legal structure of entrepreneurial business in Chapter 7, we specify in greater detail if and when an entrepreneur is responsible for the debts of the business.) If the managers of a large business had to spend their own money or were responsible for the debt of the organization, agency theory would argue that the manager would behave in a thriftier manner.

Thus, one of the greatest assets of the new business is the owner of the business due to their personal involvement in, and dedication to, the business. It is because of the owner's importance to the business that students need to consider their own abilities and resources early as they begin to look at building an entrepreneurial business.

EXERCISE 2

1. What will you do if the business fails?
2. How much time are you willing to dedicate to the success of the venture?
3. How much of your personal assets are you willing to put into the venture?

Evaluating Your Entrepreneurial Orientation

LO2-2

Discuss the importance of an entrepreneurial orientation.

There are a number of issues that potential entrepreneurs need to consider about themselves as they look at starting a new business. Examined with some depth, these issues will shape the entrepreneur's analysis of the potential of any business idea. These include (1) risk tolerance, (2) prior experience, and (3) personality orientation of the individual.

Risk Tolerance

Potential entrepreneurs must determine their own individual level of tolerance to risk. You are probably familiar with the concept from dealing with your own financial expenditures. The typical advice provided to most individuals is to spend no more than your personal risk tolerance.[4] Thus, if you have a low risk tolerance you need to spend less and save more for that proverbial rainy day. If you have a high risk tolerance, you will

Evel Knievel has become a cultural reference point for risk taking. An interesting counterpoint to this image was Knievel's very vocal stand against the risks associated with taking drugs. This dichotomy illustrates that risk levels can vary, even within the same person.

spend more, assuming there will not be a rainy day. We use a similar concept here, but we use it more broadly, asking you to consider your tolerance to a wide range of potential risks that extend far beyond just financial considerations. Initially, you need to evaluate whether you have the risk tolerance to actually start a new business. The next step is to evaluate what level of risk you will accept in a given business situation.

To illustrate, if you work for a large corporation, there is relatively low individual financial risk. In a normal economic environment, even if a large corporation has a poor year and loses money, it will still meet payroll, pay the workers' benefits, and not close its doors on short notice. On the other hand, the entrepreneur is faced with a substantially different situation. When starting a business, it takes time for the business to reach a level where the revenue coming into the firm is sufficient to cover expenses. (We examine this in significant detail in Chapter 6; the point where the revenue coming into the firm is sufficient to cover expenses is referred to as a **break-even point**.) However, the new business may quickly reach a point where the funds have run out and the business needs to close its doors quickly. If the business does close, then the entrepreneurs may find that they have to pay the debts of the firm that are left, as they had to sign personal guarantees for the loans of the business. Thus, the financial risk for the entrepreneur can be quite high. As a potential entrepreneur, you will need to consider how much debt you are willing to take on. In general, the greater the debt you are willing to take on to start your business, the higher your risk tolerance.

break-even point
The time when a new business has reached a level where revenue coming into the firm is sufficient to cover expenses.

Potential new business owners need to determine their personal willingness to accept risk in a new business and let that information help decide which business to pursue.[5] There is not one correct answer as to what level of risk tolerance new business owners should be willing to take on. Instead, the key is that individual entrepreneurs must be aware of their tolerance of risk and establish their business in a manner that is consistent with that tolerance. New business owners need to be sure that the level of risk is consistent with their background, values, and family situation. Evaluation of the risk profile for a particular type of business is more art than science.

One well-known entrepreneur provides valuable advice on risk tolerance. He suggests that entrepreneurs never do anything that does not allow them to sleep at night. This rule of thumb can help businesspeople determine the risks with which they will be most comfortable. In future chapters we will return to the evaluation of risk as we look at specific risks, such as financial risks, strategic risks, and market retaliation risks.

EXERCISE 3

To help you determine your own tolerance for risk, answer the following questions.

1. How much debt would you be willing to undertake to provide a foundation for your business idea?
2. How much of your personal savings would you be willing to risk on your business idea?
3. If you were the recipient of a $100,000 inheritance, what portion would you be willing to invest in your business?

Given your answers to the above questions, how would you rate your financial risk tolerance?

Prior Experience

The second element of entrepreneurial orientation is prior experience. Every individual brings to a new business his or her own view of the world. This view of the world places boundaries on what a decision maker will consider as he or she makes decisions. These boundaries are set by experiences, history, culture, and family values, among other things. Boundaries help each of us make sense of the world. For example, in the United States, when you see a red octagonal sign at a corner, you typically assume it is a stop sign. You automatically assume that it is a stop sign because of your history and experience.

However, if you were in another country, such an octagonal sign may not be a stop sign; it might be another highway warning. Our experiences, history, culture, and values not only help us interpret the world, but they also place boundaries on how we see that world. Thus, our experiences, history, culture, and values also establish what we consider to be both possible and practical. This is referred to as the individual's **bounded rationality**. It is the presence of bounded rationality that often leads young people to be pioneers in an area, as they are not limited by the restrictions of the past.

bounded rationality
Rational decision making that is constrained by the background and history of the person making the decision.

Bounded rationality is the reason individuals from outside an industry are able to establish a new business in a manner not previously considered. To illustrate, cattle processing historically was done by large, established firms in meat processing centers such as Chicago, Fort Worth, and Kansas City. The cattle were shipped there and processed by well-trained butchers from the moment of slaughter until they were ready for packaging. An entrepreneur had an idea for viewing the entire process differently. Rather than shipping cattle to a central location, why not process the cattle where they are raised? In addition, instead of hiring well-trained butchers, why not use individuals who make the same cut repeatedly, in an assembly-line manner? This new approach grew quickly, others copied the model, and today virtually all beef is processed this way. Those individuals who had grown up in the beef industry believed that cattle processing had to be done in a specific way. Others came from outside the industry and saw new ways to do things. Their analysis was not bounded by history in the industry.

In a similar vein we could consider the airline and industry maverick Southwest Airlines. Today it is a major employer, but it started as a new business with a few rented planes. At the time everyone in the airline industry believed that air travel was most efficiently handled with a hub and spoke system. That is, the planes would fly into a very large airport such as Chicago, Los Angeles, or Dallas Fort Worth (DFW) from all the airports in that region. Then, people from all of the feeder airports would be placed on the same flight to a given location. Southwest used a model that focused on many short-haul flights of less than an hour between airports. Herb Kelleher (one of the founders of Southwest) was trained as a lawyer and brought fresh insight on how to compete in the industry.

It is important for individuals to understand how their decision making is bounded by their own version of rationality. It is important to know your potential partners' backgrounds and how their decision making is impacted by their history. These issues will impact how you and your partners act both as you run the firm, and as you analyze problems that arise in the development of the business.

Personality Orientation of the Individual

The third element of entrepreneurial orientation is an examination of your own personality. There is a wide variety of personality tests available to assist individuals in analyzing their traits and tendencies. These tests should not be used, however, to determine whether you are capable of starting a new business. There are successful businesspeople in all personality categories. In general, you as an individual will probably score differently on the same test if you take it on different occasions.

Therefore, use these tests to help better understand yourself and your strengths, not as a guide for your career. In general, if you are very outgoing

There are varying aspects to everyone's personalities. How might knowing your strengths and weaknesses impact business decisions?

and extroverted, you may wish to focus on a business in which you have extensive interpersonal interactions. In contrast, if you are more introverted, you may wish to focus on a business, such as an Internet-based business, in which interpersonal interactions are more limited. In this section, we review some of the major personality tests that are available. If you enter the names of these tests into a search engine, you will find that there are numerous versions of the tests available online, often for free. Below we will highlight some of the more established and validated personality tests all of which you can take online.

Myers-Briggs. This is one of the most widely used tests for personality evaluations. It was developed by Katherine Briggs and her daughter Isabel Myers. The rationale for the test is drawn from Carl Jung, a Swiss psychoanalyst who sought to incorporate broader issues into his analysis than had Freud. The test focuses on four pairs of variables: extroversion-introversion (focus on outward world or internal); sensing-intuiting (how people gather information); thinking-feeling (how they make decisions); and judgment-perception (order vs. flexibility). The different potential arrangements of variables are believed to indicate the different ways that individuals deal with other people and their environments.

Enneagram. The underlying philosophy of this test is that a person is the result of all the experiences in his or her life. Thus, the factors in childhood are central in developing who we are today. A bias in this test is that adults will not change their personality over time as the assumption is that we form that personality as a child.

The test suggests that there are nine different types of personalities. Through a series of questions, the test assigns you to one of these primary types. These nine types and a few of the characteristics of each type of individual are as follows: reformer (idealist/perfectionist); helper (caring/good interpersonal skills); achiever (competent/driven); individualist (sensitive/dramatic); investigator (cerebral/focused); loyalist (committed/pessimistic); enthusiast (fun-loving/impatient); challenger (action oriented/cynical); and peacemaker (easygoing/passive aggressive).

Big Five Test. The Big Five is a popular personality test in universities. It is composed of five factors: open-mindedness, conscientiousness, agreeableness, emotional stability, and extroversion (the factor names vary a little among authors). These are considered by many researchers to be the five key components of an individual's personality.

The Big Five test was developed by two independent research teams. These researchers asked thousands of people hundreds of questions and then analyzed the data statistically. The researchers did not set out to identify the five factors; instead, the factors emerged from their analyses of the data.

ETHICAL CHALLENGE

One of the important choices that everyone has to deal with is what they may take with them when they leave a company. This becomes more critical when the person leaving is starting her own new business. Whether it is voluntary or involuntary, leaving a job can be frustrating, and sometimes individuals are frustrated enough to wish to do harm to the firm they are leaving. Beyond that, there is a question as to where the line between personal and business information exists. If the person leaving does something that harms the prior business, then the prior employer may be able to sue the former employee. The impact of such a lawsuit on a fledgling business can be substantial.

To illustrate, consider an employee who has worked for a large plumbing or electrical firm. In his former position, this employee had the opportunity to obtain the firm's customer list. However, if he takes that list and uses it to generate a customer base for the new business, the former employer might be able to sue the new business for the revenue lost.

There is a broader question that an entrepreneur must also consider—if you know you are leaving your current employer to start your own business, is it fair to your employer to do so while still being paid by your employer? Even though the budding entrepreneur may not consciously plan to take customers from the employer, how significant are those contacts to the future business? At what stage does such a setting cross an ethical line?

QUESTIONS

1. What are some ways you can build a customer base when you leave a business without running into problems with your former employer?
2. Beyond the customer list, what other things could you potentially take from a firm that would present an ethical problem?

Triggers for Starting a Business

LO2-3

List the triggers that encourage new business formations.

Starting a new business is often the result of some particular event or condition within an individual's environment. These triggers encourage the forming of new businesses, as they encourage individuals to think creatively. Individuals get comfortable with their lives, and it takes a trigger to force them to think in new ways. You may not be faced with such triggers as motivations, and still decide to start a new business. However, many people do start their businesses when one of these triggers is present, and therefore it is useful for you to understand them. The triggers in the formation of a new business can come from either positive or negative stimulus that occurs in an individual's life. Some typical triggers include the following:

1. Being laid off from established employment.
2. Being approached by one or more people with a new business idea.
3. Reaching a point financially where the risk–return level of a proposed new business is tolerable.
4. Having very little to lose financially by a failure.

5. Receiving evidence that an idea is not only doable, but there is a concrete way to improve on a given problem.
6. Being spurred to action by attending a seminar, reading a book, or talking with successful entrepreneurs.
7. Experiencing a midlife (or early-life, or even late-life) crisis.
8. Observing the establishment of an incubator, accelerator, or business development effort within the community.
9. Experiencing the inability to climb the corporate ladder due to circumstances beyond one's control. These might include not having graduated from the "correct" school, being female in a male-dominated business, having a marketing background in a manufacturing business.

Often, more than one of these triggers may be present at the same time. For discussion purposes, we segment these triggers into two categories: personal motivations and circumstance motivations. Although the exact dividing line between these two categories is somewhat fuzzy, this categorization will allow for the examination of the various issues involved in starting a business.

Personal motivations come from the individuals themselves, and as such are the strongest motivations available. Personal motivations drive people to make career and life-altering moves irrespective of "practical" advice. Entrepreneurs driven by personal motivators will tend to be more proactive, and drive relentlessly toward their goals.

Circumstance motivators tend to result in more of a defensive positioning. The environment and environmental changes make opportunities available to potential business owners, but the motivation is substantially different. This is an opportunistic start-up whose staying power is more determined by other competing opportunities.

To illustrate personal triggers, consider that today one of the fastest-growing groups of entrepreneurs are women. In large part, women are starting new businesses when their career opportunities are blocked at larger corporations. The barrier is often referred to as the "glass ceiling." It involves not formal rules, but the practical reality that in some organizations there are limits to the level in the corporate hierarchy to which women are allowed to progress. If you question the presence of such ceilings, simply note how many women are in senior management positions at most major corporations. The result is that women-led businesses are formed at a rate 50 percent greater than that of men-led businesses. A particularly fast-growing segment of entrepreneurs are minority women owners; today one-third of all female businesses are headed by women of color.[6]

Human nature is such that most people get comfortable with their current status and financial position. When they are laid off, are demoted, are forced to take reduced pay, or even survive a layoff, they are forced to think about new opportunities that they never would have considered previously. As we pointed out in Chapter 1, research has found that when a factory or military base closes, there is a blossoming of new businesses in that area.[7]

Our opening story of Friends' Home Health illustrates how personal and circumstance motivations merge. The three nurses who considered establishing their new venture wanted to have more flexibility in their lives for their families. These individuals all had small children, and they wanted to provide a better standard of living for them. In this case, the three potential business founders not only had one of the strongest personal motivators available to individuals—that of their families—they also had a strong desire to change their overall circumstances.

Supports

LO2-4

Compare and contrast various types of new business supports.

This chapter focuses on the individual who starts the business. It has been stressed in the chapter that this individual, and his or her leadership, is central to the entrepreneurial firm's success. Generally, the founder is far more important than a single individual in a large firm.

This does not mean that an individual, or team of individuals, creates a successful business without help. There are supports and resources available to the entrepreneur. No one of these supports or resources assures success, but the new businessperson should evaluate which resources and supports he or she has access to in an effort to increase the chances of success.

The supports and resources available are typically unique to the entrepreneur and where he or she lives. Not all individuals come to the process of founding the business with equal endowments or supports. The entrepreneur should seek to understand all the supports possible to make the entrepreneurial effort successful. The support and resource areas the entrepreneur might examine include (1) family, (2) social networks, (3) community, and (4) financial resources.

Like a classic architecture, a solid business is built upon a variety of support systems.

Family

Few people know you—including both your abilities and shortcomings—like your family. These individuals are a resource for support, guidance, suggestions, and potential funding for a new business. A spouse who is willing to handle the financial burden while you begin a new venture, a parent who will contribute time and money, an uncle who has been in the industry and is willing to review your plan and advise you so that you might avoid basic pitfalls are all immensely valuable to the new entrepreneur. We advise potential new entrepreneurs to work with their family members not only for their advice and potential funding, but also as a reality check and support structure. Family members are in a unique position to provide you with key insights when you may be pursuing the wrong approach to an issue. Too many other individuals will not be willing to tell you when you may be wrong. Most individuals will tell you only positive things. In addition, you will need your family's support to push you forward to success, as there will be times that you will have to deal with significant discouragements.

To fully utilize your family resources, we suggest you list those family members with whom you have regular contact, and also list the capabilities those individuals possess that might provide support to the new business. The benefit of such an activity is that it will allow you as a new business founder to think systematically through the items that need to be discussed with various family members. You need to make sure you obtain the resources desired from family members without wasting the time and effort of these individuals.

The role of family is so critical to the success of a new business that many new ventures end up being what are referred to as family businesses. In such firms, the principal staff members of the business are family members.

There may be other employees in the firm, but typically, family members hold the key managerial decision-making positions.

The long-term management of family businesses is unique when compared to that of nonfamily-owned businesses. In the initial stages of formation, the support of the family can help the entrepreneur overcome many difficulties that might cause the failure of nonfamily-supported new businesses. For example, when family members are the principal staff, a month in which payroll cannot fully be met by the company is more acceptable. These individuals' level of commitment to the founder may be high enough that they are willing to take only a partial or no salary that month. These individuals also are often willing to work at times and in conditions that other employees would not accept. For example, Christmas season is critical to all retailers, but paid staff may not be willing to work the extra hours needed at this time, whereas family will. It is this level of commitment that has produced success for many immigrant families. In these settings, the reliance on family is a key reason the firms are able to survive and prosper.

However, there are also potential negative long-term issues that accompany a family business. While family members have a greater commitment to you as an entrepreneur because of your close relationships, those close relationships make issues such as firing family members difficult. If a family member is not a good employee, how will you fire that person, or even reprimand them, without rupturing the close relationships in the family? One business founder who did fire a relative described Thanksgiving that year as horrible and silent. Similarly, since family members know each other so well, they are willing to say negative things to an entrepreneur that a regular employee would never say. These negative statements may have no connection to work, but might be issues that are simmering in the family. The negative comments can be particularly caustic in the firm because the owner may be hesitant to fire the family member, and the situation can eventually rupture all relationships with the individual and other extended family members. Finally, the presence of family in the firm can cause difficulties with other employees who are not family members. As will be discussed in Chapter 10, human resource management is one of the most important and contentious issues in a firm. Unfortunately, if it appears there are different expectations and rewards for workers depending on whether they are related to you, it can cause turmoil among employees and make holding onto key nonfamily employees all the more difficult.

Family is usually an important resource for a new business. The new entrepreneur needs to consider the balance of benefits and drawbacks to building a family-based business.

Networks

Beyond your family, another key support is the network of individuals in your life. These networks may be formed from former employers, individuals you know from a fraternal organization such as the Rotary Club, friends at school, or individuals you know from another organization including a church or synagogue. Individuals in your network can be particularly helpful in providing some legitimacy to your business, in addition to providing feedback and advice to you.

There is a rich pool of resources for networking online. For example, many communities have formed blogs and chat rooms aimed at individuals interested in forming local businesses. These online communities can be a rich source of advice on forming a business and potential sources of funding. There are also numerous crowd sourcing sites including Kickstarter.com and Crowdfunder.com. These websites allow a firm to reach out to a wide community online to get funding and often advice in the process of raising those funds.[8]

To illustrate, a start-up manufacturing business would be considered high risk until it developed a steady flow of customers and revenue. Established businesses are often hesitant to buy from a start-up business, because it is not clear if the new business will be able to fulfill an order or service the product in the future. Thus, many firms will initially buy only small amounts from a new business in an effort to observe the quality and reliability of the new firm. Similar effects are also experienced with suppliers, such that the new firm may not be able to obtain credit from a supplier for some time. Only after a history of prompt payment is built up might the supplier allow the new business to carry credit. A network can help overcome some of these debilitating issues early in the life of the business by providing a level of legitimacy. Support from companies in your network cannot only provide revenue but can also help to indicate to others your seriousness and staying power.

As noted previously we will follow two small firms throughout the text to illustrate the concepts in the text. The first one we have looked at is Friends' Home Health. The second firm we will follow in each chapter is Flow Right Brewery & Bar.

FLOW RIGHT BREWERY & BAR: A FAMILY AFFAIR*

Chris Flow had long wanted to be his own boss. Working for one of the bigger banks in the area, he sat in a cubicle processing mortgage applications. Although there was always something different in each application, he had the process down to a science. He was so good at his work that his boss gave him the unenviable task of handling mortgage workouts for people who had fallen behind in their payments. By 2014 he could see the writing on the wall. Virtually anyone involved in the mortgage processing business was eligible to be laid off as the mortgage crisis had subsided. Several of the nation's largest banks had rounds of layoffs in their mortgage divisions that amounted to thousands of employees.

Since graduating from college, Chris had a fascination with brewing beer. He worked at a microbrewery in Boulder, Colorado, during his college years and had taken a number of classes on making beer. He was a member of the local brewing club and regularly won the club awards for the beer he brewed at home. What's more is that Chris's passion to brew beer had taken over his two-car garage much to the consternation of his wife. He regularly worked with new club members to learn what he considered a craft.

On his way home from work one day he was shocked to see that one of his favorite restaurants had closed. The location was very good, but there was never much of a crowd. Chris personally knew the owner, although he was only peripherally aware that the owner had been in the heat of a divorce. Once the divorce was final the owner planned to move from the area, but there was not sufficient cash flow generated in the business to entice anyone to buy it. Thus, he had decided simply to close the business.

That night Chris and his wife talked at length about Chris taking over that location and turning it into a brew pub where aficionados of brewing could gather and enjoy locally brewed beers. He and his wife had saved up over $100,000, which they were willing to commit to the venture, and he was confident that he could bring in a set of partners who would also invest in the business. There were a lot of things to do over the next few weeks if this was going to be a reality, but Chris was truly excited about business for the first time in years.

The next day Chris contacted a real estate agent and found out that the previous owner of the restaurant had broken a 10-year lease that still had 6 years left on it but no personal guarantee. The owner of the property was anxious to get the property leased again and was willing to throw in everything inside the restaurant for no extra monthly charge if Chris would sign a new 10-year lease that Chris would personally guarantee. Even though the lease payments seemed quite reasonable—especially given that all of the kitchen equipment, tables, chairs, counters were his for free—it was nevertheless a big financial commitment as Chris would have to still pay for the lease even if the business was not a success. Chris and his wife decided to take the plunge and Flow Right Brewery & Bar was born.

*The names and small details have been changed in this running case. We will use this case throughout the text to illustrate concepts raised in each chapter and how this particular firm addressed them as they built the business.

Community

There are also more formal community supports that can lower the overall risk for a new business in the community.[9] For example, many communities have business **incubators**[10] that house new businesses and provide many critical services for the entrepreneurial businesses. An incubator will typically provide all of the office machines, basic furniture, internet connections, telephones, fax, copying equipment, and maintenance necessary for a business to begin operations. As we have noted, one of the difficulties for a new business is the establishment of some level of legitimacy. Those businesses that look as if they are ongoing businesses may have more opportunities. Most new businesses cannot afford a receptionist, whereas in a business incubator there is a common receptionist. This individual is typically trained to answer phone calls from a central location, using the firm's own name. The impression made by such simple things can be significant. In contrast to an answering machine, the ability to have a message taken by a receptionist can help build credibility.

incubator

A facility that houses new businesses and provides many critical services for the new ventures. New businesses are expected to develop and typically leave the facility often within 18 months of founding.

A business incubator also offers its space to tenant firms at subsidized rates in order to stabilize cash flow. There are professionals such as accountants and lawyers available to help the new businesses. Local community leaders hope that all this aid will lead to businesses that are more likely to succeed than unsupported new business start-ups. Thus, if an entrepreneur can locate the business in an incubator, then the firm's risk of failure drops. Business incubators work best with office-based service firms, scientific-based firms requiring lab space, or small, clean manufacturing firms. Clearly, a business incubator cannot effectively house a restaurant: A restaurant needs to be located somewhere near a flow of people. However, even for such a firm there are still supports available. In most communities there are **Small Business Assistance Centers**. These centers are funded by the Small Business Administration and advise individuals who intend to start new businesses. The supports vary widely but usually include research aids such as information on funding sources in the area for new businesses. There are other services available, such as counseling provided by the Service Corps of Retired Executives (SCORE). These retired executives work with new businesses as advisors on a wide range of issues. Still other supports are available at centers tailored to aid women or minority entrepreneurs. One specialized program is the Minority Enterprise Development Program. There are also programs targeted to veterans or those firms that are geared to export.

Small Business Assistance Centers

Centers funded by the Small Business Administration that provide free advice to individuals wishing to start new businesses.

Each community has its own unique set of resources. The federal government provides some of the funds, but it encourages the local administrators and government entities to tailor the services to what is needed locally. Therefore, each potential entrepreneur needs to survey what services are available. A quick look online for local Economic Development will provide a strong list of these services. The potential entrepreneur would be well served to take an hour or two to visit the offices identified and obtain information about their services. The potential entrepreneur should also ask these entities for leads on other agencies that have services for the start-up business. Almost all such agencies work with each other and want entrepreneurs to take advantage of all resources available, whether from them or from other agencies.

Financial Support

Another key element for a new business is the financial support it develops. The detailed evaluation of financial resources will be covered in Chapter 7 where we will examine the financing issues related to starting a firm. However, a few points need to be made briefly here. Potential entrepreneurs need to have a full understanding of the cost–benefit of the business.[11] In particular, the entrepreneur needs to account for the financial resources that may be required in starting and running a new business. It is simply good business practice to ensure that sufficient financial resources are available prior to the start of that business. It may be a waste of effort to go forward if the goals of an individual are widely divergent from the financial resources that are available. The development of the new business is not "blue sky" thinking. The processes detailed in this book are a practical and applied effort to make this a reality.

From an individual evaluation of capability, nothing more is required at this point other than a realistic vision of what resources are needed and available. If, for instance, a potential entrepreneur is considering starting a restaurant, there needs to be recognition that the equipment and setup for even a very small, modest carry-out restaurant may exceed $150,000. This cost goes up dramatically if the potential entrepreneur buys new equipment. If used equipment is purchased, that cost can be cut by over half depending on the quality of what is obtained. Regardless of the type of business contemplated, it is critical that the entrepreneur be able to fund that business or obtain the necessary funding. Therefore, the potential entrepreneur needs to have a broad understanding of what financial resources are available and a realistic idea of what will be needed to expend. Chapter 6, entitled "Cash Flow,"devotes an entire section to this exact issue.

EXERCISE 4

Using the chart below, begin to fill in the supports and resources you might be able to call on. Describe briefly the support and resource that you list. Fill in the chart as much as you can now.

CATEGORY	SOURCE	DESCRIPTION
Family		
Network		
Community		
Financial		

Form a Business Doing What You Like

LO2-5

Explain how you can evaluate those things that you enjoy the most and discover how they may lead to business opportunities.

This chapter has emphasized that new businesses are so often successful because the entrepreneur both owns and runs the business. You bring to the business a focus that simply does not exist in large businesses. You also bring unique supports that can help make the venture successful. Ultimately, the greatest contributor to your success is that you are doing something you enjoy.

An entrepreneur will need to spend considerable time at the business for it to be successful.[12] In fact, the entrepreneur will likely spend more time starting and running the business than doing anything else in life. Consider that in a typical day you have 24 hours, out of which you might typically sleep 7 hours. If you work 8 to 10 hours at a minimum in a business for five days, plus half a day each weekend, you will be spending the greatest amount of your time either sleeping or working. You need to enjoy what you do. If you do not enjoy weather extremes, do not seek to establish a heating and air-conditioning business that requires you to work on broken air conditioners and heaters (which always seem to need repair in the extremes

Positions in the retail industry are very social. The more workers can make conversation with potential customers often times more sales opportunities can result.

EXERCISE 5

1. List up to five businesses you potentially could happily work at every day.
2. List up to five businesses you potentially would not enjoy running every day.

of weather). If you do not enjoy working with people, do not establish a retail shop where you must work with the wide variety of individuals who walk in the door. On the other hand, if you like people and find conversation easy, a retail business would make much more sense than an Internet business where you see very few people and primarily work alone. It is quite possible for someone to see great potential in a new business idea; however, if the new business is not something that the entrepreneur has a passion for, history suggests that the business is not likely to be successful.

If you are considering starting a business you also need to clearly recognize the trade-off between the time commitment and the return you expect. While clearly part of the equation, the time–reward relationship in a new business involves more than simply financial reward. We will deal more with profitability as we consider the finances of the firm in Chapters 6, 7, and 8. However, your time is your most valuable asset and should be treated as such. This text is designed to help you think through the start-up business process in a formal manner and provide you with the tools necessary to be successful.

SUMMARY

The most critical resource in a new venture is the entrepreneur or entrepreneurial team. The founder(s) are the reason that a new business is so successful. In forming a start-up, the entrepreneur's choice of business needs to be consistent with his or her own individual risk tolerances. The entrepreneur also needs to be aware that one's own biases and bounded rationality will shape the interpretation of opportunities.

The thought process associated with developing the new business needs to be consistent with the actual resources that are present. The process of developing the business is both time consuming and rewarding. There are many supports available to anyone wishing to pursue this course of action in business. The potential entrepreneur should look to family, networks, and communities for assistance and honest feedback.

KEY TERMS

agency theory 22
bounded rationality 25
break-even point 24
family business 20
incubator 32
organizational slack 20
Small Business Assistance Centers 32

REVIEW QUESTIONS

1. How does the lack of "slack" resources impact new ventures?
2. Why is founder involvement in a new venture so critical to its success?
3. Is there some minimum level of risk tolerance required to start a business? Explain.
4. How does bounded rationality affect the way an entrepreneur determines what type of business to start?
5. How do you think personality differences matter in the starting of a business?
6. List some triggers that push people into starting a new business.
7. Have you experienced any of these triggers? Did it cause you to consider starting your own business?
8. Which supports do you believe you might rely on the most if you started your own business?

BUSINESS PLAN DEVELOPMENT QUESTIONS

1. How would you evaluate risk tolerance?
2. What is your risk tolerance? Why?
3. Have you formed a team before in a class or other setting? What criteria did you use?
4. If you have not formed a team, what are the criteria you think you should rely on? Are the criteria for the class teams in questions 3 and 4 the same you would use for your business teams?

5. What are your supports that you can call on for your business plan?
6. If you have a team for your business, are there gaps in the support you can call on?
7. Does your community have a business incubator? If so, what are the admission criteria?
8. How would the personality tests results you get online affect your choice of a partner or employee?

INDIVIDUAL EXERCISES

1. Individually list up to five businesses at which you could happily work every day.
2. Do the same thing for five businesses for which you would not enjoy working every day.
3. How do your personal interests impact these choices?
4. Do you think the criteria you used to decide to work for a particular business would be the same for starting a business?
5. How would these commonalities and differences affect your decision to start a business?

GROUP EXERCISES

We discuss family businesses extensively in the chapter in terms of entrepreneurial businesses. It is estimated that up to 25 percent of the Fortune 500 are family businesses. These are organizations in which a single family owns a high enough percentage of the firm's stock to have control of the business: Control can be maintained with ownership of as little as 5 percent of the shares. How do you think family-owned corporations differ from more typical corporations? Do you think these same differences apply in entrepreneurial firms?

ENDNOTES

1. C. B. Schoonhoven and K. M. Eisenhardt, "Speeding Products to Market: Waiting Time to First Product Introduction in New Firms," *Administrative Science Quarterly* 35 (1990), pp. 177–208.
2. F. K. Pil and M. Holweg, "Exploring Scale: The Advantages of Thinking Small," *MIT Sloan Management Review* 44, no. 2 (2003), pp. 33–40.
3. J. J. Chrisman, J. H. Chua, and R. A. Litz, "Comparing the Agency Costs of Family and Non-Family Firms: Conceptual Issues and Exploratory Evidence," *Entrepreneurship Theory & Practice* 28 (2004), pp. 335–55.
4. J. E. Grable and R. H. Lytton, "The Development of a Risk-Assessment Instrument: A Follow-Up Study," *Financial Services Review* 12 (2003), pp. 257–75.
5. C. Penttila, "Risky Business," *Entrepreneur* 36, no. 11 (2008), pp. 17–18
6. American Express report, "The 2013 State of Women-Owned Businesses Report."
7. R. D. Atkinson, "The Impact of the Defense Build-Down on State and Local Economies," *Economic Development Review* 10, no. 4 (Fall 1992), pp. 55–59.
8. C. Barnett, "Top 10 Crowd Funding Sites for Fundraising," *Forbes,* May 8, 2013. www.forbes.com/sites/chancebarnett/2013/05/08/top-10-crowdfunding-sites-for-fundraising/
9. H. M. Neck, G. D. Meyer, B. Cohen, and A. C. Corbett, "An Entrepreneurial System View of New Venture Creation," *Journal of Small Business Management* 42 (2004), pp. 190–209.
10. P. D. Hannon and P. Chaplin, "Are Incubators Good for Business? Understanding Incubator Practice—The Challenge for Policy," *Environment & Planning: Government & Policy* 21 (2003), pp. 861–82.
11. K. Jones and R. Tullous, "Behaviors of Pre-Venture Entrepreneurs and Perceptions of Their Financial Needs," *Journal of Small Business Management* 40 (2002), pp. 233–49.
12. H. H. Beam and T. A. Carey, "Could You Succeed in Small Business?" *Business Horizons* 32, no. 5 (1989), pp. 65–70.

CREDITS

Opener: Juice Images/Glow Images RF; p. 19: Mercury Jane/Flickr/CC-BY-2.0; p. 20: Digital Vision/Getty Images RF; p. 23: Tim Boyle/Newsmakers/Getty Images; p. 24: Ralph Crane/Time Life Pictures/Getty Images; p. 26 (both): Barbara Penoyar/Getty Images RF; p. 29: Emma Lee/Life File/Getty Images RF; p. 33: Fotosearch Premium/Getty Images RF.

chapter

3

learning objectives

After studying this chapter, you will be able to:

LO3-1 Describe a systematic means for examining skills in order to generate new business ideas.

LO3-2 Discuss the elements of opportunity analysis.

LO3-3 Analyze how to choose a business.

Business Idea Generation and Initial Evaluation

UBER CHANGES THE BUSINESS

UberCab was founded in San Francisco in 2009 as a means of connecting for-hire drivers with potential passengers. Using a mobile platform, the company connects people needing a ride with those offering rides. The system is more efficient than calling a single cab company and more on-demand-oriented than hiring a traditional limo. The application was an instant success and the name was quickly changed to *Uber* when the company purchased the website Uber.com. Uber takes 20 percent of the charge for the ride and handles the financial transaction via their mobile platform.

The founders of the business are Travis Kalanick and Garret Camp. The company started with no employees and a shoestring budget. The first prototype was developed and the app was launched in San Francisco in 2010.

Since its inception, the business has quickly grown to more than 60 cities around the world. Uber allows drivers who are not employed or even certified by the company to use their own vehicles to pick up passengers. This business model has generated some problems for the company. In 2013, for example, a class-action lawsuit was filed against the companies by taxi drivers who claim that Uber is stealing their tips. Cities have also tried to shut down the service by claiming that Uber is skirting their taxicab laws. In Paris, cabbies who were on strike slashed tires and smashed windows of cars working with Uber. In 2014, an Uber-arranged ride resulted in an accident in which a 6-year-old girl was killed. The company was sued for wrongful death.

The company started as an entrepreneurial venture but has now grown into a venture-backed company with reported revenues in 2013 of over $125 million. Uber was born from an idea to better address the needs of both drivers (who want to maximize the number of rides for hire per day) and passengers (who don't want to wait for a taxi to pull over or arrange a ride ahead of time) using technology that is now in the hands of virtually everyone.

Questions

1. Uber entered an entrenched industry using mobile technology. What other applications for this technology do you see in the personal transportation industry?
2. Why haven't the established cab and limo companies adopted these approaches?

Sources: E. Griffith, "The Uber Effect: The Hot Startup's Early Investors Are In-Demand," *CNN Money,* February 4, 2014, http://tech.fortune.cnn.com/2014/02/04/the-uber-effect-the-hot-startups-early-investors-are-in-demand; J. Brustein, "Uber Explains Why $35 a Mile Is the Right Price," *Bloomberg Businessweek*, December 17, 2013, http://www.businessweek.com/articles/2013-12-17/uber-explains-why-35-a-mile-is-the-right-price; J. Brustein, "Uber's Workforce Is Built to Do More Than Chauffeur," *Bloomberg Businessweek,* December 11, 2013, http://www.Businessweek.com/articles/2013-12-11/ubers-workforce-is-built-to-do-more-than-chauffeur; D. Streitfeld, "As It Shakes Up the Taxi Business, Uber's a Target," *The Boston Globe,* January 27, 2014; C. Matlack, "Paris Cabbies Slash Tires, Smash Windshields in Protest Against Uber," *Bloomberg Businessweek*, January 13, 2014, http://www.businessweek.com/articles/2014-01-13/paris-cabbies-slash-tires-windshields-in-protest-against-uber

FRIENDS' HOME HEALTH

Friends' HOME HEALTH

Betty and Joan had previously determined that they wanted to start a business and that they had a similar propensity for risk taking, as discussed in Chapter 2. Even though the two entrepreneurs wanted to start a home health care business, they were not sure of the dimensions of the potential business. They knew there was a very high failure rate among entrepreneurial businesses, so they wanted to be sure to examine their business ideas carefully so this would not be one of the failures. Therefore, they visited with a successful entrepreneur in their area.

This successful entrepreneur gave Betty and Joan some general ideas about the key issues in starting a new business and suggested that the two of them needed to conduct an audit of themselves to better understand what type of focus the business might need. This audit would help them to determine their views on a number of topics. The successful entrepreneur suggested that the audit include questions such as:

1. What skills had they developed in their prior work experiences?
2. What special hobbies had they pursued?
3. What things about the home health care industry did the two really like?
4. What did they want to achieve with a new business?
5. Were there home health care trends in other countries and/or other parts of the country, which seemed interesting but had not yet reached their area?

The two budding entrepreneurs initially answered these questions separately and then summarized their answers as follows:

	BETTY (RN)	JOAN (LPN)
Skills/ experience prior work	1. Inventory control 2. Establishing and maintaining complex work schedules 3. Managing people	1. Connecting with people on an individual basis 2. Customer service
Hobbies	Church Family	Church Family

	BETTY (RN)	JOAN (LPN)
Industry	Health care	Health care
Hope to achieve	1. Greater control of time to spend with family 2. Financial rewards	1. Financial rewards 2. Greater control of time to spend with family
Trends	1. Introduction of health care reforms that lead to greater control of costs and, in turn, more health care	1. Greater desire for family to both provide for elderly family members and to have time for themselves 2. Use of new technologies to monitor home health provider performance

Betty and Joan discovered through this audit process that there were important similarities and some differences in their thoughts about a potential business opportunity. Betty and Joan both shared a commitment to family and wanted more time to spend with their families. However, Betty was married and her husband had a good job with a bank. The result was that although she wanted financial rewards, the financial rewards took less priority than time with the family. In contrast, Joan was a single parent. Even though she wanted more time to spend with her family, she was the primary provider to her two children and the financial rewards were critical to her. The financial aspect was even more intense as her two children went to a private, religious-affiliated school. Both women were also very religious. Betty, an African American woman, was particularly committed and involved in her church. Joan, a Hispanic woman, was also involved in her church although the time commitment was less. The religious commitment of both women led them to agree that they wanted to form a business with the highest ethical standards and one that would show compassion and love to their mostly elderly clients.

(continued)

A fortunate series of events occurred during the early fall of 2012. The large state in which they lived began to encourage more individuals to pursue home health as an alternative to moving the elderly to rehabilitation centers, which would lower the state's Medicare costs. Medicare is a joint federal and state government program that covers a number of costs for the elderly, including nursing homes, rehabilitation centers, or home health in given situations. While a desirable program, governments are always seeking to control costs. In addition, as a minority-owned business headed by females, the two entrepreneurs learned they would receive special consideration for referral of patients from the state and regional medical facilities. Thus, there appeared to be an opportunity for this type of business.

Individuals come to the decision to begin a new business from many different perspectives and backgrounds. From this widely diverse group of individuals come many successful business ideas. Research shows that successful new business ideas are not determined by who your parents are, your race, your gender, or your religion. Instead, quality ideas are a function of the creativity and thoughtfulness of the person or persons creating the business.

EXERCISE 1

1. What similarities in the founders' answers do you see?
2. The founders chose to focus on home health care. What other options might have been open to them?
3. What is the impact if a national chain is already in your area in this industry?

So how does someone come up with an idea for a new business? Among the most popular resources is the individual's professional background or hobbies. These are domains that the individual knows very well and where it is easier to see shortcomings in the current business offerings and needs that are not being meet. Great insight can also be gained from individuals that the entrepreneur respects or those who have been successful in founding a business. There are a wide variety of sources that can be called upon for ideas about potential businesses. In this chapter we identify a systematic way in which to generate a list of potential businesses. The initial steps in evaluating the viability of these ideas will also be presented as a key element in this process.

Generating Business Ideas

LO3-1

Describe a systematic means for examining skills in order to generate new business ideas.

Even when individuals may determine that they want to open a new business, the exact type of business to open is much more difficult to determine. We encourage everyone, even individuals who feel that they firmly know which type of business they wish to open, to examine all options through the processes detailed in this chapter. We have found that potential new business owners often feel strongly about the type of business they wish to open, and yet, upon a more systematic examination, move to an alternative idea. Frequently, they do find an opportunity in the market, but it may not be the exact business concept they initially conceived. Alternatively, they may conclude after their analysis that the business they conceptualized would not be successful. Therefore, rather than reacting in a knee-jerk manner to what appears to be an opportunity, or even worse, quickly dismissing a promising idea, an individual needs to make a rational evaluation of a business opportunity and its potential.[1]

As discussed in Chapter 2, the desire to own and operate a business is a first step in entrepreneurship—but what business might that be? The generation of business ideas is not something that occurs automatically. Rather, it is a process of identifying the skills of the potential founders, identifying opportunities in the market, matching the initial financial funding available, and then marrying these together into a business idea that interests the potential founders. As noted in Chapter 1, the establishment of a successful new business is challenging. The high demands placed upon everyone involved in the process necessitate that the founders truly enjoy what they are doing. The process presented below is intended to be an open one that considers passion and enjoyment as important elements to success.

While not a sequential formula, we would suggest the following approach to the development of a quality business idea.

- First, the potential founders should list and evaluate their own personal skill sets. These skills may arise from hobbies, current work, past work experience, and/or family history.
- Second, the potential founders should carefully analyze the market and look for a gap, or some need that is not being met effectively.
- Finally, the potential founders need to compare their ability to fill those gaps with the opportunity that seems to be available. We suggest that the best means to do this is the development of a chart (see Table 3.1) that allows for an open, systematic examination. We will look at each of these steps in more detail.

Skills Analysis

You might be asking yourself why we suggest starting with the skill set of the potential founders rather than an "opportunity" in the market? The fact is that there are literally millions of "opportunities" in a wide variety of fields, but without the requisite skill set, pursuing (or even considering) these opportunities is simply a frustrating exercise of wasted money and time.

There may be tremendous opportunities in the spa services business. However, if a potential business owner had no skills in this area, then those supposed opportunities are of little use to the potential founders. Without the needed skills, the founders would be faced with not holding any advantage over competitors who have the necessary depth in the area. A founder or founding team must have not only the necessary skills, but also a depth of understanding, so that they can build a long-term advantage in the market; they need a **synergy** that connects skills, understanding, and a competitive advantage such that the sum of the parts is greater than the individual parts by themselves. Perhaps as important as the business owner's skills in a particular area is the need for the potential owner(s) to have interest in or passion for starting a business in that domain. We have found that founders without a passion for the business are not willing to devote the time and energy necessary for the business to be successful.

synergy
The connection between the entrepreneur's skills, understanding of an industry, and the ability to create a competitive advantage such that the sum of the parts of the new business is greater than the individual parts alone.

As we mentioned previously, skills come from a variety of areas and are relatively idiosyncratic to the individual. In general, skills are derived from our history, experience, and interests. Several specific areas that potential business owners might examine include hobbies, education, work experience, and family history.

Hobbies and Activities

We all pursue hobbies and activities because we love them. In these hobbies or activities we develop skills specific to the hobbies or skills.

The avid skier who opens up a ski shop, the distance runner who opens up a running store, the ham radio operator who becomes a radio equipment dealer are all examples of hobbies leading to a business. If there is a great passion associated with hobbies or activities, that passion can help the success of the new business. A rule of thumb in the founding of businesses has always been that the owner whose business is both a vocation and an avocation is difficult to beat. That person is willing to stick with the business through lean times and develop a following of fellow enthusiasts. A problem that can arise is that the "business" of running the business takes over at some point and time, and the entrepreneur does not enjoy the business like he or she once did. That problem is something we will address in later chapters.

Your hobbies can impact how you approach business ventures. Do you have any hobbies that might lend themselves to a solid business idea?

At this point the questions the potential business owner should probably ask include:

- What hobbies or activities do you pursue on an active, perhaps daily basis?
- What hobbies or activities have you pursued in any manner over your lifetime (whether or not you were serious about them)?
- What is it about your hobbies or activities that really excites you?
- What were the specific skills that these hobbies or activities required?
- What have your experiences in the hobbies or activities taught you that could help others?
- What products and services did you use in these hobbies or activities?

Education

From the time we are very young, we are in learning mode. From primary school to whatever level of education we pursue, the knowledge gained provides a skill set that can be the basis of a new business. An opportunity that uses your education (formal or informal) is another source of a business. The technological skills developed during the entrepreneur's education can be particularly valuable.[2]

- What courses did you take that were particularly enjoyable?
- What courses did you take where the material came to you very easily?
- Have you attended any unusual education programs?
- Have you taken specialized training in any specific area?
- If you had to do it all over again, what areas would you pursue now?

Work Experience

Another source of skills for a new business comes from your work experience. Your work experience builds skills that can have direct applicability to the pursuit of a new business. In each job, individuals build up skills that they take with them when they start a new business.

- In what businesses have you worked?
- What skills were critical to the jobs you performed?
- What positions have you held in business?
- In what areas would you be considered a type of expert?

Your family can be a great help in developing a business. What are some of the risks and rewards that you associate with the idea of working with your family?

- What did you *really* enjoy about the positions you have held?
- What frustrated you about the positions that you have held?
- When were you the most excited about your work?

Family

Family experiences are an often overlooked source of skills for a new business. As we are well aware, every family is unique. There are often things that you do with your family in which you develop expertise. Many times potential entrepreneurs overlook these family experiences as a source of knowledge and skills. Cooking with family members, tracing family history, working on the house or around your family property are all sources of knowledge that can grow into a new business opportunity. One of the authors regularly hires a guide when vacationing in Sedona, Arizona. This particular guide grew up hiking and exploring the Sedona area with his family. After working for the park service for many years, he decided to open his own tour operation. He takes individuals or very small groups on customized adventures in the area that cater to the desires of the customer. He turned his family passion into a business that has grown to include other guides and is a year-round operation. Your pursuits can similarly be the source of a unique skill set for a business.

- What is your family history with new business ventures?
- What types of travel and vacations does your family enjoy?
- What skill sets exist within your nuclear family?
- What are the financial resources of your extended family?
- Are there unique things your family does that others seem very interested in?
- What skills do you develop in your family activities?

Additional Skills

Beyond these categories, we suggest that you also ask yourself the following questions:

1. What are your top three personal skills?
2. What things do you like doing best each day, each week?
3. When you look back over the past year, what one or two things did you enjoy more than any others?
4. What are the magazines and books you read?
5. What are your three greatest accomplishments in life? What skills were involved in these accomplishments?
6. Do you enjoy working with people? Or would you prefer to be left alone to concentrate your efforts in a particular area?
7. In what industry (retail/wholesale/manufacturing/service) would you prefer to work?

FLOW RIGHT BREWERY & BAR: A FAMILY AFFAIR

Chris was very excited about the potential for the new brewery business but still didn't know if he could really make it work—or whether it was really even a good idea. Looking back over the past 10 years he found out that the location he wanted had been four different restaurant concepts and none of them had succeeded. Even though he thought that his concept was more in line with what might work in the area, he was also unsure about his qualifications.

Looking honestly at himself, Chris recognized that although he was a smart guy, he had no experience running any type of business. He had worked in a microbrewery in college but was a waiter and bartender most of that time. He spent a fair amount of time with the brewmaster learning the trade, which is what had sparked his keen interest in the activity over the past 10 years. He was never the brewmaster in his prior working experience, but he did have experience brewing beer at home. Therefore, Chris decided to examine some aspects of the business before he committed to the idea.

Financially he and his wife were in a sound position. They rented their house, owned both their cars outright, had retirement savings that were beginning to grow, plus they had just over $100,000 in cash to invest in a new business. Doing some quick research, Chris realized that he would probably need $500,000 to purchase everything he needed, run the business for six months until it reached breakeven, and provide him with a salary sufficient to keep up with some of the household expenses. This meant that he would either need to bring in partners to obtain the extra $400,000, take out loans, or obtain a combination of partners and loans.

The time commitment was going to be substantial. Chris knew that it was a business that would need to be open most days until midnight and that the brewing aspect was a seven-day-a-week activity. The business location was less than three miles from his house, he and his wife had no children, and they were both ready to commit the time needed.

As mentioned in Chapter 2, Chris was well known in the local brewing community. He had won a number of local brewing awards and was a sought-out teacher of home brewing. Thus, Chris felt he had the expertise to move from small amounts of brewing to running a microbrewery. However, Chris also recognized that he had to consider the competitors in the area. There was only one true microbrewery in the area, but there were many bars, restaurants, and clubs in which customers could enjoy beer. Local brews were not readily available, however, and although that was positive on the one hand, it really concerned Chris on the other. Would there be sufficient interest in local brews and in a local microbrewery to generate a real revenue stream? The only other microbrewery was part of a national chain with a very well-known name. A microbrew is typically not the cheapest beer to brew or sell. It takes a customer base that is more committed to drinking a high-quality beer that may cost a little more for a microbrewery to prosper.

After weighing all the factors and including his wife's overwhelming support for his pursuing this effort, Chris decided that he would commit to starting the business.

Clearly, the goal from all these questions is to explore the range of potential skills and abilities that each of us possesses. A few more questions can help you tailor your business to your unique skills and personality:

1. Do you prefer to work extensively with people or not? If not, you need to focus on a business that has minimal interpersonal demands (an Internet-based business or a business that performs tasks for other businesses by handling back-office operations, such as bookkeeping, billing, order fulfillment, etc.). If you thrive on people and have the corresponding skills, then a retail or service-oriented business may be ideal.
2. Do you have an intense detail orientation? If you are very detail oriented, then a business that is procedurally complex and involves managing a wide variety of details may be appropriate. Remember that there are many people and companies out there that will pay handsomely for someone to manage the details of life. For example, a supply company to large manufacturers that

customizes a product on a wide variety of details might be appropriate. Another area might be project management. Alternatively, an individual who finds this level of detail frustrating should pursue a business with a simpler or more forgiving business model.

3. Are you trained in the area in which you want to work? Your experience and educational skills will have a critical impact on the direction of the business. Someone may believe that there is a need for a computer repair shop in your part of the city. However, if the individual does not have the skills from either educational training or experience to do such repairs, it does little good to consider such a business. As a general rule, focus on what you know best.

What is clear from the questions above is that in this text we believe that the founder(s) of a business need to be intimately involved in the design, funding, and running of the new business. Although we sometimes read about individuals who like to claim they are "idea" people and plan simply to hire everyone needed to run the business, we would suggest that these individuals are not founders—they are bankers with vision. They are simply providing funding and the concept. Such a model might work for people with large amounts of money; however, this model is difficult to pursue successfully for most people. Therefore, in this text in general, and in this chapter in particular, we use the basic assumption that the founder will be intimately involved in the new business.

LO3-2

Discuss the elements of opportunity analysis.

gap analysis
A relatively simple process of systematically examining the difference, or gap, between what is expected and what occurs. One type of gap analysis, called opportunity analysis, examines opportunities in the marketplace side-by-side with the individual's ability to address those gaps.

Opportunity Identification

Once you have developed a list of your skills, abilities, and interests, the next step is to examine the marketplace for opportunities to use these in a business. The method that we use and recommend is a form of **gap analysis**. In such an analysis, individuals identify a gap or opportunity that exists between the demand for a product or service and the supply provided by firms in the market. It is then up to you to determine if you have the skills and abilities to fill that gap.

Potential Businesses

There are a variety of ways to identify gaps, or business opportunities, in the marketplace. These include the following:

1. Examining trends around the region, nation, or world that may not have reached your particular geographic location. Trends do not start uniformly. Notice that a number of regional coffee chains have developed significant businesses in specific cities throughout the United States (see the chapter-opening vignette in Chapter 1). Some of these chains (especially those in the Midwest) were developed by their founders examining how firms such as Starbucks were achieving success in major cities on the coast. These businesses achieved a strong local position before the national firms could make significant investments in their local markets.
2. Interview and talk about opportunities with key successful entrepreneurs in the area. Most successful entrepreneurs have great ideas that have the potential to be successful given the right set of circumstances and people. From their own experiences, these individuals have a keen eye for what businesses are needed in an area. However, these individuals often have too much to do with their own businesses to pursue new ventures themselves, so they are willing to share their insights. The result is that they are willing to advise new entrepreneurs, as well as to identify and

perhaps fund such opportunities. In effect, they become mentors to new entrepreneurs.

3. Discuss potential businesses with family members. Your family members know your abilities and disposition. Furthermore, they are uniquely positioned to provide a much-needed honest perspective on your efforts. Particularly if any of these individuals have a small business of their own, they might be useful in the process of helping you decide which businesses are best suited to your particular set of skills.
4. Look for environmental changes that create opportunities that did not exist before. Significant regulatory changes create new openings in an industry that did not exist before that regulatory change. Consider all the changes associated with health care reform, for example. Regardless of what you think of the law, it has clearly changed the industrial setting in health care and created new opportunities that entrepreneurs can take advantage of.
5. **Brainstorming** with key entrepreneurs and family members can also be useful to the potential entrepreneur. Brainstorming is a creative process in which a group of individuals are brought together and asked to generate ideas related to a specific topic or problem, with little effort given to evaluating the true potential for those ideas. In this case, the scenario might be one where a group is provided information on the skill set of the founder and asked to generate a list of businesses that might be appropriate. The interaction within the group leads to a dynamic that can lead to new, innovative ideas. Such brainstorming sessions work well in informal groups. Think of friends or family gathering over a meal and talking in depth about the options that are available; this is brainstorming. The conversation in Chapter 2 in which Chris's family initially talked about the options for Chris to take over the closed restaurant and open a microbrewery was a form of brainstorming.[3]

brainstorming
A creative process whereby a group of individuals are brought together and asked to generate ideas with little or no effort made to evaluate the potential for each idea rather the focus is to generate numerous ideas.

6. Take a look at the things that frustrate you and your family. Daily frustrations are an incredible source of ideas. How would you solve the frustration? What is it about the frustration that needs to be solved? You will find that you might have as many as a dozen aspects that could be solved, but only a few that truly fit with your capabilities and interests. Most (if not all) needs in a developed society are currently being met. However, the degree, level, detail, efficiency, effectiveness, politeness, or access all provide means for improving the satisfaction of a particular need being met.
7. If the potential entrepreneur has an interest and skill set based in technology, one of our personal favorites for the generation of business ideas is the examination of patent files. Millions of patents exist and are maintained by the original inventors and have never been the subject of a commercial attempt. We recommend an examination of patent files (available at www.uspto.gov) to find several that interest the potential entrepreneur. We suggest that you contact the inventor (all of the contact information is included with the patent) to see if that individual would be willing to work exclusively with you in the development of a commercial business. We have worked with entrepreneurs who started with their interest area, found a set of patents that had not been developed into businesses, successfully contacted the inventors, and then based their business on those patents.

EXERCISE 2

1. Create a list of ideas in each one of the aforementioned first six idea categories.
2. Do any of these ideas strike you as particularly intriguing for your future business? Why?

LO3-3

Analyze how to choose a business.

The generation of ideas along the way to selecting a business is a process that takes time and frequent interaction.

Choosing a Business

The process of generating ideas is not something that is done in a single sitting. Instead, it is a process that takes time, interaction, consideration, evaluation, and iteration. These steps do not occur in a linear fashion but should occur in an interactive manner. For example, if a successful entrepreneur suggests a new business that seems to fit well with your skills, then an investigation into the opportunity may be warranted. In discussions with trusted friends and family, the idea will morph and be refined. As the business idea evolves you may realize that you need new skill sets to be successful. This might require including others on the founding team. As a result, the generation of ideas is truly a process that takes time and interaction. However, done well, this effort should lead to a list of three to five business ideas where the founders have the appropriate skills and there appears (at least on the surface level) to be an opportunity.

To illustrate, we worked with an entrepreneur who had strong retail experience. This individual enjoyed working with people and had great orientation to detail. Three opportunities were initially identified by the individual. First, several family members who operated a flower shop in another city were encouraging him to pursue a similar business in his city. These family members thought the potential entrepreneur had the skills for that business, and they could coach him in the business. Second, some experienced businesspeople that he knew identified a gap in the printing services offerings that were available in their area. There was a chain copy shop in the small downtown area of town, but that shop did not provide any really high-quality business printing, despite the relatively large number of small businesses in the area. The focus of the chain store was on individuals, self-service, and low-volume printing jobs. Finally, this individual had noted a trend on the West Coast of the United States (not his area of the country): the growth of restaurants that were in-between fast-food restaurants and full-service restaurants. These restaurants typically focused on regional food offerings. This type of restaurant had an upscale decor, but individuals ordered at the cash register and had their food delivered to them at the table. Thus, it was a different format for a restaurant than he had noticed in his area.

Each of these businesses had a relatively high level of detail involved in the operation of the business, and yet the processes to operate the businesses were relatively well known. Additionally, each of the businesses required high levels of interaction with customers, and customer service seemed to be a critical element of the business model. The background and skills of the potential entrepreneur appeared to fit with all of these businesses. Now he would have to pick one business idea.

Initial Analysis

The potential entrepreneur, just as in the example above, will likely have several ideas, but will need to identify one business on which to perform a due diligence analysis. Chapters 4, 5, and 6 identify the process for performing an in-depth analysis on that single business idea. It is possible that after doing the in-depth analysis, the potential entrepreneur will decide not to pursue that particular business and will begin the analysis of business ideas all over again. However, the nature of the effort required to perform an effective due diligence study necessitates a focus on a single business concept. The analysis and thought processes require focus, time, and usually some financial investment. If the potential entrepreneur is to be successful, then the process is to move from the three to five ideas initially generated to a single idea on which to focus. Our would-be entrepreneur in the prior example had to determine whether to focus further analysis on the flower shop, the printing business, or the restaurant. One means to identify which business to pursue is through a gap analysis.

Gap Analysis

How do you decide that a sufficient business opportunity exists and that you have the resources necessary to take advantage of that opportunity? While there is more art to this process than science, starting with the list of three to five ideas that you have generated, you can now develop a chart that examines the issues that might impact the success of the new business. The business ideas are listed down in the first column, with a brief explanation of what each idea entails. (Later, each of these descriptions will be put into a short paragraph explaining the business and its opportunity for economic success.) You should be able to tell anyone succinctly—in less than two minutes—what your idea is and how it will bring substantial success. (You will see student business plan competitions called "elevator pitches" that are essentially the same concept—pitch your business in two minutes, or the time to ride the elevator to the top of a building.) Taking more time simply indicates that you have not clearly identified the opportunity or how it will work. We refer to this as gap analysis, and it should look roughly like the one in Table 3.1. We have filled in the three business ideas generated by the small business founder discussed in the previous section (flower shop, printing shop, and restaurant). However, you would use this form for your own business ideas.

In the second column, next to a given idea (and this may take several spreadsheet pages), list each category you will use to analyze the idea. We urge you to consider, one at a time, at least these five categories, which are crucial to the founding and successful running of a business: finances, time, nonfinancial resources, risk, and competitors. Each of these categories will be discussed in greater detail once we illustrate why this is a gap analysis.

In the third column, you should provide a realistic estimation of personal resources. In the fourth column, you should list your estimates of what resources are required for success. For the last column, you should qualitatively compare your skills and resources with the perceived requirements of that particular business, and record the perceived deficit or gap. Then you can answer an important question: Is that deficit surmountable, or is it one that kills the idea?

This qualitative chart can be completed with minimal or no research. What we are suggesting at this stage of investigation is a gut-level, reasonably quick analysis to see if the business passes an initial test. The gap analysis is intended to be completed by the entrepreneur or entrepreneurial team in a very short time period.

As we mentioned before, the second column lists "categories." These are categories that should be used for analysis. There are a number of categories that the entrepreneur needs to consider for a gap analysis. Following are the five important categories we have listed briefly. We will examine all of these in greater detail in later chapters. The list below is not meant to be exhaustive, as every type of new business will have its own unique categories.

BUSINESS IDEA	CATEGORY	OUR RESOURCES	RESOURCES REQUIRED	DEFICIT
Printing Shop	Finances			
High-quality; commercial	Time			
	Nonfinancial			
	Risk			
	Competitors			
Flower Shop	Finances			
Family history and support	Time			
	Nonfinancial			
	Risk			
	Competitors			
Restaurant	Finances			
Fast-food cross with service	Time			
	Nonfinancial			
	Risk			
	Competitors			

Table 3.1
Form to Compare Three Different Business Ideas

1. *Finances.* You must examine the amount of money required to start and operate a business. A principal cause of new business failure is insufficient financial resources at founding. An entrepreneur may have a good idea but then run out of funds long before a sufficient client base can be built. This will be discussed further when we examine cash flow in Chapter 6. However, we feel that at this stage of analysis, the entrepreneur needs to have a basic understanding of the financial demands of the business.
   a. Your resources—What financial resources do you have that you can realistically commit to the new venture? This should include estimates of savings, retirement accounts that may be used, your spouse's salary, and other. Do you have family resources that could be committed to the effort? How much money could you realistically raise on short notice?
   b. Business need—Estimating how much money do you expect to need to start and to stay in business for one year? Without a lot

of investigation, consider the following: rent, furniture, utilities, advertising, renovation, equipment, supplies, cost of an employee or two, taxes, and fees. Take whatever number you develop and add 50 percent to it. A standing rule-of-thumb is that start-ups take twice the money that was initially forecasted to achieve a sustainable level of operation. Is this number within the range that you would be willing to commit?

2. *Time.* It takes time to start a business. You will hear many successful entrepreneurs say that they estimate the time it will take to do something from scratch and then triple it. Again, you need to assure that you have the time necessary to start the business. Each type of business started will require different time frames. This is an area that many entrepreneurs grossly underestimate.
   a. Your resources—If you are currently employed, how much time can you dedicate to starting this new venture? Will you quit your current job to work in the new business? How much time on a weekly basis are you willing to commit to the business once it is up and running? What other time commitments have you made? Does your family support your efforts?
   b. Business need—What will the hours of operation require? How many additional hours will be required to manage the operation? Do you need staff early in the life of the business? When do you eat, sleep, and so on? What can be done concurrently versus sequentially?
3. *Nonfinancial Resources.* There are many other resources the new business will need beyond financing and the time commitment. This list can be long and should include such things as special contacts with suppliers or customer groups as well as the physical location of the business. This is a category where the entrepreneur should exercise some creativity in the analysis of the situation and the needs of the business.
   a. Your resources—What do you bring to the business beyond the financial? What unique capabilities/experiences/knowledge provide you with a competitive advantage? Are these visible to the rest of the world? Are there others, such as family members, who can provide critical needs of the new firm?
   b. Business needs—What unique skills will be required to run the business? Can you contract with individuals for the areas that you are missing? Can you obtain the resource in short order? (For example, to open a printing business, it would be very helpful to have wide experience on various types of printing presses. This could be gained by going to work for someone else for a period of time or by taking classes offered by contractors or the printing press company.) What unique resources are necessary to develop a competitive advantage in this business?
4. *Risk.* All new businesses have an inherent amount of risk associated with the starting and operation of the business. Whereas what constitutes that risk is determined by the entrepreneur, the level of risk needs to be commensurate with the rewards and within the tolerance level of the individual involved in the business founding. To determine your own risk tolerance, you should look at your own life over the past few years. When the economy

is not in a recession, do you invest primarily in high-risk stocks or in safer places such as savings accounts? If you invest in savings accounts, then you are probably somewhat risk adverse. There are two types of specific risk you should consider: personal and business.

a. Personal risk—Risk at a personal level has many definitions and potential means of examination. It is certainly well beyond just the financial. What level of risk to personal reputation are you willing to live with? If the business fails, what will you do? There is a strategic risk to starting a business when you are not ready, not committed, not sufficiently funded, and the like. A failed business idea may lead to others imitating your idea and even doing it better, or may affect your ability to pursue that or a similar type of business in the future.

b. Business risk—How aggressively does the business need to grow to be successful? Is there a competitive advantage that is fleeting? What level of product or geographic breadth is necessary to not only be a player, but be a success in the industry? What are the limiting factors in the growth of this business? What are the factors that could disrupt your supply chain?[4]

As mentioned in Chapter 1, you can also characterize and examine business risk by considering three threats to business success: (1) threats to the profit margin, (2) threats to sales generation schemes, and (3) threats to operational financing.[5] Each of these areas represents a systematic examination of business risk.

threats to profit margin
The threat of not being able to achieve a profit margin sufficient to allow the business to attain substantial returns.

1. **Threats to Profit Margin.** A significant threat to the success of a new venture is its ability to establish and maintain a high-margin product or service. That is, the firm is unable to make a high level of profit on each unit of product or service sold. What might inhibit your pricing or cost structure? Who are your significant competitors? Why do people shop with your competitor? How does pricing impact your ability to attract customers from your competitors?

threats to sales generation schemes
The threat of not being able to generate sufficient sales required to make the firm profitable.

2. **Threats to Sales Generation Schemes.** A new venture must have the opportunity to sell to many customers and to obtain repeat business. The ability to develop a sales scheme that is broad enough to appeal to a wide variety of customers is critical to the development of a successful business.[6] Can your competitors meet or exceed your quality? Undercut your price? Position themselves better physically? Lock you out of suppliers?

threats to operational financing
The threat of not obtaining sufficient financing to operate a firm.

3. **Threats to Operational Financing.** There are a number of specific threats to the new venture in obtaining the necessary financing for its growth. Some such threats are high development costs, rapid expansion plans, high inventory needs, and/or an entrepreneurial team with a low asset base. As will be discussed in Chapter 6, one of the greatest risks to a new business is fast growth. Typically, you will be selling products or services effectively on credit (delayed billing) but having to pay cash for your inputs as a new firm. Thus, rapid expansion can quickly overextend your financial resources. Research has shown that firms with higher initial capitalization have the opportunity to grow faster.[7] Why don't new ventures simply increase the amount of financial capital they need before starting the business? Why would you need additional operating capital once the business was growing? What

might impact your assessment of "enough" money to start and grow your business?

4. **Competitors.** The new business also must be realistic about its competitors. There are competitors for every business contemplated. If the potential entrepreneur cannot think of any company doing exactly the same thing as the new potential business, then what are customers doing now to satisfy that need/want? That current solution to the customer's problem is a competitor and will have to be dealt with by the new business. Most of the time, there are obvious competitors trying to lure the same set of customers as the potential new business. List who exists in this competitive set and why you believe they are competitors for your new business.

To illustrate how critical the accurate evaluation of these issues is to the success of the new firm, consider a business we worked with at the onset of the first Internet boom (late 1990s). This firm proposed to use the Internet to automate (and make remarkably more efficient) a process that previously had been done only through extensive use of the telephone—one call at a time. The former process involved making 30 or more phone calls to various individuals and then trying to coordinate their activities in a stepwise fashion while waiting for each to return the call (which usually came in while the initial caller was on the phone with another individual). The product developed by the founding entrepreneurial team was a Web page–based product that would perform this function on one screen at the same time (something we take for granted today). The initial response by the customers was immediate and positive. The software behind the product was modestly complex; nonetheless, once the Web page was available and visible, it would not be overly difficult for a well-heeled competitor to imitate it in just a couple of months. Some of the founders believed that the Web page itself and the software code that supported it was the key to success, and that the rollout could be incremental. They wanted to

ETHICAL CHALLENGE

The risk of a business increases dramatically as the investment in the business provided by family members goes up. It is one thing to tell an outside investor that you lost his money; it is an altogether more difficult conversation when the investment came from your sister. Before you accept money from your family or close friends, consider how you will handle that money in your business and how you will reward their confidence in you. All new ventures are inherently risky. As part of your risk analysis, you have to consider how much financial risk you are willing to commit to personally and with funds provided from those close to you. There are a rich set of questions that an entrepreneur should ask themselves as they move forward.

QUESTIONS

1. How would having your grandmother's retirement funds invested in the firm affect your judgment of the risk of a venture?
2. What if the business investment included your college funds?
3. What if those funds had been left to you by a relative?
4. How does the risk equation change if you had children that were young as opposed to approaching college?

limit their risk and use cash flow to fund their expansion with a systematic plan to expand the business slowly. Another group of the founders believed that the critical limiting factor was obtaining exclusive commitments from as many of the 300 core customers as soon as possible, before the competition realized what was happening to the industry. Once the key customers were secured they were less likely to change to another provider of the service.

This focus on the importance of the customers as the source of competitive advantage changed the whole approach for the new business. The owners decided that rather than rolling the business out incrementally, they would seek to sign up the core customers as quickly as possible. The solution chosen by the team was to hire a sales company that put 35 contract salespeople on the project for 90 days. The cost and risk of this approach was significantly higher for the founders. However, the result was that before competitors even realized that there was a new company in the field, the founders had locked up over 210 of the 300 customers. The first competitor showed up 70 days after they started their operation and was able to sign up only 14 customers after a year in operation.

For this new business, there was a significant strategic risk of misreading the critical factor(s) in the business, and a great idea could have simply limped along because of a poor implementation decision. If the business founders had not recognized the risk of their business idea being copied, they might have implemented the wrong approach and would likely have been replaced in the market by a larger, richer firm.

Now let's go back and take a look at our entrepreneur who is debating between a printing shop, a flower shop, and a restaurant. The entrepreneur contemplated the situation and developed the following insights about location and the associated cost. The printing shop would not have to be in prime retail space, because it was not going to focus on retail customers as did the large chain near campus, but instead was to focus on business customers. The flower shop needed to be in prime retail space to obtain the impulse purchases that are a high percentage of the flower business. The size of the space needed and the need for excellent access to customers would make the restaurant's location the most expensive of all three.

The entrepreneur in thinking through the competition and profits realized that the flower shop's competition would be the strongest, and the profit margins in that industry were lower than in the other two industries. The printing shop had good profit margins, but the investment in the equipment necessary was relatively high. The restaurant seemed to have the highest competition risk. The nature of eating out is both eclectic and faddish. Individuals might desire one type of food for a while, then switch to another type of food. Additionally, returns in the restaurant industry are historically low, although individual restaurants can be quite profitable.

Considering time, the entrepreneur realized that the time needed to start up the flower shop and the printing shop would be shortest. The time it takes to set up and start a restaurant can be quite high, due to the nature of the finish to the interior that is required in the restaurant itself. The restaurant will have to develop a character and must be decorated, whereas the print shop might just have white walls. Finally, in terms of staffing, a far bigger staff is required in the restaurant, so the need for extensive hiring and training is an inherent and integral part of the business.

The entrepreneur had financial support from his family as well as some personal savings; had been laid off from his job, so he had lots of time to dedicate to the business; was single; and was dedicated to starting a business. His personal take on the deficit analysis for these three factors is provided in Table 3.2.

As a result of this analysis, the entrepreneur decided to focus his due diligence on the printing business. The due diligence proved that there was a need for the business (this concept will be discussed more in Chapter 4); that a successful and sustainable strategy had the potential to be developed (this concept will be discussed more in Chapter 5); and that the potential business had the opportunity for positive cash flows (this concept will be discussed more in Chapter 6). As a result of that due diligence process, the small-business person established the business and has made it a success.

Table 3.2
Example of Entrepreneur's Personal Deficit Analysis

BUSINESS IDEA	CATEGORY	OUR RESOURCES	RESOURCES REQUIRED	DEFICIT
Printing Shop	Finances	Savings and some ability to get loans	Need additional funds for equipment	*Medium*
High quality; commercial	Time	Full time	Full day—high volume work with deadlines	*Low*
	Nonfinancial	Little knowledge	Need printing expertise	*High*
	Risk	Moderate—cheaper space, expensive equipment	Rapid acquisition of used equipment and cheap space	*Medium*
	Competitors	Moderate	Advertising and sales to counter	*High*
Flower Shop	Finances	Savings, loans, family money	Cooler, basic equipment, Display cases	*Low*
Family history and support	Time	Full time + family time	Full day in house; delivery	*Medium*
	Nonfinancial	Significant family knowledge	Arrangement, design, stocking knowledge	*Low*
	Risk	Smaller footprint; expensive interior	Knowledge of market, high availability	*Low*
	Competitors	Strong and many	Positioning, leverage family; differentiation	*High*
Restaurant	Finances	Savings, loans	Significant resources needed for equipment; customer face	*High*
Fast food crossed with service	Time	Full time	10–9 daily; lots of staff needed for cooking, serving, etc.	*High*
	Nonfinancial	Little knowledge	Food prep, licensing, ordering, serving	*High*
	Risk	Heavy investment and employees; could be easily copied	Attract based on concept unproven. Fickle customers; holding onto concept	*High*
	Competitors	Numerous in general; few specifically	Pricing, positioning, newness issue	*High*

SUMMARY

In this chapter we presented a method for the potential new entrepreneur to develop and perform an initial evaluation of various business ideas. This process starts with an evaluation of the skills that the individual brings to the new business. What education, experience, hobbies, and other interests do you already have in your pocket before the new business gets founded? The next step is to look at the world around you and systematically evaluate the potential opportunities. There are literally millions of ideas out there. The real question is: Do you have the ability to successfully take advantage of those ideas to create a successful business? Finally, we presented a gap analysis methodology that has been used successfully for some time to determine potential fit with a business idea.

KEY TERMS

brainstorming 45
gap analysis 44
synergy 40
threats to operational financing 50
threats to profit margin 50
threats to sales generation schemes 50

REVIEW QUESTIONS

1. Based on your *education*, what are the skills you have that could be the basis for a business?
2. Based on your *work experience*, what are the skills you have that could be the basis for a business?
3. Based on your *hobbies*, what are the skills you have that could be the basis for a business?
4. What are your top three personal skills?
5. What things do you like doing best?
6. What magazines and books do you read?
7. What are your three greatest accomplishments in life? What skills were involved in these accomplishments?
8. Do you enjoy working with people?
9. In what general industry (retail/wholesale/manufacturing/service) would you prefer to work?

BUSINESS PLAN DEVELOPMENT QUESTIONS

Conduct the following for yourself to determine which businesses would be an appropriate match for the skills and traits as you work on your business plan.

1. Think about what trends around the region/nation/world you know about that have not reached your area.
2. Interview and talk about opportunities with key successful entrepreneurs in the area. Where do they find a match between opportunity and your skills?
3. Discuss with family members what potential businesses they believe might be best for you.
4. Take the business ideas that have met your criteria thus far and perform a deficit analysis of those ideas. Which idea has the most potential for success, given your resources, time, risk position, and so on?

INDIVIDUAL EXERCISES

1. Pick a successful business in your area that is not a franchise. What was the opportunity this business identified? Does that opportunity still exist for another business in either another location or if addressed in a different manner?
2. For this business, what key skills would the entrepreneur need to be successful?
3. If you can visit with this entrepreneur, then see if you can determine if your analysis was correct.

GROUP EXERCISES

1. Break into teams of three to four. Present each of your personal deficit analyses. Help each other think through their accuracy and the means by which you could overcome any shortcomings in skills or resources.
2. The team has a combination of experiences and resources. If the team, instead of just one person, were putting together a business, how would the analysis change?

ENDNOTES

1. M. Maddock and R. Vitn, "Innovating During a Recession," *BusinessWeek Online,* November 5, 2008, p. 13.
2. D. A. Gregorie and D. A. Shepherd, "Technology-Market Combinations and the Identification of Entrepreneurial Opportunities: An Investigation of the Opportunity-Individual Nexus," *Academy of Management Journal* 55 no. 4, (2012), pp. 753–85.
3. P. Croce, "Think Brighter," *Fortune Small Business* 15, no. 9 (2005), p. 35.
4. D. Simchi-Levi, W. Schmidt, and W. Yehua. *Harvard Business Review*. 92, no. 1/2 (2014), pp. 96–101.
5. K. H. Vesper, *New Venture Strategies* (Englewood Cliffs, NJ: Prentice Hall, 1990).
6. P. P. McDougall, J. G. Covin, R. B. Robinson, and L. Herron, "The Effects of Industry Growth and Strategic Breadth on New Venture Performance and Strategy Content," *Strategic Management Journal* 15 (1994), pp. 537–54; E. Romanelli, "Environments and Strategies of Organization Start-up: Effects on Early Survival," *Administrative Science Quarterly* 34 (1989), pp. 369–87.
7. A. C. Cooper and F. J. Gimeno-Gascon, "Entrepreneurs, Processes of Founding, and New Firm Performance," in *The State of the Art of Entrepreneurship,* ed. D. L. Sexton and J. D. Kasarda (Boston, MA: PWS Kent, 1992), pp. 301–40; K. M. Eisenhardt and C. B. Schoonhoven, "Organizational Growth: Linking Founding Team, Strategy, Environment, and Growth Among U.S. Semiconductor Ventures, 1978–1988," *Administrative Science Quarterly* 35(1990), pp. 504–29.

CREDITS

Opener: Xavier Arnau/E+/Getty Images RF; p. 37: Thinkstock/Jupiterimages RF; p. 41: Royalty-Free/Corbis; p. 42: Big Cheese Photo/PunchStock RF; p. 46: © Plattform/Johner Images/Corbis RF; p. 48 (left): Monty Rakusen/Cultura/Getty Images RF; p. 48 (middle): Hola Images RF/Getty Images RF; p. 48 (right): BananaStock/PunchStock RF.

part 2

chapter 4

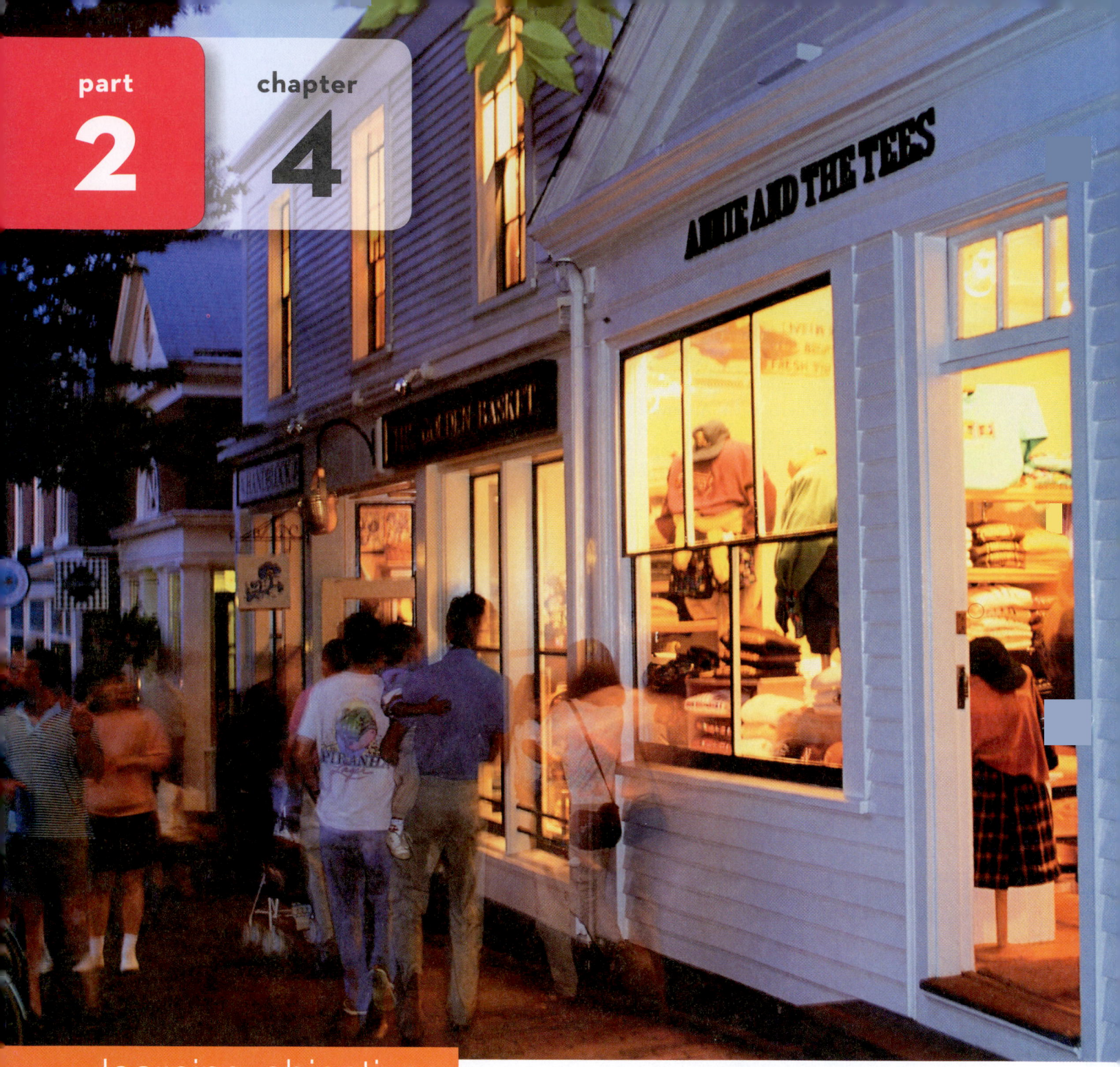

learning objectives

After studying this chapter, you will be able to:

LO4-1 Describe how to examine the industry that the new business plans to enter.

LO4-2 Discuss how to create a profile of the target customers for a new business.

LO4-3 Explain how to categorize competitors of the new business using external analysis.

LO4-4 Explain how to construct competitive maps.

LO4-5 Ensure that the entrepreneur has considered a full set of concerns in his or her external analysis.

LO4-6 Differentiate between those elements of the business that provide a competitive advantage and those that do not.

External Analysis

GUAYAKÍ SUSTAINABLE RAINFOREST PRODUCTS, INC.

Products and services that are popular in one part of the country or world may be very effective models for new businesses in other parts of the country or world. However, to be successful in starting this type of new business, you must ensure that you understand the interests of potential customers and have the ability to educate the market about the product. Based on a student project to develop a new business, Alex Pryor built a business selling Yerba Mate, a drink that was wildly popular in his native Paraguay. This product is a coffee substitute that seems to have many other benefits, including being an energy enhancer, a body system balancer, and an appetite suppressant.

Alex's friend Steve Karr joined the business in 1996 to form Guayakí Sustainable Rainforest Products. Their goal from the beginning has been to capitalize on the desire of many people to live an ecologically sustainable lifestyle. Funding in their early days included several SBA loans, Karr's entire life savings, and lots of credit cards. The founders traveled and served Yerba Mate from a rain forest mural–painted RV while operating the business out of a one-bedroom apartment. The market developed slowly as each customer was educated in the uses of the drink and the goal of the organization. Even as they provide a sustainable drink product, their organizational goal is to create economic models that drive reforestation while providing a living wage to employees in emerging economies. The entrepreneurs established a carbon-neutral business model and have recently become a significant buyer from women-based businesses that are driving the change to eliminate poverty, malnutrition, and destructive land practices from the area. The firm today has a goal of restoring 200,000 acres of South American Atlantic rain forest and creating 1,000 fair wage jobs by 2020.

Guayakí is now one of the leading providers of organic, fairly traded, rain forest–grown yerba mate in North America, with products sold at thousands of natural foods stores, cafés, and supermarkets. The firm's success led to it being invited to participate in the Clinton Foundation Global Initiative in 2010.

Questions

1. List Guayaki's competitive advantages.
2. What is your assessment of Guayaki's ability to maintain those advantages?

Sources: S. Huszar, "South America's Secret Weight Loss Tea," *Woman's World,* October 21, 2003; J. Caplin, E. McGirt, and A. Wilson, "Fortune Hunters," *Money,* August 2003, www.guayaki.com; S. Anna, "Coffee, Tea or Guayaki: A World Challenge," Presidio Graduate School, www.triplepundit.com/2011/10/coffee-tea-guayaki-world-challenge-finalist/; J. Cirillo, "Mission Possible," *Beverage World,* 2010, pp. 43–44; A. Ardichvili, R. Cardozo, and R. Sourav, "A Theory of Entrepreneurial Opportunity Identification and Development," *Journal of Business Venturing* 18, no. 1 (2003), pp. 104–24.

Starting an entrepreneurial business should be based on the observance of an opportunity.[1] The recognition of an opportunity may come from a frustration with the way that existing businesses operate (poor service, lack of selection); a new technology that makes an idea that was previously impractical become available (i.e., an Internet-based service, computer animation); a hobby that provides you unique skills and insight; or a new vacancy at the perfect location for a business. However, even though there are many ways to identify an opportunity, the entrepreneur must ensure that what he or she is observing is truly an opportunity. What may appear to be a great opportunity to one person may in fact not be viable as a business. The key to effective opportunity recognition is a detailed understanding of the external environment.

There are a number of critical steps in examining the nature of the external environment. These include the following:

1. Define the industry in which you are competing.
2. Define your customers.
3. Research the industry yourself.
4. Identify competitors within that industry.
5. Research those competitors.
6. Draw a set of competitive maps.
7. Examine and develop insights about additional economic aspects of the industry, including substitutes, elasticity of demand, ease of entry and exit, benchmarking, and industry trends.
8. Start developing an understanding of your competitive advantage.

We will look at each of these steps in turn in analyzing the external environment.

LO4-1

Describe how to examine the industry that the new business plans to enter.

Defining Your Industry

The first part of an external analysis is to determine the industry within which the new business will compete, as well as the general makeup of the industry.[2] In doing so the entrepreneur should seek to be as specific as possible. For example, if you want to open a new ice cream store, you might ask, In what industry does a new ice cream store compete? Clearly, the industry will include other ice cream stores. However, if the ice cream store will make a significant part of its revenues from selling ice cream cakes, then the industry might be best viewed as including a broader group of dessert providers, such as bakeries and other businesses that sell competing products. If the ice cream store has both dipping operations where the ice cream is sold in cones and prepackaged gallons of ice cream, perhaps the industry includes competitors that sell ice cream in grocery stores. The industry may also vary if the ice cream is high end with a high milk-fat content (referred to as "frozen custard" in many states such as Wisconsin) versus more typical ice cream that has much lower milk-fat level. Defining the firm's industry is not something that should be taken lightly.

Nowadays, most information can be obtained on the Web or via a magazine or journal that covers a broad category of firms to which you believe your new business will belong. Industry associations are another prime source of this type of data. Industry associations for virtually any industry you can think of probably exist at the national level, and many have local or state organizations as well. These associations exist primarily to support and promote their industry. They have extensive data on their industry and are usually quite willing to share that with the public.

To obtain statistical data, the potential entrepreneur will want to obtain the industry categorization. Two relatively simple means are available. The first is to locate your industry's NAICS (North American Industry Classification System) code for the industry. An NAICS code is a code that can vary from two to seven digits in length (the more digits, the more specific the classification). The codes were generated by the U.S. government in an effort to gather, track, and publish data on specific industries. You can locate this code either on the Internet via a number of sources including the U.S. government websites (www.census.gov/epcd/www/naics.html). The second way to find nationwide information is to locate a public company that might be a direct competitor to the new business and simply use its NAICS code to look up overall industry data (via Dun & Bradstreet, LexisNexis, etc.).

Housing construction slowed in recent years due to the recession with the amount of decline varying from state to state.

At an aggregated national level, the data gathered on a firm's industry has some value; however, it is the rare new business that intends to draw customers from across the United States at its founding. Most of the data available will be on a national basis, which provides you some information on national trends but provides little understanding of the local competitive environment. The national industry may be doing very poorly, but your immediate area might contain virtually no competitors and have the potential to do very well. For example, in the recent recession, housing construction businesses in California, Florida, and Nevada were severely hurt, while at the same time the housing construction industry in Texas and Missouri experienced only limited economic slowdown.

Entrepreneurs should define the industry in which they will compete broadly enough to be inclusive of all potential competitors, but not so broadly as to be overwhelming. If you are starting a new jewelry store, it is most likely that not even all the jewelry stores in your area are direct competitors. If your store will be in a shopping mall, clearly, other stores in similar malls will be competitors. However, if there is a Tiffany's in the same city, it might or might not be a direct competitor, depending on the specific customer market you are seeking to serve. Someone who buys jewelry at Tiffany's is not likely to purchase items in a small, shopping-mall store, and vice versa.

Even more important, the entrepreneur must be clear about the practical level of actual competition. An entrepreneur should ask, What is a reasonable geographic customer draw for a new business? Opening up a sandwich shop in the downtown area of a city means that the shop most likely competes with other sandwich or fast-food shops within a 10-block radius—and perhaps less, if walking is the primary means of transportation for downtown lunching workers. There are limits to how far someone will travel for a sandwich. Drawing a practical radius around your potential new business location will also help target the customers that are most likely to patronize your business. This raises an interesting question for the brew pub we are examining in each chapter. How far do you believe a potential customer would travel to get to a brew pub like Chris is planning to open? There have been four restaurants that have closed in the location he has chosen. Will customers travel further for the brew pub? If not, does he need to think of a different formula for success than have the prior failed restaurateurs? As we think of other businesses such as Internet businesses the draw may be national—people really don't care where they order things from. However, as we will discuss later in the book, the key to Internet business becomes more how to ensure a business gets through the clutter of the Internet to reach the customers they want, no matter where they live.

industry
Those direct competitors selling similar products or services within a specified geographic radius that is consistent with a customer's willingness to travel to purchase those products or services.

For a new entrepreneurial business, the **industry** is defined as those companies within a specified geographic radius (if the business has a physical presence) that will be in direct competition for the same customers and sales as that of the new business. Thinking about Chris and the brew pub he wishes to open demonstrates some of the difficulties that many new businesses have in their planning. If he defines his industry as "restaurant," this would push him to design his business in different ways than if he believes his industry is a bar. Recognize that even as Chris starts to consider in what industry he competes, he will also need to drill deeper and consider which competitors might seek the same customers. A customer normally chooses from a wide variety of restaurants within categories such as price, class, ambiance, and location. Just as we highlighted with jewelry stores—a high-end steak house such as Ruth's Chris is not likely competing against the local chicken-fried steak house. How to determine such choices will be examined next.

LO4-2

Discuss how to create a profile of the target customers for a new business.

Defining Your Customers

Once the industry is broadly defined, then the exact nature of the customer should be developed. It is important to define a narrower group of individuals whom you believe will constitute your most likely customers. Where are they located? Where do they currently obtain their product or service? A new burger place opening up near a university is not competing against all burger places in the country, so overall industry figures for the nation, state, or even city are of little assistance. Instead, the customers are going to be the students, faculty, and staff of the university, and the immediate residents of the university area.

In defining the customer, the entrepreneur should be diligent in the effort to be as accurate as possible. We will discuss promotional activities such as advertising in Chapter 11 ("Marketing"), but here we note that defining the customer to which your company caters is important for the effective use of your marketing dollars, as well as the satisfaction of core, repeat customers.

One potential restaurant owner told us that he viewed his target customer market as those individuals from ages 2 to 90, from all income ranges, anywhere within a 50-mile radius. Indeed, he became quite upset when we suggested that this was unreasonable. His view was, why not seek every potential customer he could?

What would this type of definition mean to the operation of the business? The entrepreneur would have to have food items that appealed to children, teenagers, adults, and senior citizens in all price ranges. The entrepreneur's original concept for the restaurant was that it was to be an upscale restaurant with some "flash" oriented around the extensive wine selection. However, if he defined his customers as everyone aged 2 to 90, his wine selection would have to run the gamut from alcohol-free wine to jugs of cheap wine to rare vintages, because the range of customers he was targeting would demand to be satisfied, and all of these customers would be equally valued. This egalitarian approach is probably appropriate for a political movement, but is a poor approach to business success.[3] The offering of alcohol-free wines and cheap wines turns off the customer who likes high-end wines. Similarly, a large wine list with lots of expensive wines is frustrating and intimidating to the customer looking for a $3 glass of wine.

FRIENDS' HOME HEALTH

As we discussed in previous chapters, Betty and Joan planned to start a home health agency. They hoped to develop a business that provided them an opportunity to benefit from their expertise and also be financially rewarding. A clear understanding of some of the external elements of the business was a crucial start to the design.

Industry

The two friends would clearly be in the home health care industry; however, the two knew that many businesses call themselves *home health* when the services they actually provide run a spectrum of needs, including physical therapy, car service to and from doctors' offices, running errands, providing meals, cleaning, and simple accompaniment to the elderly. The two entrepreneurs were very clear that they wanted to provide the medically necessary elements of home health care and not the routine domestic elements that could be provided by anyone with or without a college education.

Customers

Betty and Joan realized they also needed to have a clear definition of their perfect customers. They also wanted to be sure to focus their work where they would qualify as a minority-owned business for referral of Medicaid patients. Thus, they would not focus on other insurance providers or customers who are primarily private-pay customers. However, they also recognized that many times customers wanted more from a home health service than the government will pay for. For example, the family may need more hours of medical care than the government is willing to pay for. In those cases the entrepreneurs also wanted to be able to offer extra services for private payment. Therefore, they targeted an upper-middle-income section of the city as their starting point. They reasoned that the very wealthy would want only private care and the entrepreneurs' status as minority business owners would provide no benefit. The south side of their city seemed to meet their target group the best.

Competition

There were five major home health competitors in the south side of the city. One was part of a large national chain. The service from this vendor was more expensive, but there was a halo effect created by its television advertising campaign. The firm had very good systems in place to ensure efficiency and timeliness of the care, but those same systems could become very bureaucratic for the family being served.

The other four competitors on the south side were all local firms that varied widely in size. The first firm was the largest and was associated with and received most of its patients from a large, local nonprofit hospital (not the one for which Betty and Joan worked). It had a natural connection to the patients but also a history of weak customer service. Interestingly, the home health unit of the hospital was a profit center for the hospital that generated significant cash; however, it was not the major focus of the hospital, so the care of the customers was often less than satisfactory.

The second firm was a small business that had a good reputation. The firm was started by a successful entrepreneur when he could not find good care for his mother. The fact that the business was not the entrepreneur's main source of income resulted in the firm limiting its growth. The entrepreneur was mostly concerned about providing very high-quality care for his family, their friends, and their friends' families. Thus, the pricing for the service was competitive, but the profit was very low as the entrepreneur paid higher-than-average wages to his employees.

The third firm was a minority-owned business such as the one Betty and Joan planned. The firm appeared to be well run in terms of health care. Unfortunately, this business was the hardest to find information about. This lack of information made Betty and Joan wonder how well the business aspects of the business were conducted.

The fourth potential competitor was a mid-sized business that appeared to be on the verge of bankruptcy. The newspaper had run a feature story about one of their employee caregivers who had sat and texted while she thought the elderly person in her care was asleep. The elderly patient instead had gotten up out of bed, fallen, and later died. Although the business might be around for a while longer, it did not seem likely to be a significant competitor.

EXERCISE 1

1. What other questions do you think Betty and Joan should ask as they do their customer analysis of Friends' Home Health?
2. On what basis do you believe the competitors are trying to differentiate themselves?
3. Do you believe that Friends' is sufficiently differentiated from these competitors?

Once the entrepreneur realized the expansive—and expensive—scope of the plan he wanted to pursue, he decided to narrow his true target to adults aged 30 to 50 with a median income of $60,000 who lived within about 20 minutes' drive from the restaurant. This is not to suggest that he will, or would want to, turn away anyone who wishes to dine at his establishment. It does, however, suggest that the only patrons that he specifically caters to are those in his demographic target. An outcome of this approach is that if a college-aged couple comes in and complains about the wine selection being too expensive, the owner no longer has to feel the need to appeal to them and provide inexpensive wines. In fact, he specifically does not want to do that as it would affect the image and cost structure of the restaurant. The college couple is not his perfect customer.

This approach helps the entrepreneurial business clearly focus on its core customer. It also helps the business maintain a strategic distance between itself and its competitors, as the firm is not trying to do what everyone else may do. Finally, a clear understanding of the business's customers assists the owners in controlling expenses, as the business does not try to be everything to everybody. The inventory can therefore be much more focused than if the entrepreneur tries to be everything to everyone.

LO4-3

Explain how to categorize competitors of the new business using external analysis.

Developing the Information for the External Analysis of Competitors

The Friends' Home Health founders were able to develop some very good information for their external analysis. They accomplished this with a lot of legwork and by using publically available information. Next we discuss a number of ways to conduct such research.

Research Your Industry Yourself

At this point in your efforts to start a new business, you should have defined the industry that interests you, determined who your potential customers might be and why they might want to buy from your business, and gathered some information on these domains. The next issue is to identify the exact competitors within that industry. These competitors are those firms that directly compete for the same set of ideal customers as your proposed business. If the new business owners are very clear regarding their customers' needs, then the ability to identify direct competitors becomes significantly easier. For many new entrepreneurial ventures, these businesses will be geographically local. Thus, the most obvious and mundane places to look for these competitors are the local telephone book and the front seat of your car.

Although it is certainly possible to hire a consulting company to perform the type of customer research service discussed above, the entrepreneur will gain invaluable insight by handling this process personally. We assisted a small group of highly committed golfers who had the idea of developing an affordable, nonmember 18-hole golf course in the Dallas–Fort Worth (DFW) metroplex. Their idea was to offer a country club–level course without the membership commitment and expense involved with playing on some of the area's quality courses. The group had a tract of land that had been in the family of one of the potential founders and had been given to him upon the death of his father. Although this is substantially larger than the usual entrepreneurial business idea we present in the text, we believe the concepts point out the critical issues that any potential entrepreneur must address.

At the first meeting, the golf professionals were clear that they knew the market and what the market needed. However, basic market questions kept coming up that they were unable to answer. Some of the questions raised for which they had no answers included these:

When planning new development like a golf course, knowing your market is crucial. What activities would you want to control personally when developing your business?

1. How many 18-hole courses are there in the DFW metroplex?
2. How many of these courses are not tied to a country club?
3. How many rounds of golf are played on a typical weekend at these courses?
4. How far does the average golfer drive to play a round?
5. Are there capacity problems at some of the more popular courses?
6. How much does the average golfer spend in food and drink while playing 18 holes?
7. What is charged to play at various times of the day or week at each of the open courses?
8. Where is the population growth area for golfers?
9. What is the profile of a typical golfer?

It was clear that these individuals who wanted to start the business loved golf and thought they had a great understanding of the local industry; however, the golfers had not done any in-depth study of the market. These individuals were frustrated when they realized that they did not have a detailed understanding of the potential customer. In response, they were ready to hire a company to collect this information, despite the high cost of pursuing that option. Instead, we encouraged them to collect this information themselves. Doing so would make them the experts in the area and enable them to develop a plan for a business that would give them a competitive advantage. The benefits of planning and analysis are the nuanced insights it provides the individuals performing the activities. Hiring a company to gather information is not only expensive, but also limits the insights to more factual data.

Therefore, the founders prepared a list of questions about a golf course that would help differentiate their business. After doing some quick research to find every 18-hole course in the metroplex, they divided up the courses and individually visited each one. They played each course and tried to experience all the offerings at the course. The questionnaires that they developed were completed after each visit and an overall analysis was completed describing the entire market.

EXERCISE 2

Using the golf course initiative as an example, pair up with one other person and explain your business idea to him or her. Have the person role-play a friend who would be investing in your business. Have the person ask you questions about what the customer desires to get out of the product or service. Use the list as a starting point for your own competitor analysis.

Defining Actual Competitors

An effective industry analysis starts by identifying every potential competitor within that previously defined reasonable distance of your planned establishment location. What a reasonable distance consists of is a matter of interpretation, and the interpreter is the new businessperson. Although someone could argue with any individual's assessment of that distance, it must be established, and this is much more a matter of art than a matter of science. In any case, the first step is to define a radius from which you believe you will draw a majority of your customers. Make this distance reasonable, not just a wish.[4] If the business does not have a physical restriction to its operation, then it is important to create a list of competitors that can easily be found electronically by your customers.[5]

A woman in Knoxville, Tennessee, was planning a quick-serve, breakfast-oriented restaurant. She needed to define a reasonable radius from which she would draw her ideal customers. She originally said that she would draw customers from the entire metropolitan Knoxville area, and (much like our previous restaurant owner) was adamant that she did not want to forego any business. Once again, we certainly do not suggest that you forego business unnecessarily, but an assessment that a business draws from an entire region is unreasonable for many reasons. Just one is that if you try to cater to everyone in a metro area, you will distort your advertising efforts, and you will dramatically increase your costs. Instead, this entrepreneur needed to focus on customers within a reasonable commuting distance from the restaurant. She eventually narrowed that distance to 20 minutes of driving in traffic. Although you may indeed draw customers from outside this area, they are not your primary group at the outset. (Think of yourself and how much time you are willing to travel to get breakfast?) If you need to rethink this distance as your operations mature, then you can. The core information is already in hand and will still be relevant if you expand or contract the market radius later. The opening story in Chapter 1 is a great example of this. Oren's Daily Roast Coffee & Teas has opened 10 locations on the island of Manhattan primarily because customers will walk only so far for a great cup of coffee.

Once our breakfast restaurant entrepreneur had identified the area she wanted to serve, she began driving around the area, to see what competitors might be in operation. She also identified businesses through the phone book. The end result was that with relatively little expense, she was able to identify those restaurants that would be her direct and indirect competitors.

Once you have established a reasonable radius from which you will draw your primary customer, the next step is to examine each of your potential competitors. It is easy to discuss practices in the industry in general terms. For example, you might hear that all the area photocopying places have poor service, wait times are long, and the local shops have poor-quality equipment. These general feelings about the industry may help an entrepreneur believe he or she sees an opportunity, but actually running a business requires specific knowledge about the competitors. Even in a poor industry, there are probably some competitors who will be tough to beat. The entrepreneur must identify those competitors, what they do well, and where they are located.

fragmented markets

Markets in which no one competitor has a substantial share of the market and the means of competition vary widely within the same market space.

Most entrepreneurial businesses compete in what is referred to as **fragmented markets.**[6] These are markets that have no clear dominant competitor and are instead made up of a large number of similar-sized firms. If the entrepreneurial business is competing directly with well-established firms, this virtually guarantees that at a minimum, the entrepreneurial business will be operating at a cost disadvantage and will have to compete on some other basis. The number and size of all competitors need to be detailed so that the entrepreneur has a rich and full understanding of their competition. Additionally, the differences in how the various businesses compete and their competitive advantages also need to be well understood.

In the Knoxville restaurant example discussed, the ability to drive by and visit the various existing restaurants allowed the entrepreneur to understand each of those establishments in greater depth as well as which might be the strongest competitors. Straightforward observations made by an entrepreneur who understands the competitive issues of the industry can provide valuable insight. However, there is another tool available to the entrepreneur that can provide additional information. Specifically, an analytical tool that has the ability to digest information and display this information to others is a **competitive map.**

competitive map
An analytical tool used to organize information about direct competitors on all points of competition.

Developing a Competitive Map

LO4-4

Explain how to construct competitive maps.

At this point in the process, the amount of detail about competitors that needs to be organized raises the need for a systematic means to categorize that information. Thus, the next step in your external analysis is to develop a competitive map to better understand competitors and their capabilities.[7] Although there are many companies available that are in

FLOW RIGHT BREWERY & BAR: A FAMILY AFFAIR

Chris was progressing and starting to think more about his bar. He had the opportunity to sit and visit with a banker about possible financing and the banker asked a number of great questions that Chris could not answer. Specifically, he asked about the target customer and competition. Chris had thought the target customers would be people who were beer connoisseurs such as himself. However, the following week he went to his beer club, which was made up of beer connoisseurs, and began to realize that he needed to be clearer about his customers. His beer club was made up of great people, but their incomes ran the full range of virtually none to very high. In addition, it was not clear if they would come often enough to the downtown area where his bar was to be located for him to have a viable business.

Chris then made a visit to Seattle for a cousin's wedding. While there, he had the opportunity to visit a brew pub similar to the type he wanted to establish. During the time at the brew pub he got to visit with one of the pub's owners. The owner's background was similar to Chris's in that he had a love of beer. What Chris found interesting in the conversation was that the core profits of the business came not from beer but from the food that was served with the beer. The beer was what attracted the customers, but what made money for the establishment was the food and also renting the facilities out for private parties. Chris was also surprised to find that most of the customers at this brew pub were not even beer connoisseurs. They were instead young professionals who liked beer, but their actual discrimination in taste was limited. The young professionals liked the idea of craft beers, but this brew pub actually had to educate their customers on what made a great beer.

This insight on customers led Chris to realize he would have to plan his bar similar to the brew pub in Seattle. Chris may brew a great beer, but the beer alone could not be what would drive the success of the bar. Instead, he would need to be able to reach out to other customers. In thinking of the customers, Chris decided that he would pursue a customer profile like the brew pub in Seattle—young professionals.

The nature of the competition changed dramatically as Chris began to think through his customers. He now realized that he would need to have a more elegant environment than he had envisioned and that food would play a much greater role in the success of the business.

As Chris began to think through his planned business, he examined the downtown area and found approximately 40 restaurants within two miles of the center of the city. Of those he determined that 10 would be the closest in competition to him. These 10 also served a professional crowd and relied on a mixture of alcohol and food to prosper. Three competitors specifically pitched themselves as a place for beer lovers, but only one of those actually brewed any beer on-site. The other 30 restaurants included fast-food franchises and diners, which Chris did not consider to be significant competitors.

EXERCISE 3

1. Think of your campus or downtown area. Would a brewery such as Chris is planning be a viable business in this area?
2. How would customers and competitors differ around a campus versus the downtown area in a major city?
3. How would you develop a competitive map for this business?

business to examine competitors, as we have stated previously, we recommend that the entrepreneur develop this map personally, for the following reasons:

1. It is less expensive.
2. Knowledge of what is right and wrong with each of the competitors allows the entrepreneur to better position the new business.
3. Insights will be developed regarding positioning, pricing, and even facility layout.

Developing a competitive map requires that the entrepreneur visit *all* of the potential competitors in whatever form they run their business. Further, we recommend that you be a customer of your competitors. Even if your desired entrepreneurial business sells business to business, you can still seek to interact with the competitors to try to understand their activities. There is nothing like obtaining the customer perspective from a series of such visits; the comparisons to your potential competitors become easier with this type of insight. With this in mind, the entrepreneur must develop a list of criteria that they wish to take away from each visit and record that information after each visit. Although this list might change depending on the type of establishment, we suggest a list of potential items to consider if the business is a retail business selling to customers in a brick-and-mortar location:

1. Parking availability (how many spots and what quality?)
2. Access from road
3. Nearby attractions for customers
4. Size of facility
5. Décor
6. Pricing
7. Product breadth
8. Product depth
9. Staffing (number and quality)
10. Capacity
11. Brochures/advertising material
12. Customer traffic at several different times of day
13. Average sale
14. Friendliness/helpfulness
15. Unique features
16. Suppliers (what company is delivering to their business?)

Although this list is most applicable to retail businesses that have a set location, you should recognize that many of the same concepts apply to any Internet business or other business types. The key in each case is to determine the key competitive factors that you wish to understand about your competitors.

An example of a competitive map is shown in Table 4.1. This competitive map (for the Dallas–Fort Worth golf course discussed earlier) encompasses a number of criteria that could be used in the evaluations of the business. The eight-mile radius employed in this map is based on the distance the partners determined from their research that someone would drive to play golf.

Some of these items (and there will be other ones for your venture) can be easily categorized and analyzed. Others are more descriptive and

	COMPETITOR 1	COMPETITOR 2	COMPETITOR 3	COMPETITOR 4	COMPETITOR 5
Population in area					
No. of households in area					
Household income					
Average age in area					
No. of driving ranges					
No. of golf shops in area					
No. of customers per weekday					
No. of customers per weekend					
Average no. of customers per hour					
Peak flow of customers					
Average charge per transaction					
Tee charge: peak and off-peak					
Clubhouse feel					
Course feel					
Variety of menu offerings: clubhouse					
Variety of menu offerings: course					

Table 4.1
Competitive Map: Golf Course (Eight-Mile Radius)

give you a rich sense of what is available to customers right now. We have included a description of some of the findings from the group seeking to establish the golf course.

At the time of this investigation the DFW area had 74 golf courses. However, it was determined from surveys with potential customers that on average, individuals would drive no more than 30 minutes one way to the golf course. Therefore, rather than examine all 74 courses, the entrepreneurs chose to examine only those courses in Fort Worth because that is where their land was and those no farther than 30 minutes from downtown. This resulted in our entrepreneurial team visiting 24 golf courses, 25 percent of which were private. The private courses in this particular area are very difficult to join. The membership or initiation fees at these clubs are quite expensive, several are at capacity, the current members appear to be very particular about who is a member, and the benefits of belonging to the club are more about social/business connections than the golf. Therefore, the focus of the entrepreneurial team shifted to the remaining 18 nonclub courses.

Five of the 18 public courses appeared to be poorly maintained. However, the other 13 were in good shape, with at least 6 of those in excellent shape. In visiting with golfers at the courses and playing the courses themselves, the potential entrepreneurs discovered that there was no difficulty in getting on the courses. Both the access and the nature of the courses were generally excellent. The fact that they were public courses was a result of city government subsidies, which provided the operators with subsidized lease payments and some assistance with the maintenance expenses.

After completing their map, the potential golf entrepreneurs concluded that the competitive landscape was not at all what they had envisioned. They concluded that the DFW area was overbuilt and that the presence of public subsidies for many courses distorted competition. They decided that the market was not as attractive as they originally had thought.

EXERCISE 4

Develop the basis of a competitive map for your proposed venture. Outline in columns each of the items that you would like to observe while visiting your competitors. Present this to the class and ask for help in developing a complete map.

LO4-5

Ensure that the entrepreneur has considered a full set of concerns in his or her external analysis.

Additional Issues for External Analysis

There are a number of other economic issues that founders of a new business will want to consider as they develop their external analysis. These include substitutes, elasticity of demand, ease of entry and exit, benchmarking, and industry trends. Each will be discussed briefly.

Substitutes

substitute

A product that performs a similar function or achieves the same result, but is not a precise imitation.

The potential new businessperson should keep in mind potential substitutes for the activities of the business. A **substitute** exists if the service or product performs a similar function or achieves the same result as the planned business, but is not a precise imitation.[8] In the case of golf, a substitute might be tennis or boating. Any other sport that the customer can pursue in place of golf could be a substitute.

In developing a competitive map, the entrepreneur needs to be aware of such substitutes and the potential impact they can have. However, it is also important that the new businessperson not get overwhelmed with so many potential substitutes that it appears there is no way to compete in the industry. Each new businessperson must judge the potential impact of a substitute, but the important issue is the recognition that at some price trade-off point, customers will switch to substitutes. For example, if you charge $500 for a single round of golf, individuals will eventually seek out other means of entertainment (unless you are Pebble Beach). Thus, substitutes can help form a ceiling on the price that can be charged for the product or service.

Elasticity of Demand

elasticity of demand

Consumers' respond to price changes. For example, as the prices of luxury items increase, the demand usually declines as these goods are not essential and their purchase can be delayed. This would be called *elastic demand*. Conversely, items such as gas for your car typically have relatively inelastic demand as you will not stop using it as the price increases.

Elasticity of demand refers to customers switching to substitutes or not using a product as the price of the product rises.[9] A product or service for which customers are willing to pay virtually any price is said to have a very inelastic demand. In other words, for your cancer medicine, the price is irrelevant; you will still seek out the medicine and buy it. In this case, substitutes have very little impact because they do not perform the exact same function. However, for a product that has elastic demand, such as rounds of golf, a price increase of $25 for a round may create a significant substitute impact. Chapter 11 will deal more in detail with the marketing and pricing of goods; it is sufficient here to say that the presence and power of substitutes need to be considered by the new businessperson. When developing your competitive map, you will need to include those companies that are close substitutes for your product or service and determine how to evaluate a trade-off value.

Ease of Entry or Exit

Another issue that needs to be considered is the ease of entry to and exit from the industry. Once a business is in operation, expenses are being incurred. If those expenses are such that an entrepreneur cannot easily recoup the investment, then the level of competition will be more intense. This is considered an **exit barrier**[10]—that is, a barrier that keeps an entrepreneur from leaving a business she has invested in.

The ease of entering and exiting a business investment is an important detail to consider.

To illustrate an exit barrier, consider the principal investments for a clothing store, the clothes in the store. Clothes tend to be very seasonal. If a piece of clothing is not sold in season, then it likely has limited value in the near future. Think about the value of white polyester suits if you need to be convinced. (Your parents probably wore them.) To close a clothing store is easy, but to recover the initial investment is not. The owner will need to sharply discount the price of the goods just to get as much of their invested money back before they have to close the store.

exit barrier

A barrier, such as investment in capital assets, that keeps a firm from leaving an industry.

In our golf example, the initial investment for the golf course is very high, but the ease of exiting the business is also very high, as the real estate could be converted to another use such as a housing tract; thus, in the case of the golf course, there is no real exit barrier. If a business owner cannot easily exit an industry, then that owner is more likely to use predatory pricing in an effort to generate cash flow and survive. The ability to exit the industry must be taken into consideration when evaluating the competitive threat posed by existing businesses. A clothing store would have a high-intensity competition, whereas a golf course would have somewhat less. In contrast to the clothing store, a liquor store's principal investment is alcohol. If a liquor store is not doing well and needs to close, there is always a secondary market for liquor. There is little need to have deep price discounts to seek to recover the investment. Thus, exit is relatively easy, and competition would be expected to be a bit lower. The ability to exit a business relatively easily tends to limit the intensity of competition in the industry and reduces the threat posed by a new entry.

Benchmarking

There may be specific areas in your business that you have identified as potentially providing you a competitive advantage. To strengthen those

ETHICAL CHALLENGE

How far can or should you go to collect information about your competitors? Most competitors will be private companies, and their financial information will not be part of the public record. Is it appropriate to be a customer of your competitor for the purpose of collecting competitive information? At what stage does acting as a customer cross an ethical line? Can you lie about why you are there? Can you hire a private investigator to find out information that is not in the public domain? What if the existing firm is owned by a friend? At what stage can you copy ideas from your friend and still maintain your ethical standards?

QUESTIONS

1. In terms of your own business what information would be useful about your competition as you start your business. List all potential data.
2. Rank this information in order of how easy it will be to obtain.
3. Which of the data do you think would cross the line of ethics?

benchmarking
Working with and learning from a company outside of your industry that has a particular skill that is potentially critical to your operation.

areas, you may consider **benchmarking** a business that is very successful in that particular arena, but that does not compete in your industry.[11]

The ability to provide a top-flight call center for your business could be dramatically improved by your looking to companies in other industries that have excellent call-center operations. Most companies are more than willing to share their knowledge as long as you are not a potential competitor.

Industry Trends

An overarching part of any analysis of competitors is an understanding of the trends in the industry. These trends shape the long-term prospects of the industry. For example, the United States is moving toward a more self-service economy, and companies that can move that process forward or take advantage of this movement appear to have an opportunity for success. Another example might be restaurant patronage. Whereas the number of people eating at restaurants has not changed dramatically over the past few years, what they eat has been changing in a consistently predictable manner. Healthy, mid-price-range restaurant sales have been increasing dramatically. Thus, the percentage of individuals who are willing to pay a little more than fast-food prices for differentiated product is steadily increasing, while there has been little change in those willing to pay for very high-end restaurants. As a result, a restaurant that enters an emerging market (utilizing the Atkins Diet or another diet craze as a menu theme, for example) may be able to be among the first to enter that niche, and thereby gain an advantage over other firms.

LO4-6

Differentiate between those elements of the business that provide a competitive advantage and those that do not.

Competitive Advantage

Once the industry, customer, and competitor issues have been clearly identified, an entrepreneur must develop a deep understanding of the competitive advantage they expect to hold. A **competitive advantage** is made up of those things that your business does uniquely well, or better than anyone else in your industry (remember, the industry is defined by you, and consists of those businesses in direct competition with you in your area).

competitive advantage
The edge a business has over competing businesses, made up of those things that the business does better than anyone else in the industry.

Understanding the competitive advantage is the last step in your external analysis. We will discuss competitive advantage in greater detail in Chapter 5; it is important at this point to understand that these advantages (we hope there will be several) will ultimately be the reason that individuals come to your business and not to one of your competitors. Those areas that provide you with competitive advantages are the ones that are valuable, allowing the business to charge a price that exceeds that of its direct competitors, provide a product or service that might be priced the same as competitors, but at a lower cost structure or allows the new business to draw in new customers even if the price and costs are at an equivalent level with your competitors.

A competitive advantage must provide the new business with the opportunity to make money in excess of the competition. Few new businesses perform better than their competitors in all areas, nor should they be concerned about doing so. Instead, there are many functions that a business must perform (and perform well) simply to be a player in the industry. In most industries the new business is similar to its competitors, but there is one (or hopefully, several) fundamental characteristic(s) with which the firm is able to exceed the performance of the industry. These characteristics constitute the business's competitive advantage. In order to be able to define the potential areas for this advantage, it is imperative that you have completed the competitive map and are able to discuss how each of your competitors do business today.

The source of the competitive advantage can be an activity of the firm, such as the type of service or product they provide. It can also be something structural, such as a high-quality location. The new business must be clear about what its own competitive advantages will be, as well as about the current advantages of its competitors. One of the causes of failure for new businesses is a lack of focus on their competitive advantages. Individuals might believe they have a great idea and work hard to implement it, but they may not clearly understand why a customer might choose their business over that of their competitors. Your customers must have reasons to consciously choose your business, and you must know what those reasons are to maintain your advantage.

In thinking about competitive advantage, it is helpful to examine the business as consisting of performance within two areas. The **normal or ordinary parts of the business** must be done and done well, but there is little reason to do any of these things any better than the average in the industry. The **unusual or unique parts of the business** that are central to the firm's competitive advantage over others should be the focus of the energy, money, and time of the business, because they are the means by which a business can differentiate itself from its competitors.[12] What provides a competitive advantage varies by industry, and it varies with time in an industry. The standard practices in an industry move, and they inexorably move to greater and greater heights. For example, when the frequent-flyer program was initiated, it was unusual and allowed the pioneering airline to stand out, gaining customers and profit at the expense of its competitors. However, today virtually every airline has a frequent-flyer program, and indeed, many have shared programs. What starts out as unusual will (if it is effective) lead to imitation, and thus become normal in the industry. That said, we suggest that the new businessperson examine the competitive map carefully. What is normal in the industry—that is, what does virtually everyone do just to be a player in the industry? These are the standard things you will have to provide just to be a business in this arena. What is unusual in your industry? What are competitors doing that varies from one to another? What can you do that is unusual and might form a competitive advantage?

normal or ordinary competitive factor
Describing those areas of a business that are simply standard practice in the industry and are necessary for the business to be a player.

unusual or unique competitive factor
Describing those areas of a business that are unique or unusual when compared to the standard practices of the industry, and that provide the opportunity for the business to gain value over and above the ordinary returns in the industry.

The need to be complete in this area is critical. Table 4.2 explores the competitive advantage of a new restaurant. Although not complete, it provides a bit of insight into this process.

Even though this chart may appear to be a bit excessive, it is not nearly complete. It would be difficult for us to overemphasize the importance of developing this chart prior to beginning operations, so that entrepreneurs are clear as to what might form a competitive advantage for them. We have found few tools more helpful in defining the uniqueness of the potential start-up, as well as defining the potential start-up expenses.

EXERCISE 5

Develop a two-column list for your new business. Label the first column "Normal" and the second "Unusual." In the "normal" column, list everything that you will need to have (physically) and do (actively) just to be accepted by customers in the industry. In the second column, explain what your business will have or do that is rare or unusual compared to your competitors.

Resource-Based View

To understand the unique resources and capabilities of a business and develop a competitive advantage the new business owner should use a technique generally known as

NORMAL BUSINESS RESOURCES AND CAPABILITIES	POTENTIALLY UNIQUE BUSINESS RESOURCES AND CAPABILITIES
A storefront	A small, intimate facility
Tables	Fixed tile tables
Chairs	Roller, cushioned chairs
Floor covering	Tile floors
Lights	Mood lighting throughout
Cash register	Card swipe machines at each table
Signs	Custom neon signs
Menu	Touch screen at each table
Kitchen equipment:	
Freezers	
Refrigerators	
Sinks	
Stoves/ovens	
Cookware	
Safety equipment	
Fryers	
Plates, cups, silverware, napkins, salt and pepper shakers, sauce dispensers	
Shelving	
Tables and chairs	
Desk/work area	
Time sheets	
Staff:	
Cook staff	Trained chefs
Waitstaff	Unique outfits; experienced, highly trained staff requirements, formal
Bartenders	
Cleaning crew (tables, etc.)	
Host crew	
Management	
Trash cans (internal and external)	
Utilities	

Table 4.2
Company Evaluation of Resources and Capabilities

resource-based analysis
A theoretical approach and practical methodology that examines the functioning of a business in terms of whether a product or service simultaneously meets the criteria of being rare, durable, nonsubstitutable, and valuable.

resource-based analysis (although it can be found with a variety of acronyms such as VRIN or VRIST). This tool helps the entrepreneur delve deeper into what actually creates an advantage. In the prior list of potentially unique actions for a restaurant that could create a advantage for a restaurant it was noted that tiles on the table could be a normal business item. However, upon further consideration, the tiles are really just part of a larger resource that relates to the ambiance of the restaurant. The tiles themselves are good, but they need to be part of something more significant to have an impact. Resource-based analysis has been developed over the past 50 years;[13] it has become one of the most effective tools in defining a business's competitive advantages and in differentiating these from their competitors. While we will cover this topic in depth in the next chapter, we feel that some introduction to this topic is warranted in the discussion of positioning relative to your competitors. The focus of resource-based analysis is solely upon the potentially unusual products or services that you will offer in your business, which can be a source of competitive advantage.

To develop into a competitive advantage, the potentially unusual products or services offered by the new business need to meet all of the following criteria: They must be rare, durable, relatively nonsubstitutable, and valuable to develop into a competitive advantage. "Rare" describes a quality that competitors will find difficult to obtain. For example, a particular chef might be unique, or a location may be particularly valued. "Durability" has three elements to it where any one element provides the company with the ability to hold onto the competitive advantage. The first has to do with the length of time that you might be able to gain and hold a competitive advantage. The second is an evaluation of how long would it take for a competitor to imitate you or to wash away your advantage. The third is an evaluation of the desire of your competitors to compete with you with the same potential resource or capability. "Relatively nonsubstitutable" is a determination about whether the product or service may be easily substituted by something else that a competitor could provide. "Valuable" refers to your ability to gain extraordinary returns from your product or service. A product or service might be rare, durable, and nonsubstitutable, but if you cannot obtain returns in excess of your competition from its sale, then it will not provide you with a resource-based advantage.

As you examine your list of unusual products or services for the new business, consider each one along these four dimensions. Those items that meet all four criteria are your primary points of competitive advantage. These are the points on which you should concentrate your resources, time, and effort. These are the areas that will provide you with a competitive advantage relative to your competitors, and will be the reasons that customers choose you over the competition. We will discuss this in much more depth in the next chapter.

SUMMARY

This chapter examined the reasons and methods for the potential entrepreneur to develop a complete, well-reasoned, and personal knowledge of the competitive conditions for their business. This analysis is fundamentally founded upon the idea that the entrepreneur decides what constitutes the "industry." The industry does not include (except in unusual circumstances) the whole country or the world. It is important that the entrepreneur limit the defined "industry" as it relates to the specific business, to effectively analyze the competition and the potential competitive threat. We have provided these highly practical tools for the founders to personally develop their own analysis of the environment and their ability to compete within that environment.

KEY TERMS

benchmarking 70
competitive advantage 70
competitive map 65
elasticity of demand 68
exit barrier 69
fragmented markets 64
industry 60
normal or ordinary competitive factor 71
resource-based analysis 72
substitute 68
unusual or unique competitive factor 71

REVIEW QUESTIONS

1. How would you advise a potential entrepreneur define the industry for a new business?
2. How should a new business develop a profile for its potential customers?
3. Why should a potential entrepreneur research the industry personally?
4. What techniques would you recommend for identifying competitors within an industry?
5. How would you recommend developing a complete analysis of the competitors for a new business?
6. What elements are in a competitive map?

BUSINESS PLAN DEVELOPMENT QUESTIONS

1. What is the industry for your potential business?
2. Who is the customer?
3. Who are the competitors?
4. Develop a competitive map for your business.
5. What do you believe your tentative competitive advantages will be?

INDIVIDUAL EXERCISES

1. Using your map developed for the business plan exercise above, visit (virtually or in-person) the first two competitors on your list and adjust the map according to reality.
   a. What additional items might you add to the map?
   b. What qualitative areas of competition did you add to your map?
2. Using the material that you have developed in the previous exercises, write a two- to three-page description of the competitive environment in which your proposed new business will compete.
3. Develop a competitive map for the restaurants around campus. Discuss in class how everyone else designed their competitive map of this group.

GROUP EXERCISES

1. Look at the list of items for the restaurant in Table 4.2 of this chapter. What would be the resources that would drive the potential sources of competitive advantage?
2. Take the material that you developed outside of class. Break into small groups. Create a final list of resources you will need to develop your competitive advantage for the firm.

ENDNOTES

1. A. Ardichvili, R. Cardozo, and R. Sourav, "A Theory of Entrepreneurial Opportunity Identification and Development," *Journal of Business Venturing* 18, no. 1 (2003), pp. 104–24.
2. F. Delmar, P. Davidson, and W. Gartner, "Arriving at the High-Growth Firm," *Journal of Business Venturing* 18, no. 2 (2003), pp. 189–217.
3. N. Kumar, "The CEO's Marketing Manifesto," *Marketing Management* 17, no. 6 (2008), pp. 24–29.
4. C. Comaford-Lynch, "The Power of Positioning," *BusinessWeek Online*, June 3, 2008, p. 13.
5. H. Corrigan, G. Craciun, and A. Powerll, "How Does Target Know So Much About Its Customers? Utilizing Customer Analytics to Make Marketing Decisions," *Marketing Education Review* 24, no. 2 (2014), pp. 159–66.
6. G. Dess, "Consensus on Strategy Formulation and Organizational Performance: Competitors in a Fragmented Market," *Strategic Management Journal* 8, no. 3 (1987), pp. 259–79.
7. W. Bogner, H. Thomas, and J. McGee, "A Longitudinal Study of the Competitive Positions and Entry Paths of European Firms in the U.S. Pharmaceutical Market," *Strategic Management Journal* 17, no. 2 (1996), pp. 85–108.
8. M. Peteraf and M. Bergen, "Scanning Dynamic Competitive Landscapes: A Market-Based and Resource-Based Framework," *Strategic Management Journal* 24, no. 10 (2003), pp. 1027–42.
9. D. Teece, G. Pisano, and A. Shuen, "Dynamic Capabilities and Strategic Management," *Strategic Management Journal* 18, no. 7 (1997), pp. 509–30.

10. M. Porter, *Competitive Advantage* (New York: Free Press, 1985).
11. J-C. Spender and R. Grant, "Knowledge and the Firm: Overview," *Strategic Management Journal* 17 (1996), pp. 5–10.
12. L. Costa, K. Cool, and I. Diericky, "The Competitive Implications of the Deployment of Unique Resources," *Strategic Management Journal* 34, no. 4 (2013), pp. 445–63.
13. S. Alvarez and L. Busenitz, "The Entrepreneurship of Resource-Based Theory," *Journal of Management* 27, no. 6 (2001), pp. 755–75; J. B. Barney, "Firm Resources and Sustained Competitive Advantage," *Journal of Management* 17, no. 1 (1991), pp. 99–120; R. Grant, "The Resource-Based Theory of Competitive Advantage: Implications for Strategy Formulation," *California Management Review* 33 (1991), pp. 114–35; E. Penrose, *The Theory of the Growth of the Firm* (New York: John Wiley & Sons, 1959); M. Peteraf, "The Cornerstones of Competitive Advantage: A Resource-Based View," *Strategic Management Journal* 14 (1993), pp. 179–91.

CREDITS

Opener: Royalty-Free/Corbis; p. 57: PRNewsFoto/Rexam/AP Images; p. 59: Lifesize/Getty Images RF; p. 63: Design Pics/Don Hammond RF; p. 69: Glow Images RF.

chapter

5

learning outcomes

After studying this chapter, you will be able to:

LO5-1 Recognize how mission statements guide a new business.

LO5-2 Explain what constitutes a sustainable competitive advantage.

LO5-3 Identify a new business's assets and capabilities.

LO5-4 Distinguish which of those assets and capabilities are standard and which are unique.

LO5-5 Apply a resource-based analysis approach to arrive at a list of competitive advantages.

LO5-6 Determine a strategy to match the new business mission.

Business Mission and Strategy

ZANE'S CYCLES

In 1977, Chris Zane started fixing neighbors' bikes in his parents' garage. At only 12 years old, Chris was making $400 a week and building a reputation as someone who always delivered what he promised. At 16 he went to work for a local bicycle shop only to have the owner inform him that the shop would be closing in just a few months. Chris convinced his parents and grandparents to loan him $20,000 at 15 percent annual interest to buy the inventory and to allow him to take over the bike store lease. His mom ran the store during the day while he was in school and Chris worked there every day after school and on weekends.

Chris knew he would have to create a unique competitive advantage to be able avoid the problems that the prior owner suffered. Therefore, he decided to offer lifetime guarantees on everything sold in the store. He installed a coffee bar with free gourmet coffee for customers and guaranteed that he had the lowest prices in Connecticut. Anything that cost less than $1 was just given to the customer. Chris sold many products, such as children's bike helmets, at cost, helping him develop a deep relationship with his customers.

By 1995, he had grown the business to $1.2 million in sales even as many of his competitors in the region had gone out of business. Chris tried many of the strategy and management fads that came along over the years and was frustrated by the results. He decided to focus his strategy on the promises made to the customer. *Inc.* magazine called it nonstop, no-limits, no-scheme-is-too-small competitiveness. Every move was made to try and drive his competitors out of the market by giving the customers exactly what they wanted with each transaction. He unabashedly wanted it all. Chris pursued aggressive growth, which allowed him to move to progressively bigger store locations. In 2011, he published a book about his approach to business, *Reinventing the Wheel: The Science of Creating Lifetime Customers*. In 2013, Chris Zane's bike sales topped $21 million.

Questions

1. If you were crafting a mission statement for Zane's Cycles, what would it be?
2. In just a few bullet points, list what you believe makes Zane's Cycles unique.
3. What would it take for a competitor to match those unique elements of the business?

Sources: A. Danigelis, "Local Hero: Zane's Cycles," *Fast Company,* no. 108 (September 2006); D. Fenn, "A Bigger Wheel," *Inc.* 22, no. 16 (November 2000), http://www.inc.com/ss/10-inspiring-small-business-success-stories; C. Lesser, "Zane's Pursues Premiums Market," *Bicycle Retailer & Industry News* 14, no. 3 (March 1, 2005).

mission statement
A brief statement that summarizes how and where a firm will compete.

Defining the new business's mission is one of the most difficult and critical elements in the success of any business. A firm's **mission statement** is a brief statement that summarizes how and where the firm will compete.*

LO5-1

Recognize how mission statements guide a new business.

Mission Statements

Because the mission and strategy together have the power to guide the business as it develops, we believe that an early effort to craft both is warranted. Substantial research has found that as a business grows, it gets progressively more difficult to change its direction. Imagine establishing a new business oriented toward high levels of customer service with experts in each area of the business available to help customers. The customers appreciate this extensive expertise, and, as a result, the business grows. However, the founders find that the model they have developed is expensive and they wish to increase their profits. Therefore, despite the company's success, they decide to eliminate the experts and not provide the same level of ability to answer the customers' questions. The reaction from their established customer base will likely take place over time. It will not be a dramatic drop in one month, but over time customers will begin to cease doing business with the firm as they seek out other firms, which provide the expertise they desire.

This is precisely what happened to Circuit City. The firm started in 1949 (originally as Wards in Richmond, Virginia) as an entrepreneurial venture based on a well-defined strategy of hiring individuals throughout the company who were experts in the products sold. As a result, the company grew to be one of the largest electronic goods retailers in the United States. The business was crafted around commissioned salespeople who were experts in audiovisual equipment. New management decided to change the approach to use inexpensive, noncommissioned clerks in an attempt to match the cost-conscious model being pitched by the new upstart, Best Buy. A dramatic change over time in the expertise that Circuit City could offer its customers occurred, which led to a loss of Circuit City's traditional customer base and, more important, a loss in its unique positioning in the market. The result was that the entire business closed in 2009, in one of the largest retail store closures in U.S. history.

Smaller electronic stores and chains benefit from hiring employees with a high level of product knowledge.

The firm's mission and strategy are central to the new business's ability to maintain a clear vision about what it wants to be and how it will accomplish that plan. Without that consistent guidance, the firm can lose its focus and competitive advantage. Although there is great strength in building into the firm a strong common understanding of the firm's strategy, firms sometimes find that they have to change their mission and strategy. Any business seeking to radically change its fundamental way of doing business as defined by the firm's strategy will find the road ahead difficult. Once the understanding of how to do things is

*Larger firms might also have a vision statement that is a very broad statement of the firm's direction while the mission statement is a more specific statement. For a new business we believe that mission alone is appropriate. The goal is to help direct everyone who works for or with the firm in its actions and not create unnecessary work. For a new business to try to differentiate between vision and mission would be splitting hairs. Thus, the student should recognize their differences in theory, but also recognize that here they are treated as the same item.

built into the organization it becomes second nature and can be hard to change.

We use the term *mission statement* here, but there are many terms used when creating the overarching goals of an organization. It is quite easy for a businessperson to become consumed in the proper labeling of this statement rather than focusing on the goals of the organization. As a result, you will likely see terms as varied as *company mission*, *vision*, *overall strategy*, *goals*, *simple rules*, and *statement of purpose* to describe what we refer to as the *mission*. The important point for the new business is that the statement is concise and well understood by everyone who will come in contact with the business so that they will understand what the company does and what it does not do.[1]

The firm's mission helps the venture by targeting its efforts in specific arenas and on specific opportunities. No firm can be all things to all people. Instead, the new business needs to focus on performing those activities where it has competitive advantage, or doing some set of activities better than everyone else. The firm's mission helps the new business specify what the business does best in its industry (the industry consists of those businesses you believe are your direct competitors). However, the mission statement also helps the small business stay away from things that opportunistically sound promising, but which take the business away from its principal focus. Realize that if you start wandering off to another area of competition, you will lose focus in your core area of business. If that occurs, there are always single-focused companies in any market that are ready to capitalize on your judgment errors.[2]

To illustrate the benefit of a mission statement in targeting a firm's activities, let's take a look at another restaurant business. The mission statement of this restaurant read as follows (with some minor changes to protect its identity): *The Gourmet Mediterranean (Italian) Meal Experience in the Heart of the City.*

Even though this mission statement is very simple, it ultimately helped the business owner tremendously. The city was opening a new central high school basketball arena and needed someone to run the food facilities. The head of the school board asked the owner of the restaurant to consider running the concessions for the arena. The idea appeared to have the potential to be very profitable. However, the food that would be sold at the arena would be very different from what the restaurant traditionally sold. Thus, the expertise that the business owner held would largely not be applicable. Additionally, new suppliers would need to be located because the concession stands and the restaurant would use different quality inputs. The operation of the concessions would also take the business owner's attention away from what she knew best: running a high-quality Mediterranean restaurant. Thus, even though both the restaurant and the concession stands involved the preparation and selling of food, in reality they were two distinct businesses. A clear mission statement helps the new-business person focus her efforts on her expertise. The ability to be successful with one type of business does not mean that she will be successful with another type of business, even one within the same broad domain. The businessperson's earlier mission statement helped that owner keep the business targeted where it needed to compete. The owner declined the opportunity to run the concession stands in the basketball arena and instead continued to build her restaurant to become one of the most successful in the area.

There are numerous books on the development of mission statements, and the ways suggested to do them are as diverse as the individuals who write the books. There is, in fact, little empirical evidence regarding

FRIENDS' HOME HEALTH

Friends' HOME HEALTH

Betty and Joan are aware of how important a mission statement can be for their new business. As a result, they developed the mission statement below:

> Mission Statement: *Friends' Home Health uses only licensed home health workers to provide home health services for elderly patients seeking to ensure their ability to live in their own homes in a manner that provides both the patient and the patient's family the best assurance of honesty and care.*

Key Issues This Mission Statement Reflects

Positioning. The mission statement of Friends' sought to position the firm as unique in its industry by focusing on the product mix, staffing, and security. The goal was not to be the cheapest in the industry but one that offered a high quality, differentiated product.

Product Mix. Friends' is looking to provide its services to the elderly as an alternative to long-term rehabilitation services. These services can include a wide range of people who need care from illness, accident, or age.

Staffing. The staffing of the firm will consist of only licensed individuals. The skill level of home health can vary widely from those who were simply willing to work in home health care to licensed nurses. Most of the services provided by home health workers do not require the 24-hour care of a licensed nurse who can make between $80,000 to $100,000 a year or more. The key is to match the family's needs to the skill level of the person. However, Friends' is clear that whatever skill level is required, they will use only licensed and trained individuals for each specific job as required by that job.

Security. Friends' Home Health looks to provide assurances including information for the patient and the patient's family so they know exactly what care is being provided. The industry has a reputation for not providing clear information on what is happening to the elderly. Friends' Home Health is looking to counter that image in the industry of the elderly being taken advantage of.

EXERCISE 1

1. Friends' has decided to pursue a strategy in which they differentiate themselves by having licensed staff, which is expensive. How would the mission statement differ if this entrepreneurial venture had decided to be the lowest-cost provider instead?
2. What would be the range of differences in the actions of the firm if the mission statement had been set up with a focus on being the lowest-cost provider?

the most effective type of mission statement. We suggest that an effective mission statement and sustainable competitive advantage are inseparable. It should be recalled from Chapter 4 that the resources of the firm are generally constrained.[3] As a result, it is particularly critical that the new business conserve its resources and focus them on those areas that have the potential to maximize the firm's success. A key aspect to that success is the firm's **capabilities,** or those resources that combine to allow the firm to perform better than its competitors.[4]

capabilities
Resources that combine to allow a firm to do things better than its competitors.

Designing a Mission Statement

In developing the mission statement, we believe there are several key characteristics that should drive the new-business founder(s).

1. Keep it short—Make sure it can fit on a coffee mug?
2. Keep it simple—Ensure that everyone in the company can learn and understand what it means and why.

3. Make it applicable—The mission statement should be able to guide every individual in the company each and every day. It should also be something that customers cite as to why they use the company.
4. Be specific—Be so clear that it tells everyone exactly what you do, and by definition, what you do not do.
5. Establish measurable goals—Be able to develop a metric for every part of the statement.

Keep It Short We cannot overemphasize this fundamental aspect of a mission statement. The statement must be understandable and memorable for all those who come in contact with it. While it principally is written to guide the employees of the company, it must also speak to customers, suppliers, and others. It is not a tome that describes everything you have done and might do, and how you will do it, so that the organization can impress external parties. It is a short, direct statement that is designed to guide the organization each and every day.

The mission of a firm is not "to make money"; that is a by-product of a good direction; it is significantly more likely that the organization will indeed make money if the mission statement is clear, succinct, memorable, and widely known by all in the firm.

Keep It Simple A mission statement that is not shared has little, if any, value to the organization. We have watched people spend countless hours crafting a statement only to have it poorly communicated and/or not reinforced by the senior management of the company. The new-business owner must ensure that every employee can understand the statement and how it can be applied to his day-to-day decision making. The key to the ability to communicate a mission easily is that the statement be simple, direct, and appropriate.

As the firm is developed, the founder needs to ensure that the mission statement is at the center of the various activities that are developed. Whether the firm is a new high-technology firm with PhDs on staff or a quick-order restaurant where many employees have no high school education, the workers will come closer to having an understanding of the mission of the organization if the statement is simple. The firm needs to ensure that the words and concepts employed in the statement are straightforward and have a clear meaning to all who hear or read them. A great line in the 2003 Disney movie *Pirates of the Caribbean* illustrates this concept wonderfully. The captain of the ship, somewhat taken aback by the demands and high-brow, patronizing language of his recent captive, responds to her request by saying, "I'm disinclined to acquiesce to your request," pauses for a moment, and turns back to her and says, "Means NO." Avoid the use of lots of adjectives or descriptive language about how the company will accomplish its mission.

Make It Applicable It takes extraordinary care to develop a mission that guides the entire organization, and yet, for the mission to be utilized effectively by every member of the company, it must have direct applicability to even the most entry-level employee. Imagine the employees assigned to handle the customer service lines who are faced daily with customers calling in with concerns and complaints. If the mission of the organization is a long statement that fundamentally says "do good," or if it is like so many and simply exhorts the employees to "act like owners and maximize shareholder value," then what are the customer service employees to do? They will try to follow procedures and not get in trouble. Although large companies can afford to have people who just follow procedures rather than use all of their skills and creative abilities, new businesses cannot afford to limit their employees. The entrepreneurial business needs to align employees in a consistent direction and allow them to use their creativity and skills.

Thus, the mission of the business needs to be actionable. That is, the mission statement needs to help the employees to make active decisions in the moment, without having to refer everything to the founder of the firm. An advantage to a well-developed mission statement is that it is able to guide everyone in the organization toward the goals that the owners have set. A well-developed mission statement helps ensure that everyone in the organization is heading in the same relative direction, so that, although there will be some variance, there will not be decisions made that are counter to what the founder of the new business would choose.

Be Specific In order to accomplish the three keys for mission statements we have noted it is necessary that the mission be so specific that it clearly also tells everyone what *not* to do. Take a look again at the mission statement for one of the restaurants discussed earlier in this chapter: *The Gourmet Mediterranean (Italian) Meal Experience in the Heart of the City.* We know from this statement that it does not serve Chinese, or barbeque, among other items. We also know that it is located in the city and (at least with this statement) should not look to expand into the suburbs. It provides an "experience" that includes ambiance, certain types of wine, food, and service. It should not consider adding American cuisine, French wines, or rap music. The value of this limitation should be clear to everyone every day. Employees are repeatedly faced with decisions that appear to be of little importance, but the cumulative impact of such small decisions that do not lead in a consistent direction is that the firm eventually is trying to be everything to everyone. A strong focus on a single mission statement keeps everyone in the organization constantly striving to achieve the goals of the owners.

metric
A measure to evaluate whether a person or firm is meeting stated goals.

Establish Measurable Goals A **metric** is a measure used to evaluate whether a person or firm is meeting its goals. From the mission statement, a new-business owner should be able to develop a set of metrics that are meaningful to judge if the mission is being accomplished.[5]

Greater specifics on metrics and developing them will be presented in Chapters 7 and 8; however, a few brief comments are appropriate here. We typically recommend that each organization develop between five and eight measures of success for its venture. These are broken up into two categories: (1) quantitative measures—those that are tied to the financial or strategic goals of the organization and are easily measured; and (2) qualitative measures—those that are tied to the strategic goals of the organization but have more to do with the "feel" of the organization.

To illustrate, below are some of the metrics used by our example of a high-end restaurant that we have been discussing:

Mission: *The Gourmet Mediterranean (Italian) Meal Experience in the Heart of the City*

Metrics The Gourmet

1. Number of chefs who have graduated from gourmet schools
2. Ranking in annual Zagat or similar guides
3. Quality of reviews in local papers

Mediterranean Meal Experience

1. Closeness in appearance to actual Mediterranean restaurants
2. Number of employees from Mediterranean region
3. Service measure as compared to actual restaurants in Mediterranean

Heart of the City

1. Proximity to city festivals/events
2. Do people refer to other stores, events, and so on by referring to our restaurant as the starting point (i.e., "Just down the block from XX restaurant")?

Metrics are best established at the founding of the business and are evaluated on a recurring basis. The baseline position is not nearly as important as the vector (direction and level of change) that the metrics are taking. We want to see positive movement on each of the metrics. They are the direct measure of the business's mission, and the more the business improves on each metric, the closer it is getting to its fundamental mission.

Mission Statement Impact

To illustrate the range of decisions that are impacted by the mission of the organization, consider three domains (advertising, location of the business, and staffing) for the Friends' example in this chapter and how they are impacted by market choice:

1. If Friends' Home Health chose to pursue multiple types of client bases at the same time, where would the firm advertise? Each market has substantively different outlets to reach its respective customers. Which magazines do different groups of people read? What endorsements would each group of potential customers consider important? What organizations (hospice, Ronald McDonald House, and/or AARP) might you support, given your desired customer base?
2. The location chosen for the type of business would differ significantly based on the mission. A company focused on the elderly might want to be positioned near big hospitals if they offer day care for patients. However, because Friends' service is in the customers' homes, the clients and their families never go to the office. Thus, the nature of the office or its location may be very unimportant.
3. Personnel and staffing size would vary from firm to firm as well. The style, sophistication, and approach from the staff will vary dramatically with the approach and audience chosen to serve.

Thus, before the founders can begin to build the new business, they must be clear about where and how they will compete. Almost all new ventures have a wide variety of activities that can be pursued. The mission statement should help by clearly specifying in which market the firm will compete, in some cases how broad a geographic range the firm will serve, and the major ways in which it will compete. If these activities are not precisely defined, the new owners will find themselves building an entity that in some ways is targeted to one business, and in other ways targeted to another related, but inconsistent business. Having everyone in the business moving in the same direction and toward the same group of customers will provide immense benefits to the new firm.[6]

LO5-2

Explain what constitutes a sustainable competitive advantage.

Sustainable Competitive Advantage

sustainable competitive advantage

An advantage that others cannot immediately copy.

It was noted in Chapter 4 that a firm needs to ensure that it has a set of *competitive advantages,* or areas of separation where the firm performs better than anyone else in the market that it serves. Here we will go into more depth on this critical topic and discuss how it impacts the implementation of the mission statement. In particular, we will examine competitive advantages in terms of a **sustainable competitive advantage**—that is, a set of advantages that provides you with the opportunity to make money where other businesses cannot easily copy your advantages.[7]

All individual competitive advantages eventually disappear as industries change and competitors adapt. However, businesses should seek to maintain an advantage for as long as possible by continually refining their business model. A key part of building a competitive advantage is having a deep understanding of your customers' needs.[8] For example, a new business may decide that it will develop its business around the best customer service in the replacement/repair of any item it sells. If customers do not really value the ability to repair the product quickly, then this service (which is quite expensive) will not provide a sustainable competitive advantage. Consider another example: a business that sells and repairs Wi-Fi systems for businesses to use wireless throughout the organization. Having the wireless capability go down during a business day is an emergency at most companies. Businesses have come to rely on wireless to accomplish so many activities in the firm. Focusing attention and effort on the rapid deployment and quick recovery of these systems could provide a substantial competitive advantage for the right entrepreneur.

Building a sustainable business is critical to long-term success.

Many entrepreneurial businesses find that their greatest source of sustainable advantage is founded in the personal relationships with their customers.[9] The development of a compelling personal relationship is something that large organizations find quite difficult. Building the relationship with a customer for the new firm may be as simple as acknowledging the customer when you see him, or as complex as knowing what a customer buys and contacting her when a new shipment arrives. The long-term difficulty for the new-business owner comes from setting expectations now that you will be able to maintain in the future.

Prior to developing an effective mission statement, the new business must first develop a detailed list of what might constitute or what will constitute its competitive advantages. There are three steps to the process of identifying a new business's sustainable competitive advantage. Although it is quite tempting to skip ahead, we suggest that the process itself leads to unique insights and will help the founder craft a business that has a long-term opportunity for success.

Identifying a Sustainable Competitive Advantage

Step 1: Develop a list of your business's assets and capabilities (either existing or proposed).

Step 2: Break that list into two groups: standard and unique.

Step 3: Evaluate the unique resources/capabilities.

Table 5.1
Tangible and Intangible Assets

TANGIBLE ASSETS	INTANGIBLE ASSETS
Building location	Industry experience
Equipment (list)	Contacts
Initial financing (equity or debt)	Previous start-up experience
Inventory	Education
Patents or patents pending	Unique knowledge of the industry (usually from previous research)
Software and systems for business	Skill set of founders (presentation, innovation, etc.)
Build-out of facility (list detail)–walls, fixtures, built-ins, etc.	Name branding

Step 1: Develop a List of Your Business's Assets and Capabilities

LO5-3

Identify a new business's assets and capabilities.

The owner, or founding team, needs to develop a complete list of all the physical and intangible assets that the company will have at its founding. **Tangible assets** are those hard assets such as equipment or a location. The intangible assets are those things that are not physical but are just as critical to success, such as relationships with key suppliers. A key part of the **intangible assets** are the capabilities and skills of the founders or employees.[10]

tangible assets
Hard assets such as equipment or a location.

intangible assets
Things that are not physical but are just as critical to success, such as a relationship with a key supplier.

Although this inventory process may seem a bit mundane, it is absolutely critical to the later steps and the development of an effective and focused mission for the organization. In evaluating the intangible assets and capabilities, the new-business founders need to develop a clear and precise list that encompasses the breadth of knowledge within the founding team. This list will tend to be long and should include absolutely *everything* that the company has now or will have at the point that it opens for business. See Table 5.1 for a very short example.

Step 2: Split the List into Standard and Unique Assets

LO5-4

Distinguish which of those assets and capabilities are standard and which are unique.

The tangible and intangible assets can be further separated into standard and unique, much in the same way we categorized actions of the entrepreneur and firm earlier as either standard or unique. Most of the assets listed by a firm are standard to be a player in the industry. For Friends' Home Health, those assets might include a wide range of items such as an office, computer systems, telephones, and business licenses. These assets allow the firm to operate; they are not, however, things that provide a competitive advantage to the firm.

Similarly, most capabilities, or skills of the founders and employees, are also standard for the industry. For example, serving customers in a timely manner may be done very well by a new business; however, the standard expectation of most customers is that you will have a strong capability to provide such service. Therefore, this capability can only rarely be a source of sustainable competitive advantage, and then so only if it is so far above average that the customer really notices.

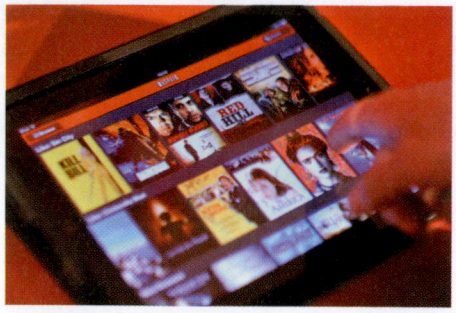

An Apple iPad is used to view Netflix, the leading global Internet subscription service for films and TV programs. Netflix offers instant and unlimited access to a broad range of entertainment.

There will also be unique assets and capabilities that the entrepreneur or entrepreneurial team possesses. These unique resources and/or capabilities can provide the business a competitive advantage for some period of time. The nature of individuals, and in turn businesses, is that they are driven by inertia. Individuals or businesses are not willing to make a change unless encouraged to do so for some reason. Your unique capabilities will be the source of that motivation to convince customers to change to do business with your new business. The previously discussed personal relationship is just such a unique capability.

To illustrate, if you were to consider opening a new video store in a strip mall, what would you consider to be your competitive advantages? Why would customers come to it rather than use Netflix or rent via a Redbox vending machine? Would your new firm have different movies when compared to the other choices? Would the firm's movies be rented more cheaply? Would access to the business be easier? If you are going to do the same thing that other firms do, or something that is considered to be a step backward, then why will anyone switch to your store?

The new business must have something that will motivate potential customers to select that business; these are your unique resources and capabilities. It will be these unique assets (or resources, if we consider the term more broadly) and capabilities that form a competitive advantage for new business.

There are a wide range of potential resources and capabilities that can be the source of a competitive advantage. For example, customer loyalty can be obtained if customers are driven principally by something other than cost and the firm is the first to market with a differentiating approach. This is referred to as a **first-mover advantage**, and those firms that arrive later are referred to as **followers**.[11] Followers can benefit by learning from the mistakes of the first movers, but they may not be able to obtain the loyalty of customers if there is any to be had. For the new business, this does not mean that you have to be the first to market with the broad concept as long as you bring some unique resource or capability to the idea. A new business could never be the first to market with a general concept such as that of a mid-priced restaurant. However, you may recall from Chapter 4 that new businesses do not compete against the entire industry. Instead, there are limits to how far someone will drive for a restaurant. Therefore, a new business only needs to be the first in the industry that is relevant to that firm. In many fast-growing suburban areas, a restaurant may be the first of its type in the area; it would then be the first mover in that area.

first-mover advantage
The benefit of gaining customer loyalty by being the first firm to the market.

followers
Firms that enter a market after the first mover.

There are other ways that a new business can build a competitive advantage. For example, a firm can have special relationships with suppliers. There are a number of Amish carpenters who make furniture. A small retailer may wish to carry that particular furniture but would need to have a relationship with those specialized suppliers before such opportunities could be arranged. Location can be another source of advantage; those firms with prime locations that have easy automobile access might have an advantage over those businesses that are hard to access. The range of potential sources of a new business's competitive advantage is as wide as there are activities in the firm. A new business's competitive advantage also needs to be defensible. That is, the advantage must be something that is not easily substituted away or matched by established competitors.

EXERCISE 2

Develop a complete list of resources and/or capabilities for your proposed new venture. Then break the list into two sections based on whether each one is standard or unique for the industry as you have defined it.

Step 3: Evaluate Competitiveness of Unique Resources or Capabilities

LO5-5

Apply a resource-based analysis approach to arrive at a list of true competitive advantages.

Once you know what resources or capabilities your new business might have that appear to be unique, you will need to examine each before you can claim any of these as a source of competitive advantage. Successful businesses generally have several sources of the competitive advantage. The new business may have a capability or resource that is unique, but as noted before, that may or may not be the best resource on which to center a new business. To illustrate further, in a manufacturing business we may be able to offer 24-hour customer service in an industry that does not value 24-hour operations. The new business needs to focus its efforts on those areas that have the potential in the market to provide the greatest competitive advantage to the business. We refer to the financial gains garnered from an asset or capability that are in excess of the ordinary returns in that particular industry as **economic rents**. Ordinary returns in an industry suggest that you are doing no more nor less than the average of the industry. This average performance should be accomplishable by simply matching the industry average for behavior, location, and the like. Economic rents imply that the new business not only matches the norms for the industry, but in several areas, far exceeds the industry in a manner that allows it to charge well in excess of its additional costs.[12]

economic rents
Financial gains garnered from an asset or capability that are in excess of the ordinary returns in that particular industry.

There are several means with which to analyze these resources and develop a small list of resources and capabilities that truly provide the new business with the potential to obtain a sustainable competitive advantage. The predominant approach by strategists is the resource-based perspective.[13] For new businesses, there are four elements that seem to be most important within this evaluation system. Each and every resource and capability that is listed as potentially unique in the previous step must be subjected to the following four questions.

ETHICAL CHALLENGE

In establishing the firm, an entrepreneur has to make some basic ethical choices based on their values about how the new business will compete. For example, how far would you be willing to go to drive your competitors out of business? Even as you consider how aggressive you wish to be, will that aggressiveness be focused on improving the capability of your new firm so that you do a better job of appealing to your customers, or will it use a range of aggressive actions such as calling regulators if you think your competitor has violated some rule? Recognize that there is not a right or wrong answer to this question. You have to do what you feel comfortable doing—it is an ethical choice that you as an entrepreneur face.

QUESTIONS

1. Would you feel comfortable cutting the prices of your business to drive the competitors out of business so that you can raise prices and/or reduce service in the longer run?
2. Would you be willing to track down the customers of your competitors and offer them incentives to do business only with your firm? Post disparaging comments about your competitor anonymously using Twitter, Facebook, or other social media? (Although it should be recognized that if it were ever discovered that you are the person posting such comments there would be serious implications.)
3. What will the ethical bounds of your business's mission or strategy be?

As mentioned at the end of Chapter 4, only those unique resources and capabilities that meet all four criteria are truly the keys to the new business's strategy.

Is It Rare?

You must evaluate the uniqueness of each resource and capability relative to the competitors in your market. Is the resource or capability relatively unique for your industry? If the resource or capability is matched by one of your competitors, it can still be considered rare. However, if it is matched by more than one competitor, then it is not rare and therefore is simply the standard expectation in the industry. These are qualitative judgments based on the research and experience of the founder.

Is It Easily Substituted?

For every resource and capability that you determine to be indeed rare, you should evaluate the market for a close substitute. A substitute is not provided by a direct competitor, but is something that satisfies the same basic need that is satisfied by your product or service. If we started up a small electronics repair operation, then our direct competitors would be other businesses that repair electronics in our area. Substitutes would consist of self-repairs, manufacturers' warranties, or throwing the item away. As you can see, these are not particularly great substitutes, and that is the question every entrepreneur needs to ask: How close are the substitutes to your unique resource and capability, and are they good substitutes? If there are not good substitutes then that element of the business is a potential competitive advantage.

Is It Durable?

If you have determined that a unique resource or capability is both rare and not substitutable, then the next step is to determine how long you might be able to hold onto those advantages. As noted before, no advantage lasts forever, but the new-business person wants an advantage to last as long as possible. The time lag between the introduction of the competitive advantage and the point where competitors can match your advantage is the window where the new business can earn unique returns. In some industries, a competitive advantage will last only a few months, whereas in other industries, an advantage might last a long time as competitors are slow to adapt.

The evaluation of durability is done by estimating both the amount of time you believe it would take for a competitor to match you in a particular area and whether you believe they would actually try to match you. Many companies have the resources to match the offering of a new business, and yet they do not always try to match the competitive advantage. The entrepreneurs' estimation of the time frame in which they will be able to enjoy the benefits of a unique advantage is a critical element in this evaluation. Said succinctly, "Can a competitor easily copy it? If it can be copied, how perfectly can it be imitated and how long would it take to be copied?"

Is It Valuable?

In order for the resource or capability to be a competitive advantage, the customer must be willing to pay extra because of these unique resources and/or capabilities. A key decision, then, is which resource or capability the customer will pay the most for. It is not uncommon to have a resource and/or capability meet all three criteria above, and yet be unable to attain value in one or more of the three means for doing so: (1) charging more to generate more profit, (2) obtaining more customers, or (3) reducing costs relative to the competition.

Table 5.2 summarizes these concepts.

CRITERION	MEANING	ILLUSTRATION
Rare	Few firms have it.	There are only four corners at an intersection. Once they are used, no other firms can locate there.
Nonsubstitutable	It cannot be replaced by something else easily.	Your firm may be able to supply original auto parts for automobiles from the 1950s. However, newly produced auto parts for such cars would substitute for those parts easily.
Durable	The length of time that the advantages will last before competitors match the offering.	Can firms match what you do in days, months, or years? Do they have the financial means to do so? Do they seem to care about what you are offering?
Valuable	Customers are willing to pay extra and/or it draws in new customers from the competitors and/or it costs the new firm less to accomplish than its competitors.	What you do is something that customers value and so they will pay more than what is charged by your competitors.

Table 5.2
Components of Resource-Based Analysis

Strategy

LO5-6

Determine a strategy to match the new business mission.

strategy
The broad approaches a small business will use to accomplish its mission.

We have presented the content thus far in a sequential manner, but the reality is that much of this is and should be done concurrently. The firm needs to build on its mission and develop an effective **strategy** for the new business. This building process in which the mission is the firm's foundation explains why such extensive attention is given to the development of a mission statement. The firm's strategy is how the firm plans to use the competitive advantages of the business to accomplish its mission. Thus, the mission is the foundation on which the firm's strategy is built. Strategy is a complex field of study, and we do not presume to cover the subject in this text. Our goal is to present the general concepts we believe will be most valuable to a new-business start-up.

Michael Porter suggests that there are fundamentally three broad means to view a business's strategy: low cost, differentiation, or focus. A low-cost strategy is one where the firm seeks to be the lowest-cost competitor in the industry. A differentiation approach is one where the firm finds a unique position in the market through product, service, location, and the like. A focus approach seeks to craft a business around a small set of customers, specialty products, or a small geographic approach. Porter goes on to argue that firms can combine their focus approach with one of the other strategies; thus, there could be a focus differentiation or a focus low-cost strategy.[14]

If you went into the cupcake-making business, what would you need to do to differentiate your strategy from a large competitor?

As a practical matter, most new firms pursue a combination of these broad categories. The result is a value strategy in which some combination of cost and differentiation is employed as the firm seeks to serve a focus population of some type. A key reason for this combined strategy is that a new business is only rarely the absolute lowest-cost competitor in an industry (especially in an industry that is well established). Similarly the new business will also find it difficult to be differentiated along all dimensions of a product or service (and actually may not really wish to be). A value strategy that mixes cost and differentiation also can help a firm evolve its strategy as its industry changes.[15]

Thus, many new businesses employ a value strategy and then also seek to employ a differentiation focus strategy. In choosing the elements where they may effectively differentiate, new-business owners should reexamine the prior discussion in this chapter on competitive advantage. The resources and capabilities upon which the new business differentiates itself will constitute the key elements on which the firm builds its competitive advantage. To illustrate, the firm may believe that customer service will be one of its competitive advantages, so that should also be where it builds its differentiation and value strategy.

There are four logical steps in developing the firm's strategy which build on the earlier discussion of the firm's mission statement and understanding of its capabilities.

Step 1: The firm's mission statement is employed to specify where the firm is to compete and how.

Step 2: A detailed strategic plan is laid out specifying a series of resources or capabilities that will be used to meet each part of the mission and strategy. This plan should include the area of the mission that is being addressed, the strategy employed, the specific action, the result desired, the person responsible, and the status of the action. This can be developed in a spreadsheet format for ease of analysis. A brief example is shown in Table 5.3 for our Mediterranean restaurant example.

Step 3: Following the approach outlined previously, the strategy needs to meet the criterion of being defendable for some length of time (depending on the industry, the length of time that would be considered sufficient may vary). The strategy should also provide the founder(s) economic returns above the industry average. If these two criteria cannot be satisfied, then the firm's strategy needs to be reexamined. However, if these two criteria can be met, then the firm should move forward with a focus on those activities that are defendable and have the potential to provide economic rents. The firm does not have to be excellent in all areas. Instead, it needs to have only those two to three competitive advantages that are its means of value differentiation.

Step 4: The firm's strategy needs to be constantly reevaluated. As noted, no competitive advantage or means of differentiation lasts

MISSION	STRATEGY	ACTION	RESULT DESIRED	RESPONSIBLE PARTY	STATUS
Gourmet	High-end, well-known chefs	Hire a chef from one of the top schools	Recognized in community	Founder	
			Has a short spot on TV news show each week	Founder	

Table 5.3
Restaurant example's strategic plan

forever. The new business must constantly evaluate its performance and its means of competitive advantage relative to its direct competitors to ensure that they are still relevant. This control function will be discussed in greater detail as we discuss analysis techniques in Chapter 12.

Applying the Strategy

Implementing a strategy is about fit and alignment within the business. Greater detail will be discussed in Chapters 10 and 11 on how to build a consistent set of activities around the strategy of the firm. However, to illustrate the key role that strategy can play for the new business, consider another illustration from the restaurant industry. A restaurant was founded by a Greek immigrant located close to downtown in a large midwestern city.* The principal customers were expected to be the individuals who lived in the apartments and condos that were close to the downtown area. The restaurant started as a café with cheaper Greek entrées, but over time it developed a dinner clientele that kept requesting more sophisticated menu items. So the owners upgraded a number of items on the menu to the point where a standard dinner entrée cost $15. Due to inertia and a desire to hold onto the restaurant's roots, the owner kept several of the original items on the menu. Then the founder wanted to expand his customer base. He noted that Cajun food was gaining popularity in the region, so without regard to his position as a Greek restaurant, he added Cajun food to the menu. The market already had several restaurants, which were part of large chains that offered Cajun food in the downtown area.

Piece by piece the owner of the Greek restaurant was working his business away from what he wanted it to be and muddling the perception that potential customers had of his establishment. Customers who chose to go to dinner at his restaurant might have found the Greek atmosphere and food appealing. However, as the atmosphere and offerings moved away from this Greek atmosphere, customers were confused by the menu choices and the eclectic nature of the offerings. The restaurant was losing

*We have referred to restaurants on several occasions as classic examples of strategic management not because we believe they are the only examples, but because they are well-known types of establishments and their positioning is obvious to even the most casual observer. They also are a classic business type with an owner/manager who typically has high involvement in the business. These businesses can be founded by anyone with a passion for the business and do not generally require the special training that many other types of business might require.

its appeal and becoming undifferentiated in a market that has thousands of choices.

The owner of the restaurant decided that his business was on its way to being a generic restaurant (and would probably need to close if changes were not made). He decided to refocus the organization around a succinct mission statement for the firm and then build a strategy or set of actions consistent with that mission. It had become obvious that although he thought he had seen an opportunity, he had failed to define his true competence and focus. As a result, the owner centered his business strictly on Greek food, eliminating the Cajun offerings. The owner also determined that his fundamental skill set was oriented toward more sophisticated meals, so he chose to offer a differentiated product at a premium price.

The owner then set out to align his business in a manner consistent with the differentiation strategy that would focus on sophisticated Greek food. The simpler, cheaper offerings were eliminated from the menu. This rationalization of the menu also allowed the owner to more efficiently use the food that went into making the products. In this industry, a key success factor, especially for a small restaurant, is control of the cost of inputs. The cost to the firm of ordering a large variety of food items entails significant storage and spoilage expenses in addition to an increase in complexity in virtually every aspect of the business. Thus, focusing strictly on Greek food and eliminating lower-priced items helped the efficiency of the whole organization, as well as situating it in a unique position within the market.

Consistent with this approach on food, the restaurant began offering only Greek wines. Previously the restaurant had served beer, but consistent with its differentiation focus, the owner wanted to focus on wine as the drink of choice, and specifically Greek wines. The hiring of staff also became much more clearly focused. There were a number of Greek immigrants in the city with detailed knowledge of this cuisine who were willing to work in a restaurant. The owner decided to hire these individuals, actually paying them a premium, in order to have highly skilled workers who understood what they were serving.

Finally, rather than advertising in the newspaper that went to all parts of the city and to numerous individuals who would never come downtown or, even if they did, would not patronize a high-end Greek restaurant, the owner began to focus his advertising. These are the specifics:

1. Since the restaurant is a part of the downtown area, the owner began to work with the concierge at the major hotels in the area in order to become one of their suggested specialty restaurants.
2. The Greek community in the city was strongly associated with the local Greek orthodox church. The owner opened a Greek restaurant because that was the food he knew. Only later did he realize that the Greek community was willing to travel from around the city to have good Greek food. Therefore, the owner began to advertise in publications and activities associated with the church to better reach that audience.

The result was that the restaurant built a consistent set of activities around its mission and strategy that helped to focus the firm clearly on what played to its strengths and gave it the best opportunity to make economic rents.

EXERCISE 3

1. As a class, pick several neighborhood bars close to campus or near downtown. Have each person write a mission statement for that bar. Compare the mission statements generated.
2. Discuss the impact each of these mission statements would have on the way the bar is operated.

FLOW RIGHT BREWERY & BAR: A FAMILY AFFAIR

Chris focused all his efforts on his new-business idea. He went to the Small Business Assistance Center and was advised to craft a mission statement. He understood that he was designing a microbrew pub and had decided that it would cater to beer enthusiasts who lived within a 10-mile radius (recall Chapter 4, in which he analyzed his external environment). He also understood he would need to sell food. However, within those parameters, Chris was not sure how he wanted to compete.

Chris had been to many microbrew pubs and talked to a number of brewmasters in the industry. There seemed to be as many strategies as there were places. One brewmaster told Chris that it was all about the quality of the beer. With this approach the whole focus of the place was on the latest craft brew, which was priced at a significant premium. Events were held around each tapping, and they had a new tapping every week.

Another brewmaster advised Chris to use the microbrew machinery as a prop for the business. Although new brews would be made there—and they should be done well—the majority of sales at the place would be for other craft beers and even national brands such as Budweiser.

The advice kept coming, but Chris eventually decided that he had to be true to his love of craft beer and his desire to share that with a community who might only just be starting to learn about the virtues of unique beers. He knew he would have to sell food to be profitable, but he did not want that to be his focus. He designed the following mission statement as his first draft.

"A Neighborhood Brewery and Bar opening the door to new beer tastes."

SUMMARY

New businesses are well served by developing a mission statement for the company. A good mission statement that is effectively implemented with a consistent strategy will help everyone involved in the organization to focus on what is needed.

Five elements to keep in mind while crafting a mission statement are as follows:

1. Keep it short—Make sure it can fit on a coffee mug.
2. Keep it simple—Ensure that everyone in the company can learn and understand what it means and why.
3. Make it applicable—It should be able to guide every individual in the company each and every day. It should also be something that customers cite as to why they use the company.
4. Be specific—Be so clear that it tells everyone exactly what you do, and by definition, what you do not do.
5. Establish measurable goals—Be able to develop a metric for every part of the statement.

The strategy puts that mission into action. The steps to identifying a sustainable competitive advantage follow:

Step 1: Develop a list of your business's resources and capabilities.

Step 2: Break the list into two groups: standard and unique.

Step 3: Evaluate the unique resources and/or capabilities.

1. Is the resource or capability rare?
2. Is the resource or capability durable?
3. Is the resource or capability relatively nonsubstitutable?
4. Is the resource or capability valuable?

KEY TERMS

capabilities 80
economic rent 87
first-mover advantage 86
followers 86
intangible assets 85
metric 82
mission statement 78
strategy 89
sustainable competitive advantage 84
tangible assets 85

REVIEW QUESTIONS

1. What is the value of a mission statement for a new organization?
2. How should a mission statement guide the actions of employees?
3. What makes a good mission statement?
4. What is the difference between a tangible and an intangible asset?
5. Why do resources or capabilities have to meet all four requirements of the resource-based analysis to provide the company with a competitive advantage?
6. Why is it important to identify the standard elements of a new business?

BUSINESS PLAN DEVELOPMENT QUESTIONS

1. What are the core resources and/or capabilities of the business you are contemplating?
2. Which of those resources or capabilities do you believe are just standard expectations in the industry?
3. Which of those resources or capabilities do you believe pass all four elements of the resource-based approach?
4. Given the resources or capabilities you listed in question 3, what mission statement would you write for your new business, and why would it be a good one?

INDIVIDUAL EXERCISES

1. Seek out a locally owned business.
   a. Ask if the owner can provide you with the mission statement of the business.
   b. Ask if the owner can talk about the unique positioning of the business in the market.
2. Seek out a locally owned business and, without talking to the owner, visit the business.
   a. Can you craft a mission statement for the business that aligns with your experience?
   b. What do you believe are the unique elements of the business compared to the competitors?

GROUP EXERCISES

1. Using the Internet, identify three large corporations that are in the same general industry as the business that you are developing. Search their Web pages and record their mission statements. For these corporations, how would you evaluate the mission statements in terms of clarity and fulfilling the goals of a mission statement identified in the chapter?
2. Discuss in your group how these mission statements might be improved.
3. Take one of these organizations and list your best assessment for what might be ordinary and unique at the company.

ENDNOTES

1. K. M. Eisenhardt and D. M Sull, "Strategy as Simple Rules," *Harvard Business Review* (January 2001), pp. 107–16.
2. B. Bartkus and M. Glassman, "Do Firms Practice What They Preach? The Relationship Between Mission Statements and Stakeholder Management," *Journal of Business Ethics* 83, no. 2 (2008), pp. 207–16.
3. R. Lussier, "A Nonfinancial Business Success Versus Failure Prediction Model for Your Firms," *Journal of Small Business Management* 33, no. 1 (1995), pp. 8–21.
4. T. Man, T. Lau, and K. Chan, "The Competitiveness of Small and Medium Enterprises: A Conceptualization with Focus on Entrepreneurial Competencies," *Journal of Business Venturing* 17, no. 2 (2002), pp. 123–43.
5. K. H. Doerr, K.R. Gue, A Performance and Goal Setting Procedure for Deadline Oriented Processes. Productions and Operations Management. May (2013), 22(3): 726–738.
6. T. Powell, "Organizational Alignment as Competitive Advantage," *Strategic Management Journal* 13, no. 2 (1992), pp. 119–35.
7. A. Davis and E. Olson, "Critical Competitive Strategy Issues Every Entrepreneur Should Consider Before Going into Business, *Business Horizons* 51, no. 3 (2008), pp. 211–21.
8. R. McNaughton, P. Osborne, and B. Imrie, "Market-Oriented Value Creation in Service Firms," *European Journal of Marketing* 36, no. 9/10 (2002), pp. 990–1013.
9. I. Chaston, B. Badger, T. Mangles, and E. Sadler-Smith, "Relationship Marketing, Knowledge Management Systems and E-Commerce Operations in Small UK Accountancy Practices," *Journal of Marketing Management* 19, no.1/2 (2003), pp. 109–31.
10. R. Hall, "A Framework Linking Intangible Resources and Capabilities to Sustainable Competitive Advantage," *Strategic Management Journal* 14, no. 8 (1993), pp. 607–19.
11. M. Lieberman and D. Montgomery, "First-Mover (Dis)advantages: Retrospective and Link with the Resource-Based View," *Strategic Management Journal* 19, no. 12 (1998), pp. 1111–26.
12. D. Miller, "An Asymmetry-Based View of Advantage: Toward an Attainable Sustainability," *Strategic Management Journal* 24, no. 10 (2003), pp. 961–76.
13. J. B. Barney, D. J. Ketchen, and M. Wright, "The Future of Resource-Based Theory: Revitalization or Decline?" *Journal of Management* 37, no. 5 (2011), pp. 1299–1315.
14. M. Porter, *Competitive Advantage: Creating and Sustaining Superior Performance* (New York, NY: Free Press, 1985).
15. R.R. Gehani, "Innovative Strategic Leader Transforming from a Low Cost Strategy to Product Differentiation Strategy," *Journal of Technology Management & Innovation*. (2013), 8(2): 144–155.

CREDITS

Opener: Stockbyte/Getty Images RF; p. 77: Purestock/SuperStock RF; p. 78: Jochen Sand/Getty Images RF; p. 84: Photo by Lynn Betts, USDA Natural Resources Conservation Service RF; p. 86: Gareth Cattermole/Getty Images for Netflix; p. 90: Matt Sayles, File/AP Images.

part 3

chapter 6

learning objectives

After studying this chapter, you will be able to:

LO6-1 Recognize the fundamental importance of cash flow analysis.

LO6-2 Prepare a cash flow statement and a budget.

LO6-3 Identify other financial tools.

Analyzing Cash Flow and Other Financial Information

NUMI ORGANIC TEA

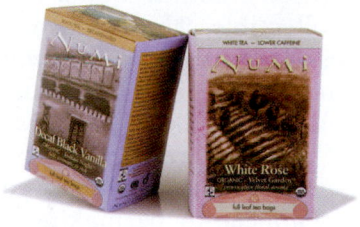

Ahmed Rahim and Reem Rahim are a brother and sister combo who have founded one of the largest tea companies in the world based on fair trade principles. Ahmed and Reem are children of immigrants from Iraq who each pursued individual careers in the arts prior to founding Numi Organic Tea. Ahmed was a photographer; Reem studied painting and has a master's degree in fine arts.

The two individually considered creating a firm to import a dry lime tea from the Middle East. When they realized that they both had the same idea, they decided to combine their efforts. Today the firm has over $20 million in sales.

Ahmed and Reem started by working out of their 750-square-foot apartment, living and working in the same space to save money. The two sought to differentiate their teas by using super-premium inputs that are organic and Fair Trade Certified. In recent years the pair has also differentiated their products by sewing teas together into flowers. Thus, rather than proffering loose tea in a bag, their teas form into flowers that bloom when placed in the water. For example, a black tea would have pearls of jasmine tea sown around the black tea to form a flower.

Since becoming so successful, the Rahims have created a foundation working to benefit the community of Oakland where their company is located. One of the key issues the two siblings had to learn was how to work together productively. They actually entered into counseling to help learn the skills necessary to be successful in this process.

Questions

1. Why were the founders able to start their business so inexpensively?
2. Do you believe that the foundation they have created is a good match for their business?

Sources: L. Budgar, "Has New Tricks," *The Natural Food Merchandiser* (2006), pp. 22, 26; C. Dunn, "Brother and Sister Brewer," *Fortune International* (Europe) 168 (November 18, 2013), p. 22; Numi Web page, "Founders Story," http://www.numitea.com/vision/founders-story/

At this point you have generated the basic concept for a business, analyzed the external environment of your proposed business, and determined what strategy the new business will employ. The next step in the due diligence process is to develop an actionable financial plan for the business. In fact, the next analytical step is perhaps the most critical in the due diligence effort, as the financial analysis of the business will most likely determine whether there is actual financial opportunity for your business. Specifically, a new firm must decide whether there will be sufficient cash flow for the proposed business to survive its early days and then thrive as an established entity. An idea that has passed your evaluations to date but that is unable to generate minimally sufficient cash flow in a reasonable time is not a practical business idea.

cash flow
Actual cash that flows into the firm, minus the cash that goes out of the firm.

It is important to understand that **cash flow** in a business is not the same as profit.[1] A firm obtains profits when its sales revenue is higher than its expenses, including depreciation of assets. However, generating profits does not put cash in the bank today. It is quite common to have high levels of products "sold" with no cash coming into the firm. Credit accounts commonly have terms that range from 30 to 90 days, which means you will not receive payment for your services or goods for 30 to 90 days. In fact, some percentage of these credit accounts will go past due and some will ultimately be uncollectible. Thus, you will not likely receive the money for your business immediately once you sell the product or service. On the other hand, a new business must generally pay in cash for its goods and supplies immediately because it has no credit history. Carrying inventory of any type results in payments for those supplies taking place long before any cash is received by the business. Thus, while many new firms appear to be making a profit, they can be suffering from a negative cash flow. Ultimately, the danger is that the entrepreneurial business will need to make payments in cash for its inputs but will have insufficient cash available from sales to make those payments.*

This cash crunch is actually exacerbated when sales are growing. A doubling in orders in a single month sounds great, but it means that twice the inputs must be ordered and paid for while there is no cash coming into the firm to pay for the dramatic increase of inputs needed until those goods are paid for by the customer. The outcome is that rapid growth by a new entrepreneurial business is actually one of the most dangerous times for that business. An entrepreneurial firm must understand and monitor its cash flow as it is typically the absence of sufficient cash flow that is the greatest reason that an entrepreneurial business fails.[2]

To prevent such a cash crunch, it is important for a new entrepreneurial business to carefully, thoughtfully, and accurately forecast its real cash flow. In its simplest form, a cash flow statement is a comparison of cash inflows to cash outflows. In this chapter we will present a thorough method that will help ensure that the business has a clear picture of its cash flow situation.

LO6-1

Recognize the fundamental importance of cash flow analysis.

Importance of Cash Flow Analysis

The role of the cash flow statement developed in the due diligence stage of a new entrepreneurial venture is substantially different from the financial analysis developed for an ongoing firm. An established business will

*For a good case regarding cash flows see T. G. Canace, J. E. Wilkerson, "A Practice Based Statement of Cash Flows Learning Experience: An Initial Public Offering for Contempri Homes?" *Issues in Accounting Education*. 29, no. 1 (February 2014), pp. 195-216.

FRIENDS' HOME HEALTH

To illustrate the fundamentals of cash flow analysis, let's examine the cash flow developed by Friends' Health Care as the two friends evaluated the potential financial viability of the new venture. The initial analysis the founders made of their projected cash flow is listed below.

The cash flow statement reflects the firm's plan for $100,000 of equity investment by the two founders and the acquisition of a bank loan in September. The founders tried to include every actual expense that would be incurred in the first six months of operation. The receipts were estimated by observing their competitors. They obtained an estimate of operational expenses by talking with owners in other cities about what they spend each month. The two largest expenses for the firm will be advertising and the cost of the personnel who will work for the business. The advertising is regarded as critical because Friends' will have to educate their community about why they should choose the level of care that Friends' will be offering. It is unclear to the owners at this stage if they will need to continue this advertising expense over time. The approach to marketing will be examined later in Chapter 9.

The professional dues are an expense to ensure that all employees who work for the firm are certified in their given profession; recall this was one of the strategic features of the firm discussed earlier in Chapter 5. The plan is to hire employees in July who will attain their initial certifications in July and August. Then in October as business grows, the firm will add more people and will need to have them certified; this is why the health insurance expense increases in October. As the firm continues to grow, the various individuals certified will work more hours for the firm so the hours increase somewhat consistently over the six months.

	JULY	AUGUST	SEPTEMBER	OCTOBER	NOVEMBER	DECEMBER	TOTAL
Receipts (Sales), $	$ 0	$ 0	$ 31,000	$55,000	$78,000	$ 91,000	$255,000
Debt Financing, $	0	0	50,000	0	0	0	50,000
Equity Financing, $	100,000	0	0	0	0	0	100,000
Equipment Purchases, $	22,250	3,850	2,500	500	1,500	0	30,600
Salaries, $	4,167	22,167	40,167	48,000	55,500	63,500	233,501
Payroll Taxes, $	375	375	375	675	675	675	3,150
Health Insurance, $	900	900	900	1,350	1,350	1,350	6,750
Professional Fees, $	5,000	2,500	0	2,500	0	0	10,000
Office Lease, $	5,208	5,208	5,208	5,208	5,208	5,208	31,248
Utilities, $	750	500	500	550	600	750	3,650
Phone Expense, $	0	850	900	1,000	1,000	1,000	4,750
Insurance, $	1,350	0	0	1,350	0	0	2,700
Advertising, $	0	7,500	4,250	2,500	4,250	7,000	25,500
Office Supplies, $	500	1,000	250	250	500	500	3,000
Interest, $	0	0	0	417	417	417	1,251
Taxes, $	0	0	0	0	0	1,695	1,695
Beginning Balance, $	$ 0	$57,000	$ 12,150	$ 30,100	$ 31,300	$38,300	
Cash In, $	100,000	0	81,000	55,000	78,000	91,000	
Cash Out, $	43,000	44,850	63,050	53,800	71,000	82,095	
Net Cash Flow, $	57,000	44,850	17,950	1,200	7,000	8,905	
Ending Balance, $	$ 57,000	$ 12,150	$ 30,100	$ 31,300	$38,300	$ 47,205	

EXERCISE 1

1. What additional items would you like to see included in the Friends' Home Health cash flow statement?
2. Do you believe that the numbers above are realistic? Explain.
3. For which items would you like to have additional information? How might this be best presented?
4. Solely based on the cash flow statement, would you believe that this venture was worth investing in if you were an investor? Why or why not?

develop a series of financial reports for either themselves or for investors over some time period such as a month or a quarter. The data generated will include an actual cash flow statement, but will also include a balance sheet, an income statement, and a small series of industry-specific reports. Each of these financial statements provides a unique look at the operation of the business, and each is valuable in its own right. We will briefly examine these statements in this chapter, and then in Chapter 8, we will provide a detailed examination of the means to use such financial reports once the business is up and running. For a proposed business, the financial analysis focuses almost exclusively on its ability to generate positive cash flows in the shortest time possible.

The focus on cash flow is due in part to the fact that in the new business, the management of the firm will also be the owners of the firm. Profitability is applauded in the public investing community, where the members of management are generally not the majority owners and therefore there is a split in ownership and control. When there is a separation between management and ownership, profits are a useful measure as a means to evaluate performance, inasmuch as such firms are typically larger and have numerous slack, or excess, resources. However, for owners of a new entrepreneurial firm, the focus is on the viability of the business, and the viability of the firm will be decided by cash flow, not profitability. The ability of the new business to generate strong profits on each item sold is indeed important; however, profit should not be the principal focus in the analysis of a potential new business. Profits have little to do with whether the business will be viable over the long term. The key to the success of a new venture (as simple and obvious as it seems) is its ability to bring in more cash each month than it spends and, more important, to bring that cash in on a cycle that is faster than the payout cycle.

equity
Investment into the entrepreneurial business by the owners of the firm.

One of the authors of the text assisted a start-up company whose founders had developed a device that sold for $199 and was used in the construction industry. The founders and their investors had invested almost $80,000 in the business (the firm's **equity**). This entrepreneurial business had been in operation for approximately four months when the founders asked the author to come to the office for a celebration. Upon his arrival there were drinks and balloons to celebrate the first sale of the product produced by the firm. One of the founders proudly announced he had just made $100, a profit margin of about 50 percent on this first sale of their product. The owners were totally focused on that profit margin and had visions of a business that would now grow and provide them a solid living for the rest of their lives. However, the owners had burned through almost $38,000 to make that $100. Total cash that had flowed into the company was $199; total cash outflow had exceeded $38,000, for a net cash flow of a negative $37,801.

Similar to homeowners, business owners invest their own money with the hopes that increased profits will pay off over time.

Regardless of the profit margin of a company's product, there is a need to bring in sufficient cash to pay all of the bills. That entrepreneurial business was going to have to generate many more sales to have any potential for staying in business. Although the firm generated lots of interest and started to gain contracts for its product, it went through all of its cash reserves before it could bring in sufficient cash from sales for the firm to survive. Unfortunately this occurs to many new entrepreneurial firms. This was another great idea that had lots of potential and a good profit margin, but ran out of cash from loans and equity before it could generate a positive cash flow.

Of course an entrepreneur wants to make a profit, but cash pays the bills and the payroll. As we stated earlier, a new entrepreneurial business will have to pay its vendors cash. Even after an entrepreneurial business is well established, it may have only 30 days to pay vendors, whereas its customers, particularly if they are large firms, may take upward of 90 days to pay their bills. The entrepreneurial business has to cover that period of 60 days between when it had to deliver the product and when it receives payment. It may even be a longer period if your customer was a government entity of some type.

This situation represents an important concept or term in cash flow analysis: **float**. This term reflects the setting where there is a difference between when the money goes out and when it comes in.[3] Banks commonly use float to their benefit. You as a business owner may deposit a check or receive an electronic transfer from an out-of-state buyer. For some period of time your bank account reflects no inflow to you. However, the bank generally receives the money for that check within 24 hours. This is because the bank is legally allowed to hold an out-of-state check for clearance for preassigned time periods. Thus, the bank has free use of the money during that period when it has received the cash but is not yet required to reflect it in your account. Even though the float from one out-of-state check may be very small, when those amounts are aggregated by large banks, they can involve millions or billions of dollars they have the ability to use at no cost to themselves during a year.

float

The difference between when the money goes out and when it comes in. For example, if you deposit a check or receive an electronic transfer today in payment for some good, you typically do not receive cash when you deposit it. Instead there is a period of float before it is credited to your account.

The entrepreneur can also benefit from float. Credit card charges (not including cash advances) are typically a free form of cash float, as the new business owner does not have to pay interest unless the bill is not paid in full each month. For anywhere up to 25 days a month, the owner has use of the funds without having any outflow to pay the bill. This is a positive cash flow situation for the entrepreneur.

Cash Flow Versus Budgets

A cash flow statement is not a budget and should not be confused with a budget.[4] A **budget** projects all the costs that will be incurred by the organization over some period of time (a year, for instance) and allocates that expense evenly over the relevant time period. This is similar to what you might do for your household expenses as you set aside money each month to pay the annual life insurance payment or school tuition. At any one time the account for that expense usually has excess funds (except for the month in which the bill comes due). An example might be an insurance payment. The annual cost might be $1,800; thus, the budget would reflect $150 per month.

budget

Statement that projects all the costs that will be incurred by the organization over a period of time and allocates those expenses evenly over the relevant time period.

An example budget for a start-up firm that sells software is shown in Table 6.1. This is the actual budget prepared by a new business that sold software to other small- to medium-sized businesses (the founders had developed a small software package and sales consisted of a CD-ROM and a small manual). This budget was what the firm relied on as it started its business, and it showed that the business should have consistent positive cash balances. Note that virtually all of the amounts in each category were the same from month to month.

A cash flow statement does the exact opposite of a budget. In the example above of an insurance payment, in each month in which no actual cash outflow occurs, the category receives a zero, and then in the month that the payment is due, the account will record a cash outflow of $1,800. Although budgets are helpful for planning purposes, nothing brings home reality like the recognition that the company must have X amount of actual cash in order to pay this month's bills.

BUDGET								
Receipts:		January	February	March	April	May	June	Total
	Sales, $	$ 1,000	$ 2,500	$ 3,000	$ 5,000	$ 7,000	$ 10,000	**$28,500**
	Consulting, $	5,000	5,000	5,000	10,000	10,000	10,000	**45,000**
Total Receipts, $		$ 6,000	$ 7,500	$ 8,000	$15,000	$17,000	$20,000	**$73,500**
Disbursements:								
	Salaries, $	$ 4,000	$ 4,000	$ 4,000	$ 5,500	$ 5,500	$ 5,500	**$28,500**
	Travel, $	1,000	1,000	1,000	1,000	1,000	1,000	**$ 6,000**
	Car Leases, $	1,000	1,000	1,000	1,000	1,000	1,000	**$ 6,000**
	Rent, $	900	450	450	450	450	450	**$ 3,150**
	Payroll Taxes, $	300	300	300	300	300	300	**$ 1,800**
	Insurance, $	121	121	121	121	121	121	**$ 725**
	Fuel/Maint., $	150	150	150	150	150	150	**$ 900**
	Benefits, $	350	350	350	350	350	350	**$ 2,100**
	Advertising, $	300	300	300	300	300	300	**$ 1,800**
	Inventory Inputs, $	50	50	50	50	50	50	**$ 300**
	Utilities, $	200	200	200	200	200	200	**$ 1,200**
	Misc., $	250	250	250	250	250	250	**$ 1,500**
Total Disbursements, $		$ 8,621	$ 8,171	$ 8,171	$ 9,671	$ 9,671	$ 9,671	**$ 53,975**
Beginning Balance, $		$ 0	$ 7,379	$ 6,708	$ 6,538	$ 11,867	$ 19,196	
Equity Investment, $		10,000						**10,000**
Net Profit, $		(2,621)	(671)	(171)	5,329	7,329	9,196	**18,392**
Ending Balance, $		$ 7,379	$ 6,708	$ 6,538	$ 11,867	$ 19,196	$ 28,392	

Table 6.1
Example Budget for Start-Up Software Firm

Compare the example firm's budget with its actual cash flow statement in Table 6.2.

The firm developed this cash flow analysis after several months of operation, when it became clear that the budget document was not proving helpful in the management of the firm's cash. The cash flow statement that was developed for the company showed some shortfalls that should scare a firm founder. The company (which started with $10,000 from the founders) was completely out of cash by March and had a negative cash position of almost $2,000 in April. The firm actually covered this shortcoming with credit card cash advances and was able to survive. Note that the company founders did not account for the interest on those advances which accrued from the date of the transaction—a cost they should have accounted for to better understand the firm's financial standing. One of the fundamental realities of starting a new business is that it takes a period of time for the new venture to ramp up sales and then to obtain cash from those sales. Much of the difficulty with this business could have been avoided with a cash flow projection prior to deciding whether to pursue the business or not, and then with use of that cash flow projection to ensure an increase in the initial equity position of the new firm.[5]

We utilize a rule of thumb (and it is only a rule of thumb) when examining the initial equity needs of a new venture that has proved to be very

CASH FLOW STATEMENT

Receipts:		January	February	March	April	May	June	Total
	Sales, $	$ 350	$ 550	$ 1,200	$ 9,400	$12,200	$13,000	**$36,700**
	Consulting, $	3,000	3,500	5,000	0	3,000	3,500	**18,000**
Total Receipts, $		$ 3,350	$ 4,050	$ 6,200	$ 9,400	$15,200	$16,500	**$54,700**
Disbursements:								
	Salaries, $	$ 4,000	$ 4,000	$ 5,000	$ 5,000	5,000	$ 5,000	**$28,000**
	Travel, $	2,304	365	558	846	1,368	1,104	**$ 6,545**
	Car Leases, $	1,000	1,000	1,000	1,000	1,000	1,000	**$ 6,000**
	Rent, $	900	450	450	450	450	450	**$ 3,150**
	Payroll Taxes, $	240	240	300	300	300	340	**$ 1,720**
	Insurance, $	0	0	0	1,450	0	0	**$ 1,450**
	Fuel/Maint., $	13	21	46	361	468	502	**$ 1,412**
	Benefits, $	350	350	350	350	350	350	**$ 2,100**
	Advertising, $	28	44	96	752	976	0	**$ 1,896**
	Credit Card, $				500	2,000		**$ 2,500**
	Supplies, $	17	20	31	47	76	112	**$ 303**
	Utilities, $	174	213	208	189	132	188	**$ 1,104**
	Misc., $	67	81	124	188	304	764	**$ 1,528**
Total Disbursements, $		$ 9,093	$ 6,784	$ 8,163	$ 11,433	$ 12,424	$ 9,810	**$ 57,708**
								$ 0
Beginning Balance, $		$ 0	$ 4,257	$ 1,523	$ 60	$ 27	$ 2,802	
Equity Investment, $		10,000						**10,000**
Credit Card Advance, $				500	2,000			
Net Cash Flow, $		(5,743)	(2,734)	(1,963)	(2,033)	2,776	6,690	**(3,008)**
Ending Balance, $		$ 4,257	$ 1,523	$ 60	$ 27	$ 2,802	$ 9,492	

Table 6.2
Example Cash Flow Statement for Start-Up Software Firm

helpful in ensuring that the new venture has sufficient cash to achieve a market position. Calculate your entire cash flow projection without adding in any equity investment, and look for the point where the ending balance is at its lowest point. Take that number and multiply it by 150 percent. We argue for multiplying by 150 percent because it always takes more cash than you expect to start the business. (It also takes more time than you expect.) That number is what we would recommend for the initial equity or equity-plus-debt investment.

For example, we take the exact cash flow statement from Table 6.2 and remove the equity-plus-debt investment from the projection to produce Table 6.3.

Notice that in Table 6.3 in April the low point for the ending balance is ($12,473). Multiplying that number by 150 percent yields a recommended initial investment of $18,709, or roughly $19,000. With that number inserted into the initial equity investment for the firm, we see that the cash balance remains well above zero. This provides a cushion to the new firm, which enables it to pursue options it did not consider at founding, more easily

CASH FLOW STATEMENT								
Receipts:		January	February	March	April	May	June	Total
	Sales, $	$ 350	$ 550	$ 1,200	$ 9,400	$12,200	$13,000	**$ 36,700**
	Consulting, $	3,000	3,500	5,000	0	3,000	3,500	**18,000**
Total Receipts, $		$ 3,350	$ 4,050	$ 6,200	$ 9,400	$15,200	$16,500	**$ 54,700**
Disbursements:								
	Salaries, $	$ 4,000	$ 4,000	$ 5,000	$ 5,000	$ 5,000	$ 5,000	**$28,000**
	Travel, $	2,304	365	558	846	1,368	1,104	**$ 6,545**
	Car Leases, $	1,000	1,000	1,000	1,000	1,000	1,000	**$ 6,000**
	Rent, $	900	450	450	450	450	450	**$ 3,150**
	Payroll Taxes, $	240	240	300	300	300	340	**$ 1,720**
	Insurance, $	0	0	0	1,450	0	0	**$ 1,450**
	Fuel/Maint., $	13	21	46	361	468	502	**$ 1,412**
	Benefits, $	350	350	350	350	350	350	**$ 2,100**
	Advertising, $	28	44	96	752	976	0	**$ 1,896**
	Credit Card, $				500	2,000		**$ 2,500**
	Supplies, $	17	20	31	47	76	112	**$ 303**
	Utilities, $	174	213	208	189	132	188	**$ 1,104**
	Misc., $	67	81	124	188	304	764	**$ 1,528**
Total Disbursements, $		$ 9,093	$ 6,784	$ 8,163	$ 11,433	$ 12,424	$ 9,810	**$ 57,708**
								$ 0
Beginning Balance, $		$ 0	($ 5,743)	($ 8,477)	($10,440)	($ 12,473)	($ 9,698)	
Equity Investment, $								**0**
Credit Card Advance, $								
Net Cash Flow, $		(5,743)	(2,734)	(1,963)	(2,033)	2,776	6,690	**(3,008)**
Ending Balance, $		($ 5,743)	($ 8,477)	($10,440)	($12,473)	($ 9,698)	($ 3,008)	

Table 6.3
Modified Example Cash Flow Statement for Start-Up Software Firm

handle rapid growth, and/or handle unexpected external shocks to the organization. See Table 6.4.

In developing a cash flow projection, the new business owner should contact vendors and suppliers to ask about payment terms and also check with credit card companies to get exact information about when accounts will be processed and what percentage will be charged to the company for each transaction. These interactions also allow the new business owner to seek out the best terms possible from vendors and suppliers. In the next section of this chapter, we will suggest a specific series of items to be accounted for as you develop your cash flow statement. Once the venture begins operations, actual cash flow should be compared monthly to the projected cash flow statement in order to produce a **deviation analysis**, an analysis of how the predicted and actual cash flows differ. This will not only assist the entrepreneur in developing realistic forecasts for the business in the future but also point out differences between actual performance and predicted performance at a point in time. Taking the time each month to examine this allows the new-business person maximum flexibility in making changes to the business as it grows (a habit that

deviation analysis
Analysis of the differences between the predicted and the actual performance.

CASH FLOW STATEMENT

Receipts:		January	February	March	April	May	June	Total
	Sales, $	$ 350	$ 550	$ 1,200	$9,400	$12,200	$13,000	**$36,700**
	Consulting, $	3,000	3,500	5,000	0	3,000	3,500	**18,000**
Total Receipts, $		$ 3,350	$ 4,050	$ 6,200	$9,400	$15,200	$16,500	**$54,700**
Disbursements:								
	Salaries, $	$ 4,000	$ 4,000	$ 5,000	$5,000	$ 5,000	$ 5,000	**$28,000**
	Travel, $	2,304	365	558	846	1,368	1,104	**$ 6,545**
	Car Leases, $	1,000	1,000	1,000	1,000	1,000	1,000	**$ 6,000**
	Rent, $	900	450	450	450	450	450	**$ 3,150**
	Payroll Taxes, $	240	240	300	300	300	340	**$ 1,720**
	Insurance, $	0	0	0	1,450	0	0	**$ 1,450**
	Fuel/Maint., $	13	21	46	361	468	502	**$ 1,412**
	Benefits, $	350	350	350	350	350	350	**$ 2,100**
	Advertising, $	28	44	96	752	976	0	**$ 1,896**
	Credit Card, $				500	2,000		**$ 2,500**
	Supplies, $	17	20	31	47	76	112	**$ 303**
	Utilities, $	174	213	208	189	132	188	**$ 1,104**
	Misc., $	67	81	124	188	304	764	**$ 1,528**
Total Disbursements, $		$ 9,093	$ 6,784	$ 8,163	$ 11,433	$ 12,424	$ 9,810	**$ 57,708**
								$ 0
Beginning Balance, $		$ 0	$ 13,257	$ 10,523	$8,560	$ 6,527	$ 9,302	
Equity Investment, $		19,000						**19,000**
Credit Card Advance, $								
Net Cash Flow, $		(5,743)	(2,734)	(1,963)	(2,033)	2,776	6,690	**(3,008)**
Ending Balance, $		**$13,257**	**$10,523**	**$8,560**	**$6,527**	**$9,302**	**$15,992**	

Table 6.4
Finalized Example Cash Flow Statement for Start-Up Software Firm

will help keep the venture responsive as the venture develops). Chapter 8 will go into greater detail on such comparisons and how to analyze and respond to the deviations that are identified. To illustrate, you can see in Table 6.5 the cash flow deviation analysis from the software firm we have been discussing.

In this example, the software company's revenues fell $2,650 short of the owners' predictions, and their expenses were $693 more than they had expected. Although the firm will still have positive cash balance, this type of cash analysis provides valuable information to the owners of this new company. Why were sales so far below expectations? Why was travel more than double the projection? We note that the firm did virtually no advertising; perhaps this is why sales were less than expected. Some expenses need to be made in order to increase the opportunity for success on the revenue side, so we are not suggesting that the new venture attempt to cut its way to success; instead we suggest a careful monthly analysis of all actual revenues and expenses.

Table 6.5
Example Deviation Analysis for Start-Up Software Firm

DEVIATION ANALYSIS				
Receipts:		January –Predicted	January –Actual	Difference
	Sales, $	$ 1,000	$ 350	($ 650)
	Consulting, $	5,000	3,000	(2,000)
Total Receipts, $		$ 6,000	$ 3,350	($2,650)
Disbursements:				
	Salaries, $	$ 4,000	$ 4,000	$ 0
	Travel, $	1,000	2,304	1,304
	Car Leases, $	900	1,000	100
	Rent, $	900	900	0
	Payroll Taxes, $	300	240	(60)
	Insurance, $	0	0	0
	Fuel/Maint., $	150	13	(137)
	Benefits, $	350	350	0
	Advertising, $	300	28	(272)
	Supplies, $	50	17	(33)
	Utilities, $	200	174	(26)
	Misc., $	250	67	(183)
Total Disbursements, $		$ 8,400	$ 9,093	$ 693
Equity Investment, $		10,000	10,000	0
Net Cash Flow, $		(2,400)	(5,743)	(3,343)
Ending Balance, $		$ 7,600	$ 4,257	($3,343)

LO6-2

Prepare a cash flow statement and a budget.

Developing Cash Flow Statements and Budgets

There are several key issues that should be noted in developing a cash flow statement. The first is that a cash flow statement for a new business is substantially different from the typical publicly traded corporate annual report that you may have seen. New businesses, unlike established companies, are unlikely to have either investing activities or financing activities (interest on notes/loans is included in the operations section of new business cash flow statements). New entrepreneurial ventures typically have only one type of activity: operations. Everything that involves cash in/cash out is related to the operation of the business.

The cash flow statement is used to describe all of the activities that provide and use cash during the period being examined (we would recommend that the statement be done monthly until the business is well established). Used effectively, this statement helps the owners accurately keep track of the overall cash position of the business and provides a well-respected and accepted means of displaying the ability of the company to meet its obligations. As the business grows, a well-developed, accurate long-term track record of cash flow statements and the comparison of the planned cash flows to reality will go a long way toward assisting the company with loans, credit lines, infusions of equity capital, and even valuation, should the businessperson want to sell the company.

Generating the cash flow statement should actually begin with the expenses of the organization, for the very simple reason that they are easier to accurately forecast than are revenues. Expenses fall into a number of categories that are inclusive of, but not limited to, the following list:

- Salaries
- Basic Benefits
- Taxes/Fees
  - Payroll
  - Income
  - Local
  - State
  - Business
  - Licenses
- Cost of Goods Sold
  - Manufacturing
  - Packaging
  - Direct Labor
  - Shipping
- Utilities (Electricity, Gas, Phone Service, etc.)
- Security Systems
- Tools/Machinery
- Office Supplies (a big and often underestimated expense)
- Travel Expenses
- Insurance
- Advertising
- Furniture/Computers
- Telephones
- Maintenance of Equipment
- Cleaning (either a service or supplies for your use)
- Rent/Mortgage Payments

In short, all actual expenses must be accounted for in the cash flow statement. If your specific business has unique expenses that do not fit into these categories, note that you also need to add those expenses to this list.

Revenues (cash inflows) should be separated into as many categories as possible in order to provide maximum insight to the owner. The firm's revenues can come from a wide variety of sources that may not automatically be recognized. A new firm may sell computers, but it may actually make more money from servicing those computers. Separating out revenue lines aids both in predicting where the firm's revenues will come from and in analyzing the actual revenue sources for the new entrepreneurial firm. Once there is a fine-grained understanding, then those categories can be collapsed together if a more general-level categorization is desired.

To illustrate further, a lawn care company found from its cash flow analysis that its cash inflow was more positively impacted by what appeared to be an ancillary portion of the business (planting the flowers for a commercial building). The firm had to have the contract to mow the lawn to get the business, but it was planting the flowers that actually had a greater positive impact on the cash flow. Thus, the firm reexamined its pricing and priced the mowing so that the firm was certain to get the lawn-mowing contract, with flower planting and other landscaping activities providing the substantial portion of the positive inflow of revenues.

Several examples of the breakout in revenues that we have seen are listed in Table 6.6. These include revenue statements from a restaurant, a clothing store, and a retail office supply operation. Note that these examples focus only on revenues to provide you an idea of how to develop this aspect of cash flow statements. We will discuss expenses later in the chapter.

As the examples above suggest, generating a cash flow statement should be tailored to the information needs of the new venture. The lists above are not meant to be exhaustive. In general, we recommend that each unique area of the business that generates income should be given a separate revenue line item.

sensitivity analysis
An examination of the best- and worst-case cash flow scenarios.

A final comment regarding cash flow statements concerns the development of a **sensitivity analysis**.[6] The cash flow statement developed above could best be labeled a "most-likely case" scenario. It is also quite prudent to look at a worst-case and a best-case scenario to examine the sensitivity of the potential cash flow to dramatic changes in the revenue or cost stream when conducting due diligence on a business idea. The sensitivity analysis is a judgment call by the new-business person about whether the business could survive the worst-case or successfully carry out the best-case scenario.

To better understand your financial situation, our advice is that you take the revenue figures developed in your most-likely scenario and create two new cash flow statements. One increases monthly revenue by 25 percent and the other decreases monthly revenue by 25 percent. What is the effect upon your net cash flow? Could your new venture survive either of these situations? What changes might you make to accommodate the new outcomes?

There are several ways an entrepreneur can help to manage their cash flow. Clearly seeking the longest time to pay for any inputs will help the firm. However, the entrepreneur can also choose to pay their hourly employees on the 15th and the 30th rather than the 1st and the 15th. The delays of several weeks help the entrepreneur to delay those payments. One thing that entrepreneurs should also consider if their cash flow is too low is that they simply may not be charging enough for their product. Another option is for the firm to use a business credit card to pay some expenses, which can allow up to a 25-day delay in paying expenses and the ability to barter for services can save the new company extra cash.

To illustrate the benefits of cash flow analysis, the owners of a new print shop developed best- and worst-case scenarios of their cash flow projections. The insight led the founders to realize that if things continued as they were the business could not survive. This did not lead the entrepreneurs to give up. Instead, they worked to control their immediate costs through methods such as negotiating with their landlord to pay lower rent until they reached the break-even point. Additionally, this situation encouraged the founders to secure several definitive contracts from the city for printing. The result was that the founders were able to revise their cash flows such that even a worst-case scenario would be survivable.

EXERCISE 2

1. To help Chris work on his cash flow statements consider his expenses—what would be the hours, the number of staff that will be needed for each day at the bar, and the hourly pay. What would be your estimate of the payroll taxes and other employee-related expenses?
2. What other expenses should Chris consider?
3. Develop a cash flow statement for Chris that incorporates both receipts and expenses.

RESTAURANT CASH FLOW STATEMENT

Receipts:	January	February	March	April	Total
Food, $	$1,300	$1,800	$2,300	$2,400	**$ 7,800**
Drink, $	350	490	600	605	**$ 2,045**
Alcohol, $	450	770	780	810	**$ 2,810**
Misc., $	110	200	205	399	**$ 914**
Total Receipts, $	$ 2,210	$3,260	$3,885	$ 4,214	**$13,569**

CLOTHING STORE CASH FLOW STATEMENT

Receipts:	January	February	March	April	Total
Men's, $	$1,100	$ 900	$ 880	$ 850	**$ 3,730**
Women's, $	800	1,300	3,900	4,010	**$10,010**
Children's, $	210	800	1,460	1,503	**$ 3,973**
Shoes, $	0	130	468	890	**$ 1,488**
Accessories, $	35	473	608	950	**$ 2,066**
Total Receipts, $	$2,145	$3,603	$7,316	$8,203	**$ 21,267**

OFFICE SUPPLY STORE CASH FLOW STATEMENT

Receipts:	January	February	March	April	Total
Paper, $	$ 110	$ 400	$ 900	$ 1,450	**$ 2,860**
Calculators, $	0	340	0	110	**$ 450**
Computers, $	0	4,060	1,300	9,400	**$ 14,760**
Peripherals, $	460	2,389	1,600	2,450	**$ 6,899**
Furniture, $	0	0	0	199	**$ 199**
Writing Instruments, $	280	300	460	730	**$ 1,770**
Presentation Materials, $	505	695	803	477	**$ 2,480**
Impulse Display Items, $	34	79	672	309	**$ 1,094**
Cards, $	250	150	172	220	**$ 310**
Services, $	120	420	1,200	1,833	**$ 3,573**
Other, $	96	388	700	271	**$ 1,455**
Total Receipts, $	$1,855	$ 9,221	$ 7,707	$ 17,449	**$35,850**

Table 6.6
Revenue-Side Examples for Three Different Businesses

FLOW RIGHT BREWERY & BAR: A FAMILY AFFAIR

Chris and his wife thought they had thought through all the key details for the bar including the supports they would use, their business strategy, and key operational issues. However, Chris initially developed only a budget for the business. When he went to the Small Business Assistance Center for advice on his plan for the bar he was told that a budget was simply not enough. It was then that Chris learned about the differences between a cash flow statement and a budget. It was like a light came on for Chris. He had always heard the owner of the brew pub where he worked in college talk about how "cash was king." Now it was becoming clear to Chris why he said that. The national suppliers of restaurant supplies wanted payments within 30 days, after which they invoked significant penalties. A small bar represents only a speck in the total sales of a big national or regional supplier, so Chris and similar establishments have very little leeway as to when payments were due.

The result of this insight and the advice of the Small Business Assistance Center was that Chris developed two high-level cash flow statements: a best- and a worst-case example of his possible receipts. The basis for these two cash flow statements was his discussions with others on how a bar of his size could be expected to perform. Talking to other bar and brew pub owners in the region who were not competitors helped Chris make many of the decisions on the cash flows.

These conversations also gave Chris insight as to the percentage breakdown in the various activities. The income side of the cash flow statement he developed is below. Much to his dismay, it became clear that food was the driver of the cash to the firm—not the custom beer. It also became clear that there would be custom beer customers who would still like to have access to national beer brands and liquor to drink (other alcohol). The miscellaneous receipts came from room rentals and catering jobs that seemed to be a natural flow for this type of restaurant.

CASH FLOW STATEMENT
BEST CASE

Receipts:		January	February	March	April	Total
	Food, $	$ 11,850	$ 11,410	$ 13,540	$ 16,900	$ 54,700
	Custom Brewed Beer, $	4,400	3,200	8,600	10,900	$ 27,100
	Other Alcohol, $	3,200	3,800	5,900	5,900	$ 18,800
	Misc., $	1,300	1,860	2,550	2,650	$ 8,360
Total Receipts, $		$20,750	$21,270	$30,590	$36,350	$108,960

CASH FLOW STATEMENT
WORST CASE

Receipts:		January	February	March	April	Total
	Food, $	$ 6,970	$8,400	$ 9,040	$ 11,100	$ 35,510
	Custom Beer, $	2,850	1,890	4,800	5,800	$ 13,340
	Other Alcohol, $	1,800	2,100	4,300	3,800	$12,000
	Misc. , $	800	1,300	1,650	2,100	$ 5,850
Total Receipts, $		$12,420	$13,690	$19,790	$22,800	$68,700

Other Financial Tools

LO6-3

Identify other financial tools.

The focus thus far in this chapter has been exclusively on cash flow. This focus is consistent with the view that cash is king in an entrepreneurial business. However, there are other financial tools that are very helpful in analyzing a new business idea. Specifically, a new business will likely want to create **pro forma** balance sheets and income statements. The term *pro forma* (Latin, meaning "as a matter of form") simply means that the entrepreneur estimates what the balance sheets and income statements will look like in the future, in order to plan well.

pro forma
A term describing estimates of what the balance sheets and income statements will look like in the future.

Balance Sheet

A **balance sheet** is a summary of the assets and liabilities of the entrepreneurial business. It is useful for the new business to analyze and understand the types of assets and liabilities the business can expect. Once the firm is up and running, the pro forma balance sheet is also useful as a comparison in order to understand how assets are being used. The analysis of balance sheets in an ongoing business will be discussed more in Chapter 7. There are two basic types of assets that should be included as separate items in the balance sheet:

balance sheet
A summary of the assets and liabilities of the entrepreneurial business.

Current assets: Assets such as cash or those assets that can easily be converted to cash, such as accounts receivable and notes receivable.

Fixed assets: Assets that have a physical presence, including land, buildings, office equipment, machinery, and vehicles.

current assets
Assets such as cash or those assets that can easily be converted to cash, such as accounts receivable and notes receivable.

fixed assets
Assets that have a physical presence, including land, buildings, office equipment, machinery, and vehicles.

The balance sheet should include separate lines for each relevant type of current and fixed asset. The level of detail in this type of document is exclusively up to the entrepreneur; however, we would suggest that one err on the side of more detail early on in the life of the new venture.

On the other side of the equation there are two types of liabilities: current liabilities and long-term liabilities. The definitions of these two types of categories and explanations of what constitutes each are as follows:

Current liabilities: Liabilities or debts that the entrepreneurial business has to pay within one year. These include accounts payable, notes payable such as bank notes, and accrued payroll.

Long-term liabilities: Liabilities that are owed by the business and are ultimately due more than a year from the current date. These include mortgages payable, owners' equity, and stockholders' equity (the latter two are the investment by these individuals in the business).

current liabilities
Liabilities or debts that the entrepreneurial business has to pay within one year. These include accounts payable, notes payable such as bank notes, and accrued payroll.

long-term liabilities
Liabilities that are owed by the business and are ultimately due more than a year from the current date. These include mortgages payable, owners' equity, and stockholders' equity (the latter two are the investment by these individuals in the business).

ETHICAL CHALLENGE

We have noted that banks are able to accept a check from out of state, and yet they do not have to place those funds in your bank account for a period of up to 10 days, even though the bank may actually obtain those funds earlier. The banks benefit from the float. Although this is a historic element of the business and certainly an element of the business model for banks, what is your opinion of the practice? Many entrepreneurial businesses use the same type of float to their advantage when they use credit cards during the month, knowing that they will pay off the balance before any finance charge is due. How could banking and businesses adjust this practice and gain a competitive advantage? Should other tools be employed along these same lines?

The assets minus the liabilities of the firm reflected in the balance sheet should total to zero. Thus, the assets and liabilities balance each other. A balance sheet is a snapshot of a firm at some point in time. For a new start-up small firm, the balance sheet is a pro forma projection of what is expected in the future. The estimate of the firm's current assets will be quite limited, as the firm will not yet have any operations. The fixed assets and liabilities can be more exact and should be estimated with some care, since the cost of items can be reasonably estimated, and issues such as debt should be well known. Since the firm is a start-up, there will generally not be depreciation of items such as machinery. The text will discuss issues such as depreciation in Chapter 8, but for now you should know that it is basically a percentage of the value of equipment that is seen as the loss of value of an asset due to wear, tear, age, or obsolescence. The current assets minus the current liabilities are referred to as the working capital, which is in effect, the liquid assets the firm could call upon quickly to meet needs that arose. Table 6.7 shows the balance sheet for a small manufacturing firm.

Income Statement

income statement
Revenue of the firm minus expenses.

A pro forma **income statement** projects the future income of an entrepreneurial firm. The focus of the income statement is profit rather than cash flow. Whereas we emphasize cash flow as a foundation for

Table 6.7
Pro Forma Income Statement

Assets			
Current Assets			
Cash, $			$ 50,000
Acct Receivable, $			0
Total Current Assets, $			$ 50,000
Fixed Assets, $	Land	100,000	
	Buildings	150,000	
	Office Equipment	15,000	
	Machinery	75,000	
Total Fixed Assets, $			340,000
Total Assets, $			**$390,000**
Liabilities			
Current Liabilities			
Accounts Payable, $	35,000		
Notes Payable (less than a year), $	4,500		
Accrued Payroll, $	15,000		
Total Current Liability, $			$ 54,500
Long-Term Liabilities			
Mortgage, $	200,000		
Total Long-Term Liability, $			$ 200,000
Owner's Equity, $			$ 135,500
Total Liabilities/Owner's Equity, $			$ 390,000

analyzing the potential viability of the new business, we believe an understanding of profit allows the projected business to understand its overall cost picture. It is not unusual for a new entrepreneurial business to take a significant amount of time to reach overall profitability.

One of the keys to developing an income statement is predicting sales for the entrepreneurial firm. Even though there is much more art than science to this process, there are some techniques available to assist the entrepreneur. The entrepreneur should initially look to similar enterprises and attempt to estimate or research their sales levels. If a restaurant with a format similar to yours is available, for example, you can estimate its sales by taking the average ticket price and multiplying that by the traffic flow through the restaurant. You can estimate traffic flow to the restaurant by sitting in the parking lot for one or two nights and keeping a count of how many customers go in the door. The ability to talk with entrepreneurs in the same domain against whom you will not compete was cited in Chapter 3 (identifying the idea) and in Chapter 4 (external analysis) as excellent sources of information. These same individuals are excellent sources of information on what sales levels could be expected at various stages in the new business's growth. The key is to be conservative, because the reality is that things never happen as fast or as smoothly as you would hope in founding your business.

Correctly predicting a business's performance can help secure better terms with vendors and suppliers.

The entrepreneur may come to the conclusion that there are 25,000 people who live in the area around his appliance rental store who are potential customers. The store owner cannot (and should not) assume he will get all or even a majority of those customers. It is better to be very conservative and underestimate demand for a product or service than to overestimate demand. What percentage of the general population rents appliances on a weekly basis? What are the demographics of the typical appliance rental customer? How far will the typical appliance rental customer drive to rent an appliance? What are the primary drivers for the rental of appliances versus the purchase of them? How is the industry tracking? These and many other questions will assist the new-business person in estimating the potential sales of his new venture. Additionally, the entrepreneur needs to realize that sales growth is a function of time and should not assume that the new venture will reach an established company's sales volume in the short run. The new business venture needs to make conservative predictions regarding demand. Again, discussion with successful entrepreneurs is the new-business person's best resource. Table 6.8 illustrates the income statement developed for the computer sales and service firm.

The income statement provides both the gross and the net profit figures for the firm. In its simplified form, gross profit generally equals the sales of the organization minus the cost of goods sold. The firm then calculates all other expenses, such as salaries and benefits, to reach a total expense for the firm. Gross profit minus all other expenses yields net profit before taxes. Lastly, estimated taxes are calculated and subtracted from net profit, to determine the company's net profit after taxes. Note that the cost of goods sold is very small, in that producing a computer disk and a manual are very cheap activities from the production standpoint. If this were a restaurant, the cost of goods sold would be much higher.

INCOME STATEMENT							
Receipts:	January	February	March	April	May	June	Total
Sales, $	$ 350	$ 550	$ 1,200	$9,400	$12,200	$13,000	$36,700
Consulting, $	$3,000	3,500	5,000	0	3,000	3,500	18,000
Total Income, $	$3,350	$4,050	$ 6,200	$9,400	$15,200	$16,500	$54,700
Cost of Goods Sold							
Inventory Inputs, $	17	20	31	47	76	112	303
Gross Profit, $	3,333	4,030	6,169	9,353	15,124	16,388	54,397
Other Expenses							
Salaries, $	$4,000	$4,000	$5,000	$5,000	$5,000	$5,000	$28,000
Travel, $	2,304	365	558	846	1,368	1,104	6,545
Car Leases, $	1,000	1,000	1,000	1,000	1,000	1,000	6,000
Rent, $	900	450	450	450	450	450	3,150
Payroll Taxes, $	240	240	300	300	300	340	1,720
Insurance, $	0	0	0	1,450	0	0	1,450
Fuel/Maint., $	13	21	46	361	468	502	1,412
Benefits, $	350	350	350	350	350	350	2,100
Advertising, $	28	44	96	752	976	0	1,896
Utilities, $	174	213	208	189	132	188	1,104
Misc., $	67	81	124	188	304	764	1,528
Total Expenses	$ 9,093	$ 6,784	$ 8,163	$10,933	$10,424	$ 9,810	$ 55,208
Profit Before Taxes, $	(5,760)	(2,754)	(1,994)	(1,580)	4,700	6,578	($ 811)
Taxes, $	0.00	0.00	0.00	0.00	0.00	0.00	0.00
Profit After Taxes, $	($5,760)	($2,754)	($1,994)	($1,580)	$4,700	$ 6,578	($ 811)

Table 6.8
Example Income Statement for Computer Sales and Services Firm

Break-Even Analysis

break-even analysis
Tool for the estimation of when a business's income exceeds its expenses.

Now that you have developed a pro forma cash flow statement, income statement, and balance sheet for your proposed new venture, it is time to look at one additional analytical tool. The initial effort to project the cash flow is critical. However, the firm needs to extend this analysis. Specifically, what are the opportunities for the new venture to really generate significant returns for the owners? Individuals have numerous alternatives to starting a new venture, and we want to suggest that a **break-even analysis** of the projected position of the company will go a long way toward determining not only the viability of the new venture, but also the realistic assessment of whether this is the best path for the entrepreneur to embark upon. A break-even analysis provides some judgment about when the firm will reach a point of being self-sustaining after the business is begun.[7]

The break-even analysis recognizes that the growth in sales does not occur all at once. Instead, the sales of the business will grow incrementally once the firm starts. However, many of the expenses of the firm will start months before the first sale. Specifically, there are **fixed costs** (e.g., rent, utilities, equipment leases), which must be paid regardless of the sales level. There are also **variable costs** that will fluctuate according to how many goods are produced. For example, if you manufacture something packaged in plastic bottles, you will have increasing costs as you produce more products, since you will need more bottles.

fixed costs
Costs that must be paid no matter how many goods are sold, such as rent for the building.

variable costs
Costs that vary according to how many goods are produced.

The traditional Fortune 500 approach to break-even analysis would suggest that once revenues exceed the total of the fixed costs plus the variable costs, then the firm has reached breakeven. In this approach, the profit margin from each sale adds to the net profit for the firm. For firms operating in a project-by-project environment, this type of analysis is relatively effective. These firms are simply trying to compare an investment in one project to an investment in another, as shown in Figure 6.1.

However, entrepreneurial ventures need to operate in a fundamentally different manner, and we calculate breakeven using cash flow rather than profit. The initial investment in the new venture is an item of concern that is not normally included in most corporate cash flow analyses. Accounting for the initial investment allows the new firm to discuss the true economic returns, or economic benefits, from the business. (Recall that we discussed earlier that the entrepreneur wants to be sure that her business is providing the economic return she envisioned and that she is not working essentially for free.) Figure 6.2 demonstrates this relationship. We begin this diagram with an initial investment level. As the new firm begins operations, it is burning cash (from both a fixed- and a variable-cost standpoint) and reporting a negative net cash flow. Depending upon the venture and the industry in which it is operating, this negative cash flow can go on for some time. However, at some point a successful business turns the corner and begins producing positive cash flows. This has been called the break-even point for the company, that is, when the firm's costs equal its sales. However, we believe that until the new venture's positive cash flow exceeds the initial investment, **entrepreneurial breakeven** has not been achieved. This analysis can be further enhanced by taking into consideration the issue of time value of money.[8] There are other uses of your investment dollars and your raw time. With inflation, $1,000 received today is far more valuable than $1,000 will be if received 10 years from now. Thus, if you invest in a business today, you will want it to produce a return that is greater than the return you could have made if you simply had put the

entrepreneurial breakeven
When a new venture's net cash flow exceeds the initial investment plus the time value of the money invested.

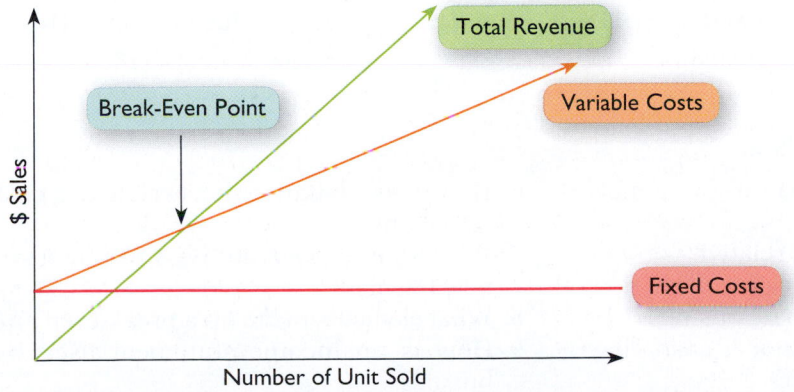

Figure 6.1
Classic Break-Even Diagram

Figure 6.2
Entrepreneurial Break-Even Diagram

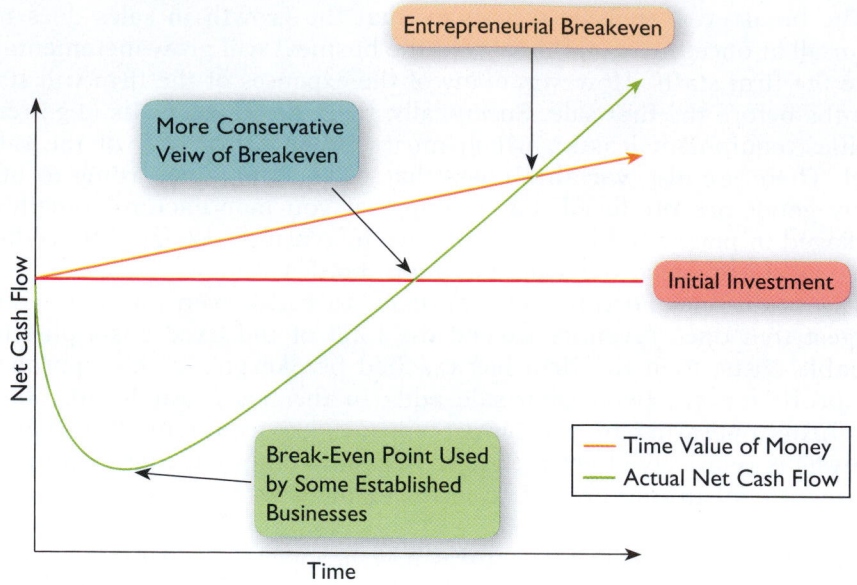

time value of money
The value of money over time at a given rate of inflation or other type of return. Calculated as the value of your investment in time and money if you did not do the proposed venture.

money in a savings account. Calculating the **time value of money** gives the initial investment line in Figure 6.2 an upward slope and creates an entrepreneurial break-even point that is farther out, but infinitely more realistic from an investor point of view.

SUMMARY

The decision process for starting a new entrepreneurial business is fraught with the unknown. This chapter has focused exclusively upon the analysis tools that are the most critical in determining the financial viability of the proposed new venture. A detailed examination of cash flow, its inputs, and its uses was provided. A brief examination of the balance sheet and income statement were provided, and finally we discussed the unique nature of an entrepreneurial break-even analysis.

KEY TERMS

balance sheet 111
break-even analysis 114
budget 101
cash flow 98
current assets 111
current liabilities 111
deviation analysis 104
entrepreneurial breakeven 115
equity 100
fixed assets 111
fixed costs 115
float 101
income statement 112
long-term liabilities 111
pro forma 111
sensitivity analysis 108
time value of money 116
variable costs 115

REVIEW QUESTIONS

1. Why is cash flow so important for a new business?
2. How are cash flow and profit related?
3. What are the basic elements of a cash flow statement for an entrepreneurial business?
4. Why is a budget statement not a cash flow statement? How do they differ?
5. How does float affect a cash flow statement?
6. How does a balance sheet relate to a cash flow statement?
7. Why is break-even analysis so important to a new business?
8. What elements make up a break-even analysis?
9. How is an income statement used by new business?

BUSINESS PLAN DEVELOPMENT QUESTIONS

1. You have all the basic tools now to create a projected cash flow statement for your proposed business. Categorize all of your income-generating areas and carefully develop a complete list of your expenses (review the list provided earlier in this chapter). Using the examples in this chapter, develop a six-month projection and then present it to a group of your peers.
2. Develop a break-even analysis for your business.

INDIVIDUAL EXERCISES

1. Talk to two entrepreneurs. Do they track cash flow? If so what is their view of cash versus profit in their business.
2. How long did it take these entrepreneurs to reach breakeven in their current business?
3. What was their advice on how conservative to be on the cash needed to start the business?

GROUP EXERCISES

1. Each person on the team should prepare a preliminary cash flow statement for his or her proposed venture. Look at each other's analysis and discuss what other revenue categories could be developed to better focus sales tracking?
2. Use an Internet search engine to look for SBA cash flow loans.
   a. What are the basic requirements of these loans?
   b. Why do you think the government supports such loans for entrepreneurial business?
   c. What insights does this provide each person on the team about his or her own proposed ventures?

ENDNOTES

1. J. Kelly and J. O'Connor, "Is Profit More Important Than Cashflow?" *Management Accounting* 75, no. 6 (1997), pp. 28–30.
2. D. Worrell, "Keeping Tabs on Cash Flow," *Entrepreneur* 37, no. 1 (2009), p. 32.
3. C. E. Chastain, S. Cianciolo, and A. Thomas, "Strategies in Cash Flow Management," *Business Horizons* 29, no. 3 (1986), pp. 65–74.
4. H. Whited, "Constructing a Cash Budget and Projecting Financial Statements: An Exercise of Short-Term Financial Planning for Entrepreneurs," *Review of Business and Financial Studies* 5 (2013), pp. 102–12.
5. K. Klein, "How Small Business Owners Can Cope with the Crisis," *BusinessWeek Online,* October 13, 2008, p. 14.
6. R. B. Lorance and R. V. Wendling, "Basic Techniques for Analyzing and Presentation of Cost Risk Analysis," *Cost Engineering* 43, no. 6 (2001), pp. 25–32.
7. J. M. Davis, "Project Feasibility Using Breakeven Point Analysis," *Appraisal Journal* 65, no. 1 (1998), pp. 41–47.
8. R. R. Crabb, "Cash Flow: A Quick and Easy Way to Learn Personal Finance," *Financial Services Review* 8, no. 4 (1999), pp. 269–83.

CREDITS

Opener: © iStockphoto.com/teekid RF; p. 97: Bob Fila/Chicago Tribune/MCT via Getty Images; p. 100: © Ingram Publishing/AGE Fotostock RF; p. 105: Nick Koudis/Getty Images RF; p. 113: John Lamb/Getty Images RF.

chapter

7

Financing and Accounting

learning objectives

After studying this chapter, you will be able to:

LO7-1 Identify key financial issues involved with starting a business.

LO7-2 Discuss the basics of funding a business.

LO7-3 Explain the importance of proper accounting when starting a business.

AEROPRESS

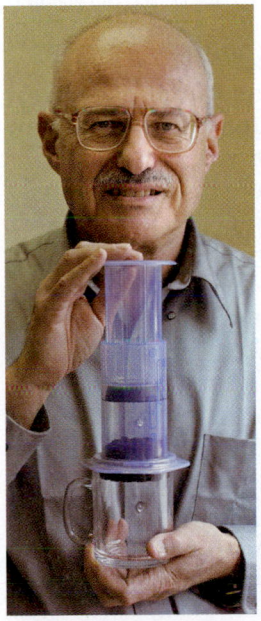

Alan Adler was always tinkering with new products. In the 1970s he was working as an engineer and a part-time instructor at Stanford University. At this time he would invent toy ideas in his garage and sell them to the big toy companies. Having taught himself how to sail and being fascinated with the aerodynamics of sailing, he wondered if there was a way to make a better flying disc. In 1984, he developed a far superior version of the flying disc that he called the Super Aerobie. The Super Aerobie made the 1986 *Guinness Book of World Records* for the farthest object thrown. It set the new record in 2003 at 1,333 feet. Ultimately he grew the business to an eight-person company in Palo Alto, California, called Aerobie. The firm focused on a variety of toys all built around taking advantage of aerodynamics. His firm ultimately became a leader in the disc golf movement.

However, Alan's frustration with coffee brought about a huge change in the life of this company. Alan was not a great fan of coffee because it would upset his stomach. He liked the taste, just not the acid. His fascination with making a better cup of coffee changed the whole company. After tinkering with more than 30 different prototypes, in 2004 he invented the AeroPress. The AeroPress uses air pressure and a plunger in much the same way that a French press coffee maker does, but forces the water through a filter at very high velocities to create a perfect cup of espresso in less than 30 seconds.

Fans of the AeroPress have created competitions around the world for the perfect cup of espresso using the product. Retailing at $26, the AeroPress now accounts for more than half the company's sales. Alan has over 40 patents to his name and, at age 75, the latest invention has taken his entrepreneurial venture in a whole new direction.

Questions

1. What other product areas would seem to fit with AeroPress's capabilities set?
2. How did Alan Adler's interest in brewing a better cup of coffee fit with the business?

Sources: http://aerobie.com/about.htm; http://aerobie.com/about/history.htm; C. Jung, "Invention Brews Good Coffee—Faster," *South Bend Tribune* (2006), http://articles.southbendtribune.com/2006-05-08/news/26971788_1_coffee-maker-espresso-filter; N. Summers, "Iterate, Iterate, Caffeinate," *Bloomberg Businessweek*, April 28, 2014, pp. 72–73.

Financing the start of a new business and establishing the accounting systems are central operational concerns in the start-up of a new business. In Chapter 6 we examined the basic financial analysis (on a pro forma basis) that should be used to evaluate the decision to start a business. The next issue to develop is the specific financing and accounting issues that impact the operational start-up of the business. Specifically, three questions are examined in this chapter:

1. How will the entrepreneur or entrepreneurial team fund the new business, and what funding level is really needed for the new venture?
2. What accounting records should be maintained, and how will they be maintained?
3. How should the business manage the paper and data flow of the new company?

All of these issues are directly related to the establishment of the financial structure and record keeping of the new company. Too often new businesspeople put these issues at the bottom of their priority list (both during and after start-up) and do not devote much time to them. However, it is far easier to establish items such as a sound system to account for the transactions of the business at the beginning of the venture. Some forethought on the process will save lots of frustration after the business is up and running.

LO7-1

Identify key financial issues involved with starting a business.

Key Financial Issues Involved with Starting a Business

There are a wide range of issues that new businesses need to be aware of that are related to financing of the start-up. The issues we address in this chapter are not ordered by their importance; instead these issues are intertwined with each other. The first is the funding and funding level of the firm. The next is the establishment of an accounting system. Finally, the flow of information in the new business needs specific attention. If the new business does not address all of these issues very early on in the process, then the owners will constantly be putting out fires related to these items rather than focusing on building the firm.

The experience of the founders of Friends' Home Health demonstrates the interconnection of a rich set of issues that any entrepreneurial firm faces. The owners were very concerned with their need for an effective means of accounting. This need really stood out when they realized they did not know the true cost of any individual service in their operation (an important issue in this business). In developing a bid for the hospital's work, the owners had not included the cost of hiring temporary workers to handle short-term increases in the number of patients, had not planned how to ensure the skills of those employees, nor how to account for the purchase of additional medical supply items that weren't in the plan for a standard patient. The opportunity to showcase their business as well as how to gain a larger, more consistent business as partners was not something they had originally addressed in their business plan. In effect, this opportunity would divert Friends' focus from its business plan during its first days of operation, a time at which the partners might not have a clear idea of what they were actually getting involved with. Whether this possible partnering with the hospital was really a good opportunity or not, was truly a question they couldn't answer. Entrepreneurial firms often face such opportunities—ones that may or may not be beneficial to the entrepreneur. However, the entrepreneur needs to evaluate clearly the pros and cons of any such major shift to their business plan.

FRIENDS' HOME HEALTH

Friends' Home Health was continuing on its path to make the new business a reality. The owners had established a banking relationship with the region's largest bank, found a place of business, and were working on obtaining the required business licenses for the firm, and the certifications for their employees. The two founders had left their employer by this time and, to help start cash flow for the firm, the two opened for business with just two home health patients that the owners handled personally. In the process of spending money and receiving invoices, the two founders quickly realized they needed a means to track their transactions. For the first few weeks they simply kept a classic accounting T-chart with all the expenses on one side and all the income (of which there was very little) on the other.

During this time they also received their first bank statement and, more importantly, a call from someone at a nearby hospital who had learned of their new operation. The hospital had decided to add home health care as part of their offering but wanted to partner with a local company to actually provide the services. The hospital had a policy of supporting local businesses and wanted to know if Friends' Home Health could handle the volume of patients the hospital expected to generate. They also wanted Friends' to consider being an exclusive partner with the hospital, which would mean they would only accept patients who were referred to them from the hospital.

The founders traveled to the hospital and worked out a deal to be the exclusive operator of the home health care operation for the hospital. On average, the hospital discharged 14 people per day who required home health care. The average patient needed this care for less than two weeks, but there would be patients who would require long-term care. The hospital wanted to announce the new arrangement as soon as possible and asked the founders of Friends' to be ready to start accepting patients within three weeks. The hospital agreed to handle all the medical payment processing for 10 percent of the total bill. In addition, they agreed to pay Friends' one-fourth of the total estimated weekly bill up front, with the remainder payable when the hospital was paid by the insurance company or government.

Betty and Joan were thrilled with the prospect of this business and went straight back to develop a plan. The founders initially thought they could run ads to hire workers. However, as they thought more about this, they realized they did not have time to hire workers and still develop the business they planned. The entrepreneurs still wanted to offer a differentiated service so the employees would need training. They contacted several temporary ("temp") agencies and began to realize that the potential employees from these agencies would still need to be trained, and further, they could not control for the quality of the potential employees. Betty and Joan found that their cost estimates were not accurate when they realized the hourly rate they were going to have to pay to get the workers from these agencies. Betty and Joan also were concerned that if they were a captive unit of the hospital they would not have the control they wanted of their business, nor would they necessarily capture the profits they wanted. In their position as a captive unit of the hospital, pricing and most key strategic decisions would most likely be determined by the hospital. Thus, the founders decided to not align with the hospital.

This episode made the entrepreneurs realize they did not have a full understanding of the potential costs they may face. The human resources issue above was simply one of many areas that they had to understand more fully. For example, the medical supplier they wanted to use for the goods for their patients had a policy regarding new businesses that required full payment up front for the first 90 days that they did business together. After that time period, the supplier would start extending a 2/10, net 30 policy to them (2/10 meant that Friends' could get a 2 percent discount on its purchases if the business paid its bill within 10 days, and if the bill was not paid during that 10 days, then the full amount would be due in 30 days).

Betty and Joan determined that they needed to track every item that they would use at each patient location so that they could tell if their plan for a 100 percent markup would in fact cover their other costs. The owners came to see that their business was a lot more complex than they had initially thought, and they needed to have a much better system to track all of their finances. The realities of the business were confronting them.

Betty and Joan called an accountant they found in the phone directory. This accountant told them that

(continued)

(Continued from previous page)

maintaining accurate records was going to be critical, and the sooner they got a computer accounting package and used it, the better. The accountant recommended a straightforward package that was available at most office supply stores and was easily understood. They quickly acquired the software and went about learning it and setting up all of the business records. The result was that they were learning how to use the system and seeking to adapt it to their needs while, at the same time, preparing to run the business.

QUESTIONS

1. What is your assessment of the potential deal the founders were offered by the hospital?
2. How important will inventory control be to this business? What do you recommend?
3. What do you think the most critical cash flow issues will be with the business as it is currently crafted? What do you recommend the founders do to manage cash flow?

Extra expenses, especially early on in a business's life when no (or virtually no) income is coming in, can quickly use up the cash intended to found and grow the business. By the time Friends' pays for all the additional expenses related to this opportunity, the business could well be out of cash. How much initial funding does a business need to survive the first year of operation? What type of financial cushion should be in place to help buffer the business when an unexpected cost such as the one facing Friends' arises? Central to a financial cushion is the nature of the firm's funding. When considering funding, the firm needs to evaluate not only the amount provided but also the sources of that funding. A key aspect of how the funding will be used is found in the information provided by the business, and that comes through the accounting system and the data flow management. Thus, all of these issues are interconnected and will be discussed in turn.

LO7-2

Discuss the basics of funding a business.

Basics of Funding a Business

Funding for almost any new business starts with the founder(s) and his or her personal resources. However, at some stage (often prior to actual start-up), the firm may need to find other sources of funding. These sources may be small and may or may not be tied to an equity (ownership) interest in return for the funding.

equity investment
Funds received by a business in exchange for a percentage ownership of the business.

crowdfunding
Funds received by a business by soliciting a large number of very small investors usually via the Internet.

In contrast, other investors will make **equity investments**, where someone provides funding in return for some ownership in the new business. Each of these types of funding will be reviewed in turn. First, we review those funding sources that do not require equity in the firm, followed by a review of equity investments, and wrap up with alternative sourcing tools, such as crowdsourcing and **crowdfunding**, that have become so popular.[1] Separately we will discuss a means for determining the actual amount of funding a new business should seek, to ensure it has sufficient resources at the outset of the business.

Non-Equity Funding

There are several sources for non-equity capital to start a business. Debt is a major source of such non-equity financing and can come from banks, credit cards, asset leasing companies, individuals, and/or suppliers. Grants are another type of non-equity funding to which some businesses may have access. A grant may come from the government or a nonprofit agency; it is simply money designed to help the new business begin operations with no expectation of repayment.

Debt. A firm can obtain **debt** in many forms, each with positives and negatives for a new business. Debt is any form of capital infusion that must be paid back with interest. Debt allows the new business to manage its cash flow through the various peaks and valleys in the operation of a business, or more importantly, to handle the disparity between when goods must be purchased and when money will be received from a customer to pay for those goods. The most common forms of debt for new businesses can be classified as follows:

debt
A generic term to describe any type of non-equity funding tied to the business.

1. Loans from
   a. Bank or finance company
   b. Individuals
   c. Founders
2. Credit cards
3. Supplier credit

Loans. A **loan**, regardless of its origin, involves a contractual agreement whereby the business receives some amount of money that must be repaid over a specified period of time at a specified interest rate. Loans are most often repaid monthly from cash flow and, especially early in the life of a business, are secured by assets or a personal guarantee. In the case of business failure, debt must be paid back prior to any equity investors receiving a distribution.

loan
Contractual agreement whereby the firm receives some amount of money that must be repaid over a specified period of time at a specified interest rate.

Banks have traditionally been a major source of funds for established firms but are quite restrictive in their lending to start-up firms, as the risk is perceived to be too high. However, there are some specific ways that banks lend to new businesses. For example, banks will make loans for the purchase of some types of equipment. In this type of lending, the bank will estimate the residual value of the equipment if the bank had to repossess the equipment and then lend the business a percentage of the difference between that number and the sale price. This discount is typically quite significant. This type of lending is referred to as **asset-based lending**. As will be discussed in Chapter 12, a relationship with a bank is critical to the new business's ability to obtain bank financing.[2]

asset-based lending
A loan provided for the purchase of a necessary asset for the business.

Banks will also lend money for the establishment and maintenance of inventory by arranging a revolving line of credit. A lender will periodically perform an on-site examination of the inventory to ensure that the inventory is being accounted for properly. A particular problem with lines of credit for inventory is that a firm may have old inventory that has not been sold for a period of time. Such inventory needs to be discounted, as its value in the market has shrunk. Too often firms still reflect that old inventory on their books at full market value.

A classic source of entrepreneurial finance is friends and family. Although the conditions for borrowing from friends and family may be a bit more relaxed, the new business owner should view the loan as he would one from a bank. One issue to consider in such loans is that if the business fails, the inability to repay such loans can permanently rupture the family relationship or friendship.

The founder(s) of the business may also choose to personally lend money to the new business. Even though it may strike some as odd to lend money to your own business, debt is a secured investment. Therefore, if you lend your firm $1,000, then you, along with the other debt holders, have the right to the firm's assets if the firm fails to pay off that debt. An equity investor generally receives only those proceeds that are left after paying off all other debts.

credit card
Card entitling one to revolving credit that is not tied to any particular asset, does not have a set repayment schedule, typically has a set upper limit, and is usually tied to a much higher interest rate than that of a bank loan.

Credit Cards. Credit cards are another form of non-equity investment. A **credit card** is simply another type of credit. However, a credit card is not tied to any particular asset, nor does it have a set repayment schedule (other than a minimum payment).

We have worked with a number of new businesses that decided early on to finance their operations with credit card debt. One new businessperson running an advertising agency would, when faced with a new bill for the company, go to the center desk drawer to look through more than 60 active credit cards to decide which one should be used to pay the bill. Not only is this a very poor management system that is extremely expensive, but it is also one where the debt is almost always tied personally to the founder(s), thus exposing them to personal bankruptcy. That said, credit cards can be a wonderful short-term method of managing your cash flow, especially during peak times in the early stages of the business. If paid off each month, business-issued credit cards provide the company with an excellent financial tracking system that can be divided up by individuals within the company, and payment can be delayed by up to 25 days, allowing for a unique positive cash flow situation. However, the new business must be able to manage such debt carefully if it is going to be employed. The interest rates can easily exceed 30 percent and will quickly bankrupt a firm if allowed to build.

What are the risks and rewards of using credit cards when financing a business?

supplier credit
Another form of non-equity funding that is available. Suppliers often will provide credit on both physical assets (refrigerators, molding equipment, etc.) and the actual supplies provided.

Supplier Credit. **Supplier credit** is another form of non-equity funding that is available.[3] Suppliers will generally provide credit on both physical assets (refrigerators, molding equipment, etc.) and the actual supplies purchased. A firm such as IBM Credit LLC is an example of a firm that you may be familiar with that exists primarily to fund the acquisition or lease of IBM products and services although they also finance purchases from other organizations. The credit terms offered by such firms can be quite generous, but they are a liability for the company and need to be managed as such. Accepting supplier credit can tie you to that supplier, limiting your ability to shop around for a cheaper source. The terms can be quite generous and the rates are usually more competitive than those available from traditional bank sources.

grants
Special funds that do not require repayment and are designed to aid businesses in specific areas.

Grants. The new business should also explore **grants** from both governmental and private foundation sources. There are special funds that are neither equity nor debt funds that are designed to aid businesses in specific areas. These grants typically target disadvantaged groups, economic areas, or particular industries. There are also grants for target groups such as veterans and women-owned businesses. The presence of such grants vary widely based on the given funding year and where you live. Grants should be explored through groups such as your local Small Business Assistance Center.

Equity Funding

The new business should employ all non-equity funding mechanisms available to it. In the long run (assuming a successful business operation), the cost of such capital is generally less than that of equity investment. However, a growing business might need to seek equity funding beyond founders' capital.

In the founding process, the business generally receives funds from the founder(s) as well as other investors. An evaluation is needed to determine the percentage of ownership each founder will have in the business and the percentage that will be reserved for investors. We will cover valuation of the business in Chapter 13, and we recommend that prior to allowing any nonfounder to invest in your new business, you have a fair and valid estimation of the value of your company. That said, we would like to address several key issues related to equity financing of the new business with outside sources.

Obtaining equity investment from investors has a number of potential operational impacts. Investors can be active or passive, majority or minority, companies that might ultimately wish to buy the whole new venture, and/or suppliers looking to add new volume for their products. Each of these potential sources has characteristics that can have a major impact on your business. Additionally, accepting an equity stake from an outside investor adds a dimension of accountability to the founding of a new business and opens the new venture up to new concerns. Therefore, seeking outside funding is a significant decision.

To illustrate the impact of outside investors, we worked with an entrepreneur who started a new high-end restaurant. The initial investment needed to make the venture work was substantial and well more than the founder could invest. She sought outside investors for the business from her country club, social friends, and business acquaintances. She ended up with 47 total investors with separate investments that varied from $8,000 to $110,000. The restaurant was built and opened to great fanfare. Thursday, Friday, and Saturday nights were packed, with an average wait for a table of two hours. The founder worked nonstop on those evenings, but had continuous problems with her fellow "investors."

A number of these investors believed that they deserved preferential treatment at the restaurant because they were "owners." Many of them demanded special favors, such as being placed first on the wait list for a table; walking through the kitchen with guests (not a helpful thing to do on busy nights); talking to the chefs about their ideas; or even having their meals "comped" (received for free). Some investors similarly felt free to discuss employee performance with the individual employees. These investors would also call at will to talk to the founder about the restaurant's direction, as well as expecting to be able to meet with the founder at their convenience.

The founder finally had a meeting with all of the investors to lay out the problems involved with their behavior and the disruption to the success of the business. Several of the investors were indignant and demanded their investment be returned. This was not something that the business could afford at this early stage, and legally it did not have to comply with their request. The result was fractious relations with some investors, and an enormous amount of time being taken away from the business to handle "bruised egos." A little care in the initial setup of these relations could have prevented a series of problems later in the operation. Eventually each of the upset investors was bought out and all of the other investors agreed to end their disruptive behavior.

Equity investment traditionally involves selling a percentage of the business to an outside party. This should be done in consultation with an attorney who is well versed in this area of the law. The founder(s) must be very clear that in the case of dissolution, each investor is entitled to the percentage of the break-up value (after all debts and obligations are paid) equal to their investment percentage of ownership. However, even more critical to the success of the business is to carefully and clearly outline what rights and expectations each investor has as the business grows. Equity investment does not necessarily carry with it an equivalent percentage of control in the firm. An entrepreneur needs to clearly specify how ownership will be handled. Similarly, the entrepreneur needs to clearly specify how the profits of the business will be handled. Will the new venture divide up all profits at the end of each year? What will be retained in the business for future growth? How can each investor "sell" his or her shares? Does the company have first right of refusal in any share sale? Working with an attorney to develop a clear document that details all of the concerns about an equity investment should be completed prior to approaching a potential investor.

As previously mentioned, the sources of equity investment include other firms, venture capitalists, and business angels.

Businesses as Equity Investors. Many established businesses are willing to make equity investments in other start-up firms. Large firms such as Microsoft, Intel, and Cisco have traditionally been among the most active equity investors in new start-up firms in the technology sector; corporate venture capital from these firms is actually one of the leading sources of venture capital in the United States. (Venture capital is discussed in greater detail below.) There are two scenarios that we have dealt with regularly in the funding from such firms. The first involves a company that will invest in a new venture with the idea of ultimately purchasing the operation. The second type is a large supplier that is willing to invest in a new operation as an additional outlet for its products.

The company that invests with the idea of an ultimate purchase does so because it is one of the least expensive means for trying out new ideas/products/methods and for maintaining access to the latest thinking in the field. For the established company to try to develop every idea in-house, it would have to redirect significant resources away from the core focus of its business. Instead, the large business invests in a series of businesses that are trying new things within its industry, and in effect, it has taken out a series of strategic options without having to detract from its core business.[4] Those options that turn out to be successes are then purchased and brought into the core organization. This can be a wonderful harvest strategy for the entrepreneur to capture the value in a newly founded business; however, the founder(s) may not wish to sell the business at the exact point in time that the larger company wishes to close the sale. Depending on the nature of the investment, the founder(s) may not have the option to decide when the business is sold.

Intel is an active equity investor in start-up firms. What are the pros and cons of equity investment from a firm like Intel in a new small business?

Having a supplier invest in your new business is somewhat simpler, in that the supplier is generally not trying to run your business, nor looking to take the business over if it does particularly well. Instead, the issue with this type of equity investment is one of restriction. The deal usually involves an exclusivity agreement to use only that supplier's products. This can be a significant (and in some cases a business-killing) proposition. The founder(s) must be careful not to trap themselves into an agreement that prevents flexibility that may be needed in the future.

Venture Capital (VC). A form of equity investment that seems to garner considerable press because of the sheer size of their investments is venture capital. A **venture capital fund** is a fund that is usually organized as a limited partnership.[5] Limited partners in the fund, which may include very wealthy individuals, insurance companies, other businesses, and retirement funds, invest in such funds seeking high returns. The general partner in the fund is the venture capitalist, who then investigates and invests in each new

venture capital fund
A fund that is organized to make significant equity investments in high-growth new ventures.

business. Venture capitalists might invest in less than one out of the thousand business plans they see in a year. They are seeking extremely high-growth businesses that have an opportunity to "cash out" with an IPO or sale to a larger company within a set period of time. VCs are looking to make a significant investment, generally something greater than $2 million. As such, they are not a source of funding for very many new businesses, and we spend very little time in this text on venture capital.*

Business Angels. Business angels are a form of equity investors that are more widely available to new businesses. **Business angels** are high-net-worth individuals that invest widely in businesses.[6] These individuals may include entrepreneurs who have built one or more businesses and have cashed out (i.e., sold their businesses and have the excess cash in hand), executives with large organizations that have high incomes, professionals such as doctors and lawyers, and individuals with significant inheritances. These individuals can be very helpful sources of expertise and contacts in the area. However, the new businessperson should seek individuals who have relevant knowledge (not just money) to add to the firm. When seeking investment from such individuals, we suggest that you evaluate the nature of their advice, how intrusive they will be, the nature of their business experience, and what other contacts and relationships the angels may have that can help the new firm.

business angels
High-net-worth individuals who invest in businesses not as a business, but as an individual.

Crowdfunding. Crowdfunding is a relatively new means for raising capital that may result in either an equity approach or an in-kind exchange for the firm. Companies seeking to raise capital without using the traditional approaches have found that the Internet is an excellent means to try to reach out to potential investors.[7] Internet sites such as Kickstarter.com, EquityNet.com, Indiegogo.com, and others have systematized the process. Entrepreneurs seeking capital make their pitch on the site and let potential investors know what they will receive for their funding. This might be equity (depending upon the size of the investment), but is more often a product/service, or gift.[8]

Other Financing Tools

Several other financing tools are available to the new business as it starts. These mechanisms include asset leasing and factoring.

Asset Leasing. A form of funding for a new organization is an **asset lease** arrangement. Similar to leasing a car, many of the assets needed by the new business can be leased from the manufacturer, or from a third-party reseller. Instead of owning the assets, the company simply leases what it needs. In fact, there are companies (third-party resellers) that have a significant part of their inventory in equipment that they lease to other companies. The advantages are relatively straightforward. The new business is able to acquire the assets that it needs to begin operations with a minimal cash outlay. The company pays the lease from production that is a direct result of using the equipment that it has leased. Furthermore, it is not stuck with an aging asset. As newer, higher-quality machines become available, the entrepreneur is able to trade up.

asset lease
A form of lease tied to a particular asset used by a business to conserve cash and maintain the latest versions of whatever equipment is available.

The big disadvantage to leasing is that over time the new business may spend more money for the equipment than if it had bought the unit outright. However, the net present value of the lease may actually work out to a net positive as the new businessperson does not have to put as much cash initially into the lease as in a purchase. Therefore, the decision maker

*If the student wishes to locate more information on venture capital and venture capitalists in his or her area, the National Venture Capital Association is an excellent source of information.

should evaluate two areas: (1) How much cash does the new business have to invest in equipment up front? and (2) Given the pace of equipment obsolescence in that industry, would it be more advantageous to lease or own the equipment needed to operate the business?

Factoring. With the exception of new businesses that operate strictly on cash, as the business begins to make sales it will generate accounts receivable—that is, sales that have been made, but not yet paid for. If the firm needs to generate cash in the short run, these accounts can be sold at a discount via a technique known as **factoring**. Numerous businesses provide this service. They will discount the dollar amount of such accounts based on the quantity and quality of the receivables. The quality of the receivables is determined by such issues as: (1) who owes the new business money; (2) the debt age; (3) the size of the transaction; and (4) the debtor's credit rating. For example, if a blue-chip firm such as ExxonMobil or a government entity owes you the money, there is a virtual 100 percent chance of being paid. In contrast, if your accounts receivables are from a small building contractor (an industry segment with a considerable history of turnover), then the accounts will be more heavily discounted. The benefit for the entrepreneur is that the new business gets the money from the accounts receivable immediately. Aside from obtaining the cash up front, the new business does not have to spend time and effort trying to collect the accounts receivable. The negative is that the new business will not receive the full amount of the debt that is due to it.

factoring
Accounts receivable that are sold at a discount to another company to receive immediate cash.

Initial Funding

The new businessperson needs to calculate how much money will be needed to start up the business. Although it would appear that more initial funding would be somewhat better than less, it must be tempered by what the founder has to give up to obtain the money. In Chapter 6 we examined the financial issues associated with breakeven and basic cash flow analysis. The complexity of capital funding increases substantially as the new business requires external investment to begin operations.

To calculate the maximum amount that you may wish to obtain in outside financing, recall from Chapter 6 that we recommend the entrepreneur calculate the entire cash flow projection without adding in any equity investment and look for the point where the ending cash balance is at its lowest point. A safe rule of thumb suggests taking that number and multiplying it by 150 percent. The resulting amount is what we recommend for the initial equity or equity-plus-debt investment. The new businessperson then connects this amount with the percentage of the firm that was previously determined would be made available to other investors. The two points frame the new businessperson's investment parameters. Consider the following example:

Value of the Firm Prior to Beginning Operations (See Chapter 14)	$100,000
Lowest Point in Projected Cash Flow	$ 20,000
Required Investment	$ 30,000
Amount Invested by Founder	$ 10,000
Amount Needed from Outside Investors	$ 20,000
Potential Percentage of the Business to Be Expected by Investors (20,000/100,000)	**20%**

It is important to remember that negotiations between the founder(s) and your investor are just that, negotiations. It takes two willing parties to reach an agreement. You may see the investment in your firm as worth X, whereas an investor sees it as worth Y. It will take negotiation to determine the ultimate value. A review of Chapter 13's discussion of valuation and negotiation should be helpful in conceptualizing these issues.

EXERCISE 1

1. How much funding will you need for your new business?
2. How do you plan to fund the new business?
3. What assumptions have you made regarding your funding?

Importance of Proper Accounting When Starting a Business

LO7-3

Explain the importance of proper accounting when starting a business.

We do not presume in the next few pages to show you how to do all of the accounting that you will ever need to know to manage your business. There are many fine texts and courses available that focus tightly on this huge and complicated area of business. Furthermore, we covered the basics regarding the balance sheet and income statement in Chapter 6. That said, we would like to suggest that the needs of most new entrepreneurs are very straightforward and can best be met with one of the numerous computer software programs available.

The new businessperson will need to quickly decide whether she will use a cash- or accrual-basis accounting system. In its simplest form, cash-based accounting recognizes expenses as they are paid and recognizes revenue as it is generated. Accrual-based accounting is the more typical form of accounting used, with expenses and revenues recorded when they actually occur, regardless of when the cash is received. Accrual accounting must be used if you have inventory; if you have to report your financial statements; and if your business is a Subchapter C corporation, partnership, or trust. The end result is that only the smallest businesses use cash-basis accounting.

The new businessperson will need to carefully evaluate which accounting program would be the best for his business. Choosing a package that will be useful for your business is a process of understanding your new business first and then finding a package that will accommodate your needs with the least impact on the business. Most of the packages will provide any report that could be demanded by the owner(s), potential investors, auditors, or loan officers. Some of the key reports that the new

ETHICAL CHALLENGE

You have seen in this chapter that there are different types of investors, and there can be different levels of investment. These investors come into the business facing potentially different types of risk and return.

QUESTIONS

1. Think about and discuss the ethical obligations you have to early-stage investors versus later-stage investors. Do you promise more returns to someone who shows faith in you at an earlier stage?
2. What are the ethical obligations if some investors are family members and some are not? Do family members deserve different investor treatment?

businessperson should be prepared to generate include these: (1) chart of accounts, (2) petty cash register, (3) check register, (4) expense accounts, (5) inventory accounts, (6) accounts payable, and (7) payroll.

Chart of Accounts

The chart of accounts is the master system for tracking the activity of the business. It requires a bit of care up front in its establishment and will need updating as the business grows. This chart is not complex; however, the new businessperson needs to ensure that the system designed provides the information necessary to analyze the business and its performance. This topic will be discussed more in Chapter 8 as we examine business performance of the going concern and ensure that the firm is performing as desired.

A chart of accounts is simply a listing of each type of activity (income or expense) and each type of asset within the company. The account number used is completely at your discretion, but income categories are usually first, expense categories next, and asset categories last. You may use two-digit or three-digit numbers as you wish and in accordance with the level of detail you anticipate in the future. There are usually far more expense categories than there are income categories. Table 7.1 shows the chart of accounts of an electronics manufacturer, which displays some of the expense categories for the firm.

The new businessperson will want to leave room for new account detail to be put into the chart of accounts. As the business develops, you will find that you want to obtain additional detail, as new income/expense categories will appear. Notice that the chart tracks not only income and expense accounts but also asset accounts.

EXERCISE 2

1. Develop a preliminary chart of accounts for your new business.
2. Have fellow classmates review the chart and add or delete as necessary.

Table 7.1
Chart of Accounts—Electronics Manufacturer

ACCOUNT NUMBER	CATEGORY	ACCOUNT NUMBER	CATEGORY
10	Basic Tube	142	Office Supplies—Other
20	Premium Tube	150	Internet Supplier
30	Basic Service	160	Auto Leases
40	Unlimited Service	170	Insurance
101	COGS*—Wooden Tubes	180	Advertising
102	COGS—Diodes	200	Payroll
103	COGS—Circuit Boards	201	Benefits
104	COGS—Resistors/Capacitors	210	Telephone (Cell and Office)
105	COGS—End Caps	220	Licenses
106	COGS—Packaging	300	Production Machinery
107	COGS—Shipping	310	Tools
120	Utilities	400	Building Mortgage
130	Security System	500	Payroll Taxes
140	Paper	510	State Taxes
141	Letterhead/Business Cards	520	Federal Taxes

*Note: COGS = cost of goods sold.

Petty Cash Register

There are numerous expenses that are simply too small to write a check for, and there are times when a check is simply inappropriate (for example, if you had pizza delivered for everyone because the whole group was working late to meet a deadline). A petty cash fund operates much like a bank savings account. The founder purchases a small lockbox and writes a check to "Petty Cash" for whatever amount they would like to keep on hand (this is not the same as cash register money, which should be handled as a separate deposit/expense account). A register is maintained to track the amount of money in the box, much like a savings account register. For example, if you decide that $100 is the amount that you would like to have on hand, you would start the box off with $100. As withdrawals are made, each is recorded and all change is put back in the box. The founder should be able to glance at the register and know exactly how much money is in the petty cash fund at any point in time, as well as know how the money has been spent. As it depletes, a new check should be written to "Petty Cash" to fill the box back up to the $100 level.

Check Register

As simple as it sounds, it is important to create a listing of all checks that have been written and all that have cleared through the bank. Today, with online banking and the ability to transfer data directly, this process has become quite easy. Regardless of how the entrepreneur might maintain her personal checking account, it is very important to record and balance the company account on at least a monthly basis.

A young woman looking at the First Direct Bank website. Online banking is not only efficient but convenient.

Expense Accounts

Depending on the volume of business that your venture processes, you will have either a daily or a weekly listing of expenses. These will allow the entrepreneur to perform a monthly tracking of expenses and ultimately form an annual record of all expenses. The process requires you to have both your check register and your petty cash register available to record all outflow of funds. Credit card payments should be handled by recording the interest as an interest expense, recording the payment made to the account, and then recording each line item with a notation of "Visa," "MC," "Am. Ex.," and so on, next to the expense. The only other expenses that are truly handled in a different manner are those related to travel. The IRS has very specific requirements related to the record keeping necessary to deduct these expenses. You should be sure to familiarize yourself with the latest rules regarding these expenses.

Inventory Account

Any business that has even a small inventory should maintain an inventory record that lists a description of the item, the quantity, an item number, a unit cost, and a total cost. Inventory should be taken at scheduled times during the year and an exact match should be completed between starting inventory, units sold, and ending inventory. A second record should be kept to track inventory ordered and inventory received. It is a fact of business that **shrinkage** will occur. This reduction in inventory can come from poor record keeping on any of the fronts mentioned previously, but can also result from either employee or customer theft.

shrinkage
The difference between what is sold and what was brought into the business.

Accounts Payable

A separate accounts payable record should be maintained for each creditor. All invoices received should be recorded and a record of payment toward each invoice should be included (Date Paid, Amount Paid, and Check Number/Transfer Tracking Number).

Payroll

A payroll record should be maintained for every employee, tracking time for hourly employees and attendance for exempt (salaried) employees. Additionally, an employee record should be maintained that tracks every payroll check (electronically or in paper form) issued to the employee. This record will list all of the items that make up the check:

- Date
- Check number
- Number of hours worked (or 40, for exempt employees)
- Base pay
- Overtime hours worked
- Overtime pay rate
- Gross pay
- Taxes (federal, state, local, Social Security, and Medicare)
- Benefit deductions (if appropriate)
- Net pay

Table 7.2
Profit and Loss Statement

PROFIT AND LOSS STATEMENT					
Period:			Month		
Income, $	Gross Sales		$114,560.00		
	Less COGS		34,900.00		
	Net Sales			79,660.00	
	Other Income			13,400.00	
	Total Income			**$93,060.00**	
Expenses, $	Acct No.	120	$ 1,084.00		
	Acct No.	130	35.00		
	Acct No.	140	110.00		
	Acct No.	141	320.00		
	Acct No.	142	45.00		
	Acct No.	150	79.00		
	Acct No.	160	1,340.00		
	Acct No.	170	367.00		
	Acct No.	180	1,100.00		
	Acct No.	200	47,900.00		
	Acct No.	201	14,370.00		
	Total			66,750.00	
	Misc. Expenses			1,780.00	
	Total Expenses			**$68,530.00**	
	Profit (Pretax)				**$24,530.00**

Accounting software packages the entrepreneur may buy have the ability to produce all of these records plus many more. These become both the control records and the input records to produce your financial statements (Cash Flow, Balance Sheet, and Statement).

One additional statement is a must-have for most businesses and comes directly from the effective collection of all this information: the **profit and loss statement (P&L statement)**. This statement represents your business performance over time. It is a brief, easily understood document that should be prepared monthly. An example is shown in Table 7.2.

profit and loss statement (P&L statement)
A financial statement that summarizes the revenues, costs, and expenses incurred during a specific period of time.

Developing and maintaining effective records is essential in the operation of a business, and some forethought to the process and needs of the business will pay off in the knowledge and understanding developed by the founder(s). We will examine a number of analysis tools in Chapter 8, but for analysis to have any value, good records must be kept.

Managing Data Flow

The entrepreneur needs to recognize that new businesses will differ in the time frames that they need to obtain data based on their industry and experience. The founder(s) should seek to visit with other similar firms and find out what reasonable time frames might be for the monitoring of data. The experience of other firms can be very helpful in the start-up phase of your business.

Well-established firms have aggressively moved to using just-in-time (JIT) inventory. This method of inventory control seeks to minimize excess capital investment in inventory. These firms seek to have inventory present only shortly before it is used. New firms do not have the

FLOW RIGHT BREWERY & BAR: A FAMILY AFFAIR

Chris spent several weeks visiting an extensive line of relatives and friends of the family. Over that period of time, he was able to put together the entire $500,000 he estimated he needed to purchase the business and ensure its survival for the first year. He had managed to raise the money with just eight investors. Three of the investors put in $100,000 each, which was the same amount that Chris and his wife were investing financially in the business. The other four investors each put in $25,000. Chris took a 25 percent stake in the business; the three $100,000 investors each took a 20 percent stake, while the four $25,000 investors each got just 3 percent. The remaining 3 percent was held out to use in the future as incentives for valuable employees.

Having cleared that hurdle, Chris faced a significant issue in the design of statements and tracking of funds in the business. He had no formal accounting training, and during several conversations with other entrepreneurs he had been told repeatedly to purchase an accounting software package—which he did. Not knowing what he might need for the business, Chris decided to just set up some rudimentary categories and then add new ones as he needed.

The business was developing nicely. Even though the location came with a lot of equipment, Chris was excited about the opportunity to buy the remaining things that he thought he needed on the used market. One of the beer distributors told him about a big, national chain restaurant that had closed less than 90 miles away. Chris contacted the agent handling the dissolution and was able to buy some excellent furniture that he really wanted for the business.

As the equipment, furniture, and supplies began arriving, Chris was simply too busy trying to set everything up to spend time entering all of the information into his accounting package. He wasn't worried because he had a good head for numbers and knew that he was right on track for what he had predicted for the business. He thought that he might ask his wife to enter the information from the invoices over the weekend. When he and his wife took a look at the invoices, the two of them quickly realized that Chris's temporary system was not working. There were bills that did not appear to be accurate, but no one had asked about them when the shipment of supplies came in. Similarly, there were a few bills that had already gone past due.

EXERCISE 3

1. How could Chris have done a better job setting up the accounting system?
2. What kind of data flow system should Chris use to track his business?

same complex data measurement methods of large firms, but they should be driven by the same basic philosophy. The key to this ability is obtaining data in a timely manner that is tied to the strategic needs of the organization. We worked with a restaurant that wanted to serve fresh vegetables and meats; however, the owner wanted to perform his inventory check only once a week. "Freshness" as a strategic position would dictate that the data collection cycle should be shortened. If deliveries are constant, then a high-turnover firm should monitor its inventory needs on a daily or every-other-day basis. The accounting system of a firm is a powerful tool asset that should be used as a fine-grained tool to provide data about when and how inventory is needed.

SUMMARY

This chapter examined two important operational issues directly tied to the start-up of a new venture. Obtaining sufficient initial funding is a key method to allow for the variances inherent in any business. We examined several means of obtaining that financing. We then examined the development of the firm's accounting system and method of data gathering and handling. Establishment of a quality method for data gathering at the outset will allow the founders to focus their efforts on the running of the business.

KEY TERMS

asset-based lending 123
asset lease 127
business angels 127
credit card 124
crowdfunding 122
debt 123
equity investment 122
factoring 128
grants 124
loans 123
profit and loss (P&L) statement 133
shrinkage 131
supplier credit 124
venture capital fund 126

REVIEW QUESTIONS

1. How can using loans help the new business grow?
2. Explain the best use of credit cards in a new business operation.
3. What are the negative impacts of supplier credit on the new business start-up?
4. How can a new business take advantage of grants?
5. Why should a new businessperson be wary of equity investments by other companies?
6. How will venture capital impact a growing business?
7. What are the pros of having angel investors in a new business?
8. How can asset leases be used to improve the income generation of a new business?
9. Why might a business choose to factor its accounts?
10. How might an entrepreneur find out how much a business is worth?
11. What factors impact how much equity a new business gives away for a set dollar investment?
12. How does a new businessperson use a P&L statement?
13. Why should a new business spend time setting up a chart of accounts?

BUSINESS PLAN DEVELOPMENT QUESTIONS

1. At this point in your business development, what mix of equity and debt are you planning on using? Why?
2. Develop a plan for fundraising. Make a list of who you will approach and why.
3. Create a potential chart of accounts for the new business.

INDIVIDUAL EXERCISES

1. Given the needs of your business, examine at least two widely available accounting packages and choose one for your business.
2. Why did you choose that one and not one of the others?
3. How robust is the package that you chose? Will it still be useful if your sales reach $1 million per year?

GROUP EXERCISES

In a group, take one of the companies that a group member is designing (or alternatively, use the Flow Right Brewery & Bar) and set up a spreadsheet in Excel (or other similar program) that will form the basic accounting system for the company. To follow are suggestions for such a project.

1. Start with the Cash Flow Statement:
   a. Create a worksheet (tabs) for each of the 12 months and label each one.
   b. Enter all sources of income and all expenses that you can think of for January.
   c. Put in a formula to subtract expenses from income and determine the net cash flow.
   d. Copy January's data to the other 12 months and then modify any month that needs to be adjusted. Remember, this is just the start of the effort. You will have plenty of time to modify this spreadsheet as you develop the company.
   e. Create formulas on the Summary sheet to capture the data from the 12 months.
2. Repeat this process and create a Cash Budget.
3. Repeat this process again to create an Income Statement.

ENDNOTES

1. R.J. Shiller, "Capitalism and Financial Innovation," *Financial Analysts Journal* 69, no. 1 (January/February 2013), pp. 21–25.
2. R. Cole, L. Goldberg, and L. White, "Cookie Cutter vs. Character: The Micro Structure of Small Business Lending by Large and Small Banks," *Journal of Financial & Qualitative Analysis* 39 (2004), pp. 227–52.
3. N. Wilson and B. Summers, "Trade Credit Terms Offered by Small Firms: Survey Evidence and Empirical Analysis," *Journal of Small Business Finance & Accounting* 29 (2002), pp. 317–52.
4. R. McGrath, "A Real Options Logic for Initiating Technology Positioning Investments," *Academy of Management Review* 22, no. 4 (1997), pp. 974–96.
5. D. DeClercq, V. Fried, O. Lehtonen, and H. Sapienza, "An Entrepreneur's Guide to the Venture Capital Galaxy," *Academy of Management Perspectives* 20, no. 3 (2006), pp. 90–112.
6. S. Prowse, "Angel Investors and the Market for Angel Investments," *Journal of Banking & Finance* 22 (1998), pp. 785–83.
7. Crowdsourcing Industry, "Will the Rise of Crowdsourcing and Crowdfunding Help Unemployed Young Americans?" www.crowdsourcing.org/editorial/will-the-rise-of-crowdsourcing-and-crowdfunding-help-unemployed-young-americans/32881
8. E. Weitzman, "Crowdfunding Sites Are Making Hard-to-Finance Indie Films Easier to Achieve," *New York Daily News*, July 13, 2014, www.nydailynews.com/entertainment/movies/crowdfunding-indie-films-easier-finance-article-1.1859003

CREDITS

Opener: Glow Images RF; p. 119: Rick E. Martin/KRT/Newscom; p. 124: © Comstock Images RF; p. 126: © Intel Corporation; p. 131: © David J. Green/Alamy.

chapter

8

Comparative Stock Performance
Dow Jones Industrial Average
News
Portfolio
Mibtel News
Security
Jul. 2008
Aug. 2008

Financial Analysis

learning objectives

After studying this chapter, you will be able to:

LO8-1 Describe the importance of a solid financial foundation in an entrepreneurial business.

LO8-2 Discuss techniques for measuring performance.

LO8-3 Explain ratio analysis.

LO8-4 Explain deviation analysis.

LO8-5 Explain sensitivity analysis.

LO8-6 Describe the use of short surveys in business.

LO8-7 Analyze the importance of having a measurement focus.

VAVAVROOMONLINE.COM

As Bank of America was getting ready to take over LaSalle Bank, the executives from LaSalle had some big decisions to make about what they would do in the future. For Denise Maple, it was a no-brainer: Take a buyout from Bank of America, which was being offered to reduce the staff at the acquired bank and hit the open road on her new, dual-sport motorcycle. The former vice president for corporate development also became an entrepreneur, investing $31,000 in VaVaVroomonline.com, a Chicago start-up that sells hoodies and snug, multicolored riding tops she helped design, alongside accessories and apparel of other brands.

Even though motorcycle sales overall had declined at the time, the number of female buyers had increased 20 percent since 2003. In 2008 she told *BusinessWeek*, "I saw a need in the market. When I started riding five years ago, there was almost no motorcycle gear in women's sizes, let alone with style." "The company's most famous T-shirt says 'I'm one of those girls.'" The business is helping to unite women who ride to not only buy on the firm's website but form a community in which they share their stories and thoughts. The women are often professionally successful and find they have to challenge the norms of society and its thoughts on who a motorcyclist is. Serving a profitable niche, VaVaVroom had 2013 revenues of less than $500,000.

Questions

1. There is evidence that women are more likely to be entrepreneurs than men. What do you think drives most women entrepreneurs to form their own businesses?
2. Do you think Denise Maple is driven by this same motivation?
3. If you were to start an Internet clothing business, what would you propose to focus on? What could you learn about success by looking at VaVaVroom as a model?

Sources: "America's Most Promising Startups: For Cool Biker Chicks," reprinted from *BusinessWeek* (July 7, 2008) on VaVaVroomonline.com; "Denise Bio—VaVaVroom.com," www.vavavroomonline.com/index.php/denise/; "Manta," www.manta.com/c/mt4ptbs/vavavroom; "MIC Forecasts Decline in U.S. Motorcycle Sales for 2012," http://blog.motorcycle.com/2012/03/15/industry-news/mic-forecasts-decline-in-us-motorcycle-sales-for-2012/; "VaVaVroom Races to Fashion," *Sport Rider Magazine*, www.sportrider.com/vavavroom-races-to-fashion-cafe-style

With the new business up and running, the focus of the firm shifts from developmental activities to day-to-day operations. In starting a successful business, good initial development is important, but perhaps as important are the efforts of the business as it grows. Once in operation, the business exists within the competitive marketplace and is subject to competitive attack, customer response to the product offering, supplier problems, inventory management issues, collections issues, and more. No operating business ever matches the proposed business exactly. The reality of operations and the ability to adjust to those realities is the key to managing a successful business. Adjusting requires an in-depth analysis of the firm's progress, particularly its financial progress.[1]

LO8-1

Describe the importance of a solid financial foundation in an entrepreneurial business.

Importance of a Solid Financial Foundation in an Entrepreneurial Business

The evaluation of a firm starts with the mission of the organization and is (as was pointed out in Chapter 5) always relative to the industry in which the firm competes. The key measures of the firm should focus on the key aspects with which the firm hopes to build its competitive advantage. For example, if the mission of the organization is to be a low-cost operation, then rigorous control of expenses would be the focus. This would suggest that very little money would be spent in such activities as research and development, or new product introductions. The firm's outcomes would be measured at intervals that were relevant to the business, which, in the case of evaluating cost savings, might mean measuring such items very frequently, perhaps even daily. To illustrate, consider a restaurant that plans to have broccoli as a side dish this week and receives its order of fresh broccoli on Monday. Unfortunately the sales of broccoli during the week are significantly less than expected. If the firm accurately monitors its broccoli supply, it can determine that it needs to offer broccoli soup as an option on Thursday and Friday. Hopefully this will result in a significant reduction in the waste of the broccoli. (The development of potato skins as a snack food that appears at so many restaurants is a direct result of the way the potatoes that were used for mashed potatoes from the prior day were used to prevent wastage.) Poor monitoring of the situation will result in waste for the business and the same mistake being made week after week.

In this chapter we will examine the development of the various metrics (measures) that should be used to evaluate the business. These analytical techniques are easily available and readily understandable by any business owner.

LO8-2

Discuss techniques for measuring performance.

Techniques for Measuring Performance

There is virtually an unlimited number of items upon which you could perform an analysis of your business, its activities, and its performance. However, taking the time to do this analysis means time away from running the business, and we therefore like to limit the analysis to those areas that are critical to the business's ability to make real profits. Any company analysis, large or small, should proceed from the general and move toward

FRIENDS' HOME HEALTH

Friends' Home Health Care had been in business for almost six months when the founders realized they needed a major change in operations. Although Friends' Home Health Care sold goods to the patients, the entrepreneurs found that often the level of what was sold did not equal the amount that had been bought by the firm; an insight working with their accountant helped to identify. The entrepreneurs did not think people were stealing from them, but they did think employees were being sloppy in recording what was being supplied. Currently the system is very simple: the employees write down what they take from the storeroom and to whom the good is to be charged. That information is entered into their accounting software each week. But it is clear that the system is not working. After pondering the alternatives, the founders decided they would buy a new software package for the computer system in which employees would scan the goods as they were removed from the storeroom. If they did not report which client used the goods, then they personally would be charged for the items. Betty and Joan intended to be in business to stay and wanted to have the best operating system for such goods as possible.

Through a well-known businessperson and personal friend, the founders arranged to meet with the national sales representative from the leading supplier of such software. The system they desired cost approximately $75,000 as they needed both the software and the assorted equipment for scanning the goods. However, rather than closing the deal that night, the saleswoman seemed almost hesitant. The next day the personal friend of the founders and the saleswoman came to see Betty and Joan.

The friend began to question the entrepreneurs as to whether they could really afford the total package they had picked out. The friend asked pointed questions about their true returns and whether this included the cost of capital. What was the depreciation on their existing equipment? What was the nature of the financing they would rely on for the new system? When this friend asked the owners to think about whether they actually were profitable, they realized they had performed no real analysis of the business to date. They had customers and their checking account had maintained a nice balance; they were making payroll every month; they had money to make the payments on their loans; and they felt that things were good. Unfortunately, they didn't really know how much profit they were making, nor did they really know if the business could continue to expand. The reason that the mutual friend had come to ask these hard questions was that the salesperson selling the system had told him she had seen the scenario many times. A new business starts to do particularly well and the founders decide to splurge. However, too often the owners of the business are not making as much money as they believe they are, and the new system contributes to the business failing. As a salesperson, she felt she could not say she would not sell them the system, but she had asked their mutual friend to visit with Betty and Joan to ensure they knew the implications of making such a large purchase on credit.

The questions asked helped the founders of Friends' Home Health Care realize that the time had come for them to start doing some serious analysis of their business in order to determine how they could proceed.

QUESTIONS

1. As you think about Friends' Home Health Care, what other options do they have to the simple system of individuals signing out goods or buying the expensive software program?
2. How does a firm create incentives to help the firm watch its costs?

the specific. In that light, we review four classic analysis techniques prior to our discussion of designing and monitoring the core metrics for a particular organization. These four classic techniques are as follows:

1. Ratio analysis
2. Deviation analysis
3. Sensitivity analysis
4. Short surveys

Figure 8.1
Balance Sheet

BALANCE SHEET (in U.S. dollars)			
	12/31/2013	12/31/2014	Difference
Assets			
Current Assets			
Cash	$ 50,000	$ 61,000	$ 11,000
Acct Receivable	12,400	16,700	4,300
Inventory	29,000	31,000	2,000
Total Current Assets	**$ 91,400**	**$ 108,700**	$ 17,300
Fixed Assets			
Land	$ 100,000	$ 100,000	$ 0
Buildings	150,000	150,000	0
(Accumulated Depreciation)	(15,000)	(30,000)	(15,000)
Office Equipment	75,000	82,000	7,000
Machinery	45,000	45,000	0
(Accumulated Depreciation)	(3,500)	(7,000)	(3,500)
Total Fixed Assets	**$ 351,500**	**$340,000**	($ 11,500)
Total Assets	**$453,000**	**$430,000**	($23,000)
Liabilities			
Current Liabilities			
Accounts Payable	$ 35,000	$ 42,000	$ 7,000
Notes Payable (less than a year)	4,500	7,000	2,500
Accrued Payroll	15,000	23,000	8,000
Total Current Liabilities	54,500	72,000	17,500
Long-Term Liabilities			
Mortgage	200,000	192,000	(8,000)
Bank Loan	35,000	30,000	(5,000)
Total Long-Term Liability	**$ 235,000**	**$ 222,000**	($ 13,000)
Owner's Equity	**$ 163,500**	**$ 136,000**	($ 27,500)
Total Liabilities/Owner's Equity	**$453,000**	**$430,000**	($23,000)

Before examining these four techniques of analysis, students should quickly review the sample balance sheet in Figure 8.1 and the income statement in Figure 8.2. This data will be employed to illustrate the financial analytical methods.

Figure 8.2
Income Statement

INCOME STATEMENT (in U.S. dollars)			
Receipts:		2013	2014
	Sales	$ 178,790	$ 241,650
	Less Returns	4,000	7,000
	COGS	54,700	67,662
	Gross Profit	**$ 120,090**	**$ 166,988**
Expenses			
	Salaries	$ 28,000	$ 37,000
	Travel	6,545	7,650
	Car Leases	6,000	6,000
	Rent	3,150	3,600
	Payroll Taxes	1,720	2,450
	Insurance	1,450	1,800
	Fuel/Maint.	1,412	1,733
	Benefits	2,100	3,600
	Advertising	1,896	3,000
	Utilities	1,104	1,946
	Misc.	1,528	1,255
Total Expenses		**$ 55,208**	**$ 70,034**
Operating Income		**$ 64,882**	**$ 96,954**
Interest		11,975	13,800
Taxes		14,274	22,299
Profit After Taxes		**$ 38,633**	**$ 60,855**

Ratio Analysis

LO8-3

Explain ratio analysis.

Ratio analysis is a tool for the entrepreneur to use to examine the overall health of the organization.[2] Ratios by themselves are of little value. Instead the ratios for any given firm need to be evaluated in comparison to other similar organizations, an industry average, or simply the previous month's or year's performance.[3] We will discuss four basic categories of performance ratios: liquidity, activity, leverage, and profitability (Figure 8.3). We will first provide the means by which these ratios are calculated and then provide some insights that each brings to the business owner.

ratio analysis
A series of ratios along four areas of company performance (liquidity, activity, leverage, profitability) that provides a picture of the health of the company.

Liquidity Ratios

Financial liquidity is critical to the success of the firm.[4] **Liquidity ratios** measure the short-term ability of the firm to meet its obligations. These obligations would include debt or accounts payable that must be paid by

liquidity ratios
Ratios that measure the short-term ability of the firm to meet its obligations.

Figure 8.3
Commonly Used Ratios

Liquidity Ratios		
	Current (Note: current assets = cash + accounts receivable + inventory)	$\frac{CurrentAssets}{CurrentLiabilities}$
	Quick (or Acid Test)	$\frac{CurrentAssets - Inventory}{CurrentLiabilities}$
Activity Ratios		
	Inventory Turnover	$\frac{CostofGoodsSold}{Inventory}$
	Accounts Receivable Turnover	$\frac{CreditSales}{AccountsReceivable}$
	Total/Fixed Asset Turnover	$\frac{NetSales}{FixedAssets}$
Leverage Ratios		
	Debt to Equity	$\frac{TotalLiablities}{TotalAssets - TotalLiabilities}$
	Debt to Assets	$\frac{TotalLiablities}{TotalAssets}$
	Times Interest Earned	$\frac{OperatingIncome}{Interest}$
Profitability Ratios		
	Gross Profit Margin	$\frac{GrossProfit}{NetSales}$
	Operating Profit Margin (or EBIT)	$\frac{OperatingIncome}{NetSales}$
	Net Profit Margin	$\frac{NetProfit}{Netsales}$
	ROA (return on assets)	$\frac{NetProfit}{TotalAssets}$
	ROE (return on equity)	$\frac{NetProfit}{Equity}$

EXERCISE 1

1. Using the information from the income and balance sheet provided to you, calculate each of the ratios in Figure 8.3 and fill in the chart provided in the figure for 2014.

the business in the near term.[5] Financing institutions generally require that liquidity ratios be kept within certain ranges. If the business drops below the lower bounds of its liquidity level, then the bank may limit the line of credit to the firm or require a higher interest rate on the debt, as the risk position of the firm will have increased. Even for companies that appear to be growing well and have good prospects, the ability to meet the short-term obligations of the firm is a significant concern. Two specific types of liquidity ratios are of interest: current ratio and acid ratio.

Current Ratio: Current Assets divided by Current Liabilities. The current ratio measures those assets that can be quickly turned into cash and used to pay for immediate liabilities. In general, this is the cash balance of the firm plus inventory divided by all short-term liabilities.

Quick (Acid) Ratio: Current Assets minus Inventory divided by Current Liabilities. The quick ratio removes the ability to sell inventory and examines the pure cash position relative to the current liabilities. The term used here is *quick ratio,* but it is also sometimes referred to as an *acid test.*

Calculating Liquidity Ratios. Using the balance sheet (Figure 8.1), let's take a look at these two calculations. Look for the lines labeled Current Assets, Current Liabilities, and Inventory.

Current Ratio	2013	$91,400/$54,400 = 1.68
	2014	$115,362/$72,000 = 1.602
Quick Ratio (or Acid Test)	2013	$91,400 − $29,000/$54,400 = 1.147
	2014	$115,362 − $31,000/$72,000 = 1.079

Interpreting these items relative to each other, you can see that this business has held relatively constant over these two years in its ability to meet its short-term obligations. The current ratio is over 1.0, which tells us that the company has enough money to meet all of its short-term obligations. The quick ratio tells us that the firm has slightly decreased in its ability to pay cash for its short-term liabilities. However, the firm relies extensively on inventory to pay its current liabilities. That is not a concern in and of itself, but it can be problematic if the inventory in this industry becomes dated quickly. Therefore, it would be useful to evaluate the firm's ratios against the ratios for the industry (if available). An important issue in ratio analysis is ensuring that you are comparing apples to apples. However, often the ratios you may find are based on Fortune 500 firms, and these will have little or no relevance to an entrepreneurial business. We suggest for comparison purposes that an entrepreneurial business use sources such as the data published by the Risk Management Association (RMA). This alliance of community banks gathers data from the portfolios of all of its member firms and then provides typical ratios by industry. The firms in the database are generally smaller than those in most other generic data sources. For our example firm, the data show that the quick ratio is very consistent with the industry averages.

Activity Ratios

activity ratios
Ratios that measure the efficiency with which the entrepreneur is handling the resources of the business.

Activity ratios measure the efficiency with which you are handling the resources of the business. They are particularly helpful as the business develops, since you will be able to compare from month to month (or more often if you wish). There are three specific ratios in which we are interested.

Inventory Turnover: Cost of Goods Sold divided by Inventory. Cost of Goods Sold is the direct costs involved with a product. As this inventory turnover rises, the firm is getting closer to a just-in-time system. There are pros and cons to operating in a just-in-time system, and in some cases, the reality of the industry means that this is not a reasonable approach. Generally an inventory turnover ratio that is better than the industry average or one that is improving each month means that the firm is operating more efficiently.

Account Receivable Turnover: Credit Sales divided by Accounts Receivable. This metric examines how fast the company turns credit sales into cash. The faster the firm is able to turn credit sales into cash, the better the cash flow position of the firm is. Credit sales should also be aged into categories based on how long it has been since the sale. Unfortunately, this is necessary because the older the debt is, the less likely it is that you will be paid. Almost all debt 30 days and under is considered highly likely to be paid. After 90 days past due, however, only a small percentage of the debt will be realistically recovered. We will discuss this topic more when we examine collections at the end of this chapter.

Total/Fixed Asset Turnover: Net Sales divided by Fixed Assets or Net Sales divided by Total Assets. Entrepreneurial businesses will likely use one of these numbers more often than the other. The difference principally turns on whether or not the business has large amounts of fixed assets. For example, a small manufacturer will want to focus on the productivity of its fixed assets. How efficiently the business is in using those fixed assets is crucial in determining how competitive the firm is in the marketplace. In contrast, a retail store will be more interested in total assets. Such a firm has limited fixed assets but does have extensive inventory. In either case, the founder is attempting to examine the ability to generate sales from the assets employed by the organization. As this number increases, the firm is being more efficient. New businesses should try to minimize the amount of both fixed and total assets in order to conserve cash.

Calculating Activity Ratios. To calculate activity ratios requires information from both the balance sheet and the income statement. For example, the inventory turnover ratio derives the numerator (cost of goods sold) from the income statement, while the denominator (inventory) comes from the balance sheet. Using the numbers provided in Figures 8.1 and 8.2, we calculate the following activity ratios.

Inventory Turnover	2013	$54,700/$29,000 = 1.88
	2014	$67,662/$31,000 = 2.18
Accounts Receivable Turnover	2013	$178,790/$12,400 = 14.42
	2014	$241,650/$16,700 = 14.47
Total Asset Turnover	2013	$178,790/$453,000 = 0.39
	2014	$241,650/$430,000 = 0.56
Fixed Asset Turnover	2013	$178,790/$351,500 = 0.51
	2014	$241,650/$340,000 = 0.71

To interpret these numbers (in the absence of industry comparisons), the entrepreneur should focus on the relative change. Such a comparison would tell the business that the inventory turnover rate has gone up in 2014. The business then would want to determine the cause for this greater efficiency. The firm could have been inefficient in 2013 and may be just now gaining the experience necessary to gain the efficiencies of more mature firms. However, another reason might be that the firm has discovered some activity or method that provides the firm a level of efficiency greater than those of its competitors. If this is the case, the business will want to identify that source of competitive advantage and nurture it. Therefore, the business will likely want to have industry information on industry turnover. The evidence from the RMA suggests that the business is more efficient than its peer group in that region of the country.

The other ratios changed little over the time period and appear consistent with those of other similar firms in that region of the country. Therefore, the entrepreneurial business probably does not want to focus its attention on those issues.

EXERCISE 2

1. Using the pro forma statements that you developed for your business (as discussed in Chapter 6), calculate each of the liquidity and activity ratios for your business.
2. How do these compare with the industry averages?
3. If this causes you to reexamine your forecasts, explain why.

Leverage Ratios

leverage ratios
Ratios that are used to examine the relative level of indebtedness of the entrepreneurial business.

Leverage ratios are used to examine the relative level of indebtedness of the entrepreneurial business. Specifically, all creditors (whether they are suppliers of goods or banks with outstanding loans) want to ensure that the entrepreneurial business has the ability to generate sufficient funds to pay the supplier or repay the loans. High levels of debt are dangerous when the economy turns down, as we have all seen these past few years. Three ratios are commonly used to evaluate the relative level of indebtedness of a business.

Debt-to-Equity: Total Liabilities divided by Total Assets minus Total Liabilities. The denominator of this equation (Total Assets minus Total Liabilities) is effectively the owner's equity. This ratio provides the information on the portion of the business owned by the lenders and that portion owned by the founder(s).

Debt-to-Assets: Total Liabilities divided by Total Assets. A slight variation of the debt-to-equity ratio, this measures the percentage of the assets of the firm that are actually owned by the creditors.

Times Interest Earned: Operating Income divided by Interest. This figure estimates the number of times that the firm could repay the current interest owed on its debts. The higher this number is, the more capable the firm is of servicing its debt load.

Calculating Leverage Ratios. The information for most of the leverage ratios will come from Figure 8.1, the balance sheet. However, calculating times interest earned will require information from both the balance sheet and Figure 8.2, the income statement. Using the data for our firm we can generate the following data.

Debt-to-Equity Ratio	2013	$289,500/$163,500 = 1.77
	2014	$294,000/$136,000 = 2.16
Debt-to-Assets Ratio	2013	$289,500/$453,000 = 0.64
	2014	$294,000/$430,000 = 0.68
Times Interest Earned	2013	$64,882/$11,975 = 5.42
	2014	$96,954/$13,800 = 7.02

In calculating these ratios, what appears is a pattern with a significant change in the debt-to-equity ratio between 2013 and 2014. Similarly, the times interest earned appears to have undergone a significant shift that year. These areas should attract the businessperson's immediate interest. The businessperson would want to compare these numbers to the industry to identify if this was an industry-wide pattern. In the case of times interest earned, the industry-wide numbers are very similar to what our sample firm experienced. The reason for this was the overall drop in interest rate costs in the United States during that time. The increase in debt-to-equity is more troubling. The industry averages are closer to 1.15 than they are to 2.16. Even more disturbing is that the increase in debt-to-equity ratio appears to be due to lower equity in the firm. This raises a troubling picture. It appears that the business is slowly eating away the equity position of the firm. In other words, more is being taken out of the firm than is being put back into it. This may be the result of a negative net cash flow or something as simple as the founders' drawing more off in salary than the business can support. The result is not an immediate failure of the business but a slow spiral downward that ultimately results in failure. In a normal business that has achieved a break-even position, we would expect the equity position of the business to increase over time, not decrease. Therefore, the entrepreneur should flag this result and question what type of long-term pattern of performance is being established.

Profitability Ratios

Although profitability is the focus of much of the business press, it should be recognized as an outcome of the business's other activities. Thus, profitability is a result of effectively managing the assets and cash flow of the firm, not the activity of focus itself. **Profitability ratios** examine the performance of the firm and its ability to make economic returns over and above its costs. There are five profitability ratios that generate the greatest attention.

profitability ratios
Ratios that examine the performance of the firm and its ability to make economic rents over and above its costs.

Gross Profit Margin: Gross Profit divided by Net Sales. This ratio is used to determine the overall profit that is obtained from all sales during the period being evaluated. Gross profit is a category created by taking the total net sales of the firm and subtracting returned merchandise as well as the direct cost of the goods sold. This is the most basic of the profitability measures.

Operating Profit Margin: Operating Income divided by Net Sales. A finer-grained measure, this looks at the gross profit minus all of the operating expenses. This figure is also known as Earnings Before Interest and Taxes (EBIT) and represents the operating efficiency of the organization.

Net Profit Margin: Net Profit divided by Net Sales. Net profit is the bottom-line calculation from the income statement. This figure presents a picture of the relative margin earned after all obligations and expenses are considered.

Return on Assets (ROA): Net Profit divided by Total Assets. This is one of the two overall calculations that are standards in almost any industry. This ratio examines the ability of the firm to return an overall profit compared to the amount of assets that the firm has invested into the effort.

Return on Equity (ROE): Net Profit divided by Equity (Total Assets minus Total Liabilities). This ratio is used to provide all investors with an evaluation of how much each dollar of their investment is generating in profit.

Calculating Profitability Ratios. The calculations for the first three profitability ratios come from Figure 8.2, the income statement. The last two ratios combine information from both Figure 8.1, the balance sheet, and Figure 8.2, the income statement. Using the information from our sample firm, the following calculations are generated.

Gross Profit Margin	2013	$120,090/$178,790 = 0.67
	2014	$166,988/$241,650 = 0.69
Operating Profit Margin	2013	$64,882/$178,790 = 0.36
	2014	$96,954/$241,650 = 0.40
Net Profit Margin	2013	$38,633/$178,790 = 0.22
	2014	$60,855/$241,650 = 0.25
Return on Assets	2013	$38,633/$453,000 = 0.085
	2014	$60,855/$430,000 = 0.141
Return on Equity	2013	$38,633/$163,500 = 0.24
	2014	$60,855/$136,000 = 0.45

The profitability ratios present a firm that appears to be improving in all aspects. All of its margins increased nicely year after year. Its ability to make a profit on the assets and owners' equity provided improved ratios. This was partially due to a reduction in the value of the asset base and partially due to a very pleasant increase in sales without an equivalent increase in expenses. However, it was also due to a serious erosion of owners' equity in the business. Although it is nice to efficiently use the equity, we would normally look for owners' equity to increase as sales were growing. This needs to be looked into and given serious consideration by the founders.

Summary of Ratios

The ratios provided in this chapter can be valuable tools to the firm. All of the statements necessary to calculate these ratios are standard with any accounting package that you might choose. In fact, most of these accounting packages will automatically calculate these ratios. As an owner

Even though businesses vary, the core concepts involved in a healthy financial endeavor are universal. What are some of the similarities and differences between the financials for a restaurant versus a clothing store?

of an entrepreneurial business, you will likely choose only one or two of the ratios in each category (liquidity, activity, leverage, and performance or profitability) to use for examining the company, because you can be buried in data if you do not. It is important to understand the broad indicators of the different types of ratios to be able to pick them intelligently. Establishing a good data collection system is necessary for any of this analysis to be useful or effective for the entrepreneur. Finally, it is important in analyzing ratios that the entrepreneur remember that it is only through the comparison of those ratios over time or compared to some other firm or group of firms that the ratios can be interpreted. The ratios by themselves are interesting but do not provide much insight.

LO8-4

Explain deviation analysis.

deviation analysis
Analysis of the differences between the predicted and the actual performance.

Deviation Analysis

A second analysis method that is valuable for examining the firm, its activities, and its performance is a **deviation analysis**. This type of analysis is simply a chart tracking various performance measures from one time period to the next (month to month or year to year). The deviation chart has two additional columns, one showing the actual change and the other showing a percentage change. A deviation chart should be maintained for all important metrics. These might include several of the ratios listed above as well as other metrics that the organization deems to be important. An example is shown in Figure 8.4.

Notice that whether a particular item is good or bad for a company depends on the direction desired by the entrepreneur. As you can see, the drop in current ratio from 2013 to 2014 is a negative event, whereas the drop in number of complaints during this period, from 27 to 21, is a positive event. A deviation analysis allows the entrepreneur to quickly evaluate the performance of the organization on those items that are considered most important to the success of the firm.

Although this particular example shows only data from one year to the next, significantly greater insight would be gained by comparing data on more frequent intervals. The resulting picture of the firm's trends is always more revealing about how the company is performing. The business is encouraged to develop a chart using shorter time periods so that the patterns and deviations can be observed and used in the analysis of the business. As a result, we suggest that this chart be maintained at least monthly. Most businesses have some type of seasonality that could be significant for ordering, staffing, advertising, and more. In addition,

Figure 8.4
Deviation Analysis

ITEM	2013	2014	ACTUAL DIFFERENCE	% DIFFERENCE
Current Ratio	1.147	1.079	−0.068	**−5.90%**
Inventory Turnover	1.88	2.18	0.2	**10.60**
Gross Profit Margin	0.67	0.69	0.02	**2.90**
Net Profit Margin	0.22	0.25	0.03	**13.60**
No. of Complaints	27	21	6	**22.20**
Hours of Operation/Week	42	56	14	**33.30**
No. of Employees	2	7	5	**250**
No. Who Say We Are Their First Choice	47	117	70	**148.90**

an annual chart should also be prepared that allows comparison across the years as the firm matures.

In this particular example we also included several metrics that went beyond the basic financial ratios. As will be discussed shortly, we believe that measuring the performance of a business goes well beyond the financial aspects. The success of the company in pursuing its strategy should be a part of the analysis maintained by all companies.

EXERCISE 3

1. Prepare a deviation analysis for your business using your financial forecasts.
2. What unique items might you include in your deviation analysis that go beyond the basic ratios?

Sensitivity Analysis

LO8-5

Explain sensitivity analysis.

sensitivity analysis
A chart using current cash flow statement, income statement, or balance sheet to create a pro forma projection based on a dramatic increase in sales, a dramatic decrease in sales, or the complication of a major change in the business.

A third method of examining the ability of the organization to handle changes in the future is for the firm to perform a **sensitivity analysis**.[6] This type of analysis involves taking the current cash flow statement, income statement, or balance sheet and making projections based on a dramatic increase in sales, a dramatic decrease in sales, or the business undergoing a major change. This method of examination allows the entrepreneur to look at how sensitive the business is to various factors. In the example on pages 150–152, we use a cash flow statement to contemplate the impact of a dramatic sales increase or decrease. If the firm experiences a sudden 50 percent increase or decrease in sales, what will the impact be on the overall organization? In the case of an increase, how many new staff must be hired to accommodate these sales? What might the impact be on travel or insurance? First we list the projected cash flow statement for the firm (Figure 8.5 on page 150), and then we provide one with a 50 percent increase (Figure 8.6 on page 151) and another with a 50 percent decrease in sales (Figure 8.7 on page 152).

Under the rapid increase in sales scenario, the firm is hurt during its first two years, but then recovers for an extraordinary third year. The

FLOW RIGHT BREWERY & BAR: A FAMILY AFFAIR

Chris had been in business for several months. He felt that the business was doing pretty well, although he really only knew that he was busy all the time. His sister was proving to be very valuable to him. During the first week of business, she saw Chris simply placing in a shoebox receipts and invoices that he planned to review at the end of the day. Unfortunately, he missed a few days and they started to pile up. She convinced him to actually use the computer-based system he had invested in. The system was not complex and relied on a relatively cheap, standard PC from a local retail chain. He would enter the invoice and receipts as the transaction happened so there was a complete tracking of his work.

At the end of the second month, Chris's sister printed out the totals of a few basic items for the month, such as total sales, revenue received, receivables, total expenses, the amount actually paid out on bills, and what was still owed on bills. Chris was very happy to be able to see the numbers but really did not know how to analyze them. Then his sister started a basic tracking and ratio performance chart for him like the one below:

	MONTH 1	MONTH 2	CHANGE
Current Ratio	1.147	1.079	−0.068
Gross Profit Margin	0.65	0.70	0.02
Net Profit Margin	0.20	0.26	0.03

This triggered a conversation with his sister and his wife about how the business was doing and what these numbers really meant.

EXERCISE 4

1. What do these numbers mean for Chris's business?
2. What would you need to be able to analyze these numbers?
3. Using data that you can obtain on the Internet about restaurants and bars, compare Chris's business performance for the first two months to those averages.
4. If Chris opened in June and these numbers reflect June and July, how might that impact your analysis?

firm will need more funding if this scenario occurs and should have a plan for handling such situations. Under the decrease in sales projection, not only is the firm not making any positive net cash flows, but the net cash flow number is actually increasingly negative. For the firm to miss its projections by this amount would be devastating for the future of the business. Sensitivity analysis provides the businessperson an opportunity to test out assumptions and view the potential impact of those assumptions prior to committing any new resources.

LO8-6

Describe the use of short surveys in business.

Use of Short Surveys in Business

The fourth and final means to analyze the business, its activities, and its performance is the survey. The prior three methods examined (ratios, deviation, sensitivity) focused on financial data. As has been mentioned several other times in this text, the new businessperson should also recognize

Figure 8.5
Cash Flow—Projected (in U.S. dollars)

	YEAR 1	YEAR 2	YEAR 3
Receipts:			
Sales, $	$ 25,000	$325,000	$675,000
Consulting, $	20,000	20,000	60,000
Total Receipts, $	$ 45,000	$345,000	$735,000
Disbursements:			
Salaries, $	$ 45,000	$ 95,000	$210,000
Travel, $	4,050	31,050	66,150
Car Leases, $	4,000	6,000	7,500
Rent, $	900	6,900	14,700
Payroll Taxes, $	2,700	5,700	12,600
Insurance, $	5,500	6,000	7,500
Fuel/Maint, $	960	4,500	8,000
Executive Comp, $	64,000	72,000	78,000
Benefits, $	13,500	28,500	63,000
Advertising, $	2,000	26,000	54,000
Supplies, $	225	1,725	3,675
Utilities, $	3,150	24,150	51,450
Misc, $	900	6,900	14,700
Total Disbursements, $	$ 146,885	$ 314,425	$ 591,275
Beginning Balance, $	0	98,115	128,690
Equity Investment, $	200,000		
Net Cash Flow, $	(101,885)	30,575	143,725
Ending Balance, $	$ 98,115	$ 128,690	$ 272,415

Figure 8.6
Cash Flow—50 Percent Increase in Sales (in U.S. dollars)

	YEAR 1	YEAR 2	YEAR 3
Receipts:			
Sales, $	$ 37,500	$ 487, 500	$1,012,500
Consulting	30,000	30,000	90,000
Total Receipts	$ 67,500	$ 517,500	$1,102,500
Disbursements:			
Salaries	$90,000	$ 190,000	$420,000
Travel	6,075	46,575	99,225
Car Leases	8,000	12,000	15,000
Rent	1,350	10,350	22,050
Payroll Taxes	5,400	11,400	25,200
Insurance	7,500	8,500	10,000
Fuel/Maint.	2,200	6,000	10,200
Executive Comp	64,000	72,000	78,000
Benefits	27,000	57,000	126,000
Advertising	3,000	39,000	81,000
Supplies	338	2,588	5,513
Utilities	4,725	36,225	77,175
Misc.	1,350	10,350	22,050
Total Disbursements	$220,938	$ 501,988	$ 991,413
Beginning Balance	0	46,563	62,075
Equity Investment	200,000		
Net Cash Flow	(153,438)	15,513	111,088
Ending Balance	$ 46,563	$ 62,075	$ 173,163

that there are nonfinancial methods of analysis that can be useful to the entrepreneur. So much of what we would like to know about our customers, suppliers, and employees is contextual information that is not easily categorized and is subject to interpretation.[7] This is the ideal reasoning for using a survey to gather information. Although survey methodology is virtually a science unto itself, we believe that anyone can develop an effective survey with just a little care.

Short surveys can be given to any party to a transaction with your business and provide you with the opportunity to evaluate your company's performance on dimensions that may lead to financial success. If there is a very large set of customers, the entrepreneur may choose to sample every third customer. This is a type of random sample, and the expectation is that this subset of the total customers (presuming that the sample is sufficiently large) will in fact reflect all customers (within a small margin of error). Alternatively, an entrepreneur may choose to try to survey all of his customers.

In either case there will be some bias in your survey, since only those individuals who wish to fill out the survey will do so. Therefore, the information from the survey can be useful, but judgment is still required to interpret the results. The questions on the survey should be designed to answer questions

Figure 8.7
Cash Flow—50% Decrease in Sales (in U.S. dollars)

	YEAR 1	YEAR 2	YEAR 3
Receipts:			
Sales	$ 12,500	$ 162,500	$ 337,500
Consulting	10,000	10,000	30,000
Total Receipts	$ 22,500	$ 172,500	$ 367,500
Disbursements:			
Salaries	$45,000	$ 95,000	$ 210,000
Travel	2,025	15,525	33,075
Car Leases	4,000	6,000	7,500
Rent	450	3,450	7,350
Payroll Taxes	2,700	5,700	12,600
Insurance	5,500	6,000	7,500
Fuel/Maint.	480	4,500	8,000
Executive Comp	64,000	72,000	78,000
Benefits	13,500	28,500	63,000
Advertising	1,000	13,000	27,000
Supplies	113	863	1,838
Utilities	1,575	12,075	25,725
Misc.	450	3,450	7,350
Total Disbursements	$140,793	$ 266,063	$ 488,938
Beginning Balance	0	81,708	(11,855)
Equity Investment	200,000		
Net Cash Flow	(118,293)	(93,563)	(121,438)
Ending Balance	$ 81,708	($ 11,855)	($ 133,293)

directly related to the mission or strategy of the company. Some examples of questions for a high-end manufacturer are as follows:

1. How do you rate our prices:

Lower than most		**Same**	**Higher than most**	
1	2	3	4	5

2. Is the quality of our product:

Lower than most		**Same**	**Higher than most**	
1	2	3	4	5

3. The nature of our service is:

Lower than most		**Same**	**Higher than most**	
1	2	3	4	5

This particular sample firm wants to be competitive in most regards, but given its goals, wants to be better than competitors on both service and quality. Ideally each survey will have several questions that look at various aspects of the same issue. We would want to see some consistency in the pattern of answers within the survey as well as between surveys.

Survey data can be tabulated and examined with some fairly simple statistical techniques, such as percentages. Therefore, a fact as simple as "only 55 percent of your customers indicated that your service is better than the service of your competitors" would be a trouble signal for a firm where service was presumed to be a key competitive advantage. However, with just a slight increase in sophistication in the analysis techniques, quite a bit more can be learned from the data. Cross tabulation of related items and simple regressions can form a picture of the organization that leads it beyond its competitors. Both of these are available in virtually every spreadsheet package, and while the level of statistical sophistication can get quite complex, the basics are relatively easy to use and comprehend. A cross tabulation displays the distribution of two or more variables in columns. Thus, you could see, for example, how your drinks matched your entrées in a restaurant.

	MEAT DISH (%)	SALAD ONLY (%)
Wine	35	25
Beer	40	15
Coffee	5	60

A regression is a more complex analysis and concerns how well points of information fit along a line. The results allow you to see how different variables explain the impact of a given measure, such as profits.

Importance of Having a Measurement Focus

LO8-7

Analyze the importance of having a measurement focus.

This understanding of your key competitive advantages and the ability to develop measurements that ensure you are fulfilling your strategic goals is worth greater focus. Remember from Chapter 5 that there are two aspects to any business, the standard and the unique. The standard parts of a business are those that must be done just to be considered a part of that particular industry, whereas the unique represents those areas where the business really tries to differentiate itself. A business needs to do the standard and they need to do it well, but only as well as the rest of the industry. Thus, the standard parts of the business should be managed in the simplest way possible, with very little extra analysis. As long as the firm is performing as well as the rest of the industry, then sufficient effort has been placed in these areas.

A very simple example illustrates just how easy it is to overinvest in the standard. An owner of a bus tour company said he was contemplating getting a postage machine. The natural question to ask the owner was how many pieces of mail he sends out in a day. Putting stamps on more than about 10 pieces a day easily justifies a postage machine, if for no other reason than the savings in time spent purchasing stamps, maintaining a supply, and putting stamps on envelopes. This company was sending out between 170 and 225 pieces of mail a day. This is a standard activity for a company, and no matter how much time or effort is spent, no customer will pay you extra for a stamp versus a postal imprint. We felt that this was an easy, standard decision that should take virtually no time away from the core of the business. That said, the founder decided to make a project out of this decision. He invited three companies to meet with him and demonstrate their machines. He analyzed the amount of time it took to place stamps on the envelopes (about 20 minutes a day) and added in the time for traveling to and from the post office (another 20 minutes or so a week). After all the analysis, the company decided to get a postage machine. The owner

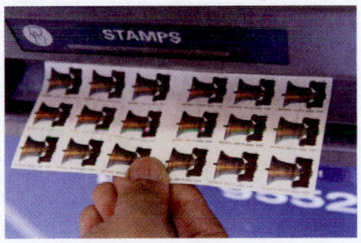

wanted to track the success of the decision by having the person who ran the envelopes through the machine record the amount of time it took each day and to include the time it took to periodically recharge the machine. This type of analysis is of no value to the ultimate success of an organization. Not only did it waste the time of the people involved, but it also meant that they were not doing their core jobs during this time. Unfortunately, it is very easy to become consumed with the minutiae of analyzing a business and fail to focus on those operations that are most critical for the customer.[8]

The focus should be on those areas that provide competitive advantage to the firm. In the example of the bus tour agency, there was no competitive advantage to be gained from either a stamp or an imprint. This firm made large segments of its income from arranging annual foliage bus tours for senior citizens to look at the changing colors of the leaves in the mid-Atlantic states. Therefore, measuring the efficiency of the buses employed, the advertising dollars spent reaching that population, the experience on each tour, and the time spent to secure each account would be much more critical. Concentrating the analysis efforts on those areas that are unique puts the founder's focus on those areas that can create a differentiation for the business compared to those of the competitors.

ETHICAL CHALLENGE

In the process of doing an analysis of your business as well as those of your competitors, you realize that the data for one of your competitor firms are quite unusual. Despite the fact that its customer count is very low and its suppliers deliver less than one-fourth of the goods supplied to you and the other retailers, this one operation is reporting sales to the government that far exceed your own. During several conversations at a local business social club meeting, you are told by several businesspeople that you should steer clear of that business because they are laundering money.

QUESTIONS

1. Do you have an obligation to tell the authorities?
2. The business that you suspect is a major advertiser in the local media and is always putting down the competition. You'd like to see the firm out of business. Does this confuse your ethical obligation?

SUMMARY

Entrepreneurial businesses have very few slack resources relative to their larger competitors. The result is that a large firm can make a series of mistakes and still maintain a going concern. With a much tighter margin of error, an entrepreneurial business should actively monitor its performance relative both to itself and to its competitors. This chapter provided a series of relatively quick, easily maintained techniques for developing and maintaining an effective picture of the company.

KEY TERMS

activity ratios 143
deviation analysis 148
leverage ratios 145
liquidity ratios 141
profitability ratios 146
ratio analysis 141
sensitivity analysis 149

REVIEW QUESTIONS

1. What are the four means to evaluate the firm, its activities, and its performance?
2. What do liquidity ratios seek to measure? What are the major types of liquidity ratios?
3. Why are industry averages important to the interpretation of ratios?
4. What do activity ratios seem to measure? What are the major types of activity ratios?

5. What do leverage ratios seek to measure? What are the major types of liquidity ratios?
6. What do performance ratios seek to measure? What are the major types of performance ratios?
7. List two performance measures and explain their significance.
8. How is a deviation analysis used by a business?
9. How is a sensitivity analysis used to protect a business?

BUSINESS PLAN DEVELOPMENT QUESTIONS

1. Throughout this chapter you have done a variety of financial exercises related to your business. Which of these would be the most useful for you to track on a weekly basis?
2. Are there other data you would follow on a monthly or quarterly basis?
3. What is the specific industry you wish to compare your performance to in order to judge how you are doing?

INDIVIDUAL EXERCISES

Locate an entrepreneur in your area who would be willing to discuss the method he or she uses to track financial performance. (Note the entrepreneur will likely not give specific information such as profits, but he or she will discuss general concepts.)

1. What financial ratio does the entrepreneur focus on most often?
2. How frequently does the entrepreneur sit and analyze the business's performance?
3. Are there specific warning signs the entrepreneur focuses on as he or she does financial analysis?

GROUP EXERCISES

Go to the Internet and pick one of the following large firms: Coca-Cola, Facebook, or Home Depot. Conduct a ratio analysis for this firm using at least six key ratios. Ensure that you find comparable ratios for its industry. Have the other members of the group do the same company. Compare your findings.

1. Which ratios did you pick and why?
2. What was the financial performance for this firm in 2014?
3. Predict what you believe the financial performance of the company will be based on the pattern of performance in 2014 and before.
4. What was the actual performance of the firm last year?

ENDNOTES

1. "Understanding Financial Ratios For Entrepreneurs," *Inc42*, http://inc42.com/resources/understanding-financial-ratios-entrepreneurs/
2. P. Back, "Explaining Financial Difficulties Based on Previous Payment Behavior, Management Background Variables, and Financial Ratios," *European Accounting Review* 14 (2005), pp. 839–68.
3. M. Bujaki, "Industry Identification Through Ratio Analysis," Accounting Perspectives 11, no. 4 (Winter 2012), pp. 315–22.
4. O. Sharifi, "Financial Risk Management for Small and Medium Size Enterprises (SMEs)," *International Journal of Information, Business and Management* 6, no. 2 (May 2014), pp. 82–94.
5. W. Davidson III and D. Dutia, "Debt, Liquidity, and Profitability Problems in Small Firms," *Entrepreneurship Theory & Practice* 16 (1991), pp. 53–65.
6. C. Praag, "Business Survival and Success of Young Small Business Owners," *Small Business Economics* 21 (2003), pp. 1–17.
7. S. Horng-Cherng. "A Study of the Practical and Theoretical Applications of Second Order Customer Perceived Value Analysis." *International Journal of Organizational Innovation* 6, no. 4 (April 2014), pp. 160–73.
8. I. MacMillan and R. McGrath, "Discovering New Points of Differentiation," *Harvard Business Review* (July/August 1997), pp. 154–56.

CREDITS

Opener: Antenna/Getty Images RF; p. 137: © Callie Lipkin; p. 143: © D. Hurst/Alamy RF; p. 147 (left): © John Lund/Marc Romanelli/Blend Images LLC RF; p. 147 (right): Inti St. Clair/Digital Vision/Getty Images RF; p. 153: Kathy Willens/AP Images.

part 4

chapter 9

learning objectives

After studying this chapter, you will be able to:

LO9-1 Discuss the various legal forms of business to determine the best design for a proposed new business.

LO9-2 Explain the basics of contracts.

LO9-3 Define the role of leases in the legal formation of the new business.

LO9-4 List how laws, rules, and regulations benefit new businesses.

LO9-5 Explain the importance of copyrights, trademarks, and patents to a new business.

LO9-6 Define the role that insurance plays in the risk portfolio of the new business.

LO9-7 Discuss how to develop an effective board of advisors or board of directors.

Establishing the Legal Foundation

WEEDMAPS: THE YELP OF MARIJUANA BUYING

How do you take something that is considered illegal in much of the United States and make a legal business out of it? Regardless of one's opinion on the subject, legal marijuana sales exist in the United States. As of 2014, 21 states as well as Washington, DC, allowed for the purchase of medical marijuana, whereas two states, Colorado and Washington, allowed for any adult to purchase marijuana for recreational use. Despite being legal in these settings, running a business in this industry is still a legal minefield.

According to the federal government, marijuana is a Schedule 1 narcotic with no accepted medial value. In addition, there are thousands of people in jail for past possession of the product. Add to that, it is still highly regulated even in states where it has some form of legality. The Marijuana Enforcement Division in Colorado issued a 230-page document prescribing how it must be advertised, sold, and distributed in the state. At this point, the federal government has decided not to pursue their established enforcement actions in those states where it is legal; however, it is unknown how long that decision will last. Any business enabling the sale of an illegal substance is subject to seizure and jail time for the owners.

Weedmaps was founded by Justin Hartfield and Keith Hoerling in 2008 and navigates this legal minefield as it provides menus and pricing of legal marijuana dispensaries across the United States. The firm makes money not by charging visitors to the website but by charging the business owners who list there. Weedmaps helps customers find legal marijuana suppliers and also helps the firms that list with them manage their products. Hartfield says the site is tracking half a million products in real time, "not just strains but also edibles, lotions, tinctures, salves, balms, clothing, bongs, and vaporizers. Anything a dispensary sells is on our weed menu." Today, the firm has over $18 million in annual revenue with more than 2 million visitors a month to the website.

Like all businesses, the firm makes efforts to reach out and connect with its customers. As one aspect of this marketing effort, the firm hosts social events for the users of medical marijuana to meet each other. Another aspect of this connection to customers is its association with NORML (a lobbying group seeking to legalize marijuana), which is an official partner of Weedmaps. In part, this partnership reflects the view that Hoerling and Hartsfield have of Weedmaps as playing not only a role to make a profit but as supporting the community that smokes marijuana. This view of the community can also be seen in Hartsfield's founding of the first venture capital fund (Ghost Group) focused on funding emerging companies in the legal medical sectors.

There are legal constraints on every business. Some are just more intense than others.

Questions

1. Does this change the definition of a "drug-free" workplace in Colorado?
2. What type of legal organization would you consider if you were running this business? Why?
3. What insurance issues concern you about this business?

Sources: B. Eha, "High Hopes and Blunt Truths for the $2.3 Billion Legal Marijuana Market," *Entrepreneur*, January 13, 2014, www.entrepreneur.com/article/230772-1; T. Hughes, "Legal Pot Becomes a Touchy Workplace Issue," *USA Today*, April 7 2014, www.usatoday.com/story/news/nation/2014/04/07/marijuana-pot-workplace-employers-hiring-jobs/7272467/; B. Weiss, "Thank You for Smoking Marijuana," *Wall Street Journal*, March 14, 2014, http://online.wsj.com/news/articles/sb10001424052702303630904579419033028056534

Legal issues are critical for any new business to consider. Even though we present issues sequentially in this text, you should recognize that often things happen simultaneously. Thus, legal issues may occur at the same time as some of the financial issues discussed earlier in the book and, in fact, may impact your financial decisions. In addition, the information in this chapter is not meant to be definitive or exhaustive of all the legal concerns related to starting a new business. The material is factually correct; however, we strongly believe that you should hire a qualified attorney to assist you in building the foundation of the new business. The laws in each state vary, and the consequences are often serious enough that you will want to ensure you have a full and complete understanding of the legal issues related to the business.

In the previous chapters we have set out a means for you to develop the type of business you want to create, determine its strategy and/or mission, and perform a detailed analysis of the potential cash flow position for the new firm. However, prior to the beginning of any actual operations, the founder must ensure that the proper legal foundation for the business is established.

Mature economies are based upon laws.* To fully appreciate the reliance in the United States on the legal institutions, one need only compare the United States to China.[1] There is a legal system in China, but in most cases this system is one that is evolving. Often the laws are on the books in China but will be enforced only sporadically or in an inconsistent manner. How those laws are enforced and the penalties for violations of those laws will vary widely across the country. Whether laws and their enforcement are the concern of the central government, province, or city is often unclear; instead, there are competing authorities who may interpret what is to be done very differently. To work in this environment, a business survives by developing good relationships with administrators, regulators, and/or the police. It will be the relationship between these individuals and the entrepreneur that determines if the laws are enforced and, if so, how they are enforced. The relationship between a businessperson and government officials may originate from a variety of sources, such as being related by blood or marriage, going to school together, or making a payoff, but without such relationships the new businessperson will most certainly find that he has significant legal problems.[2]

In contrast, the laws of the United States, and many other mature economies, are relatively clear, reasonably well enforced, and the amount of corruption relatively low. As a result, legal conflicts are decided based on the facts, not on who you know. This does not mean that the legal system in a nation such as the United States is not a source of irritation for businesspeople. For example, obtaining a license to sell alcohol at your premises involves approval from numerous independent authorities—local, state, and federal (the federal agency is the ATF—the Bureau of Alcohol, Tobacco, Firearms, and Explosives).

Although they are frustrating, entrepreneurs must realize that legal structures in society are critical for businesses. The abilities to collect money owed, to trust that contracts will be honored, to operate without fear of being arbitrarily shut down, and to prevent ruinous interventions by the government are all the result of laws. Indeed, in a developing country, or in one recently ravaged by war, one of the first major steps in building the nation's economy is to establish the police and the courts so that basic business can be transacted.

Our view is that new businesspeople need to acknowledge the central role and importance of the legal system, recognize how it will impact their

*The law present in a country is referred to as an *institution*. Other issues such as culture and ways that a given profession may conduct business are also institutions. These institutions shape the way business is conducted in subtle and pervasive manners. To fully understand how business is conducted in a given area, such institutions must be understood.

business lives, and be prepared to compete in that arena. The businessperson cannot ignore legal issues. As a result, entrepreneurs need to recognize that it is likely they will at some time go to court to resolve disputes. If, on the other hand, a supplier or customer did not live up to an agreement in China, the entrepreneur might go see a powerful person who would mediate the dispute between the two parties using his personal judgment and experience as a guide. If the entrepreneur's relationship with that mediator was poor or if the other party had very strong ties to the mediator, the entrepreneur would likely lose. In the United States, the entrepreneur has the ability to use the court system for a legal remedy that is bound by precedent and the Uniform Commercial Code. The nature of business is that there will be

FRIENDS' HOME HEALTH

The Friends' Home Health Care founders had determined the type, mission, and fundamental positioning of their new business idea. However, before they began operations they felt that this business idea might need another investor or two. The resources from these investors would allow them to position the business to grow faster. Betty and Joan started their discussion with several local bank managers and loan officers regarding their initial financing, but were stumped in the process when they were asked "what type of business" they had. Initially they thought this question referred to their positioning or plan for success, but they quickly found out that the financiers were asking about what legal form of business the entrepreneurs would choose.

Having given this topic very little thought, the partners were not sure they understood the different forms of business they could pursue, but they also did not have much time to worry about such issues (or so they thought). They wanted everything to be fair and even between the founders and the new investors, so, with very little thought, they announced that they were going to form a "partnership." They mistakenly believed that this form of business would indicate their commitment to the business and their desire to have investors involved in the business. After all, in law firms and accounting firms, being made a partner is considered the highest honor and confers upon the partner rights to the profits of the firm.

The founders had made great progress in developing their business plan, and their next step was to approach the person they expected to be their key financial investor. This individual was a very successful entrepreneur that one of the founders had loosely known since childhood. Over the years he had started and run a variety of retail businesses. Although the investor had not had a business in the health care industry, he was interested in the idea and was familiar with the business domain as his mother had just recently passed away after a long period of home care. His prior success in business led the founders to also believe he could provide great insight to them on running the business and therefore would be an ideal investor.

The founders met with this investor and made a presentation of their business idea. It had taken two weeks to get on his calendar and the meeting was going to be quite brief. He was intrigued by the business idea and by their "numbers." He then asked them what type of business entity they had formed, and Betty and Joan responded that they had formed a "partnership." The potential investor fell silent. After what seemed like an eternity to the Friends' founders, he responded that he would not invest in a partnership because of the personal liability and problems associated with the lack of liquidity. He finished up with a few polite comments, wished them the best of luck—and the meeting was over.

Betty and Joan were shocked, but in analyzing the meeting afterward, they realized that the type of business they intended to form was of significant interest to potential investors, bankers, and perhaps themselves. They realized that the legal foundation for their business needed to be reconsidered as it was a more central issue than they originally believed. The opportunity to obtain any investment from the ideal investor with whom they had just met was probably lost forever owing to the lack of an adequate legal foundation. They were now determined to investigate the legal issues in more detail before they went forward any further.

QUESTIONS

1. How would you describe the liability issues that concerned the potential investor?
2. Do these concerns seem relevant? How would you address them?

disagreements, and as a result, you as an entrepreneur are likely at some point to be in court. Although this may not be the ideal path to arbitration, it is better than the alternative of having no legal system, or a weak one.

An important part of operating a business is having a fundamental understanding of the basics of commercial law and the potential remedies when there is a dispute. The establishment of a basic legal foundation will help the entrepreneur navigate the legal environment much more easily.

Significant time and effort can be saved in the long run with some careful thought at the founding of a new venture about legal issues. This chapter will examine a number of legal issues that impact the founding of the new business, including:

- The forms of business
- Contracts
- Leases
- Regulations, including licensing requirements
- Copyrights, trademarks, and patents
- Insurance
- Board of advisors or directors

sole proprietorship
The simplest form of business organization, characterized by the fact that the person who owns the business and the business itself are treated as the same entity.

LO9-1

Discuss the various legal forms of business to determine the best design for a proposed new business.

Various Legal Forms of Business to Determine the Best Design for a Proposed New Business

There are three basic types of legal business organization: sole proprietorship, partnership (including both general and limited liability), and corporation (C, S, and limited liability company). Each of these will be examined below.

Sole Proprietorship

A **sole proprietorship** is the simplest form of business to establish, as the person who owns it and the business itself are treated as the same entity. Driven by the belief that new business is good for the economy and should be encouraged, most communities have made the process for obtaining a sole proprietorship license quite simple although there can be distinct differences between communities that will affect the rate of sole proprietorships formation.[3] A quick trip to the local courthouse or public administration building, filling out a simple form, and paying a small fee is usually all that is required to establish a sole proprietorship. More and more communities are making this process even simpler with a complete online process. All of the business income and losses for a sole proprietorship are treated as part of the individual's overall income and are reportable on schedule C of your 1040 tax form. Absent other licenses that may be required to operate your business (a topic we will cover in more detail later in this chapter), the establishment of a sole proprietorship allows an individual to legally transact business.

Many single-person businesses are set up as sole proprietorships.

The major benefit of this form of business is that it is very easy to form and easy to dissolve. There is virtually no separation between the founder and the business. There are strict rules regarding record keeping, and it is important that the founder maintain a firewall between personal and business expenses since the government does not want to pay for the daily living costs of the entrepreneur. However, the entrepreneur may be able to deduct relevant business expenses from the business income.

The drawbacks to this type of business are numerous, and for businesspeople who develop a substantial business, these drawbacks will outweigh the ease of establishment. The first disadvantage is that a business that involves more than a single founder cannot be a sole proprietorship. Friends', by its very nature of having been founded by two individuals, could not be a sole proprietorship unless the founders placed 100 percent of the authority with a single individual, and the other founder was considered an employee (not a very attractive prospect to the founder treated as an employee). The law does not recognize other equity investors in this type of business. This limitation is a significant drawback for the growth potential of a new business, not only from an initial investment perspective, but also because as the business develops it may need additional outside investment, which a founder may get in exchange for part ownership of the business. Such investment would be virtually impossible in this legal form. This inability to have additional owners also means that equity incentives to attract top employees and executives are not possible as you could not give them any ownership as part of their compensation. This leaves the founder with two options: either obtain all new monies as personal debt or go through the process of changing the legal form to a more robust one as the firm grows.

A second significant disadvantage of a sole proprietorship is the liability for the owners associated with it. In the sole proprietorship all of the liabilities of the sole proprietorship are the direct responsibility of the owner of the business. Thus, a debt for the firm is a personal debt for the business owner. The result is that if the business does something relatively risky, such as trading commodities, or even something mundane, like taking delivery of a substantial level of inventory that ultimately cannot be sold, then those debts of the business are treated as debts of the owner.

A third issue is one of legitimacy with suppliers and customers. Owing to the fact that this legal form is so easy to dissolve, suppliers typically require personal guarantees for the debts of the firm from the founder of the business. The result is that the value of the business is limited since it is so tightly tied to the founder. If the founder should seek to sell the business it can be difficult to accomplish.

Thus, a sole proprietorship is very popular among individuals who:

1. Are unsure of their business idea and just want to see what might happen (if the business proves successful these individuals often re-form the business later, using another business form).
2. Have a very small business where the time limitations of the founder will keep the business from growing significantly.
3. Have a business where the costs of equipment are low and therefore so are the risks. For example, a new business that embroiders names on shirts and hats can have relatively low costs and low risks.

Partnerships

A more complex business form is a **partnership**. There are two broad categories of partnerships: general and limited. The two differ significantly from each other and will be reviewed separately.

partnership
A type of business formed between individuals directly. It includes both general and limited varieties.

General Partnership. If two or more people are involved in the founding of an organization, they can form a partnership. Similar to the founding of a sole proprietorship, the means of forming a basic partnership is relatively simple; however, it does involve an extra step beyond that of a sole proprietorship. When filing for a partnership, most local communities

draw

A distribution of funds from the business. It is usually in the form of a cash dispersion in advance of salary, bonus, expected year-end distribution, and the like.

require a partnership agreement. Although there are no set requirements that such an agreement must take, these agreements generally specify who is involved; what each party is expected to contribute to the founding of the firm (whether it be cash, services, or property); how profits, losses, and **draws** by the partners are to be treated; how one partner can buy out the other(s) if that individual decides to leave; how new partners are brought into the partnership; and how disputes are to be settled.

We periodically hear from potential partners that they simply do not need such items to be specified. These individuals may have known each other for years and feel very comfortable with each other, so that they trust each other and are ready to tie up their combined financial wealth. As a consequence these individuals do not take the time to develop a rich and full partnership agreement. However, recall what we stressed at the beginning of this chapter. This is a legalistic society, and a business is fundamentally a financial transaction, which should be treated as such. The time to prevent problems is early in the relationship, prior to any conflict (which, by the way, is inevitable in any interaction between two or more people). We recommend the early establishment of clear and legally binding dimensions of the partnership. Thus, our advice is to get assistance from your accountant or lawyer in drawing up such an agreement. The time spent up front on an agreement will save hours and hours of frustration and conflict later.

To illustrate the importance of this process, we will describe a partnership we worked with that had been formed to develop a landscaping business. The business developed quite well for several years and grew to where the firm had more than 50 employees and annual revenues in excess of several million dollars. When the partners began, both were married, had known each other for years both personally and professionally, and attended the same church. One partner worked in the field operations while the other handled new business development for the company and managed the office operations. The wife of the partner who worked in the field was the in-house accountant for the business. Unfortunately, after several years it became clear that there was an affair between the partner working in the office and the wife of the other partner who was also working in the office. During the next few months, both partners filed for divorce and the pair having the affair moved in together. The rift in the business became obvious to customers, suppliers, and the employees of the business to the point that the business was on the verge of collapse.

The two partners had developed a short partnership agreement when they formed the business, but it was based on one they found online for free, and they had simply deleted passages that they did not want to address. At the time the two were best friends and believed that they did not need an extensive agreement. The document the two partners had generated was not clear on how they would split the business if either partner wished to terminate the agreement without the agreement of the other partner. The result was that the case ended up in court, connected to two messy divorces. Of course, the business continued to suffer. Employees left, customers chose other landscaping companies, and suppliers changed their credit terms for the business because they were concerned about the dissolution of the business. The result was a costly battle for both parties, with the field partner retaining the business and the office partner receiving a cash payment. Unfortunately for the partner who got the business, there was not a noncompete clause in the partnership or termination agreement. Once the legal case was over, the partner that left with the cash payment set up a new business in the same area and sought out customers from the previous partnership.

In general, breaking the partnership among partners has a negative impact on new businesses.[4] However, in the case of the landscaping business, a better-constructed partnership agreement could have allowed for a fair and less costly dissolution of the partnership. Plus it could have protected the existing company from the partner who left and set up a competing business.

If a partnership agreement is not developed and signed, the partnership will be governed by either the Uniform Partnership Act or the Revised Uniform Partnership Act. These partnership laws were developed as suggested formats and adopted by each state. Thus, although there is some variation among the states, they are nonetheless a relatively effective means to handle the basics of partnership. Although the laws vary somewhat from state to state, certain standards are in place in the absence of a preformation agreement. The rules in the acts are reasonable, but they rarely match exactly what most individuals would prefer for their business. For example, in these acts all assets are treated as equal for the partners. However, we find that rarely is there a true 50–50 partnership. Inevitably, one or more partners contribute more capital or take more of a role in running the business than the other(s). Given this situation, new-business owners would likely want to write a partnership agreement that recognized the larger contribution and perhaps provided a larger ownership stake. Similarly, issues like noncompete agreements are not covered in these acts.

A general partnership shares some of the characteristics of the sole proprietorship. The owners report their shares of losses or profits on their own personal income tax returns in proportion to their interest in the firm. Business expenses have some flow-through to personal tax forms, but the restrictions are significant. General partnerships require little more in the way of formal paperwork than sole proprietorships and dissolution can be quite easy, although it does require a formal record with the local authorities.

Some of the drawbacks of general partnerships are the same as they are for sole proprietorships. The issue of liability is usually a bit more of an issue than it is for a sole proprietorship. Partners are generally held to be jointly liable for all debts incurred by the partnership. This means that a debt agreed to by your partner for the business becomes your total responsibility if the partner fails to meet her obligations. Each partner is assumed to be involved with all decisions, which translates into a fiduciary relationship between partners. In other words, partners have the responsibility to watch out for the best interests of the other partners.

Whereas a sole proprietorship virtually eliminates the firm's ability to bring in new equity investment, a general partnership opens this door just a bit. To accept new equity investment in a partnership, each established partner must surrender a portion of her ownership position. This is usually a process in which the new "partner" buys out a portion of each of the existing partners in a transaction that also adds some financial muscle to the organization. A new partnership agreement is required each time this process occurs, and there are limits in some communities as to the number of partners a business may have.

Limited Partnership. Some of the drawbacks to a general partnership encouraged the development of another type of partnership: a limited liability partnership (**LLP**). An LLP still has at least two individuals who are partners in a venture (although technically, one person can form an LLP and declare a full pass-through of all income on his or her federal taxes); however, there are two classes of partners in such a venture. The first is a **general partner**. The general partner is considered the manager of the firm and, as such, has unlimited liability for any debts or judgments against the firm. In contrast, the other partners are considered to be passive investors, and as such, their liability is limited to their investment in the business. The other partners are called *limited partners* and can work for the firm, but may not be active in the management of the organization. The only requirement of an LLP is that at least one partner is considered

LLP
A limited liability partnership.

general partner
In an LLP, the individual considered the manager of the firm, who, as such, has unlimited liability for any debts or judgments against the firm.

to be a general partner. Otherwise, the positives and negatives discussed in the previous section for general partnerships also apply to LLPs.

Corporations

The result of forming a sole proprietorship or a general partnership is that the business debts flow directly to the owner(s), meaning that all owners are responsible for any debts of the firm that arise. Thus, owners can have their life savings disappear if the business goes bankrupt. The critical issues of personal liability and the desire to limit exposure to the original equity investment led to the development of other forms of organization. A corporation addresses both drawbacks by viewing the business not as synonymous with the individual but as a separate entity.[5] If a corporation suffers substantial losses, the founder(s) will lose only his investment in the business.

AT&T's corporate headquarters in San Antonio, TX. What are the advantages of working for a corporation?

There are a variety of corporations that the U.S. legal system has developed, and we will address the three most common forms. Historically, a new business formed a simple protected corporate form known as a **Subchapter S Corporation**, while a business that was larger, or one that was developing into a large business, formed as a Subchapter C Corporation. These corporation types take their names from subchapters in the Internal Revenue Code. However, today another form of corporation, the Limited Liability Corporation (LLC), has become a predominant business form in the United States. We discuss S, C, and LLC corporations in greater depth next.

Subchapter S Corporation
An organizational form that treats the firm as an entity separate from the individuals. This allows the owners to treat the income as they would if the firm were a sole proprietorship or a partnership. It has limitations in the number and type of shareholders.

Subchapter S Corporation. As with all corporate forms, the Subchapter S has the benefit of protecting the owners by treating the firm as a separate entity. Thus, the liability is generally limited to any investment the owners might have in the organization. However, a Subchapter S allows the owners to treat the income of the firm as they would if the firm were a sole proprietorship or a partnership. Thus, the owners report their income or losses on their own personal income tax returns. The business must file informational tax returns that report each shareholder's portion of the business that allows the IRS to ensure the owners of the corporation are reporting their income.

The benefits of a Subchapter S can be summarized as follows:

1. Limited liability for owners of the corporation.
2. The potential to consolidate financial statements of business and personal income for the tax benefit of the owners.
3. Relatively easy formation compared with a Subchapter C Corporation.
4. Legitimacy in the market as a more established form of business (the right to put "Inc." after your business name).

However, there are negatives to this form of business as well. Although the effort to form this type of organization is substantially easier than that involved in forming a Subchapter C Corporation, it is nonetheless quite cumbersome and expensive when compared to either a sole proprietorship or a general partnership form. We strongly recommend that an entrepreneur who wishes to form a Subchapter S Corporation get an experienced professional (lawyer or accountant) to process the paperwork. A second consideration is the limitation to the number of shareholders in this type of organization. Historically, a Subchapter S Corporation has had a numerical limit to the number of shareholders. Currently that limit is set at a maximum of 75 shareholders.

This limitation is fine for a closely held or family corporation but is a significant limitation to a rapidly growing organization or one that has any thought of going public in the future.

New York Stock Exchange

Subchapter C Corporation. Subchapter C solves some of the issues raised regarding Subchapter S Corporations, while creating others. Subchapter C Corporations also have limited liability for the owners, but the corporation pays an income tax.[6] This leads to the situation where the corporation pays a tax on its profits. Then those profits after taxes can be paid as dividends to the owners. However, the owners will have to pay taxes on their personal tax returns for the income distributed as dividends by the **Subchapter C Corporation**. This is the double taxation situation that is often discussed in the United States.

It is possible for the developing new-business owners to mitigate the double taxation cost. The owners are also considered employees of the Subchapter C Corporation and as such are paid salaries and bonuses. The costs of these salaries and bonuses can be viewed as costs to the business. Thus, the owners can pay themselves virtually all of the profits each year, so that little actual profit is reported by the corporation, and therefore, little corporate tax is owed. Profits that are not paid out for such items as salaries, bonuses, and/or dividends are then retained by the corporation for future expansion. A Subchapter C Corporation also has the advantage that fringe benefits that are paid out are not treated as income for employees. Thus, owners can have their health insurance and other benefits paid by the corporation, which then expenses each of these as a cost of business.

Subchapter C Corporation
An organizational form that treats the firm as a unique entity responsible for its own taxes. There are no limitations to shareholder participation and the "owners" are protected beyond their equity investment.

An important feature of a Subchapter C Corporation is that there are no limits to the number of shareholders that the organization may obtain. The only real limit is the number of authorized and distributed shares in the organization. Shares in the firm must have an initial value at which they are offered, a "par" value. Thus, the corporation has a floor value that is equal to the par value times the number of shares distributed, and this translates into the shareholder equity of the firm. We recommend that the par value be set very low so that the new company can authorize a very large number of shares (millions or even tens of millions). In both Subchapter C and S Corporations, authorizing more shares, holding annual board meetings, and reporting standards to local, state, and federal authorities are among the issues that must be formally addressed by the corporation. The result is that a corporation has higher administrative costs than is typically seen in a sole proprietorship or a general partnership. For example, a Subchapter C Corporation requires a rather detailed corporate charter; software packages are available to guide the new businessperson through the process.

The entrepreneur forming either a Subchapter S or a Subchapter C Corporation will have to have the following:

1. *A corporate name*—the new organization cannot choose a name that is considered a replication of another company's name. Patent and trademark attorneys offer services that include detailed searches of company names (and allow business owners some level of comfort with their choice) all the way to obtaining a nationwide trademark on the name.
2. *Location of the corporate headquarters*—for a new business this is generally the same as the business address.
3. *General nature of the business*—specified for the filing.
4. *Names, addresses, and titles*—of all corporate founders and initial investors.

5. *A so-called time horizon for the firm's existence*—for all intents, this is usually "in perpetuity."
6. *Authorized stock and capital*—the par value times the number of shares issued is considered the initial capital of the organization. Some states require the company to have that amount on deposit in a business account with a bank.
7. *By-laws of the organization*—the basic rules that will govern activity in the new company.

LLC
A limited liability corporation (LLC).

Limited Liability Corporation. In recent years the **LLC** has become one of the most popular forms of incorporation for new businesses.[7] This business form is still relatively new; for example, it was only in 1994 that California passed a law to allow such entities. The limited liability company has many similarities with the Subchapter S Corporation. There is the limited liability feature, which exposes each shareholder only to the amount of their investment. However, the LLC allows the new venture to have more investors, and it allows other corporations to hold stock in the company (a feature not available to Subchapter S Corporations).[8] An LLC may have as few as one individual listed as an officer of the company, referred to as a "member" of the corporation. The LLC is similar to a Subchapter C Corporation in that all of the information required is the same but is unlike a Subchapter C Corporation in that profits from the organization can be handled flexibly. The owners are allowed to flow the profits through to their personal returns to avoid double taxation, which occurs with a Subchapter C Corporation. Furthermore, there is substantial flexibility (unlike with a partnership) regarding the amount of income that is designated for each individual. It does not have to be in proportion to that owner's holdings.

The cost of formation of the LLC is very low as this type of organization is formed by simply submitting the paperwork to the state government and having a charter issued prior to beginning operations. State governments establish how this business entity is formed and a few states, such as New York, also require that the founder of the new business publish notice of forming the LLC in the local newspaper. Some states limit their use and will not allow professionals such as accountants and lawyers to form such business entities. As we have stated before, professional advice in regard to what is appropriate within your state is money well spent.

EXERCISE 1

1. What form of business do you believe will be the best for your new venture? Why?
2. Looking five years down the road, what form of business will be best if you meet all of your forecasts? If there is a difference in your conclusion, why would that be so?

LO9-2

Explain the basics of contracts.

Basics of Contracts

contract
An agreement between two parties to perform certain activities for some consideration.

Beyond the legal form of the new organization, there are a number of other legal issues that entrepreneurs should consider prior to beginning operations. A **contract** is an agreement between two parties to perform certain activities for some consideration. A contract does not have to be written, but it should be consistent with the theme presented in this chapter; we strongly recommend that the entrepreneur employ formal written contracts whenever there is an agreement with another party.

As with our other recommendations, we strongly suggest the use of an attorney in the creation of any legal agreement. In general, a contract should include several items that are reasonably straightforward, following on the next page:

1. Who the parties are in the contract. This preamble describes briefly who the parties are so that it is clear who is involved and in what manner.
2. What each party agrees to do and for what consideration (i.e., their cost, pay, product received, etc.).
3. When the transaction is to take place.
4. The timing of payment, if other than immediately.
5. When the activity is to take place and how long the contract is in place.
6. Warranties.
7. How the contract can be terminated. There may be damages specified.
8. Whether the contract can be transferred.
9. If the firms are in different states, which state's law applies?

ETHICAL CHALLENGE

Peter Roberts was a clerk for a Sears, Roebuck and Company store in Gardner, Massachusetts, in the 1960s. In 1964, when he was only 18 years old, Roberts invented the quick-release socket wrench. He presented the idea to Sears's managers and waited to hear back from them while they did market studies and considered the manufacturing implications. Peter was offered $10,000 for his invention, which was a sizable sum of money for a teenager in the mid-1960s. Sears told him that they saw only limited sales for the product but wanted to reward his ingenuity and also keep the rights to sell the tool. Unbeknownst to Roberts, Sears's market studies had suggested that the market would love the tool and the company had made plans to sell 50,000 per week. Roberts sued Sears and after more than two decades was awarded over $8 million. He later settled with Sears for an undisclosed sum of money.

QUESTIONS

1. Would you fight a legal case for more than 20 years?
2. Do you think it was ethically wrong for Sears to tell Roberts that his invention was not very valuable when in fact it appeared to be a significant new product?
3. Since both parties would like to benefit from a new invention, how should each approach a situation like this one?

Role of Leases in the Legal Formation of the New Business

LO9-3

Define the role of leases in the legal formation of the new business.

One of the most significant contracts that a new business is initially involved in is the lease where the business will operate. Lease contracts may be of any term length that is agreeable between the parties. Whatever the length of the lease, there are several issues that the new business owner should consider:

1. What exactly is the new business owner leasing? Beyond the basic address and exclusive access to the premises, leases should address utilities; access to parking (either exclusive or shared); responsibility for the external premises (including lawn care, painting, etc.); structural repairs/improvements; approval of leasehold improvements; and responsibility for permanently installed equipment (heating/air conditioning, plumbing, electrical, etc.).

2. Can the business owner renew the lease? The lease should specify how long it is in effect and if there is the opportunity to renew the lease. Such renewability is not critical in all leases, but the entrepreneur needs to evaluate such details in light of their business. The initial space that is leased may not be critical for some types of businesses, such as an Internet-based business where no customers will be coming in on a daily basis. For these businesses, the website and telephone are far more important issues. However, if you have a bakery that makes specialty cakes, your customers grow accustomed to where you are located. If you have to move such a retail-based business, there are significant limitations to maintaining a customer base.
3. Who is responsible for improvements? Who has responsibility and authority for physical plant improvements? A lease that includes the responsibility for making improvements to the facility should be accompanied by a lower lease payment. One entrepreneur bought an existing hair salon and negotiated what she believed was a reasonable lease with the landlord. During the first summer that she occupied the building, the air conditioner stopped working, and the lessee found out that she was responsible for replacing the air-conditioning unit; however, the landlord had the exclusive right to approve the unit. The landlord wanted a top-of-the-line unit to replace the old unit, while the lessee just wanted to install a functional mid-priced unit. The decision had to be made quickly, as it was midsummer in the southwest United States, with temperatures over 100 degrees. The owner of the business had no choice but to put in the unit the landlord wanted. The unit and the related improvements cost more than $25,000.

Leases help protect long-term businesses.

4. Who has responsibility for maintenance and other facilities issues? Who has responsibility for issues such as the utilities, landscaping, janitorial costs, trash removal, parking lot maintenance and security, window washing, and real estate taxes? Can you place the signage you want, or are there restrictions?
5. Who has to carry the liability insurance and at what level? Many leases require the tenants to carry insurance not only for themselves but also to cover any liability of the landlord. Insurance can be expensive, and it merits particular attention to be clear who has what responsibility for insurance.
6. Can your landlord enter your place of business? Most leases give the landlord some rights to enter your business to inspect it. The landlord wants to make sure you are taking care of the rental location and that nothing illegal is occurring. However, it can feel like an invasion if the landlord can come into your business whenever he or she desires.
7. If there are problems, what are the procedures for addressing and resolving them? If you cannot use all of your space and have a financial need, can you sublet some of your leased space to others? Many leases prohibit such subleasing. Most leases also do not allow you to cancel the lease unless you meet the specified conditions in the lease. To illustrate, recently a developing business was looking for a location for a new retail store. There appeared to be a number of good opportunities in the area where there were multiple buildings with empty space. Unfortunately, the business owners found that one space they really liked was already leased by a

business that no longer existed. The lease had been written with the personal guarantee of the business founder. Most states do not allow a landlord to charge two individuals for rent on the same space. Interestingly, the landlords chose to leave the space empty and collect full rent for the remainder of the old lease rather than rent the space to the new start-up at a lower rate. The individual who had personally guaranteed the lease before going out of business could only get out of the lease by filing personal bankruptcy, which he was not willing to do. If there are other problems and disagreements between the landlord and the business owner, how will these be solved—mediation, arbitration, or other means? If there are problems, can you withhold your rent?

Hopefully you can see that a lease is multidimensional and should be carefully crafted before signing. Consistent with our belief stressed in this chapter, new business owners can prevent many problems by ensuring that legal issues are thoroughly investigated and that they employ experts where needed.

EXERCISE 2

1. Put together a list of all the items you think are critical to discuss with your potential landlord.
2. What are the three or four most important items? Write down your minimal acceptable negotiation position for each.

How Laws, Rules, and Regulations Benefit New Businesses

LO9-4

List how laws, rules, and regulations benefit new businesses.

New businesses generally deal with fewer regulations than do established larger businesses. Many regulations enacted by the federal government do not apply to businesses with fewer than 50 employees (this number varies with the regulation). Some industries are highly regulated regardless of size, whereas others are only loosely regulated even for the large, well-established organizations. If a new business deals with toxic waste such as asbestos, it can expect to have to file extensive registration documentation and be subject to significant regulation immediately, regardless of the size of the firm. Thus, regulation-related issues need to be carefully considered as the business is developed. This same issue will also apply in industries involving alcohol, medical-related industries, and military-related businesses. However, at the other extreme, an Internet business that sells retail goods faces only minimal regulation.

There are some basic regulations that cut across the spectrum of businesses. Virtually all businesses must have an Employer Identification Number for tax purposes. Additionally, a business with employees will be required to calculate and deduct various taxes for federal, state, and, in some cases, local authorities. The payroll requirements are specific and well developed. Fortunately, an entrepreneur can simply purchase a canned package for doing payroll and should be able to meet all of these various requirements.

Some states, such as California, have far more expansive laws governing business practices. Although environmental regulations at the federal level are typically designated for large businesses, in some areas the states will also apply those laws to all businesses. Similarly, specific cities may have unique sets of special regulations. A city such as New York has extensive additional regulations for all businesses. A restaurant in New York City has to post information on the calories and fat content in all of its products, and any food that is deep fried must use very specific types of oil.

Obviously, the special rules and regulations for your industry and location should be explored before you start your business to ensure that you

Do you think the food regulations including health inspections, display of health code grades, liquor licensing, calorie information, and ADA certifications are fair to new business owners?

are meeting all requirements. Excellent sources of information regarding regulatory requirements are the Small Business Assistance Center (run by the Small Business Administration) in your area, the state or local department of economic development, and the local chamber of commerce. More and more government agencies are developing websites to provide all this information and, in some cases, even allow for online submission of materials. All states and cities are critically aware of the role new businesses play in their economic viability. The result has been the establishment of offices to help new businesses to navigate these laws and regulations.

One set of regulations that bears particular mention is the Americans with Disabilities Act (**ADA**). This law applies fully to any firm with more than 15 employees and in some communities has been applied to all businesses.[9] The law requires that there be no discrimination in the hiring, management, or dismissal of employees with disabilities. If the firm has someone with a covered disability, the business must make reasonable accommodation for that individual. Additionally, virtually all retail and most office businesses must make their places of business accessible to people with physical disabilities. The requirements of the ADA have spawned lawsuits in every region of the country. So many aspects of the law are still being litigated that specific requirements associated with the law can be hard for a business to pin down. The requirements of the law can also change after the new business has opened.[10] The result is that this area of the law must be constantly monitored by the new business owner.

ADA
Americans with Disabilities Act—specifies protections in business for those with disabilities.

Licensing

Related to the topic of regulation are the licenses that the business must obtain to operate. A license can be as simple as a business license that is used by communities to track business performance (and thereby tax income), or it may be specifically related to the fundamental operations of the business. Examples of licenses and permits include the following:

1. Business license.
2. Local ABC (Alcoholic Beverage Control) liquor license.
3. Occupancy permits.
4. Federal liquor license (Bureau of Alcohol, Tobacco, Firearms, and Explosives).
5. Business license (from the local city and county authorities).
6. Sign permits.
7. OSHA permits for food handling.
8. Fire safety permit.

The above list is illustrative and does not represent all the licenses that a business will likely need. However, looking at this list a few things should be noted. At a minimum, most businesses must acquire a license to do business in the county or city in which they will be operating. This type of license is quite simple to obtain, as it normally requires only that one of the principals of the business fill out a form (more and more often online), pay a set fee (usually less than $100 and often quite a bit less), and agree to report basic information about the business's performance on a set schedule. The business will be required to pay a business license tax each year; the tax is often based on company sales. While completing this procedure, we suggest that the new businessperson search for other licenses that might be required for the operation. Because lack of knowledge is no excuse for failing to have the proper licenses, we always recommend talking with current business owners and/or local authorities concerning the procedures and licenses required in each locale. For those firms who are facing more challenging licensing, such as one that involves disposing of hazardous waste or serving alcohol, it is best to visit with a lawyer.

Importance of Copyrights, Trademarks, and Patents to a New Business

LO9-5

Explain the importance of copyrights, trademarks, and patents to a new business.

A topic that merits brief mention is intellectual property protection through copyrights, trademarks, and patents. A **copyright** can be claimed on creative materials generated, such as books, magazines, advertising copy, music, artwork, or virtually any other creative product, whether published or unpublished. In the United States, a copyright is assumed to apply to anything that is your own original work (whether that original work itself is filed with the U.S. government or not). The copyright is valid for the life of the author plus 70 years.

copyright
The legal means to protect intellectual property. It grants ownership on creative materials generated, such as books, magazines, advertising copy, music, artwork, or virtually any other creative product, whether published or unpublished.

A **trademark** is legal protection of the intellectual property that is associated with a specific business. This may be the name of the firm, a symbol representing the firm, or the names of its products. Most large companies have trademarked their company name, symbols, and tag lines.

trademark
Claim of intellectual property that is associated with a specific business. This may be the name of the firm, a symbol representing the firm, or the names of its products.

You may not use a product's name such as Sprite, as it is the trademark of a specific product for the Coca-Cola Company. Although not as universally recognized as a copyright, a trademark is assumed in place once a firm begins to use the symbol or name. However, a firm can and probably should register its use to ensure the protection of the trademark. A new business is well served to perform a search to ensure that it is not violating a trademark. A firm that is violating a trademark can be sued and is required not only to pay damages, but also may be forced to change its name. A trademark is valid for 10 years and can be renewed as long as the firm or product is active.

The last intellectual property protection is the most complex and expensive. A **patent** covers a specific innovation. A patent is good for 20 years from the point that it is filed, fees are paid, and it is accepted by the U.S. Patent and Trademark Office for processing. Recent changes to the patent regulations have meant that patent protection is being granted on a "first to file" basis rather than a "first to invent" basis. This might have significant impacts on the timing of efforts by new businesses.[11] Patents are expensive to obtain and expensive to maintain, so they should be used only in the case where obtaining the patent is part of the sustainable competitive advantage of the organization.

patent
Claim of intellectual property that covers a specific innovation.

There are three types of patents: Utility, Design, and Plant. A Utility patent is for a new process, machine, article of manufacture, or composition of matter, or any new and useful improvement of those. A Design patent is for a new, original, and ornamental design for an article of manufacture. Finally, a Plant patent is for someone who invents or discovers and asexually reproduces any distinct and new variety of plant.[12]

A patent can be a potent entry barrier for a business, as it prevents direct imitation for that period of time. Unfortunately, close copies may skirt the patent laws, so a patent should be but one avenue of competitive protection.

Coca-Cola names "Share a Coke," the promotion for summer of 2014.

For businesses that founders hope will expand internationally, one issue to recognize is that copyright, trademarks, and patents filed in the United States only apply in the United States. If the firm moves to expand abroad, the entrepreneur will have to file each of those documents in each of the markets in which they plan to sell.

LO9-6

Define the role that insurance plays in the risk portfolio of the new business.

Role That Insurance Plays in the Risk Portfolio of the New Business

A topic related to the legal concerns of all types of business is insurance. One of the key concerns that should have been clear in the discussion of the form of organization is that the new business chooses the level of liability it is willing to risk. One means to limit liability concerns is through the effective application of insurance.

There are several basic types of insurance, but a key one is a firm's property insurance. Property insurance covers the building, fixtures, and inventory in all of the buildings in which the business has a function. One key concern is whether the insurance covers replacement cost or only current value. Much like owning an older car, you may have equipment that has only limited value in a resale market but is very expensive to replace if you have to buy it new. The firm must decide what types of risks it will accept and cover itself versus those that it will purchase insurance to cover. It is fairly standard to obtain coverage for fire, windstorms, hail, and smoke. However, the firm may also wish to obtain a special form of insurance that covers issues such as floods and earthquakes. The greater the insurance coverage obtained by the new business, the greater the cost. Thus, each firm needs to take some care to balance risk and cost.

The other forms of insurance an entrepreneurial business might obtain include liability insurance, bonding insurance, and workers' compensation.

- A new business can also obtain liability insurance, which helps to protect the business against lawsuit judgments. Such insurance does not cover intentional acts of malice; however, it does cover the business for accidents. Product liability insurance is expensive, but it can also be obtained to provide a legal defense fund in the case of a negligence lawsuit.
- Bonding is a type of insurance in which the business is covered in case the workers cause any damage in the performance of their work. To illustrate, a plumber may hire an assistant who makes some of the calls on customers. The assistant may make a mistake that leads to a pipe breaking, which floods the house or apartment. The damage done can be very costly and perhaps even cause bankruptcy. However, through bonding, the insurance company agrees to pay for such damages. In an office setting the owner can also purchase bonding to cover losses from employee embezzlement.
- Workers' compensation insurance covers liability for workers who are injured on the job. In many states, workers' compensation insurance is required and can represent a major expense for a business.

Insurance is such a critical issue that it merits spending time with an insurance agent, or multiple agents, to discuss the needs of the new business. Discussion with multiple agents will allow the new businessperson to obtain different viewpoints on the issue. The new business owner should seek out agents who have expertise in the industry in which the business operates.

FLOW RIGHT BREWERY & BAR: A FAMILY AFFAIR

When Chris was still developing his brewery and bar business, he really believed that getting all the equipment and supplies in place would be the biggest time holdup to starting the new business. Several weeks into the process, his uncle asked him how long it would take to get his business, liquor, and food preparation licenses. In all the effort to craft up the business, Chris simply had not taken the time to start the licensing processes.** He was stunned to find out the substantial number of licenses he was going to have to acquire, and some were going to take real time. These included:

1. A local business license just like that for any new business.
2. A license for producing alcoholic beverages, which included a federal permit from the Bureau of Alcohol, Tobacco, Firearms, and Explosives.
3. A license from the local police department to serve liquor.
4. A food preparation license.
5. An environmental disposal permit for the waste products.
6. A specialized "fry fat" recycling unit structure and permit.
7. A license for a sign. (A recently passed city ordinance required each store owner to apply for a license to put a sign on the building and/or the street. The restrictions on new signs were substantial.)

On the whole, these licenses were not particularly expensive to obtain; however, the time and effort it took to address these licenses was not a small matter. The regulation associated with each license had typically arisen in response to an abuse by a preceding business. In addition, there was so much sensitivity around the serving of alcohol and issues such as drinking and driving that there was simply no flexibility on the part of the regulators. Chris had to allocate time to attend classes for some of the licenses and, in hindsight, he wondered if some of the licensing was still relevant.

QUESTIONS

1. What are your thoughts about the nature of licensing for Chris's business?
2. What licenses do you believe will be required for your business idea? Check with the local Small Business Assistance Center to see if you are right.
3. If you are dealing with a product or issue that is highly sensitive, such as alcohol sales, how will that affect your licensing effort?

**Recall as we noted at the beginning of this chapter that even though we present these tasks sequentially, the steps of the process often happen simultaneously. Thus, legal issues like those Chris is facing may occur at the same time as some of the financial issues.

How to Develop an Effective Board of Advisors and Board of Directors

LO9-7

Discuss how to develop an effective board of advisors or board of directors.

Two related entities that can help the new business owner foresee potential legal liabilities are boards of advisors and boards of directors. These boards are composed of people who have both insight and experience with which to advise the founders. An effective group of advisors will not only help the new business owner foresee if legal problems might arise, but also help the new business wind its way through a full range of other issues and opportunities where experience is the best teacher. The new business should have at least one of these entities that will advise the founder. A business that chooses to form a corporation must have a board of directors. These are individuals who have a fiduciary responsibility to the shareholders of the organization. In new corporations, the shareholders and board of directors are often the same individuals. In contrast, a **board of advisors** may be formed at the discretion of the founders (regardless of the legal form chosen); it is composed of individuals outside the new business who will advise the firm.[13]

board of advisors
A group formed at the discretion of the founders (regardless of the legal form chosen) and composed of individuals outside the business who advise the founders.

Although the size of the board of advisors is a matter of choice, as a practical matter, it is better to have a few, well-placed individuals who are motivated to help the firm through the start-up process rather than enlist a large number who serve as a means of false showmanship. There is a set of basic needs for most new businesses; thus, we suggest choosing individuals who have experience navigating the following:

1. Licensing requirements for your type of industry in your locality (if such licensing is relatively complex or difficult).
2. Regulations for your specific industry.
3. New start-up experience and success.
4. Financial and accounting background with new start-ups.
5. Human resources experience, especially establishing basic personnel criteria.

This board can formally meet on whatever schedule seems appropriate. Many boards of advisor meetings are held virtually using applications such as Skype. The reality is for a new firm to obtain highly knowledgeable people willing to help, the new firm cannot ask the potential advisors to commit too much time. Often these highly knowledgeable individuals may be happy to have the entrepreneur contact them as issues arise without the formality of calling for a meeting to resolve the problems. Asking busy people to travel and spend a half day or more in a formal meeting may be too much of a commitment of their time.

In keeping with the efficient operation of a new business, we suggest that the board size be maintained at fewer than six individuals. Some advisors may be investors or else are involved in a professional capacity working with the firm. However, many expert advisors get involved with start-ups because of their love of seeing a business flourish. As the firm develops, formality and compensation can be considered.

SUMMARY

This chapter covered a wide variety of legal issues related directly to the starting of a new business. The legal form that the founders choose has implications from an operational, tax, and legal perspective. The new venture owners must be aware of and deal with regulations imposed by local, state, and federal authorities; obtain all relevant licenses; and be sufficiently savvy regarding the evaluation of contracts, leases, and insurance. All of these areas can be quite complex, and throughout the chapter we suggest that awareness of the issues is the first step, but getting some professional advice is the most prudent long-term move.

KEY TERMS

ADA 170
board of advisors 173
contract 166
copyright 171
draw 162
general partner 163
LLC 166
LLP 163
partnership 161
patent 171
sole proprietorship 160
Subchapter C Corporation 165
Subchapter S Corporation 164
trademark 171

REVIEW QUESTIONS

1. Why is a legal system so critical to a new business?
2. Do you think such legal protections are more or less important to a new business than to an established business?
3. What are the impacts on a business that chooses to form as a sole proprietorship?
4. What are the impacts on a business that chooses to form as a partnership?
5. What are the impacts on a business that chooses to form as a Subchapter S Corporation?
6. What are the impacts on a business that chooses to form as a Subchapter C Corporation?
7. What are the impacts on a business that chooses to form as an LLC?
8. What are the major differences between a board of directors and a board of advisors?

BUSINESS PLAN DEVELOPMENT QUESTIONS

1. What licenses or permits will be required for your new business?
2. Develop a spreadsheet with all the licenses or permits that must be obtained. Provide columns for Entity Administering License or Permit, Process Started, Application Complete, License or Permit Obtained, Fee, and Renewal Period.
3. What insurance products seem to make the most sense for your new business? What will this cost the company?

INDIVIDUAL EXERCISES

1. List the attorneys in your area who are recognized experts in new business startups.
2. Do an Internet search for contracts that can be used by new businesses. What did you find out?
3. What licensing requirements affect Web-based businesses?

GROUP EXERCISES

Break into teams of three or four people. Develop the following information and then present it to the individuals in your group, discussing why you made those choices.

1. Create a small chart outlining the varied types of people you would want to sit on your board of advisors, and explain why you would choose them.
2. Make a contact list of seven to nine people to invite onto your board of advisors; include their names, telephone numbers, e-mail addresses, positions, and what you believe they would bring to your new business.

ENDNOTES

1. W. Scott, *Institutions and Organizations* (Thousand Oaks, CA: Sage Publications, 1995).
2. Q. Huang, R. Davidson, and J. Gu, "Impact of Personal and Cultural Factors on Knowledge Sharing in China," *Asia Pacific Journal of Management* 25 (2008), pp. 451–71.
3. P. Coomes, J. Fernandez, and S. Gohmann, "Entrepreneurship: Theory & Practice," 37, no. 4 (July 2013), pp. 745–70.
4. C. Galbraith, "Divorce and the Financial Performance of Small Family Businesses: An Exploratory Study," *Journal of Small Business Management* 41 (2003), pp. 296–310.
5. R. Lewis, "Why Incorporate a Small Business?" *National Public Accountant* 39, no. 11 (1994), p. 14.
6. L. Hodder, M. McAnally, and C. Weaver, "The Influence of Tax and Nontax Factors on a Bank's Choice of Organizational Form," *Accounting Review* 78 (2003), pp. 297–326.
7. J. Freedman, "Limited Liability: Large Company Theory and Small Firms," *Modern Law Review* 63 (2000), pp. 317–55.
8. T. Taulli, "The Right Number of Shareholders for Your Company," *Bloomberg Businessweek*, December 12, 2008, www.businessweek.com/stories/2008-12-12/the-right-number-of-shareholders-for-your-companybusinessweek-business-news-stock-market-and-financial-advice
9. ADA website, "Information and Technical Assistance ADA," www.ada.gov/2010_regs.htm
10. Sun Sentinel Editorial Board, "Rein In Runaway Lawsuits on Small Businesses," *Sun Sentinel*, January 26, 2014, http://articles.sun-sentinel.com/2014-01-26/news/fl-editorial-disability-lawsuits-dv-20140126_1_small-businesses-ada-federal-lawsuits
11. U.S. Patent and Trademark Office website, http://www.uspto.gov/inventors/patents.jsp. Accessed July 20, 2014.
12. Ibid.
13. N. Upton, E. Teal, and J. Felan, "Strategic and Business Planning Practices of Fast Growth Family Firms," *Journal of Small Business Management* 39, no. 1 (2001), pp. 60–74.

CREDITS

Opener: John L. Marino/Public Domain; p. 157: Weedmaps.com; p. 160: © RL Productions/Digital Vision/Getty Images RF; p. 164: Jack Plunkett/Bloomberg via Getty Images; p. 165: Royalty-Free/Corbis; p. 168: Art Wager/E+/Getty Images RF; p. 170: Calgary Reviews/Flickr/CC-BY-2; p. 171: Mike Mozart/Flickr/CC-BY-2.

chapter

10

Human Resources Management

learning objectives

After studying this chapter, you will be able to:

LO10-1 Explain the elements of human resources.

LO10-2 Discuss the process of hiring employees.

LO10-3 Analyze the means for retaining employees.

LO10-4 Determine the pertinent aspects of employee probation and firing.

LO10-5 Understand Broad Coverage Regulations and Laws.

LO10-6 Distinguish the unique aspects of human resources within a family business.

USA GYPSUM

In 1998 Terry Weaver was working in farming and construction when a local agronomist suggested he use gypsum left over in drywall scraps for his land. This interaction led Terry to recognize a business opportunity. Gypsum (calcium sulfate) is a mineral that results from dried sea beds. The most widespread use of the mineral is to place it between paper to form insulation and the surface for most walls in buildings. The term *drywall* is also used for gypsum board, and gypsum is a good form of fertilizer. Historically George Washington and Ben Franklin both advocated the use of gypsum on farmland, especially for alfalfa fields. The PH neutral mineral acts to loosen tight soils.

Today approximately 90 percent of gypsum board scraps are placed in landfills, which creates a huge environmental problem. The gypsum board scraps can, however, be recycled by removing the paper and other items that may be in the scrap and salvaging the gypsum for use in agriculture and landscaping.

The firm built their first 2,000 sq ft factory in 1998 and in 2000 moved to a new 16,000 sq ft place. They added a second plant in 2003. Terry's business today is rapidly expanding. The small plant today can recycle 100 tons of gypsum a day, but this growth did not come without struggles. Initially local home builders saved any leftover gypsum board and gave it to USA Gypsum if the firm would haul it away. However, this proved to be inefficient because other tradespeople often dumped their trash into the bins provided by USA Gypsum. Also, these bins took up space that the central contractor needed. To solve this problem, Terry set up a unit of the company that goes to the construction site to support the gypsum board hangers by cleaning and taking out the scraps as they hang the board. Other firms existed to provide this service, but they had no incentive to help USA Gypsum by saving the scraps. Terry's unit prices its services very competitively, and workers also bring USA Gypsum hauling bins with them. USA Gypsum fills these bins and haul them away instantly, a service the central contractor likes. Thus, USA Gypsum provides a valuable service to the contractors and at a very competitive price. This arrangement allows Terry to create his own supplier of inputs.

Today, USA Gypsum works with more than 70 contractors, and the gypsum for Terry's business comes from within 100 miles of the home office. The firm continues to expand and prosper, and in 2012 was named as one of the outstanding U.S. firms aiding the environment.

Questions

1. What other recycling-oriented businesses can you conceive for the building trade?
2. How would you expand this business?
3. Do you think there are regulatory issues with expanding the types of recycling?

Sources: R. Brickner, "Gypsum Wallboard Recycling: Closing the Loop in the Middle Atlantic States," *C&D World* 1, no. 6 (2008), pp. 29–31; "Made in Berks: USA Gypsum," *Reading Eagle Business Weekly*, April 23, 2013, http://businessweekly.readingeagle.com/history; H. Stauffer, "SCORE Names USA Gypsum Outstanding Green Small Business," *Central Penn Journal* 28, no. 37 (2012), p. 2; "USA Gypsum Recognized as Outstanding Green Small Business," C&D World 5, no. 5 (2012), p. 8.

FRIENDS' HOME HEALTH

Friends' Home Health was within a few days of accepting its first patients.* Betty and Joan had initially hired 22 people, of which 15 were ready to start working after their training. These 15 encompassed a range of skills and personalities. The plan was to rotate all employees through various assignments so they would get as many hours of work as they wanted. This put the entrepreneurs in a position where they recognized that all employees needed to work well together so that the handovers with patients would be smooth. Some patients needed just a few hours of care a day while a family member went out, but others needed up to 24-hour care, which required a minimum of three shifts of workers.

The two partners designed the procedures for employee interaction based on some guidelines they found on the Internet. Employees took basic training at the junior college to ensure they were certified and knew basic health-related issues, but the founders also wanted to be sure the employees were trained to act specifically in the manner they wanted in the client homes. For example, the firm required that all employees call into the central office system to inform the founders when they arrived and started work. Betty and Joan hoped this would ensure that their employees were on time to the client's site. The new businesspersons also wanted to be sure that employees knew how to record goods used so the proper client could be charged for items such as disposable gloves. Friends' Home Health wanted their employees to be courteous, friendly, professional, and highly knowledgeable about both patient care and the procedures of the firm.

Problems with the employees started occurring the first day the employees saw patients. Several of the employees had significant problems dealing with each other, so the handoffs with the same clients were not handled well. Tardiness by several employees was also a problem. Tardiness not only reflected poorly on the firm but also resulted in detaining other employees who work the shift before them and cannot leave until the new employee arrives. The tardy employees said they were late because of traffic or automobile problems, but the end result nevertheless was that they were late.

The most difficult situation that occurred on the very first day of operation was one employee who cursed at a family member who was instructing the employee on how to get the patient into the bed. The patient was very elderly and fragile. The home health aide was in fact correct about how to get the patient into the bed, even though it was a different approach than the family had been using. Regardless, the two entrepreneurs knew that that it was never acceptable to curse at a customer even if the situation was frustrating. Thus, the employee had to be let go.

Even though letting the employee go was difficult and resulted in the firm being understaffed, it was a blessing in disguise: The fact that Betty and Joan had stood firm on the rules became a model for all the employees. The two entrepreneurs also realized then that they needed to be very clear about the rules and procedures for their employees if they were going to have to fire some of them over these issues. As a result, the entrepreneurs developed more detailed rules and policies tailored specifically for their firm rather than relying on a list of rules downloaded from the Internet when faced with a human resources issue. For example, every time an employee was late to a patient's home was recorded and a warning was provided. An employee was allowed to be late three times in a six-month period of time; the fourth time in a six-month period resulted in termination regardless of the reason for being tardy. Similarly, the two entrepreneurs were very strict with employees who did not get along with each other and had a policy that a patient is never to be impacted or to see such difficulties. If that rule was violated, then one or both employees could be terminated.

QUESTIONS

1. What other standards beyond tardiness and working well with fellow employees do you think Friends' Home Health will need for employees?
2. In your proposed business what would be the key human resources issues you might need to consider?
3. If you have two employees who cannot get along and it is disrupting patient care, how would you work out a solution?
4. If there is no solution, how would you determine whom to let go?

*Recall as noted earlier that the activities in each chapter are laid out to imply sequential behaviors.

Human resources management includes the hiring, inspiring, and managing of personnel, which is one of the toughest and yet most important functions for an entrepreneurial firm to develop.[1] For example, hiring personnel who are consistent with your business strategy and style is critical to business success, since without them it is unlikely that you will be able to implement your strategy. Similarly, managing the firm's personnel so that you increase employee skill development allows the firm to develop a key resource. This type of resource is one that other firms cannot easily copy and one that may, in turn, lead to better firm performance.[2] The business of simply meeting the basic legal requirements of your human resources function can be daunting—yet is insufficient for the firm to be successful. This chapter will explore the rich set of issues, both legal and nonlegal, that a start-up business must consider.

The Elements of Human Resources

LO10-1

Explain the elements of human resources.

human resources

As defined in economics, the quantity and quality of human effort directed toward producing goods and services.

Human resources has been defined in economics as the quantity and quality of human effort directed toward producing goods and services. What this means to an entrepreneur is far more than simply having the right number of people with the right skills for a particular job. As Friends' Home Health discovered, you can hire people and train them well but still have problems. The success of entrepreneurial firms pursuing new opportunities requires a number of deliberate actions by the business founder concerning human resources issues.[3]

The elements that this chapter will explore include hiring employees (job descriptions, job advertisements, discrimination, job interviews, testing, job offers); retaining employees (compensation and benefit systems, wages and hours requirements, performance reviews); and dealing with difficult employees (probation, firing). After dealing with these issues, the chapter will also examine several other issues specifically relevant to dealing with family in a business. We specifically address family business in this chapter. One of the most important differences between a typical entrepreneurial start-up and one that is a family business are issues related to human resources as some of the employees are family.

The Process of Hiring Employees

LO10-2

Discuss the process of hiring employees.

To visualize how important hiring is to an entrepreneurial firm, compare the impact of one person in a large organization to that of one person in a small organization. If a large organization has 1,000 employees, one problem employee represents only 0.1 percent of its workforce. In a small entrepreneurial firm with five employees, one employee causing problems represents 20 percent of the workforce. An unhappy person not working at full capacity will result in the entrepreneur spending an inordinate amount of time dealing with the problems caused by the troublesome employee. Thus, a poor employee has a triple impact on the entrepreneurial firm: (1) the owner's time is lost; (2) the organization does not fully benefit from the employee; and (3) the problems may bleed over to other employees. Where larger firms can absorb the resulting difficulties due to their built-in slack (excess resources), an entrepreneurial firm can be devastated by a bad hiring decision. The process of finding and hiring new employees is critical and should involve a series of deliberate steps.

Job Description

job description
Document that describes the job that is to be filled.

A **job description** describes the job that is to be filled. In an entrepreneurial business, this document is not meant to be a formal, highly structured document as it might be in a large corporation.[4] Nonetheless, we highly recommend that all positions that are hired into the business have a written job description. Too often entrepreneurs say they know what they want in an employee, but they never write it down. The reason is probably multifold, including a lack of time, an unclear picture of the new position, or a desire to remain flexible for the right individual. However, the process of generating a job description will assist the founder immensely as he carefully considers the skills, background, and ability of a potential new hire. All too often, the entrepreneur who fails to develop a job description ends up hiring someone because he "likes" the person.

Taking the time to write down those skills and capabilities will go a long way toward ensuring that all dimensions of the job are considered. For example, today the operation of a computer and the ability to do word processing is widespread. However, if you do not ask the job applicant if she has those skills, you may be unpleasantly surprised after hiring the person. You may even need to be more specific than simply saying you want those general skills. For example, you may need someone who can work particularly fast at typing or entering data into and using an Excel spreadsheet. However, the skills that the average person may have in these areas may not reach the level you need for the specific software program you are using. You will need to determine what skills are critical at the stage of hiring and those that you are willing to help develop after you hire someone.

In a similar vein, there is information you need to share with the potential employee. For example, if you require uniforms, will they be provided or are they an employee's responsibility? This kind of information may be seen by the founder as a small matter, but it may be enough to impact whether or not an employee will be happy in the job. Imagine the impact if an employee arrived on the first day only to be told that he was responsible for bringing in his own tools, but no one had mentioned that to the employee. When making a hiring decision, the new businessperson needs to consider whether there are skills not required today, but which may be needed in the near future. Putting the job description in writing helps in this process by ensuring that all the elements of the job are considered, as well as forcing the business owner to consider changes as the firm grows. A brief example of a job description is shown below:

Job Title: Furniture Refinisher

Salary: $26,500–$32,400 per year

Benefits: Medical for employee is provided at no cost to the employee. Medical for family is provided whereby the employee pays a premium equal to the difference between the family-policy premium and the employee-only premium.

Vacation: Two weeks of vacation will be earned after six months of employment.

Sick Days: The individual will accrue one sick day for every two months of employment.

Description: This individual will be responsible for evaluating, repairing, and refinishing a variety of office furniture, including desks, cabinets, file cabinets, bookcases, and chairs.

Skills: Skills needed in woodworking, metal fabrication, upholstery, as well as general carpentry skills. Having completed a carpenter apprenticeship program is a plus.

Many businesses today are virtual, whereby the employees all work remotely and stay connected via the Internet. There can be a tendency in the fast-paced, Internet-based society to not take the time to write up such items as job descriptions. In that setting, however, it is critical that the entrepreneur be even clearer on expectations and sharing information since the direct interpersonal connection is reduced.

EXERCISE 1

1. What jobs will be necessary in your new business during the first year?
2. Briefly outline the skills needed to handle each job.
3. Based on your cash flow statements, how much do you expect to invest in salaries and benefits during the first year?

Job Advertising

Once the entrepreneur has generated the job description, she needs to try to attract the largest pool of applicants possible for the job. Although word of mouth is a means to advertise for a job, we suggest that it is but one of many possible methods for attracting a wider audience. There are a variety of ways to advertise and a large number of organizations that can help promote information on your job opening at little or no cost. These include:

- College placement offices
- Trade associations
- Employment agencies

Similarly, if the business is in a very visible location, then a sign can be posted outside the office. If the business is a virtual business, then placing a notice on discussion boards where people with the specific skill set you desire visit.

A more expensive means to locate potential employees is a traditional help-wanted ad, placed either in a newspaper or on a formal Internet website dedicated to such businesses. These advertisements vary widely in cost and ability to reach the audience you desire. Information from the advertising location on readership or viewership, statistics on reply rates, and rates charged are all important pieces of information for the entrepreneur seeking to place an advertisement.

Finally, for very unique skill requirements, there are companies that do an extremely good job recruiting and placing people. These companies traditionally charge the company seeking to hire the employee, and that fee can range from a set fee to a significant percentage of the placed employee's first-year salary. This can be very expensive, so the new business owner needs to clearly think through the benefits of casting a more professional net.

In writing the advertisement for the new hire, the entrepreneur should keep it concise and oriented toward the basic information needed for a potential applicant to evaluate his qualifications for the position. However, there are thousands of generic advertisements placed every week that look identical to one another. You will want your advertisement to be distinct enough to stand apart so it will draw the attention of potential applicants. If possible, your ad should communicate the culture of the firm and your desire to have the right person join your organization. The advertisement should also express excitement about the business. Overall, remember to write the ad to sell the job and the business honestly to the potential employee. Even though many people who read the advertisement may decide that they are not qualified, you would like them to walk away with a positive view of the business from their reading of the advertisement.

The advertisement should ask applicants to submit a résumé and a short list of references. Virtually all potential candidates will have résumés prepared unless they are applying for jobs at the very lowest skill levels. A deadline should be established for applying in order to fairly evaluate the applicants in comparison to each other. A typical wording might state, "The application deadline is January 15, 201X, or until the position is filled." This allows a comparison across candidates after January 15, and also allows for the possibility that no one will meet all of your requirements by the deadline.

discrimination
In the workplace, hiring, dismissal, level of pay, or promotions based on race, color, gender, religious beliefs, or national origin of the employee. Such actions are prohibited by federal and state laws.

Discrimination. It is important in designing the advertisement that the firm use nondiscriminatory language. Title VII of the Civil Rights Act prohibits **discrimination** in hiring, dismissal, level of pay, or promotions on the basis of race, color, gender, religious beliefs, or national origin. This law currently applies to all firms with more than 25 employees. However, there are also state laws that may apply to firms with fewer than 25 employees, plus other federal laws that put the entrepreneur at risk even if the firm has fewer than 15 employees. Therefore, the entrepreneur should avoid any discrimination or even the appearance of discrimination. The adherence to a nondiscrimination posture takes effort by the entrepreneurial business.[5]

Supreme Court rulings have played a huge part in how human relations function in modern business.

The entrepreneur should write job descriptions and advertisements in a nondiscriminatory manner. Terms such as *salesman*, *handyman*, *young*, or *counter girl* should be avoided. Antidiscrimination laws do not require that you hire any one particular person; however, you must give everyone an equal opportunity to be considered. The wide advertising of a job and the establishment of a job description will help the entrepreneur establish that he or she acted in a nondiscriminatory manner. If you advertise widely, you have not prevented anyone from applying. The job description helps to ensure that all individuals are judged on the same basis.

EXERCISE 2

1. Pick a position in your new business and outline the needs for the business.
2. Write an ad for this position in your new business.
3. Have your fellow classmates evaluate it for effectiveness and proper language.

Interview

Regardless of whether the candidate has or does not have a résumé, you should ask each one to fill out an application for employment. It is important to establish set criteria for every applicant and to have the ability to track exactly who applied for each position. A variety of generic forms are available at any office supply store or via any one of several software packages. We believe that at a minimum, the following information should be obtained in the application and interview process:

- Name, address, telephone numbers (home, cell), e-mail address (if applicable)
- Other addresses for the past three years
- Social Security number (SSN)
- Driver's license number and state of issue
- Work history

- Date available for work
- Position for which the candidate is applying
- How the candidate heard about the job
- Education and training
- Professional organization memberships
- Any record of conviction and, if so, details of that conviction
- If not a U.S. citizen, the appropriate documentation authorizing the candidate to work. (Note that sometimes very good people will come and apply for a job and ask you to sponsor them. This typically requires several thousand dollars, which the applicant may be willing to pay. You as a business owner will have to be willing to take the time to act as a sponsor. You will also have to verify that this job requires some unique set of skills that only this person has.)
- References

Once the candidate pool has been set, the founder must winnow the candidate list down to a group to be interviewed. If possible, we recommend that you sit with the applications and the job description at one set time period, so that a direct comparison of the applications and job needs can be completed. Many businesses use some type of video feed program (e.g., Facetime or Skype) to interview candidates without having to incur travel costs. Those candidates who do not have the minimum requirements for the position should be rejected immediately. Those who closely match your job description should be the ones where you focus your next effort. Those that appear to be the best fit in that group should be considered for an interview.

During the interview process (whether it is in person or done electronically), it is important that the entrepreneur not discriminate against any given individual. There is a short list of topics that should not be asked about in any interview. You should not ask questions about, nor can you consider in the hiring decision, any of the following:

- Age
- Race
- Disability
- Gender
- National origin
- Religion or creed

Note that you can ask about prior convictions, but you may not ask about the candidate's arrest record. An arrest is not the same as a conviction. In summary, the discussion during the interview should be based on the needs of the job.

The interviewer should also use the interview to provide a realistic preview of the job and the company to the interviewee. You should not overpromise what the job will be or the relevant job security present in the firm. Too often firms try to sell the employee on the job by overpromising what the job is or underselling the expectations the firm has of the employee. Instead, you should provide a valid and realistic perspective that promotes the firm but also sets appropriate expectations for the potential employee.

Although it is a tedious process, the founder needs to check as many references as possible. However, the entrepreneur should balance the checking of references with the nature of the job. If the job requires very low skills, then perhaps the need for references might be a bit less important. However, if the job is more central to the organization and has higher required skill levels, then the importance of the references increases. The entrepreneur should also closely check references if the employee might be in a position to put either the business or its customers at risk. Thus, someone mowing lawns for you in a lawn mowing business might require only a simple employment check. In contrast, a new plumber, who will have access to clients' homes and must be covered under your liability policies, requires a more rigorous background check. The references proposed by the interviewee and any others that the founder believes would have knowledge of the person should be contacted. If the job requires driving, as it does for many salespeople, then the entrepreneur should inform the job candidate that he will be checking the candidate's driving records. In order to make these contacts and receive information, the person hiring must have signed permission from the candidate.

The interview process and the checking of references is a time-consuming process. It is for this reason that the screening of résumés or applications prior to beginning this course of action is important. However, the entrepreneur does not want to shortchange the interview and reference process. As a result, you should keep your mind open about which candidate to hire after an initial interview and background check, and then conduct a second round of interviews.

Some organizations go even further in making sure that the person is right for the firm and the firm is right for the person. For example, several organizations that we have worked with over the years require the candidates to spend a full day at the company. During the day the applicant will work with other members of the team, have lunch with the other workers, and get to see and be seen in the day-to-day environment. An evaluation by the employees of the company and the candidate at the end of the day provides the needed feedback to management prior to a hire decision. The entrepreneur should keep continuous records of all advertisements that have been run whether a physical publication or on Internet, who responded, and the criteria for the job. If there are ever questions and/or if discrimination is charged, this type of record keeping will be quite helpful in defending your actions.

Testing

Ultimately, the entrepreneur should choose the employee that best meets her needs. Testing can be a part of that decision process, and testing comes in many forms and in response to many concerns. Some business owners wish to assure a drug-free workplace, and the founder has the right to insist on testing.[6] In fact, some states, such as Florida, offer a reduction in the rates of workers' compensation insurance if the business has a drug-free workplace program. This can be encouraged by requiring all new employees to submit to a drug test as well as requiring all employees to periodically submit to random drug testing. Most entrepreneurial businesses choose not to have drug testing, and they face risks in conducting such tests. The privacy rights of employees can come into conflict with the desire to have a drug-free workplace. Entrepreneurs are encouraged to consult a local lawyer before beginning such a program. An interesting question that faces many entrepreneurial firms in a state like Colorado or Washington is how to deal with a drug-free workplace when marijuana is legal in the state.

Another level of testing consists of testing candidates on the basic requirements of a position. For example, we know of one business that requires all of its potential employees to pass a 10-question, multiple-choice basic mathematics test to be eligible for an interview. The founder's explanation for this is that every employee is handling cash, and basic mathematics is a fundamental need of the organization. A number of companies extend this testing to include personality testing or work behavior testing. All of this is perfectly acceptable if a direct link between performance on the test and the skill set necessary for success on the job is made.

EXERCISE 3

1. Prepare a set of questions for an interview of the potential employees you identified in Exercise 2.
2. What types of testing might be appropriate for your business?

The Offer

Once you have selected your top candidate, you need to extend an offer. We suggest that all of the details of the offer be developed prior to any conversation with the candidate. Consideration should be given to the possibility that the candidate might wish to negotiate the deal. You should decide on your negotiation position and how much you are willing to offer for this particular candidate. While this negotiation is primarily an art, we do recommend that once an offer is made, you allow the candidate the opportunity to accept the offer or return to you very quickly with a counter position (establish the amount of time that the offer will remain in effect before you withdraw it and offer the position to another candidate). At that point, you can make whatever concessions you think are appropriate and then respond to the candidate. Once an offer is agreed upon between the parties, it should be put in writing by the founder, signed, and sent to the candidate. Only when the candidate returns a signed original of the offer letter should you consider the position closed. We don't wish to be too formal with this process, but we have watched many entrepreneurs be frustrated by employees who thought their agreement differed from that actually offered by the firm.

The Means for Retaining Employees

LO10-3

Analyze the means for retaining employees.

Once you have actually hired each new employee, you'll want to retain the employees that perform well. The above process takes a lot of time and effort. If it is done poorly and you don't retain the employee, then this process can simply be a waste of valuable time and money, not to mention the loss of productivity as each new employee has to be brought up to an acceptable level of performance. Therefore, the entrepreneurial business needs to retain those employees that add value. The key issues here are the compensation and benefits offered as well as the method and means of reviewing performance.

Compensation is going to be a hot topic among employees, which makes equitable treatment in an employer's best interest. Are there ever instances in which paying two employees a different amount for the same job and experience might be a good idea?

Compensation

The compensation system chosen by the firm is the aspect that is often highest in the minds of employees. In building the compensation system, the entrepreneur needs to maintain a fair and equitable system for all employees, both now and as the firm progresses into the future. Salary and benefits may appear to be a private matter between you and your employees; however, history would suggest that all information quickly becomes public knowledge among fellow employees. Even if the firm is a virtual one and no one works in the same office, the employees will easily communicate with each other on issues of compensation.

equity theory
The theory that we all judge how we are treated relative to how we see others being treated.

Equity theory is helpful to understand how to avoid problems with compensation. This theory argues that we all judge how we are treated relative to how we see others being treated. Thus, employees have a powerful need to feel that their compensation given their level and performance is equitable relative to that of other employees in their firm or other individuals in similar situations. As a result, all employees need a clear rationale for how their compensation stacks up against that of others in the organization. Employees can accept that someone who has been in the organization longer has a better overall package; however, they will have difficulty accepting it if they are hired at the same time as another employee and do the same job but receive less pay. The owner might have a reason for that difference, but the presence of the difference would be difficult for the employee to understand.

Owing to the level of complication within the workforce of most large firms, these firms require a systematic program that evaluates comparable employees both in the region and around the country. This systematic review of the employees will often include the following: (1) how they performed relative to their objectives; (2) plans for future employee growth through experience and training; (3) defined objectives for the next year; and (4) pay raise being awarded.

An entrepreneurial business needs a significantly less developed system than does a Fortune 500 company. The entrepreneur should decide on a basic form of compensation. The options might include the following:

- Hourly wage
- Salary
- Commission
- Hybrid/profit-sharing system

hourly wage
The amount paid per hour for work performed.

salary
A set amount of compensation for a given time period.

commission
Payment by the entrepreneur of some percentage of sales, typically associated with the compensation of sales representatives.

An **hourly wage** is simply the amount paid per hour for work performed. A **salary** is similarly straightforward, as it is a set amount of money for a given time period. A **commission** is involved when the entrepreneur pays an individual a percentage of sales, and is typically associated with the compensation of sales representatives.

A commission compensation system can be abused and may be a source of frustration for employees and the entrepreneur. Abuse of the system can occur when the salespeople are so focused on their commission that they fail to watch for the overall good of the firm. For example, a commission can be based on sales made, and those sales could involve financing instead of immediate payment. A difficulty might occur with a particular salesperson who books a large number of clients who are financially weak and who later default. The salesperson got the commission, but the firm is stuck with bad accounts.

hybrid compensation system
A compensation system where there is a salary along with commission.

profit sharing
An example of a hybrid compensation system. The firm may set some relatively low level of salary but offer to share a percentage of the profits at the end of the year or some other period of time with the employees.

Another potential for frustration with commissions comes when the firm either does, or does not, change the commission program to reflect the growth of the firm. To illustrate, when the company is young, the first salesperson may be paid a commission of 20 percent on sales. As the firm expands and hires more salespeople, the business would suffer if the owner attempted to continue paying a 20 percent commission. At this stage the firm is more established, with customers contacting the firm directly. Yet, the founder would have difficulty telling the new salespeople that he would be making less per sale than the existing salesperson. Similarly, the founder would have difficulty in cutting the existing salesperson's commission. Therefore, when you set the first salesperson's commission, realize that you may be establishing the standard for a long time in the organization. Any change will be viewed by those already in place as a negative.

The entrepreneur can also build a **hybrid compensation system**, where a sales commission can be paid in addition to a basic salary. **Profit sharing** is another example of a hybrid system. The firm may set some relatively low level of salary but offer to share a percentage of the profits at the end of the year or some other period of time with the employees. A **bonus** system is similar to profit sharing; a bonus is offered to the employees based on their performance. Typically, bonus systems are not as well defined as profit sharing; instead, the level of reward is left to the discretion of the entrepreneur. The time period for which such profit sharing or bonuses are given should be relevant to the individuals in the firm and within the realities and constraints of the business. It is important that the entrepreneur provide bonuses in a timely manner. An entrepreneur may visualize a year as a relevant time frame, whereas workers may be looking for monthly or quarterly feedback on their performance through a bonus. It is very useful for the entrepreneur to consider the industry standards in developing her compensation system. Those in your industry who have developed a compensation system that works have the potential to provide information not only on the level of total compensation but also on how to structure it.

bonus
Similar to profit sharing, a reward offered to the employees based on their performance. Typically, bonus systems are not as well defined as profit sharing; instead, the level of reward is left to the discretion of the entrepreneur.

Legal Issues with Pay. The **Fair Labor Standards Act (FLSA)** establishes a minimum wage for workers. Virtually all workers (other than workers on small farms and administrative employees) are covered by the act. This law requires that employees be paid a minimum wage, which in 2014 was $7.25 per hour. However, states or cities may have higher minimum wages. For example, in 2014 the minimum wage in Seattle became $15.00 per hour. It is even possible for local governments to pass their own minimum-wage requirements as long as they exceed the federal requirement. Many major cities have what they call "living wages"; a living wage is an index wage that requires the minimum wage to be at least what someone who works 40 hours a week needs to stay out of poverty. If your business is covered by the FLSA, it is also covered by the Equal Pay Act, which requires that an employer not discriminate in pay to men and women who do the same job.

Fair Labor Standards Act (FLSA)
The act that established a minimum wage for workers.

The FLSA requires that all nonexempt employees who work over 40 hours a week be paid at the rate of time and a half. Compensatory time is not typically allowed from one pay period to the next. Therefore, if the pay period is only one week and you have employees work overtime this week, then you must pay the overtime rate for those hours. You cannot give them time off next week as compensation. If, however, the pay period is two weeks, then time off in one week can be used as compensation for time worked in the previous week. Thus, the firm needs to be very clear on its time frame for issues such as pay. Another legal issue related to pay is child labor. The government closely regulates the use of children under age 16. The entrepreneur would be well advised to seek out legal advice if he plans to employ children, even his own, in the business if they are younger than 16 years of age.

Benefits

There are a wide variety of benefits that any business can choose to offer. For example, benefits can include the following:

- Paid vacations
- 401(k) plan
- Paid holidays
- Medical care
- Retirement plans
- Sick leave
- Life insurance

The package of benefits the firm chooses to offer can have as much impact on the success of the entrepreneurial business's human resources efforts as the compensation offered.[7] Some benefits represent costs to the entrepreneurial business but are relatively easy for the entrepreneurial business to provide. For example, a two-week vacation after an individual has worked at a firm for a year can be provided by most firms. There is an expense since you are paying an employee that is not working; however, calculating when the benefit is due and managing the process is relatively easy. The same may be said of paid holidays and sick days; the sick days build up over time as the employee is working with the entrepreneurial business.

Benefits that are more difficult to effectively manage include medical care and retirement plans. Medical care is one of the most expensive costs for any business, and yet it is also one of the most desired benefits by employees. On average, private businesses spend in excess of $4,000 per person per year providing health care for their employees.[8] However, historically, the plans most entrepreneurial businesses provide are not the full-coverage plans provided by large businesses. In fact, at one time many small businesses did not offer any insurance to employees. Now under the Affordable Care Act, firms with more than 50 employees are required to offer their employees insurance. Federal and state governments have established exchanges grouping individuals and small firms together in an effort to seek to lower the health care insurance expense. There are also tax incentives for small entrepreneurial firms to encourage them to offer health insurance to their employees, even if it is not required. One of the biggest beneficiaries of this act, in fact, are the entrepreneurs in a business that employs only themselves and their family. Now under the exchanges these individuals can obtain a more reasonably priced health care product.

The impact of such costs to the entrepreneurial business compared to the large business cannot be overestimated. One of the biggest differences in the cost of auto plants for such large American auto manufacturers as General Motors versus those from Japan, such as Toyota, who have plants in the United States, is health insurance. The Japanese-owned plants' pay is equivalent to that of GM, but the Japanese auto plants are all new, and they have hired young, healthy workers. The American auto plants, on the other hand, are staffed by older workers, a trend that only gets more severe with every layoff, since workers with seniority get laid off last. The result is that the health benefits cost GM far more than they cost Toyota. Health insurance can be a competitive disadvantage when U.S. companies have to compete against companies from countries where health care is provided by the government.

For the entrepreneurial business, the cost of health insurance per employee will be more than that for a large firm. Large firms have the advantage of spreading losses across a large number of people, whereas the entrepreneurial business can be dramatically impacted by a single significant claim. To illustrate, out of 100,000 employees you may expect 23 heart bypass operations and can budget for that with insurance. In an entrepreneurial firm, you may have only 10 employees—but what if one employee needs a bypass? The insurance company has likely not charged you enough to cover the costs of the bypass, no matter what it has charged you in the past. The result is that the entrepreneurial firm is a much greater risk than the large firm. This leads to higher deductibles, user copayments, and out-of-pocket costs for employees of an entrepreneurial business. The entrepreneurial businessperson will need to investigate the costs and packages offered by a variety of insurance companies. The sources for such insurance can be located through other entrepreneurial businesses in the area, the chamber of commerce, national trade associations, and the Internet.

ETHICAL CHALLENGE

You were part of a two-person team that was assigned to interview candidates for a new sales position. The new employee will be on the road five days a week and will need to be able to work with a wide variety of people. The main client companies that the salesperson will have to work with are filled with former military officers.

During the interview, your partner starts asking a series of questions that make both you and the candidate very uncomfortable. After the first interview you talk to your partner about the questions that he asked. They included these: (1) Are you married? (2) Do you own a car? (3) When did you graduate from high school? (4) Do you have any small children at home? (5) What church do you attend on Sundays?

Your partner explains that knowing these answers will really improve the chances of choosing the right candidate and will make it more likely that you will keep that person. He tells you that if the candidate is bothered by the questions, then he or she doesn't have to answer, and that will tell you all you need to know.

QUESTIONS

1. What should you do? Is there any justification for asking these questions?
2. What if the candidate doesn't mind answering the questions?
3. What if the candidate does mind answering the questions—how should you respond?

The entrepreneurial businessperson would be well served to investigate and compare various medical programs closely before choosing one. One option that is now also available to entrepreneurial firms is simply to have employees sign up under the health care exchanges created under the Affordable Health Care Act passed in 2010 and affirmed by the U.S. Supreme Court in 2012. The entrepreneurial firm can either provide the employees some funding, which they can apply to the cost of buying insurance from such exchanges or simply tell the employees to join them.

Although traditional retirement plans have fallen out of favor, some types of personal retirement plans have become quite popular. Referred to generally as 401(k) and Roth 401(k) programs, they are usually offered by an employer so that employees can contribute to their retirement on a tax-free basis. Most entrepreneurial firms do not provide any matching, although many larger firms offer matching funds for these accounts.

Performance Reviews

No matter the size of an organization, whether the business is brick and mortar or virtual, performance reviews should be a part of the management system.[9] In a **performance review**, the entrepreneurial business owner reviews the employee's goals and outcomes on those goals over some given period. Workers are motivated by more than salary. The formal conversation with a worker who is doing a good job, showing that her work is appreciated, is another form of compensation. If the worker is not performing as expected, then the employer should also be very clear about that fact. Although we recommend that all performance reviews be done in writing, we do not suggest that a complex form need be used. Providing effective feedback can be handled in a number of ways but should cover each of the areas of the employee's responsibility.

performance review
Review by the entrepreneurial business owner of the employees' goals and outcomes on those goals over some given period.

During this feedback, the founder is well advised to provide praise where it is warranted and detail any deficiencies and areas that need to be developed. As will be discussed in the next section, it is critical that the employee know exactly how his performance is compared to expectations. Too often the entrepreneur does not want the confrontation, so will give only positive feedback but then later fire the person. The result is a surprised employee who may seek legal representation to get compensation for being unfairly fired. As will be discussed in the next section of this chapter, if you have not provided accurate performance reviews, the individual may win if the parties do go to court.

Central to being able to do any review is the setting of goals for the employee. The setting of such goals allows the entrepreneur to judge how well the employee is performing. These goals should be realistic, tied to the performance of the company, based upon some measurable outcome, and reset periodically. Again, the time frame for these goals should be one that is relevant for the employee. Thus, for some jobs it may be weekly or biweekly, a time period that relates to the pay period. For most jobs, the relevant time frame will be quarterly or perhaps longer.

LO10-4

Determine the pertinent aspects of employee probation and firing.

The Pertinent Aspects of Employee Probation and Firing

Despite your best efforts, you will at some point hire the wrong person. At times you may find it necessary to fire that person. The entrepreneur has the right to hire and fire employees. However, you still must have legitimate, well-documented reasons for the firing. If you do not, you are opening yourself up to a lawsuit by the dismissed employee. Furthermore, you should provide all employees (short of their having done something illegal) the opportunity to rectify their performance.

Struggling employees are a reality that most entrepreneurs will have to deal with at some point.

Thus, you must develop a paper trail regarding all employees and must be particularly diligent in your efforts to assist a poorly performing employee. Recall that in discussing reviews, we argued that an employer needs to be honest about an employee's performance and document those times when she is not performing as desired. This can form part of your paper trail. You specify over time what is expected of the employee and then document how she is or is not performing to expectations. Firing someone for poor performance that has been documented over a time and in which you have offered a means to correct the problem will go a long way toward providing a defense in any legal proceeding and a proper justification for the employee. If there are concerns about firing an employee, the entrepreneur should not hesitate to contact a lawyer for advice.

When hiring an employee, an entrepreneur typically does not consider issues such as a non compete agreement or a secrecy agreement (one designed to protect the competitive advantage of the business). However, when you dismiss an employee these issues may become critical. If you are a restaurant owner and have several secret recipes that are central to your success, then you do not want a disgruntled kitchen worker to post that information on the Internet. Therefore, at the initial hiring, you can limit later problems if you consider having your employees sign the appropriate documents. These documents are available via many software packages and are relatively easy to understand.

LO10-5

Understand Broad Coverage Regulations and Laws.

Broad Coverage Regulations and Laws

There are a series of issues related to employees that all entrepreneurs must be concerned about, although not all companies may be directly impacted by each in the same way.

FLOW RIGHT BREWERY & BAR: A FAMILY AFFAIR

Now that the business was up and running, Chris and his wife had a number of family members who wanted to help them and who had skills related not only to a bar and restaurant, but also to the running of an entrepreneurial business. Chris had originally planned to run the business without any aid from his family, but he rapidly found that he needed all types of help. He and his sister had always been close. She was within a month of earning a degree in accounting from a national career school and wanted to work with her brother. As a result, Chris hired her to maintain all of the books, which included keeping track of every item that came into and out of the business. Unfortunately, Chris originally had no idea how much he should pay her or how he would interact with her in the business.

Chris and his sister sat down together at a local coffee shop one morning to talk about her coming on board. He desperately needed someone. Even before the business was formally opened, he was struggling to keep track of his expenses with so many vendors to work with. He knew it would only get worse when he actually opened for business and there were customers to take care of. Therefore, he asked her how much she wanted to make and what she thought would be reasonable. She told him that she was willing to take a minimal salary and virtually no benefits if she could participate in the profits of the business. She suggested that if she really did her job well, then the whole company would do well. Chris liked the idea of sharing the business's fortunes with his family, since they were so central to his life and to starting the business. He also liked the fact that she would be taking very little from the business unless it did well. Thus, Chris and his sister decided that she would start the next day and that she would work whenever she wasn't in class. They established a set of company milestones, which, if achieved, would lead to her taking home 5 percent of the profits of the business. However, she would not have an ownership stake.

The relationship between Chris and his sister worked very well. With her help, Chris was able to push the business toward opening more aggressively. Inasmuch as his sister was such a big help, he started to think about other relatives to bring into the business in some manner. He needed bartenders, servers, another hostess, more cooks, and a dishwasher. Chris shared his ideas about hiring more family with his father. Chris's dad suggested that he especially consider hiring one particular cousin to help manage the restaurant side of the business. This cousin had almost 20 years of experience in restaurants, but he had been in some legal trouble. His personality was a bit rough and, while he was talented, he did not seem very motivated. This suggestion proved very troubling. Whereas Chris was open to hiring family, as shown by hiring his sister, he was not sure if he should hire his cousin. Chris had extensive cash flow coming through the business, and he worried about the cousin's interaction with the customers. Even though Chris could not imagine his cousin stealing from him, he was not sure of his cousin's friends. Finally, how could he ever fire his cousin if it did not work out?

On the other hand, he was also not sure how his father and other family members would respond if he did not hire the cousin. Although his father did not say so, he was almost certain his father had made the suggestion because Chris's uncle (his father's brother) had made the request.

QUESTIONS

1. What would you do in terms of hiring the cousin if you were Chris?
2. What alternatives would you suggest in staffing?

Workers' Compensation. **Workers' compensation** laws are designed so that employees who are disabled or injured while on the job are provided with some type of compensation. Workers' compensation insurance is regulated by each state, with some states running their own insurance funds, whereas others use private firms. The rates of the insurance can differ widely in the various states, depending on the regulations and generosity of the state legislature. However, the rates for individual firms within that state are fairly standard and are generally based on the industry and size of the firm. The payments are typically given to the employee if he qualifies, whether or not the entrepreneurial business owner was at fault for the injury from an unsafe workplace. However, the payments to the

workers' compensation Laws designed so that employees who are disabled or injured while on the job are provided with some type of compensation.

employee are limited to partial wage replacement and medical bills. The employee cannot receive workers' compensation for pain and suffering. The employee usually cannot sue the entrepreneur for his injury if he accepts workers' compensation payments.

OSHA
The Occupational Safety and Health Administration, which is charged with protecting the health of workers.

The Occupational Safety and Health Administration. The Occupational Safety and Health Administration (**OSHA**) is charged with protecting the health of workers. OSHA has attempted to shape its regulations to be more lenient toward small business. For example, whereas all employees of any size firm are covered by OSHA, firms with fewer than 10 employees do not have the record-keeping regulations that apply to larger businesses. Additionally, any fines are lower for entrepreneurial businesses with fewer than 25 employees than they are for large businesses. Effectively, OSHA will not impact many new entrepreneurial businesses, such as small retailers. However, other entrepreneurial businesses, such as manufacturing firms, need to pay specific attention to OSHA requirements regardless of their size. We would advise an entrepreneur to consult with industry associations and your local chamber of commerce to judge the potential impact on your firm. If the impact looks to be significant, then a visit with your attorney is merited.

OSHA Assistant Secretary Dr. David Michaels holds an "All Hands On" meeting for members of the OSHA Team in Washington, DC.

unemployment compensation
Financial assistance for some period of time to those people who lose their jobs through no fault of their own; provided in every state by law.

Unemployment Compensation. Every state has an **unemployment compensation** law, which was put into place to provide financial assistance for some period of time to those people who lose their jobs through no fault of their own. Unemployment compensation pays to the former employee some set amount of money for a given period after she loses her job. During the time she receives these payments, she is required to look for a job. The entrepreneur is required to pay an unemployment tax to help fund this system. That tax will vary by state depending on the unemployment benefits that state provides, as well as the experience rating (the history of unemployment) of the company.

The Americans with Disabilities Act. The Americans with Disabilities Act (ADA) generally covers those firms with 15 or more employees and provides that each and every business must provide unfettered access to all disabled people. This means at a minimum that ramps or elevators and Braille signs must be provided in the business. The entrepreneurial business may also be required to offer special accommodation to employees who need physical adaptations to work at the firm. Some states and cities have additional requirements beyond the ADA that may impact the entrepreneurial business in this regard.

LO10-6

Distinguish the unique aspects of human resources within a family business.

The Unique Aspects of Human Resources Within a Family Business

Chris and his experience at the bar/restaurant illustrates a situation that occupies a special category of human resources management, that is, family businesses.[10] A family business is one that is generally run by and for a particular family. Human resources in such businesses are still critical, but since family members make up many of the significant employees in the company, everything becomes more delicate.[11] The combination of father, mother, uncles, aunts, and children all in the business has impacts well beyond the standard human resources practice. The introduction of family brings new issues into the business that must be considered. One difference that arises in such businesses is that hiring does not always occur in the manner described previously in this chapter. Instead, the family member is simply hired. You should recognize that this does not eliminate issues of discrimination if the firm is large; placement of family members because they are family members into positions in a large business can still result in charges of discrimination. The key issue in discrimination is that everyone is not given a fair chance at a job.

Managing family members can be difficult, as these individuals know all of the "hot buttons" that make a fellow family member angry. However, there is no effective way to fire or truly discipline the person without causing major ruptures in the family structure. The result is that family businesses and the human resources in them have more in common with family counseling than they do with the legalistic methods described in the earlier part of this chapter.

One especially tricky human resources issue that occurs in family business is succession. The business may have been founded by the father or mother. He or she is ready to retire and has a son and daughter in the business. Who in the next generation becomes the leader of the business? Too often the parent will put off the tough choices. The parent dies and a battle results in the family. To avoid this situation, the parent needs to choose a successor and prepare that person for the position by ensuring that he or she has all the contacts and understanding necessary to be successful. If the parent then decides to leave the business early, that parent needs to step back and let the designated son or daughter lead the business as he or she sees fit. Firms struggle to survive with two leaders of the business. The fact that the other child is not selected can result in difficulties in the family. Again, part of the means to overcome these difficulties is to work with professionals who act almost as family counselors to help the family see the rationales for the choices and how to deal with them positively.

SUMMARY

This chapter examined the wide range of issues involved in the human resources aspects of hiring, rewarding, and compensating employees. Many legal issues are involved in this arena, which explains why there are books devoted exclusively to the topic. We have endeavored to develop a basic checklist for the new entrepreneur to use in the process of developing the firm's human resources requirements.

The chapter examined a number of complex issues related to human resources and the hiring process, including the following:

1. Hiring
2. Job descriptions
3. Job advertising
4. Discrimination
5. Interviewing
6. Testing
7. Making an offer

The chapter also examined the means by which companies retain employees, including these:

1. Compensation
2. Legal issues
3. Benefits
4. Performance reviews

Human resources is intimately tied to keeping businesses within the legal structures that affect all companies. These include the following:

1. Workers' compensation
2. OSHA standards
3. Unemployment compensation
4. ADA—the Americans with Disabilities Act

The chapter finished with a short discussion about how human resources actions are changed by being in a family business.

KEY TERMS

bonus 187
commission 186
discrimination 182
equity theory 185
Fair Labor Standards Act (FLSA) 187
hourly wage 186
human resources 179
hybrid compensation system 186
job description 180
OSHA 192
performance review 189
profit sharing 186
salary 186
unemployment compensation 192
workers' compensation 191

REVIEW QUESTIONS

1. What means would you suggest to improve the process of hiring the right people for a new business?
2. What elements should a good job description contain?
3. What are the various ways to advertise a job opening?
4. What means would you suggest to help avoid job discrimination?
5. What techniques improve the interviewing process?
6. How can testing be used to improve the hiring decision?
7. What is the best method for making an offer to a candidate?
8. How does compensation impact the ability to retain an employee?
9. What legal issues are related to the retaining and firing of employees?
10. What benefits might be offered to new employees?
11. How are performance reviews related to employee retention?
12. Describe the impact that OSHA could have on a new restaurant operation.
13. How does ADA affect retail organizations?
14. What is the impact on hiring decisions when the business is family owned and run?

BUSINESS PLAN DEVELOPMENT QUESTIONS

Develop a human resources plan for your new business that consists of the following items:

1. Pay scale plan
2. Benefit plan
3. Advertising plan
4. Interviewing and hiring plan

INDIVIDUAL EXERCISES

Identify an entrepreneurial business in your area and ask the entrepreneur the following questions:

1. How do you recruit new employees?
2. What is your turnover among employees?
3. How do you compensate individuals to try to retain them at the firm a long time?
4. Do you employ family members? Why or why not?

GROUP EXERCISES

Rewrite the following poorly worded job descriptions

1. JOB TITLE: Coffee Room Lady

She has to do everything to keep the coffee room running smoothly: ordering and stocking merchandise, as well as collecting money and controlling credit. She is told what to do by verbal instructions from the supervisor. If she has any problems she tells him about it and he tells her what to do.

One of the things she does is to order the merchandise from various vendors. When it arrives she puts it on the shelves for the employees. When they buy the stuff she collects the money or IOUs using a calculator or paper and pencil. Every day she has to clean the coffee room. This includes the coffeepot.

2. JOB TITLE: Break Room Attendant
Perform duties to order and stock merchandise, maintain cash and credit control, and clean break room. Work from instructions. Buy merchandise from vendors. Stock merchandise for purchase by employees. Maintain bookwork for cash and credit transactions. Clean break room and equipment daily. Notify supervisor of problems. Use cleaning equipment, coffeepot, calculator, paper, and pencil. Follow safety rules and keep work area in a clean and orderly condition. Perform other related duties as assigned.

ENDNOTES

1. S. Haber and A. Reichek, "The Cumulative Nature of the Entrepreneurial Process: The Contribution of Human Capital, Planning and Environment," *Journal of Business Venturing* 22 (2007), pp. 119–45; B. Marint, J. McNally, M. Kay, "Examining the Formation of Human Capital in Entrepreneurship: A Meta Analysis of Entrepreneurship Education Outcomes," 28 (2013), pp. 211–24.
2. J. Hayton, "Strategic Human Capital Management in SMEs: An Empirical Study of Entrepreneurial Performance," *Human Resource Management* 42 (2003), pp. 375–92.
3. R. Baptista and M. Karaoz, "The Impact of Human Capital on the Early Success of Necessity Versus Opportunity-Based Entrepreneurs," *Journal of Small Business Economies* 42, no. 4 (2014), pp. 831–47.
4. M. Carroll and M. Marchington, "Recruitment in Small Firms," *Employee Relations* 21 (1999), pp. 236–51.
5. R. Carlson, "The Small Firm Exemption and Single Employer Doctrine in Employment Discrimination Law," *St. John's Law Review* 80 (2006), pp. 1197–273.
6. E. War, "Employee Drug Testing: Aalberts and Walker Revisited," *Journal of Small Business Management* 29 (1991), pp. 77–84.
7. S. H. Appelbaum and R. Kamal, "An Analysis of the Utilization and Effectiveness of Non-Financial Incentives in Small Business," *Journal of Management Development* 19 (2000), pp. 733–64.
8. Bureau of Labor Statistics. "Employer Costs for Employee Compensation—News Release," 2014, www.bls.gov/news.release/ecec.nr0.htm
9. S. Appelbaum and R. Kamal, "An Analysis of the Utilization and Effectiveness of Non-Financial Incentives in Small Business," *Journal of Management Development* 19 (2000), pp. 733–64.
10. K. Eddleston, F. Kellermann, and T. Zellweger, "Exploring the Entrepreneurial Behavior of Family Firms: Does the Stewardship Perspective Explain Differences?" *Entrepreneurship Theory and Practice* 36 (2012), pp. 347–67.
11. S. King and G. Solomon, "Issues in Growing a Family Business: A Strategic Human Resources Model," *Journal of Small Business Management* 39 (2001), pp. 3–14.

CREDITS

Opener: © Chris Ryan/AGE Fotostock RF; p. 177: Sam Beebe/Flickr/CC-BY-2; p. 182: Hisham F. Ibrahim/Getty Images RF; p. 185: James Brey/Getty Images RF; p. 190: Jamie Grill/Tetra Images/Getty Images; p. 192: Department of Labor.

chapter

11

learning objectives

After studying this chapter, you will be able to:

LO11-1 Discuss the basics of a marketing plan.

LO11-2 Explain how to develop a pricing model.

LO11-3 Differentiate between the various types of promotion available to a new business.

LO11-4 Identify the methods for sales management.

Marketing

JAMES MONSEES AND ADAM BOWEN: PLOOM

James Monsees and Adam Bowen met in graduate school at Stanford while smoking out back of a classroom building. Both of them were working on their own unique new product designs: Monsees was working on a chair that could mold into different shapes, while Bowen was working on systems to reduce workplace clutter. They spent their time together talking about the drawbacks of their smoking habit. They decided to see if they could craft a better way to get their nicotine fix along with the taste of real tobacco while not actually burning the tobacco. The two started their new business as Ploom in 2007. PAX, the product they created, is a vaporizer powered by a rechargeable lithium battery that uses pure tobacco leaves. The product was named one of 2014's best products by both *GQ* and *Fast Company* magazines. The PAX is not inexpensive: It sells for $250, but it is reusable, stylish, and slim.

Marketing the device has been fraught with problems. The first is that the company cannot make any claims about the health benefits of the vapor cigarette as opposed to a traditional cigarette. The FDA (Food and Drug Administration) prohibits unregulated companies from making health claims. The FDA is also considering banning the e-cigarette from being sold online or from being advertised on television. Despite these limitations *Bloomberg Businessweek* reported that the PAX "has become almost ubiquitous at concerts and music festivals throughout the United States." The website refers to the product's devotees as "Ploomers."

E-cigarettes are predicted to grow from a $2 billion market in 2014 to a $10 billion market by 2017. This fast-growing market has plenty of competitors including the biggest in the industry, Blu by British tobacco maker Lorillard. Ploom offers a less-expensive penlike product called "modelTwo," which sells for $40. Its LED light glows bright or dim depending on the charge in the battery.

Ploom currently has 35 employees. The success of the San Francisco-based e-cigarette start-up may be founded on its ability to widely market the product. The firm received a round of funding from Japanese tobacco company JTI and is now working to expand its market internationally.

Questions

1. What methods would you consider for marketing this business?
2. Would you advertise on television at this point?
3. How would you differentiate the PAX in your sales materials?

Sources: B. Stone, "Thank You for Vaping," *Bloomberg Businessweek*, November 20–December 1, 2013, pp. 30–31, www.fool.com/investing/general/2014/03/26/e-cig-market-grows-up.aspx; Ploom website, www.ploom.com/about; Gizmo website, "Ploom Model: Two E-Cig Review: Welcome to Flavor Country," http://gizmodo.com/ploom-modeltwo-e-cig-review-welcome-to-flavor-country-586563052

At this point in the process of building a new business, you should have developed a unique product or service to offer and established its business operations so that it is physically able to offer that product or service to the public. However, if the public does not know about the product or service, regardless of how much effort has been put into the business to date, all of that prior work will accomplish very little. The old axiom "if you build it they will come" works fine in the movies, but the reality of business is that you must do quite a bit to make potential customers aware of your business. People are creatures of habit, and in order to get some form of change in their behavior, marketers must stir the target customers to action.[1] Thus, a new business must aggressively seek to make its target customers aware that they have a product or service that offers a solution to a problem of those customers. A central part of this is that the business needs to build a credible case as to why individuals need to use their product or service, either because it is better, cheaper, higher quality, or reparable, or has some other characteristic that other existing products or services do not offer.

LO11-1

Discuss the basics of a marketing plan.

Basics of a Marketing Plan

Creating the business and the means to operate it is a necessary but not sufficient condition for business success. An underlying theme throughout this book is that planning and preparation are critical to the success of an entrepreneurial business. This does not mean plans do not change. Rather, with a plan a firm is better able to evaluate its past actions, changes in the environment, and what actions need to occur in the future. The same is true of marketing. There is little to manage, record, or evaluate without having customers. Therefore, to be successful, the entrepreneurial business also needs specific a plan for its marketing effort. Then when faced with changes, the firm can adapt that plan rather than begin anew with each small problem faced.

marketing plan
The plan developed by the entrepreneurial business to specify who the customers are and how they will be attracted to the company.

The **marketing plan** is developed by the business to specify who the best customers are and how they might be attracted to the company. Developing a marketing plan can be a complex undertaking. Furthermore, marketing is a complete discipline whose level of complexity can be daunting. There are many consulting companies and business courses available to aid you in developing your marketing plan. As the new business grows, it may be advantageous to employ an outside firm to help focus on its marketing efforts. However, hiring experts or consulting firms at start-up will cost you resources at a time when it would seem that the business could least afford the expenditure. Because such expenses can be very high in some cases, they can be hard to justify when you have limited cash despite the additional knowledge gained. The information garnered in the process of researching and evaluating the market that you are operating within will return substantial benefits to the owners.

The focus of this chapter is the establishment of a workable marketing plan that can be developed by any entrepreneur. This plan should, at a minimum, include identifying your market, specifying the ideal and general target customer, determining a pricing policy that is in line with the strategy of the firm, developing promotion, determining sales management procedures, and finally, forecasting sales. After developing each of these areas for a marketing plan, we will spend some time discussing unique distribution channels.

Identifying Your Market

In Chapter 4 we outlined a means for the entrepreneur to identify her target market and identify the "industry" in which she will be competing. This was done in the context of developing the idea for the business.

FRIENDS' HOME HEALTH

To build their business Betty and Joan developed a plan to purchase data provided by a national survey company to help identify potential customers. The data would give them the names and addresses of individuals who had recently been hospitalized and were over the age of 65. Friends' Home Health hired a small, local marketing company to develop promotional material for the business. They decided to mail to each person on the list information about the firm. After a month of mailings they had only two inquiries and no new customers from all their efforts.

The founders met with the marketing company again to discuss what could be done. Early on in the development of the business they had decided to create only a one-screen Web page figuring that their customer base would not be users of the Internet to make any decisions. Upon reflection, however, the partners began to realize that their target customer was not likely the person hospitalized but often those who loved and cared for the person who was hospitalized. Often these individuals were children of the elderly person, who may not even live in the area. Thus, Betty and Joan wondered if the more technologically savvy children of the target market would be using the Internet to evaluate providers. However, developing a complex and creative website was projected to cost $10,000, which they thought was a lot of money for marketing.

So the founders thought through the process of hospitalization and recognized that there was an intermediate step in the care of an elderly person. After a hospital stay, an elderly person typically would go to a rehabilitation hospital where care would be provided for a period of days, weeks, or months depending on when the unit believed the patient could be released to less intensive care. Another issue is the amount of time that insurance will pay for a rehabilitation stay. Many policies limit this care to a set number of days after which the patient and/or patient's family must assume financial responsibility. The unintended consequence of this is that many patients are released who are not capable of self-care.

The care in a rehabilitation hospital is typically not as intense nor is performed by as highly trained a staff as in a hospital, but it occurs when a patient is not thought to be able to be home alone. Thus, the founders of Friends' Home Health began to consider the potential need to seek out key referral agents such as rehabilitation hospitals or the doctors themselves who may refer the patient to them.

QUESTIONS

1. Do you think that Friends' Home Health Care's original target market should still be its target market?
2. What forms of marketing and advertising should Friends' create to generate greater customer knowledge about the service with its target audience?
3. Out of all of the marketing outlets available, which will be the most productive for Friends'? Why?
4. How would you evaluate the website expenditure? Is it a good value for Friends'?

The new business now needs to use that information as a foundation to develop a practical and actionable plan for attracting those customers.

An initial point needs to be made about the marketing effort for a new business. These marketing efforts need to be as clearly stated as the business's mission statement.[2] The use of such a mission and/or strategy statement helps to ensure that the firm is focused and will not seek to be all things to all people. The same focused approach needs to be used by the new business to market the firm's products to those customers that are most likely to buy its products at the price desired. As appealing as it may sound, an entrepreneur is not trying to get every person in the city to his business in the hope that they all buy the company's product or service. Instead, the entrepreneur is trying to reach those individuals most likely to actually buy from the business.

You will recall from our prior discussions that for a fixed location, business customers will travel only a given distance to buy from that business. This distance grows shorter as the number of competitors in the area increases. Therefore, a sandwich shop, hair stylist, dry cleaner, or similar business could reasonably expect to have large numbers of competitors and should

Geography and marketing can work hand in hand for business success.

expect customers to drive only a very short distance to shop at their location. If you market to too broad an area, the costs can be financially draining. A newspaper advertisement in a paper that serves a large city has virtually no targeting to specific consumers—it is a shotgun trying to hit a small target for the entrepreneur. A new business would simply hope that someone who had a need for its product or service would happen to see the advertisement, live close by, and respond to the advertisement. The entrepreneur needs to target their advertising very specifically to the market they are pursuing.[3]

Therefore, recall from Chapter 4 the exercise where we asked you to develop a reasonable geographic estimate of the radius your business might draw customers from if you are not starting an Internet business (we will discuss how this analysis changes for Internet businesses below). As we stated in an earlier chapter, if you open a sandwich shop in the downtown area of a city, the shop most likely competes with other sandwich or fast-food shops in a one- to two-mile radius, and perhaps less, if walking is the primary means of transportation for downtown lunching workers. There are limits to how far someone will travel for a sandwich. Drawing a practical radius around your potential new business location will help the business target the customers who are most likely to patronize your business.

In considering the geographic area, the entrepreneur should also consider how he will reach the potential customers in the area. Every contact outside his market area is really wasted money. There is a wide variety of potential marketing activities that can be pursued, including flyers, sponsoring events within the area, and affiliating with complementary businesses. As you look to define your geographic area, there will be several methods that fit naturally with part of your geographic area but which may not be consistent with another geographic region. Thus, the new business must target the right geographic area and do so with the right marketing tool to be successful.

To illustrate, consider a business that plans on using direct mail to contact potential customers. You may find that a given zip code covers 85 percent of the market you planned to target. The other 15 percent of your target geographic area is split between two other zip codes. The cost of addressing those two zip codes, owing to the smaller size and special attention, may exceed the addressing costs for the other 85 percent of your market. Therefore, the reasonable thing to do at this stage would be to limit your target market to the one zip code. Defining a geographic market served should be a more complex analysis than simply drawing a circle around your potential business. The drawing of a circle is only a start. Building on that, the entrepreneur should make a reasonable estimate of what she can do with the least resources to reach the most people as efficiently as possible. Once the geographic area is defined, then the business owner should remember that the money invested in her marketing effort should be primarily, if not exclusively, aimed at her target market area.

Target Customer

Once the geographic area is defined, the entrepreneur needs to define the particular segment of the market that he is seeking to serve. For example, if the entrepreneur is establishing a children's consignment and resale store, it is not likely that parents who send their kids to an exclusive private school in the area will shop there. Even though the private schools may ask you to advertise in the programs for their school events, spending your scarce advertising dollars in that venue would be a wasted effort if you expected these parents to buy there (although seeking their clothes to sell might be useful).

As part of the basic market/customer identification performed in Chapter 4, you have identified broad customer groups that the new business would serve. Now your operational marketing plan needs to go deeper and specifically identify potential customers. Most new businesses have restricted resources, and this is one of the things that differentiate an entrepreneurial business from a large business. It is this lack of funds that pushes the entrepreneurial firm to direct all of its marketing resources toward reaching the ideal customer. Therefore, once the entrepreneur has identified the target market, she needs to identify the specific customers who meet those criteria in the market area chosen.[4]

To illustrate, consider a new athletic club that was opening in an upper-income area of a large city. Most gyms in the region charged $100 to $150 per month for someone to belong to the club. That represents a cost of $1,200 to $1,800 per year, not including any initial membership fees. An individual would need a reasonable income to support that expense. The owners of the gym also believed that the distance that individuals would drive to a gym was slightly farther than the distance they would drive to a sandwich shop. A brief survey by the founders of members enrolled at a friend's gym in a nearby city found that most customers drove approximately two and a half miles or less.

The owners drew a circle of two and a half miles around their location and found that a relatively high population lived in the area. However, this region of the city had a mixture of individual homes and apartments. The newer apartments typically had their own small gyms. Additionally, many of the older apartment complexes were relatively inexpensive and populated by individuals who worked service jobs in the restaurants and retail outlets in the area. The result was that the owners came to realize that their perfect customers were the individuals who lived in the houses in the target area. This realization helped the owners pinpoint their customers very specifically. Those individuals they needed to reach were homeowners in their area who had a high enough income to join the gym and renters who did not have the service already in their apartment complexes. Advertising could now be targeted using real estate records. The methods used could be direct mail or phone calls (to those not on the national do-not-call list).

This is not to suggest that the gym would turn away potential customers who did not meet their ideal profile. There might be some customers who joined the gym because they heard about it from another source. There might be others who would join with a friend. However, these customers would not be a direct result of the firm's marketing, so the cost of obtaining those customers would be much lower.

Once the target population is identified, the entrepreneurial business should try to answer questions such as these: (1) How many of these individuals exist within your market area? (2) What percentage of these individuals do you believe is reasonable for you to attract as customers? (3) What is the percentage in the general population of people that belong to a gym? (4) Do these numbers match your cash flow projections? (5) What do you need to change if they do not?

Of course the analysis above changes for a business that is operated exclusively or primarily on the Internet. This type of business serves a wide geographic footprint that must be accounted for in the design of the business. The company's Web presence may be a significant factor in a purchase or inquiry.

This is part of the issue Friends' Home Health faces. In their case, the business is primarily delivered in person, whereas much of the information may be gathered by the paying customer (a loved one) via the Web. For Friends' Home Health the customer may actually not live within commuting distance of the relative that needs the daily care. On the other hand, Friends' Home Health is also not a national firm.

The definition of a customer for businesses that primarily use the Internet is the same as for all other firms. However, these firms are clearly not limited by geographic limits in the same manner. Thus, a firm has to be clear about its reach whether that is local, regional, national, or international. As always, a key issue becomes how to cut through the clutter on the Internet such that the target customer can locate the business.

For example, a simple term such as *home health firm* can generate thousands of responses on a search engine such as Google. Designing the site appropriately and even paying for placement will allow your business to appear in the first page of views when a search is executed. This all falls under the category of Search Engine Optimization. Search Engine Optimization is the application of techniques for improving your chances of being "seen." All search engine programs (Google, Bing, Yahoo, etc.) offer companies the opportunity to pay for special placement at the top of particular word searches.[5]

EXERCISE 1

1. Identify your ideal customer. Describe in short bullet points what characteristics this customer has that makes your product or service attractive.
2. What is the geographic range of your business?

LO11-2

Explain how to develop a pricing model.

How to Develop a Pricing Model

Pricing of your product or service is a critical consideration for the new business. One approach is to value your products for what you believe they are worth to the market. Most entrepreneurial businesses charge a premium for their products or services. However, the higher the profit appears to be, the faster competitors will challenge the business.

One method for an entrepreneurial business with specific products that are comparable to other products in the market is a cost-plus pricing method, where the firm determines its cost and then adds onto that cost some level of profit it determines to be appropriate. This method can be difficult to implement effectively.[6] The method requires that the entrepreneurial business initially determine what the total cost is for a particular product. This break-even point is referred to as the **pricing floor**, since the entrepreneur will not want to price a product at a loss. In calculating the floor cost of your product, you will need to include your estimated cost of marketing and an administrative overhead allocation. The cost of your estimated marketing might change as you develop your marketing plan. As a result, you would need to go through the pricing process several times as you refine the marketing plan.

pricing floor
The break-even point, or the lowest amount that can be charged for a product or service while still making a minimal profit.

Occasionally, the new business owner may choose to have a product that is referred to as a **loss leader**. In other words, a business may sell something at a nonoperating loss (i.e., the price only accounts for the actual cost of the product) to simply get customers to patronize the business. Our advice is that the new business owner not employ loss leaders until the business has developed some substantial momentum. The entrepreneurial business owner needs to get the firm on solid ground before employing such actions, which take considerable skill and have high risk associated with them. A loss leader can become quite a burden if customers buy the leader without buying the other services or products of the company.

loss leader
A product or service that is sold at a nonoperating loss (i.e., the price only accounts for the actual cost of the product) to simply get customers in the store.

In determining the cost of a product or service, we also suggest that the new business owner avoid the time-consuming nature of making detailed calculations for every product, especially if there is a wide product selection. Instead, the entrepreneur should place products in reasonable categories that balance the need for detailed pricing, as compared to managing an ever-expanding database of information. The major airlines are large enough to have the resources and the technological ability to manage a system where every person on the plane may pay a different price, depending on when the ticket was bought, and on predicted occupancy of the plane when it takes off. As an entrepreneur, you will not have that level of sophistication, nor is it necessary for an effective pricing policy. Therefore, having a data system that generates information that is useful and manageable should be the focus.

Information on the costs of the business is the foundation for determining **cost-plus pricing**. Although the "plus" aspect can be determined in a variety of ways, the most common approach is simply adding a given percentage to the cost basis for the business.[7] A new business can seek a profit of 10 percent, 15 percent, 20 percent, 25 percent, or 100 percent or more on product categories. Part of the desired profit margin will be determined by how competitors price their products and how much overhead the business has. There will be a comparison effect as consumers evaluate different firms' products and make decisions based on an internal cost–benefit calculation. For example, you may have a retail clothing store. Your prices may be higher than those at a large mall store, but your personalized service may be evaluated by consumers to be worth that premium. Alternatively, you may be able to charge a premium if you have an image that consumers believe to be valuable. If another clothing store opens up down the street and has clothing lines similar to yours that are priced at 15 percent less, then your business might have some difficulty. Significant deviation between your prices and those of your competitors will have to be justified internally and will have to have merit with customers. The entrepreneur needs to keep abreast of his competitors and their pricing to be able to make such judgments.

cost-plus pricing
Pricing in which the entrepreneur initially determines her cost structure and then determines what profit margin is desired and adds that to the cost.

Pricing a service is a bit more complex. With a product, you have a potential price floor based on costs, whereas a service such as counseling, financial advising, or interior decorating has only time as the base operational cost. There will still be overhead expenses (rent, utilities, etc.); however, the principal value inputs are your education and experience, which are difficult to establish as a cost. In the case of services, we encourage the entrepreneur to more closely examine the pricing of competitors. These prices can be critical information in determining how to value your service. We would suggest that you do not underestimate the value of experience. A consultant with extensive experience delivering expert testimony in courts will be able to charge far more than a consultant just starting out.

The entrepreneur providing a service should also recognize that pricing is a valuable tool to balance customer flow with the time he has available. There are price-sensitive customers who will make decisions based solely upon price; therefore, for those customers, as the price goes down customer flow goes up, and vice versa. Entrepreneurs who have been in business for a while may find they have too many low-margin customers and cannot provide the level of service they would like to provide. Thus, as their customer base increases, they might need to raise prices to limit the customers coming in at an unprofitable level so that they can serve them and profit from their business adequately.

In establishing pricing, there are several caveats that the entrepreneur should remember. Typically, a business starting out will need to offer an even greater value for the money charged to build a customer base. Once the business has developed a positive reputation, the value offered to the consumer can be changed to provide a bit more financial benefit to the company. Recall that individual consumers are generally unwilling to change the suppliers of their goods and services. As the business grows, the entrepreneur can shift from a cost-plus type of pricing to one that is based more upon what the market will allow.

A second caveat applies to the actual price charged. Small increments of money should be avoided regardless of the exact percentage of margin desired. Thus, rather than charge $1.01 for a low-cost item, a more attractive pricing would be $0.99. The $0.02 difference makes a reasonably large difference in appeal to consumers. Similarly, when prices are over $1,000, the entrepreneur should avoid using cents in the price.

Finally, the new business owner will have to determine if she wants to offer a quantity discount. Much of this decision is based on the nature of the business that the entrepreneur establishes. For example, a retailer typically does not sell in large enough quantity to be concerned with such issues.

EXERCISE 2

1. How will you price your product or service? Why?
2. What do your competitors charge? Why should your price vary from that industry standard?

LO11-3

Differentiate between the various types of promotion available to a new business.

The Various Types of Promotion Available to a New Business

promotion
The means by which a business advances its product or service.

Although it is only one part of marketing, people often think of marketing as the promotion of the product or service. **Promotion** is the means by which we make our product or service known to potential customers. The most readily seen versions of such promotion are the visual advertisements seen in a newspaper, viewed on the Internet, heard on a radio station, or seen on television. However, there are many means of promoting the business and each has varying costs and impacts. Promotion must be targeted to the market and customer groups within the industry, as we discussed previously in this chapter. Furthermore, you will want your promotional efforts to reach the specific target consumers in the most efficient manner possible.

pure promotions
Promotions that are strictly financial arrangements in which you pay for some outputs, such as radio advertisements.

mixed-model promotions
Promotions that cost something but also have an element of community support.

virtually free promotions
Promotions that have very limited financial cost but have time-commitment requirements from individuals in the firm.

Although most promotional efforts involve some type of financial commitment, there are some promotions that are strictly financial arrangements in which you pay for some outputs, such as radio advertisements. These are referred to as **pure promotions**. There are other promotions that cost something but also have an element of community support, and are referred to as **mixed-model promotions**. Lastly, there are promotions that have a very limited financial cost but have a time-commitment requirement from someone in the firm; these are referred to as **virtually free promotions**. We will briefly discuss each of these ways to promote the business.

Pure Promotions

This category encompasses the majority of promotional efforts targeted by the firm. Any form of advertising that is purely designed to promote the products or services of the company falls into this category. This type includes use of signs, flyers, Web pages, newspapers, radio, trade shows, and television. Each of these will be reviewed briefly.

Signs. An oft-overlooked means of advertising the company comes in the form of a sign on the building or on the street, and on the letterhead/checks/business cards of the firm. A catchy name, a well-designed logo, and some substantial efforts to get the logo and name out can pay significant benefits in recognition and impression management. For most customers, there are myriad businesses with which they can spend their money. Why a customer spends that money with your business is at least partially a result of what that customer thinks of your business when that purchase decision comes about. Most sign firms will be willing to aid you in the development of whatever signage you purchase, although the quality of that advice may vary widely. The key thing to remember as you design your signage is that "simple but distinctive" is the goal.

Flyers. As we mentioned earlier in this chapter, if you can target a very specific geographic area and perhaps identify a likely customer profile, then using something as simple as a flyer might be very effective. Flyers can be delivered directly to the potential customers' businesses or homes, or they can be posted at appropriately visible spots. Flyers can be changed frequently, printed cheaply, and delivered with low-cost labor. Unfortunately, these very characteristics also mean that they have a smaller impact upon customers.

Black Friday, the day after Thanksgiving, is the busiest shopping day of the year. It has often been considered the unofficial start to the holiday shopping season.

Web Page and Internet Promotion. All companies must have a well-designed Web page. Although a Web presence was considered a unique competitive advantage just 10 years ago, today it is an expectation. Customers look to Web pages for basic company information, information about products and services, and the ability to purchase online. The sophistication of your Web page is dependent on the goals of your organization, but particularly for a business that sells a unique product with a wider target market, this may be one of the primary means to reach clients who live outside your region. The first step, acquiring a domain name, is an easy process available from a number of third-party providers on the Web. The second and third steps include purchasing time on a server (almost always a service provided by the same acquisition provider, as well as a number of Web design firms) and having a company design a Web page for your business or developing yourself if you have the skill set. For any Web design beyond the most basic, we suggest that you hire a professional website developer.

In addition, the Internet provides a ripe and growing means for promoting your company. There is a wide variety of banner ads, pop-up ads, and promotional placements available for purchase. Companies can use the search engine companies (Google, Yahoo!, Bing, Firefox, Chrome, etc.) and/or can also work directly with other companies to advertise complementary items on their sites. An advertising agency that specializes in the placement of ads online is the best way to develop this area of promotion. The cost of this advice is relatively inexpensive since there are so many companies providing these services. However, their knowledge and expertise can be critical to an entrepreneur's success.

Newspapers. A standard method for promoting your business is through a newspaper advertisement. This process involves two steps: One is designing the ad, and the second is placing it in the newspaper. Your local paper will work with you on both parts, or you can hire an advertising agency to design and place the ad for you. Either method is effective; however, newspaper advertisements mean that you will be paying for "views" by many individuals who will never be your customers. This a broad-based "shotgun" type of advertising. It should also be recognized that in many large cities there are specialized newspapers that may be better suited to your business.

Radio and Television. As with newspapers, a radio/television advertisement can be designed and aired by the station, or you can employ an advertising agency to develop and place an ad. Although there may be only one major newspaper in a market, it is likely that you will have a number of radio and television stations reaching your target group. This fact encourages us to recommend the use of an advertising agency whose loyalty is to you and which will place the ads regardless of the desires of a particular station. Radio and television advertisements are qualitatively more difficult and

ETHICAL CHALLENGE

How far would you go to sell a product or service? How far would you expect an employee to go for you in selling a product?

Consider a salesperson who worked for an entrepreneurial business. In order for the salesperson to earn his bonus he needed to sell another $36,000 worth of product this month—and it was the last day of the month. He was the only income earner for the family, so they depended on his income, and they had come to depend on his bonus to pay some of the bills. The salesperson had heard of other salespeople in the industry who would work with clients so that they would book a sale in one month and take delivery later, in the next month. Another salesperson in the company would regularly book phantom sales in one month if she were sure the company would actually make the purchase early the next month.

QUESTIONS

1. If you were the salesperson, would you book a sale in this manner?
2. If you were the owner, how would you respond to the salesperson if you found that he or she was actually doing this?
3. Why would each of these parties perhaps see this situation differently?
4. Could this lead to broader ethical concerns in a firm?

financially more draining than the other approaches. A radio or television advertisement must be designed to make your points, not upset anyone, and be sufficiently creative to draw customers to your business.

Trade Shows. Trade shows are events established around a particular theme where individuals are allowed to set up booths to promote their goods or services. In an industry such as toy manufacturing, there is an annual trade show (as well as numerous regional shows) in which all toy manufacturers display their products to sell to retailers. Similarly, for services, there are often trade shows in which an entrepreneur may wish to participate. If you have a wedding planning service, you will likely want to participate in bridal shows that happen in a number of cities. Trade shows can be expensive to participate in. However, a business can successfully participate by strategically focusing its efforts and ensuring that pre–trade show promotion makes potential customers aware of the presence of the firm at the trade show.[8]

Mixed Promotions/Community Support

There are a number of opportunities to promote your business and help out the community in a way that targets your customer base. Schools are in constant need of sponsors. Angling your sponsorship to those activities that will provide maximum exposure to your potential client base is an effective and relatively inexpensive means of keeping your name in front of them. Depending on the business, sponsoring sports activities, clubs in the school, events (dances and fundraising activities), and the like, allows you to put your stamp on positive activities and hopefully reach the parents/children in your target customer group. For example, if you have a sports store in a city suburb, then sponsoring sports teams in the immediate area will allow you to be viewed as the official outfitter of those teams. The members of those sports teams, their families, and their friends will more than likely buy what they need from you in the future because of that relationship.

A second group of mixed promotions/community support are churches within your target area. Church groups look for sponsors to help in various activities for the community or for their youth. Carefully targeted efforts can help the new business reach an audience that is not normally as targetable.

Virtually Free Promotion

Virtually free promotions are also widely referred to as **bootstrap marketing**, because they require little capital. There are many opportunities to speak with groups about your business or even a specific area of expertise. To illustrate, the individuals that started the athletic club we discussed earlier in this chapter sought out speaking opportunities to groups in their area. The age of the typical Lions, Optimist, or Kiwanis Club member was within the range of the target market for the club. Additionally, those individuals that have time to commit to such organizations typically have sufficient income to belong to a health club. Therefore, the owners actively sought out opportunities to talk about health programs and how to start exercising to a variety of groups. To arrange such talks, they contacted leaders of the groups and offered their services, particularly at the beginning of a new year, which is when many people start off each year with fresh resolutions about their weight. Incidentally, that is when gyms have their greatest increase in membership.

bootstrap marketing
Marketing efforts that require little capital.

There are speaking opportunities with schools, clubs, and religious groups throughout the year. If the group is relevant to your business, you should take advantage of talking to it. The presentation should be more generic than a simple promotion for your business. For example, an owner of a garden supply store may visit with a club such as the Optimists about what flowers to plant in the spring or how to maintain lawns. After you make these presentations, it will hopefully be your business that the consumer considers when she seeks out a business in your field. There are other free opportunities that an entrepreneur should seek out—for example, if an opening arises with the local news to comment on current events. There are also many local morning talk shows for which you could put together something interesting for a show spot. For example, if you have a restaurant, then you may be able to prepare a favorite dish on the local morning show.

In any case, it is important to remember that no single advertisement will be sufficient for the business. The attention of your target market is pulled in many different directions. It can take numerous "impressions" for an individual consumer to take notice of your firm or product.[9] When the firm develops its promotional program, it is important that a systematic effort take place that will commit the time and effort needed to be sure that the firm obtains the recognition of the consumers.

EXERCISE 3

1. Think of the promotional activities that are relevant in the area where you live.
2. Which of these would be most economical for a new business?

The Methods for Sales Management

LO11-4

Identify the methods for sales management.

Sales management refers to the individuals who build and maintain relationships with customers, as well as to the methods and means by which they do this. To a certain extent everyone in an organization is involved in sales; however, sales management refers to how that whole sales process is managed. Issues that need to be considered include the following:

sales management
The methods employed to, and the individuals who build and maintain relationships with customers.

1. How many contact points will the business have with each customer?
2. How will each customer be greeted?
3. What is the process for managing a customer once an order has been placed?
4. What look will the sales force present?
5. What controls are in place to ensure the quality of the product delivery?
6. How much information will be collected on each customer?
7. What will the business do with the information collected?

FLOW RIGHT BREWERY & BAR: A FAMILY AFFAIR

Chris had been operating the business for a short while and felt that most of the bugs had been worked out of the operation. Employees were handling everything quite well, and he knew that he needed to get publicity about the new business out to the community. He first looked for as many free methods to publicize the business as he could. He started by hosting a private beer tasting for the local beer-making club. He knew if he did a great job that the group would provide significant word of mouth and that this group could make up the core of his initial business.

Chris contacted a high school classmate of his sister. She ran a late Saturday night talk show on a local radio that focused on their neighborhood. It was a public service to the community. Chris knew that on Saturday night the number of listeners was probably not very high. However, Chris thought that if he could get on the show and talk about the unique experience that people would have with a locally owned business that some exposure had to be better than none at all.

He then stopped by to see the editor of a newspaper that served the local community. Chris lived in the northern suburbs of a major city that had several very large newspapers for different communities. He stopped in to see the editor, as he wanted to know about local advertising costs for an ad and he hoped to get a small story about the opening of his brewery. As is often the case, the newspaper seemed very interested in running a story about the new business, especially if Chris would buy some advertisement space.

As Chris thought about running the ad, he realized that the newspaper covered a much larger area than he saw as his target market, but the cost seemed reasonable. Chris knew full-page advertisements in a newspaper such as *The Wall Street Journal* could cost over $200,000, whereas a similar advertisement in the *Los Angeles Times* would cost over $70,000. He was gleeful to find out that a full-page advertisement in the local weekly paper cost less than $1,000. Chris knew he would not run a full-page advertisement, but instead he would run smaller advertisements. The newspaper had four columns (there can be four to six columns on a newspaper page and the length is typically 21 inches). Thus, a quarter-page advertisement would be 21 column inches (4 times 21 divided by 4) and would cost $500. He thought that for the first four months, he would run the advertisement once each month.

QUESTIONS

Beyond these choices, Chris was not sure what other advertising he should consider.

1. What do you think of Chris's choice to advertise in the local newspaper?
2. What other things could Chris do for advertising that would be relatively cheap?
3. Would these be better than the local newspaper?

Designing and maintaining a sales management system is certainly part art and part tedious coding; however, a consistent approach and image that is designed around your mission statement will pay off tremendously as your business develops. The process starts with the hiring of a sales force.* One of the real keys to entrepreneurial business success is the development of a relationship with the customer. A popular television show (*Cheers*) was set in a bar and every time one of the regulars came into the bar, the employees in the bar would loudly greet him. That is the level of recognition that many customers desire from a business, whether they are being provided a haircut, buying clothes, or being advised on their investments. Indeed, one of the reasons for patronizing a new business could well be this expectation for exceptional recognition of loyal customers.

Beyond that level of recognition, returning customers are looking for an understanding of their needs, not just a fixation upon making a sale. A client of ours loves good wine and while he could go to any of a dozen

*The role of the sales force considered here in Chapter 11 and the role of human resources considered in Chapter 10 illustrate an issue that the authors have highlighted several times. The chapters here present the material in a sequential manner, but many of the issues that the entrepreneur must decide occur simultaneously. The entrepreneur cannot know whom to hire for the sales force until she knows how she wants to market the product or service. Therefore, while the two issues are separated here, it is actually difficult to makes such splits easily.

stores that sell a wide selection of wine, he chooses a business run by a small group of wine enthusiasts. Every time he walks into the store, they greet him and make suggestions to him based upon their personal knowledge of his tastes. If he chooses a wine, even an expensive wine, that they believe he will not enjoy, they are quick to point this out to him and try to steer him to wines that he will enjoy. They are not fixed on the label, the price, or the fact that they have 30 cases of another wine back in storage. Relationship management is a process and a practice.

Forecasting Sales

Estimating sales without any history is an act of guesswork that is dependent on the founder's ability to narrowly focus a customer group as well as to attract that customer group to purchase. There are many ways to estimate sales, all of which should be modified as real sales data become available. The two methods we will examine are market potential and customer demand.

Market potential methods take a macro look at the market and estimate potential sales for the firm based on the number of potential consumers in the target area. This data is then modified by a likely percentage of those potential consumers that will be attracted to the specific business. This can be estimated by looking at the direct competitors in the area or looking at close competitors in another, similar area. As we pointed out in Chapter 4, your direct knowledge of the market and your competitors will be essential to your sales forecast. To illustrate, the founders of the gym we have been discussing believed that their customer base would exist within a two and a half mile radius of the business and that those customers would own houses. Data from the census bureau and the local government helped identify the number of homes that met the criteria. The individuals starting the gym estimated there were one and a half potential consumers per house and limited their analysis to those individuals who had full-time employment. The result was a potential population of almost 50,000 customers in their geographic area of interest.

The entrepreneurs must then estimate what percentage of their total market potential might use a business in a given area. For some companies, there will be industry information from industry associations. However, even without this it is relatively easy to estimate. For example, several of the fitness websites estimate the number of people who are members of a gym. Armed with that information and a quick search to find out how many gyms there are in the United States, our founders estimated the size of their likely customer base. They then talked to a gym owner in another state to find out how long it took that gym to ramp up to its current level of customer traffic. They made a logical estimate of monthly growth and then modified it as customers actually signed up for memberships.

The second method is customer demand. This method takes a micro look at the market and estimates how many customers the business can handle given its location, staffing, and other details. The founder then estimates how many individuals it will take to break even, make X profit, and so on. For example, one business made the following estimate:

1. The business had parking for no more than six cars at one time.
2. It was estimated that each customer would be in the storefront for an average of 30 minutes (two-thirds of the time browsing—20 minutes; one-third of the time purchasing—10 minutes).
3. Staffing meant that most of the time they could handle only four customers actually making a purchase.
4. The average sale was expected to be $850.
5. It was estimated that during a typical day, only twice per day would the storefront be full of customers.

With this information, the business was able to establish a sales forecast and staff the business appropriately. The owners modified their forecasts based on the experience of the firm once it was actually in business.

Distribution Channels

The prior discussion focused on entrepreneurial businesses that establish a fixed location and serve customers from that location in retail or wholesale. However, there are other methods of distributing one's products and services. These methods do not require as extensive an understanding of geographic location, since, for example, they may be selling an industrial product that has the potential for a nationwide distribution, or they involve situations, such as Internet services or sales, where there is no limit due to geography. These methods include the following:

1. Independent sales agents
2. Contract sales force
3. Web pages
4. Mail-order catalogs

Each of these will be discussed in turn.

independent representatives
Representatives for a variety of products for a number of companies in a given domain who try to sell those products.

Independent Sales Agents. **Independent representatives** can be used to sell industrial products.[10] The independent distributor is the representative for a variety of products for a number of companies in a given domain. The independent representative agrees to sell or distribute each of the products for a percentage of the sales price. The percentage that the representative will receive depends on the demand for the product and how much effort the manufacturer wishes that representative to invest in promoting its product. A new business starting out needs to negotiate carefully the price paid to such representatives. Clearly, these representatives will promote those products for which they make the most money. Securing the right representatives for the right price can be crucial to achieving success when using this distribution channel.

For example, a new medical device company that we worked with for some time used distributors to sell its products. These distributors already had the necessary relationships with specific doctors, and these relationships are critical in the sales of any new medical product. Some doctors will actually allow representatives from certain sales agents into the operating room to help demonstrate the use of a new product. For this to occur, the distributor has to have salespeople with the proper training and relationships with the doctors. In this setting, choosing the right independent distributor was probably more critical than any other hire in the firm.

contract sales force
Independent salespeople with a wide variety of experiences and contacts, provided by a company on a contract basis.

Sales and marketing depend on each other for success.

Contract Sales Force. A second distribution channel is a **contract sales force**. Contract sales companies provide independent salespeople with a wide variety of experiences and contacts on a contract basis. Thus, you can hire a sales force for your firm for a given period of time. Even though it is a relatively expensive means of jump-starting sales, it can be the difference between success and failure. We worked with a company whose entire business plan was dependent on quickly locking up venues in long-term contracts. Then, armed with those contracts, the company could market its service to potential clients. The process envisioned in the plan required more than 20 experienced salespeople for a period of nine months. After that time, all sales could be handled by four inside salespeople who were to be hired during this process. A contract firm provided more than 80 résumés, from which the founders selected 21 salespeople to initiate the business.

Web Pages. We have previously discussed the value of Web pages as a means of promotion, and they can also be used as a distribution channel.[11] Internet-based marketing employs the Web in much the same way that a fixed-site store uses its physical location as an advantage. The Web page displays the products, provides the means to ask questions about those products, and in many cases allows the customer to buy the products. The list of Web page capabilities and its uses for marketing is expanding daily. Such sites can be used by businesses that focus purely on Internet sales or by those that use it as a supplement to the other marketing efforts of the firms. Web-based businesses rely on the designs of their Web pages to present the information about the products and their benefits. Thus, Web page design is a crucial part of the company process. However, it is important to remember that the Web page is there to sell products, not to show off some technical prowess in Web page design.

To illustrate, consider the wonderful graphics and animations that are capable of being included in a business website. These graphics take time to load, however, and that delay can be frustrating for your customers, especially if you are loading videos as a part of the Web page. Similarly, if you walked into a local store and no one offered to help you within five minutes, you would likely leave the store with no intention to return. That time frame is compressed when it comes to navigating a website, as customer patience is very short. Similarly, in designing the website, the entrepreneur should ensure that they do not design a site that works only with a particular browser type. The site must be usable, with the minimum number of clicks necessary for the clients to achieve what they wish to accomplish. Individuals will not roll endlessly through a series of screens to reach what they desire. Lastly, the content of the Web page must be timely. Time and effort must be dedicated to maintaining the Web page so that the information is accurate. A Web page is not something that can be created and forgotten.

The classic example that individuals can look to for a Web-based business that started small, although it is now huge, is Amazon.com. Amazon's website is accessible and easy to use. The site not only provides information but also allows customers to browse, purchase, pay for, and arrange shipping for any of hundreds of thousands of products.

Developing a system to the level of Amazon is prohibitively expensive for a new business. Every firm needs to determine if the Web will be its only outlet or if it will use the Web to supplement the business's fixed location. Web sales reach well beyond any physical boundaries and generally reach low-cost customers for the business. However, the business must offer very unique items that cannot be easily obtained elsewhere for there to be sufficient demand to warrant the time and effort involved with the mixed model. The end result may be that the time and effort to develop the Web page correctly may be more than the new business is willing to invest. If this is the case, the new business should still consider a basic Web page that provides information and directs customers to call to place their order. Such a site is relatively easy to prepare and maintain. The level of complexity increases dramatically as the business attempts to increase the capability to include the ability to order and pay for products.

Mail-Order Catalogs. The last type of distribution method is mail-order catalogs. Many businesses do not have a fixed retail location but instead reach customers through the mail. These individuals will mail a catalog to customers at their homes. The catalogs will display a consistent set of products and provide a means to order those products—typically over the phone. A professional company can be hired to receive the calls and send the orders to your business. Mailing out the goods themselves is typically not difficult, unless it is the Christmas season, where time sensitivity is critical and the standard delivery systems are overloaded.

As could be predicted, identifying which customers to mail the catalog to is a critical part of the process. A new firm cannot afford to mail a catalog to every person in the country. Thus, understanding and targeting your customer once again becomes critical. One useful means to do this is to buy a mailing list from a group that may have an interest in products that you wish to sell. For example, if you wished to establish a mail-order business for historical guns such as flintlock rifles, you could consider buying the mailing list of the National Rifle Association. Similarly, if you wished to sell environmentally sound cosmetics, you could seek to buy the mailing list of the Sierra Club and send the catalog to women on the mailing list.

One difficulty in running a mail order or catalog business is the need to be able to handle credit card sales and returns. Credit card fraud has been particularly troublesome for this industry, and transaction fees need to be accounted for in the pricing of products.

SUMMARY

Marketing is a critical function in the entrepreneurial business. Too often the new business focuses strictly on the technological aspects of the product produced and not the customers.[12] To be successful, the new business must know which customers would be ideal targets for its products or service. It is clear as we examine this chapter that marketing of the product and the strategy of the firm share a great similarity. The new business must use its developed mission and/or strategy to narrowly target the perfect customers. If the new business does not understand these issues, it is easy to spend the firm's scarce resources in a manner that produces no tangible benefit.

KEY TERMS

bootstrap marketing 207
contract sales force 210
cost-plus pricing 203
independent representatives 210
loss leader 202
marketing plan 198
mixed-model promotions 204
pricing floor 202
promotion 204
pure promotions 204
sales management 207
virtually free promotions 204

REVIEW QUESTIONS

1. Describe the basics of a marketing plan.
2. What advice would you provide to a potential new business owner about establishing a marketing plan?
3. What elements are necessary for a target customer profile?
4. How is a target customer profile used in the operation of a new business?
5. What are the means by which products or services may be priced?
6. How can a new business leverage free promotions?
7. What promotions might a new business use and why?
8. In what context might independent sales agents be used?
9. How is a contract sales force used in new businesses?
10. Explain how the Web is used by businesses for advertising.

BUSINESS PLAN DEVELOPMENT QUESTIONS

1. What are some of the ways that you can identify competitors in your market area?
2. How will you create sales for your business?
3. How will the Web be used in your business? How do you ensure that your site becomes known to your potential clients as they search the Web?

INDIVIDUAL EXERCISES

1. What channels do you intend to use to market your product or service?
2. What are the costs for each?
3. Develop an overall marketing plan that encompasses a defined customer target area, the methods of promotion, the pricing, and the distribution channels.

GROUP EXERCISES

Throughout history, well-known companies have lowered prices to increase sales. History suggests, however, that this technique simply reduces profitability and leads to a decline in the overall business. The business then has a harder time justifying its place in the market. Customers generally associate a lowered price with lowered quality. First individually and then in your group, answer the following questions:

1. Can you think of examples of products that would suffer if their prices were lowered?
2. Why can some businesses easily lower prices and gain customers whereas others cannot?
3. Can you think of any products or services where lowering prices could result in enough of an increase in sales to justify the lower prices?

ENDNOTES

1. R. Grewal, R. Mehta, and F. Kardes, "The Timing of Repeat Purchases of Consumer Durable Goods," *Journal of Marketing Research* 41 (2004), pp. 101–16.
2. M. Gruber, "Research on Marketing in Emerging Firms: Key Issues and Open Questions," *Journal of Technology Management* 26 (2003), pp. 600–21.
3. Romaniuk, Jenni, "Five Steps to Smarter Targeting," *Journal of Advertising Research* 52, no. 3, (2012), pp. 288–290.
4. T. McCollum, "High Tech Marketing Hits the Target," *Nation's Business* 85, no. 6 (1997), pp. 39–42.
5. How to Increase Website PageViews, SEO Chat, www.seochat.com/c/a/Search-Engine-Optimization-Help/How-to-Increase-Website-Page-Views/
6. T. Nagle and R. Holden, *The Strategy and Tactics of Pricing* (New York: Prentice Hall, 1995).
7. Guerreiro, Reinaldo, Cornachione Jr., Edward, Dassai, Carlos. "Determining the 'Plus' in Cost-Plus Pricing: A Time-Based Management Approach, *Journal of Applied Management Accounting Research* 10, no. 1, (2012), pp. 1–15.
8. J. Tanner, "Leveling the Playing Field: Factors Influencing Trade Show Success for Small Firms," *Industrial Marketing Management* 31 (2002), pp. 229–40.
9. J. Gregan-Paxton, J. Hibbard, F. Brunel, and P. Azar, "So That Is What That Is: Examining the Impact of Analogy on Consumers' Knowledge Development for Really New Products," *Psychology & Marketing* 19 (2002), pp. 533–51.
10. K. Blois and S. Albers, "Sales Force Management," *Oxford Textbook of Marketing* (Oxford, UK: Oxford University Press, 2000), pp. 292–318.
11. T. Chitura, S. Mupenhi, T. Dube, and J. Bolongkikit, "Barriers to Electronic Commerce Adoption in Small and Medium Enterprises: A Critical Review," *Journal of Internet Banking & Commerce* 13, no. 2 (2008), pp. 1–13.
12. D. Stokes, "Entrepreneurial Marketing: A Conceptualization from Qualitative Research," *Qualitative Market Research* 3, no. 1 (2000), pp. 47ff.

CREDITS

Opener: © Lars A. Niki RF; p. 197: © 2014 Ploom. All Rights Reserved.; p. 200: MBI/Alamy RF; p. 205: Andrew Harrer/Bloomberg via Getty Images; p. 210: © UpperCut Images/SuperStock RF

chapter

12

Establishing Operations

learning objectives

After studying this chapter, you will be able to:

LO12-1 Discuss the use of a critical path chart.

LO12-2 Describe how location can be used as a competitive advantage.

LO12-3 Discuss the important issues in the financing considerations of new firms.

LO12-4 Distinguish between the various methods with which a new firm establishes legitimacy in the market.

LO12-5 Explain the importance of production management in start-up ventures.

LO12-6 Explain how production charting is accomplished.

LO12-7 Describe the importance of quality as a competitive tool.

LO12-8 Discuss the type and condition of equipment needed at start-up.

LO12-9 Explain how timing is a competitive advantage.

LO12-10 Recognize the issues related to time management in the starting of a new business.

INDIGO IT

Indigo IT is the 2014 Small Business Administration's winner of the Procurement Award for services provided to the federal government. The firm is headed by Denise Van Wynsgaardt, who is a Mexican American native of Texas. Denise graduated from St. Mary's University in San Antonio and received her master's in public policy from Georgetown University in Washington, DC.

The firm was founded in 2001 to focus on IT support services with a focus on information assurance and security engineering, infrastructure analysis and planning, business continuity/disaster recovery, project management, enterprise integration and operations, and systems engineering. Today the firm employs approximately 70 people.

Denise is principally engaged in outreach activities with customers. Under her leadership the firm emphasizes a values-based philosophy with a strong ethical code of conduct and a commitment to Indigo IT's core values of Responsibility, Initiative, Service, and Excellence. In addition to her overall CEO responsibilities, Denise provides management oversight of Indigo IT's human resources and financial functions. As a female-headed firm, the company has been able to obtain a number of contracts that might not have been open to a new business. And the firm has had to deliver on its commitments.

The firm is organized as an LLC with Shane Van Wyngaardt and Rob Craig as the other principals in the firm. The growth of Indigo IT has faced its challenges. Specifically, in 2013, the firm had to restructure to ensure greater price competitiveness and alignment between the contracts they pursued and their competitive strengths.

Questions

1. What are the advantages of tying the business to federal government contracts?
2. Will winning the SBA award help future business with nongovernmental organizations?

Sources: M. Hoover, "Soul Searching for Success: Indigo IT Steps Back and Makes Changes to Fuel Growth," *Washington Technology*, www.zoominfo.com/CachedPage/?archive_id=0&page_id=6647462554&page_url=//washingtontechnology.com/articles/2013/05/06/indigo-it-story.aspx&page_last_updated=2013-05-13T23:00:28&firstName=Shane&lastName=Van%20Wyngaardt; "Indigo IT Wins SBA Prime Contractor Award," *HispanicBusiness.com*, May 15, 2014, www.hispanicbusiness.com/2014/5/15/indigo_it_wins_sba_prime_contractor.htm; Ms. Denise Van Wyngaardt, *Zoominfo*, www.zoominfo.com/p/Denise-Van%20Wyngaardt/648138143

Planning is the first step in the entrepreneurial development process. A great many individuals do little more than this initial investigation. During this initial process, the individuals that stop may find a fatal flaw, decide that the business is not nearly as lucrative as they had originally thought, or simply determine that they do not want to take the risk. The decision to not pursue the business is completely legitimate, and it is better to make it early if you believe that the business does not present the right opportunity for success. The process provided in this book, in fact, is designed to encourage the student to fully examine the business opportunity prior to actually starting a business. Our expectation is that the specific plan you develop in this class may not be one you open, but you will learn a process that will allow you to keep examining potential businesses until there is one you do want to open.

However at some stage, if the business is one that is viable, the entrepreneur must decide that she has investigated the idea sufficiently and that it is time to actually begin operations. While we would advocate good research and examination of your idea, the critical point of difference between an entrepreneur and someone with an idea is *action*. This chapter examines the practical, process-based actions that must occur to actually begin operations.

The position reached by Friends' Home Health discussed below is quite typical of most new business start-ups. During the initial start-up period, the expenses of the firm are often higher than expected, and the time to reach the break-even point takes longer than expected. A root cause of many of the problems for a new business can be traced to the lack of development of an operational plan.[1] It is this lack of operational plans that can lead to a cash crunch in the organization as the new firm stumbles while trying to actually put its ideas into action. As a result, the firm may have a great idea and be on a clear path to breakeven but run out of cash before it has the opportunity to achieve that success. The firm should have a solid understanding of the specific operational issues related to that business prior to starting the new venture.

There are a number of distinct actions that must be taken in order for a new business to begin operations. Although there may be some crossover among these actions, we separate them into the following categories:

1. Critical path chart
2. Location
3. Financing considerations
4. Legitimacy
5. Production management
6. Production charting
7. Quality
8. Equipment
9. Timing
10. Time management

Each of these will be examined in turn.

FRIENDS' HOME HEALTH

The time had arrived for the founders of Friends' Home Health to put their plan into action and start the business or decide they would continue to work for other companies. Betty and Joan realized this need to make a choice during a time when the area's economy appeared to be taking a nasty turn for the worse, with several major employers in the city announcing plans for layoffs. In addition, both of the potential founders had been informed by their employer that there would be no raises during the next year.

These economic conditions might look like a poor time to start a new firm, but our founders viewed the conditions as only limited barrier for starting their particular business. They knew from the analysis that their potential success depended on their customers. However, Friends' Home Health was targeting an upper-income area of the city with a differentiation strategy (better product due to the specialized training of their employees). In addition, the service of home health care is not something where demand is elastic; that is, the demand does not change dramatically as price changes. If someone's mother needs home health care then the adult children are not going to eliminate that care from their budget. The alternative is a nursing home, which many people will avoid at any cost. The issue that the founders next faced was to actually begin to set up the operations of the home health care business.

The founders raised their initial investment from themselves, friends, and family. The funds they hoped would be able to pay for a number of things including the rent on the office they would establish, initial supplies, and some basic training of employees. The founders had sought out a relatively cheap location because they did not believe that they needed a place that was highly visible; no one would drive by and decide to hire a home health care worker for a loved one after seeing their sign. Unfortunately, they realized they did not have enough capital for the business to reach the six months they estimated it would take to reach breakeven. Therefore, they took their business plan to their local bank and worked out an initial working line of credit from which they could draw to pay expenses and then pay back as accounts payable were paid to them. Armed with this initial financing, they proceeded to complete the next steps critical to starting the business over a three-week period of time. The steps they took included the following:

- Betty and Joan employed a stationery store to design a simple logo for the operation. The cost was only $400, and the service would be free if they purchased all their business cards, letterhead, and envelopes from the store. The founders realized that visual items such as letterhead and cards would help to legitimize their appearance (a concept discussed in more depth later in this chapter). They agreed to this immediately.
- Betty and Joan started advertising to recruit staff. They wanted all of their staff certified to some degree. Although they wanted to hire people with their certification in hand, they knew for the largest segment of their potential workers—those who most often worked with individuals in their homes, delivering very basic services—that this would not be readily available. Therefore, they reached out to the local community college, which had a two-week program offering such training. If the firm could hire a set of 25 part-time workers who would deliver these services, then the local community college would offer the two-week intensive class just for Friends' Home Health Care employees.

The class would cost Friends' Home Health only a fraction of the total cost as the population of students would be considered low skill and there were subsidy programs for technical training. In the economic setting of the city, this course was seen as a valuable service to provide this group of jobs. However, Friends' knew that the potential employees might not go to the class if they were not paid for their time. Therefore, Friends' also had to have in place a means to pay them. To make such an investment pay for itself, Friends' would need to have a number of customers already in place to generate the needed revenue as soon as the employees were trained.

- Betty and Joan contacted the phone company, electric company, water department of the city, and gas company to establish service at the facility.
- The two owners realized they were in a delicate position, that is, by needing to recruit and train employees and also having the accounts waiting in place for these employees to start to work almost immediately after the training. Thus, the two owners agreed to take no salaries for themselves until cash flow was positive.

(continued)

(Continued from previous page)

The partners had begun the operations of their entrepreneurial business. They had a plan for when they should reach breakeven, but unexpected expenses also started almost immediately.

- Friends' Home Health hoped to offer a rich range of services in addition to the direct care of patients, including occupational (OT) and physical therapy (PT). The founders quickly recognized as they started looking, however, that such employees were very expensive and they needed guarantees of hours worked. The two entrepreneurs also realized that they could not financially make that work at the outset of the business. Therefore, they decided to create a contract relationship with local OT and PT firms. However, these contracts required that Friends' guarantee minimum revenues for the OT and PT firms. Therefore, as the firm started there was an immediate cash flow out that was not matched by a cash flow in.

Betty and Joan also soon found that whereas they were willing to pay the new employees even while they were in training, that these individuals had little loyalty to the business, and the resulting turnover rate was very high: Approximately 15 percent of potential employees dropped out during the two-week class. The typical employee was female with a high school education. The work was not seen as appealing to most individuals since they are frequently just sitting with a person who is often bedridden or in a wheelchair. The activities that must be done as a part of the position included helping to feed the client and helping him or her with their bodily functions. Although Friends' had planned to pay above-city averages for such work consistent with their differentiation strategy, as a start-up, their reputation for such efforts was not well established. The outcome was that they found they were paying for people's education, although some of those who received the education would never work for the firm, and this extra service was yet to be appreciated by the firm's potential customers.

Betty and Joan immediately recognized that their plans for the operations of the business were not leading to the break-even point (the point where revenue equals expenses) that they had projected. Instead, the company was faced with a negative situation well beyond their expectations.

QUESTIONS

1. What steps would you take now to start this business if you were in the Friends' Home Health founders' position?
2. In what order would you suggest they proceed with these steps?
3. What are your suggestions for Friends' to overcome the negative cash flow setting they now face?

LO12-1

Discuss the use of a critical path chart.

The Use of a Critical Path Chart

The first operations-related concept we want to introduce in this section is also one of the most popular for organizing a wide range of activities in a firm. An absolute imperative for any organization, but most especially for a new business, is the efficient use of time. Many tasks can be handled concurrently, but others must be performed sequentially. Identifying the actions that must occur, in what order they should occur, and what order will be most efficient is one of the first operational steps for a new business. Although it is often not possible to identify every action item that will be required prior to the start of a new business, the effort to develop a complete list will allow the new business to have a faster, more thorough, less expensive start-up. Failing to plan may leave the new business waiting weeks for some small step that could have been completed earlier, concurrently with other actions taken by the firm. For example, items such as obtaining a state tax ID or a city license are not difficult but may take some time, depending on the requirements. However, the firm may not be able to buy equipment for the business or rent facilities until these licenses are obtained.

STEP	TASK	TIME TO COMPLETE	ACTUAL TIME INVOLVED	PREVIOUS TASK REQUIRED	RESPONSIBILITY
1	Establish business bank accounts	1 week	3 hours		James and Margaret
2	Obtain bank loan	2 weeks	4 hours		James and Margaret
3	Establish accounting system	3 weeks	1 week		Margaret
4	Lease Facility	2 weeks	20 hours	2	James and Margaret
5	Obtain equipment (office and manufacturing)	4 weeks	8 hours	2 & 4	James (manufacturing) and Margaret (office)
6	Acquire raw materials	4 weeks	30 hours	2 & 4	James
7	Make initial sales calls	8 weeks	90 hours	2 & 4	James and Margaret
8	Produce initial inventory	4 weeks	150 hours	4, 5, 6, & 7	James and Margaret

Table 12.1
Critical Path Table

Although there are a number of methods and formats for completing a critical path analysis, we present a relatively common, easily understood format that we have used with a number of new start-ups.[2] Initially, the entrepreneur must identify the most likely amount of time it will take for each of the key tasks to be completed, the actual time one of the owners will be involved, any prerequisite tasks, and who is responsible for the task. The chart of critical activities might look something like the one in Table 12.1 for a small manufacturer. This process could be the same for many different types of manufacturing. However, it should be noted that the initial efforts of the entrepreneur, concern so much more than the actual manufacturing. It should also be noted that while we have specified the tasks for a manufacturer, the tasks will be different for different types of businesses.

Note that the assigning of responsibilities and estimated times is more than an intellectual activity. When you specify who will do a task and how long it will take to be completed, you set for yourself a control mechanism to ensure that you are going to be ready when you intend to open. If you do not set timetables and responsibilities, it is possible for the founding of the business to drag on, using up precious financial and emotional resources. The founders setting the schedule allows them to get a solid handle on how soon they can begin operations. The owners understand that while they must wait on some tasks, they can complete other tasks so that their time is used efficiently. The owners also can set some priorities on where their time should be focused. For example, it would be difficult to acquire raw materials and have them delivered prior to the leasing of the facility. Thus, if the leasing of the facility took more time than estimated, then the entire process would be delayed.

Underestimating the amount of time it will take to begin operations is a mistake that harms many new businesses. You should estimate the times very generously, since many critical steps may take significantly longer than originally planned. New businesspeople often do not recognize a given step they will need to accomplish in order to successfully develop their business. It is for this reason that you will hear many new entrepreneurs say getting the business to the state it could generate revenue often takes 2 or 3 times what they first thought. The listing of critical tasks and the resulting critical path chart can help to overcome this problem.

From the lists of critical tasks identified in Table 12.1, the new business can then develop a chart that demonstrates how the activities fit together.

Figure 12.1
The Critical Path Chart

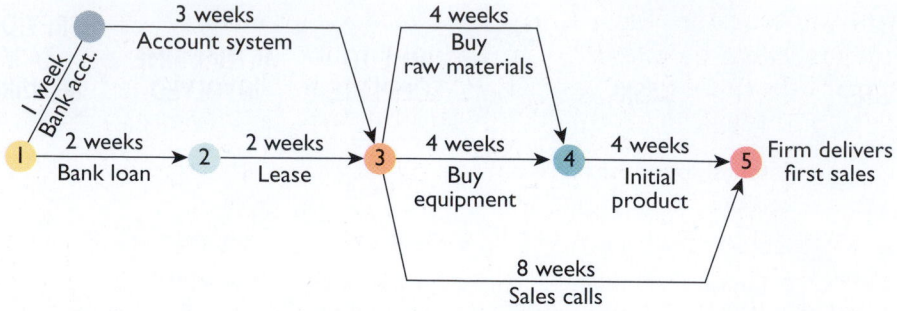

critical path chart
Chart that demonstrates how the activities necessary to start the firm fit together and build on each other. This chart allows you to understand which activities can occur concurrently and which must already be in place before the next activity can occur.

The chart of how your actions fit together is your **critical path chart** that shows the set of activities that are dependent on each other (i.e., the longest path) and which take the longest time. The chart listing the critical tasks provided in Table 12.1 will produce the critical path chart shown in Figure 12.1.

As you can see from the critical path in Figure 12.1, it will take a minimum of 12 weeks to open the business in this case. There are some things the firm can do at the same time, such as setting up the firm's bank accounts and starting to work on bank loans. However, the new business will likely not be able to start to lease a facility until it has its financing in place. Potential landlords will initially screen out those individuals they do not think are serious as they seek to lease a property.

The businessperson can make the critical path as detailed as is necessary. The chart for the small manufacturing firm in Figure 12.1 is actually quite simple. The new businessperson should be guided by developing a chart that provides the most assistance and information. The purpose of the chart is not to be a formal document to place solely in a business plan. Instead, it is designed to help focus the founders' efforts so they are not slowed down by some simple activity that was not visualized. Therefore, it may be useful for the founders to create a more complex form of a critical path chart that can be developed by estimating three different time needs for each task: minimum, most likely, and maximum. For complex start-up operations, there are several project management software packages that will assist you in developing a task chart and producing a critical path chart. They are available at most office supply stores. The new businessperson must judge the level of detail that he desires in a critical path chart and whether purchasing such a program will aid him or not. The process for an Internet-based business is somewhat simpler than for a manufacturing business. However, there are critical steps that can delay the start of any business such as obtaining the required licenses.

To further illustrate the importance of such planning, consider one of the entrepreneurial businesses that students in one of our classes wished to start. The students wanted to start a Study Café that would be open from 4 P.M. to 8 A.M., seven days a week. The business design was simple but elegant and potentially quite lucrative. The café would provide a well-lit, open-forum, safe space to study individually or meet with groups. It would make a majority of its money by selling basic food and drinks, and leasing out the conference rooms in the facility. There was cheap space available close to the campus where a restaurant had gone out of business. (The prior restaurant had appealed to students, but closed every night at 9 P.M. and strongly discouraged students from "hanging out.") The students' original intent was to open just prior to the start of classes in the fall semester. However, after completing the critical path chart, they realized that they would complete everything necessary to open their doors in April. This would mean the business would open for operation at the end of the spring semester. The city in which the Study Café wanted to open was a college town where only the resident college students would be interested in staying up until the early hours of the morning. As a result, the business would have to suffer through the summer months of limited business while the expenses just piled up.

As a result of their critical path analysis, they approached their opening from a completely different perspective. Rather than starting the process immediately and seeing when they could open, they went to the end of the chart and set the opening date as August 1. They then calculated the critical path chart in reverse, with the date they were to open being the starting (and therefore missing) element. Estimating the longest path for opening the Study Café, they were able to establish a date to begin the process of putting together the operations of the business so as to minimize wasted effort and money while still opening for operations by August 1.

Is the Study Café a lucrative business idea? Why or why not?

Entrepreneurs should constantly update their critical path analysis as they develop the plan for a business. Entrepreneurs should also share that critical path analysis with potential suppliers, friends, and industry experts—with anyone who will look it over for you and add, modify, or delete activities. The critical path analysis is a living document that should be modified during the process of actually accomplishing the tasks. We have worked with a number of new businesspeople who take large flip chart sheets of paper and post a critical path chart on the wall of their home, office, or wherever it can be easily viewed. As tasks are accomplished, delayed, added, or changed, the chart is continually updated.

EXERCISE 1

1. Develop a list of all activities necessary to start your business.
2. Develop a critical path table of activities. Think very carefully about what activities can be completed concurrently.

How Location Can Be Used as a Competitive Advantage

LO12-2

Describe how location can be used as a competitive advantage.

One of the most important steps in the critical path chart will be the identification and purchase or lease of a location for the new business. The old axiom from marketing is that the three keys to business success are location, location, and location. Although this might be a bit overblown, we certainly agree that location is a critical factor in the successful operation of a new non-Internet business.[3] How do you decide upon the best location for the money? The method that we use involves breaking the business down into the critical design features of the business. You may recall from Chapter 5 that you should develop a list consisting of all of the resources or capabilities of the organization.

It is very easy to simply fall into the trap of trying to locate a business based on the capital available or some convenience factor that has little to do with the actual strategy of the business. This is a mistake that can, by itself, send all of the other planning down the drain. For example, one of the authors met a young couple for dinner several years back, both of whom had been students in his classes. They were very excited because they had decided to open a restaurant and wanted us to come by once it was open. It was a reasonable restaurant idea, but its location constituted a fatal flaw. They were opening the business near their home because they knew the area "so very well." This decision also allowed them to return to the area where they had both grown up.

strip shopping center

A small retail center located typically along a major road. The center has only small businesses and the center itself occupies only a small strip of land along the major street.

anchor stores

Major retail stores, such as department stores in a mall. They serve as the anchor for the retail establishment.

However, the area the couple wanted to locate to was more than 60 miles from any major city and, worse than that, they had selected as their location a **strip shopping center** with very cheap rent. A strip center is a small, one-story retail center typically located parallel to a well-traveled road. This type of center is referred to as a strip center since it is often developed on a strip of land irrespective of the development in the area; a strip center generally has no major **anchor stores** to draw in customers. The fact that the entrepreneurial couple were locating in the strip center itself was not the problem. Instead, it was the specific strip center that they had selected. The reason the rent was so cheap was that the shopping center was virtually empty. It was empty not because the center was too new to have tenants; instead, the customer base in the area was too small and poor to support any of the businesses that had previously operated there. Their proposed location was more than two miles from the interstate. Therefore, they would not be getting the interstate travel traffic that would be passing through this isolated location. Despite our warnings and suggestions, they went ahead with the business with their father's seed money (almost $50,000) only to see the small restaurant collapse within six months. Even the best idea can be killed by a bad location.

What businesses are best suited for a strip shopping center? What businesses might not work in such a space?

Although there are many very sophisticated methods for performing a location analysis, in simple terms, locations can be graded by the type and amount of traffic that the particular location draws. If you are setting up a warehouse, then you neither need nor want an "A" location in a mall, on a busy street, or in a tourist-heavy downtown area. Match the type of business and the amount of money that you wish to invest in the first years of operation. Take the time to analyze the long term as well. If you will need to move within a short period of time because you achieve all of your targets and outgrow your space, then you may want to consider a location that includes an option to allow for expansion.

To illustrate the rich options that a firm can pursue, we helped a small group of founders of a real estate firm that started out as three people renting space from a travel agency (literally, three desks in the back of the building). As luck would have it (for the new business at least), the travel agency was struggling, which allowed the new business owners to rent more and more of the building as their business expanded. Within 18 months the team was renting 80 percent of the building and approached the travel agency owner about taking over the entire building and setting up a lease-purchase agreement. The travel agency finally closed and the entrepreneurial team was able to acquire the building location. Having established a client base, they really wanted to hold onto their location. As will be discussed later in this chapter, location is one of the things that provide a business with legitimacy. If you have a location and maintain it for some period of time, then you are more accepted and acceptable with potential clients and suppliers, because your business appears to be more stable.

ETHICAL CHALLENGE

Entrepreneurs often face serious ethical challenges in their operations. For example, in obtaining supplies for products such as shoes, balls, clothing, and agricultural products, the cheapest supplier may be able to provide that price by cutting corners in worker safety or by polluting the environment. For major corporations it is often not the law but the potential of bad publicity that pushes them to take certain operational actions. In 2012 more than 100 people were killed at a factory fire in Bangladesh. The supplier who employed the people had violated many laws such as locking all doors with chains so no one would skip out from work. However, it was not only the local Bangladeshi factory owner who suffered, it was also their large U.S. and European retailing customers who suffered as the bad publicity did major damage to their reputations. The result is that some large corporations now have an entire staff, or hire consultants, to ensure that they are not using a supplier who keeps costs low by using methods that most of the world would condemn.

New entrepreneurial firms will not have the staff or the slack resources to send individuals to check out how well potential suppliers treat their employees or their environment. In addition it is far less likely that adverse publicity will negatively impact a relatively small entrepreneurial firm. However, the ethical challenge remains for the entrepreneurial firm. How is the entrepreneur responsible for ensuring that its suppliers are meeting its own ethical standards? If the entrepreneurial firm sells sporting goods and buys a container load of soccer balls from Pakistan, do they have the responsibility to make sure children were not used in this process? (It is a shame that in some places children work long days to make soccer balls because their small hands are flexible enough to perform the stitching work inside the ball.)

QUESTIONS

1. What would you do to get something that you deemed to be critical for your new business?
2. At what point do you have a responsibility to find out the nature of the supplier of a product?

Commercial real estate firms are a source of unparalleled information for the new business owners trying to locate their business. Building owners pay agents in a leasing agreement that is usually based on a percentage of the first year's lease and the signing of a two-year lease. Although commercial real estate agent income can be quite substantial, the commercial real estate market is relatively small and an individual's reputation is critical to future bookings. Therefore, agents focus extensively on ensuring that the new business signing the lease is successful. The fact is that the cost for all this expertise is paid by the building owner, and a successful business that pays its bills is very desirable. Thus, commercial agents can be a valuable asset to new business owners as they seek to locate properties that match their needs.

The Important Issues in the Financing Considerations of New Firms

LO12-3

Discuss the important issues in the financing considerations of new firms.

While not addressing the details of financing operations here (we have covered those issues in depth earlier), we nonetheless want to acknowledge the gamut of financial issues related to the operational start-up of a new business. Financing the initial operations begins with the variety of initial payments and the process of setting up the business and ends with the first completed sale. The new organization has to be in a position to make initial payments for

1. Security deposits.
2. Utility setup fees.

3. Purchase or lease of initial equipment and installation.
4. All licenses and inspections.
5. All initial supplies (this is a significant and often overlooked expense).
6. Hiring and training of initial staff.
7. Initial advertising expenses.
8. Bank set-up fees.

These costs can be substantial, and the new business must ensure that it has the proper resources to conduct these activities. (For an interesting discussion of start-up costs in the artesian cheese industry, see the 2014 article by Bouma, Durham, and Meunier-Goddik).[4] Recalling our critical path analysis, if one element, such as purchasing of some key inputs, must be delayed because of a lack of resources, the impact can be to place the entire development of the new business's operations behind schedule.

It was highlighted earlier that the issue of establishing a bank relationship is critical. The new business is well served to establish a variety of financial relationships with its bank. Some of these key issues include establishing a revolving line of credit (working capital), acquiring a business credit card account, and setting up a basic business checking account. These accounts should have a primary signatory and a confirmation signatory as an audit safety condition. No one individual should be able to write checks for the business in excess of a specified amount (usually $500) without a countersignature. Using confirmatory signatures ensures both parties know where major expenses occur and that the bill is accurate.

Picking which bank to work with is more than a choice of which branch is closest to you. Working with small businesses is a specialized skill that all banks will say they possess, but which, in fact, may be very limited at a given institution. Some banks develop expertise in large commercial accounts such as Fortune 500 customers. Other banks have an expertise in retail banking, primarily serving individuals. Still other banks have their principal focus on small and medium-sized businesses. A bank may have a range of customers, but you want to ensure that it has an expertise in your type of business and understands issues such as timing of payments from customers. If you have a small retail firm, you may need large draws on your lines of credit to get the Christmas merchandise onto your shelves. If you are a small oil and gas exploration firm, you will have other specialized needs, such as determining the value of given leases that you include in your assets. Whether your bank can work with such issues is an important question for a new business owner. The expertise of other successful entrepreneurs in your area provides valuable insight into these issues.

LO12-4

Distinguish between the various methods with which a new firm establishes legitimacy in the market.

The Various Methods with Which a New Firm Establishes Legitimacy in the Market

legitimacy
The acceptance by key stakeholders such as customers and suppliers that you are a genuine business that will still be in operation next year.

A topic rarely discussed in the establishment of a new business is the issue of legitimacy. **Legitimacy** is the term we use to discuss acceptance by key stakeholders, such as customers and suppliers, who believe in the firm as a genuine business that will still be in operation next year. Developing the perception of legitimacy for both customers and suppliers can be difficult, although it is critical to the long-term survival of the business.[5]

The new business will need to look like and act as an operation that will be in business for the long run in order to achieve some level of legitimacy. If a customer buys a product and the company is then no longer in business, who does she turn to when she has a problem? When a supplier sells goods on terms of 90 days, where will that firm get its payment if the firm that bought the goods goes out of business before the 90 days? Thus, both customers and suppliers want to ensure your business will be operating for the long term before they do business with you.

You will recall from our discussion of community supports in Chapter 2 that business incubators were discussed. These institutions are a potential setting for new businesses (especially non–food service businesses) to locate their initial operations. They offer new businesses office space at reduced rates, as well as providing services such as a receptionist who answers the phone with the business name, conference room facilities, and basic office equipment (copying, fax, Internet, telephones). The effect of these supports is that it helps to build the perceived legitimacy of the business with the look of a more professional presentation as well as the endorsement provided by the incubator operator. Incubators are usually swamped with new businesses that would like to be considered. The incubator operators try to pick those businesses that have the best chance for success.

EXERCISE 2

1. What do you look for in a business before you patronize it?
2. If you were going to sell equipment and supplies to a new entrepreneurial business on credit, what would you want to see from the new business before selling to them?
3. What small items might aid to your legitimacy as a new business with little cost?

Regardless of the business location, the entrepreneur needs to consider the potential means with which to establish the legitimacy of the business in the eyes of the customers and suppliers. Below is a list of classic items that may help establish more legitimacy for your new business:

1. A business checking account with the firm's name printed on the checks; start the check numbering higher than 001 or even 101.
2. A business credit card.
3. A bank line of credit.
4. Professional business cards.
5. Professional letterhead, billing slips, envelopes, and so on.
6. Professional advertising material.
7. The prestige of the business address
8. Job titles—titles cost you very little, use them liberally.
9. Telephone answering support.
10. A high-quality Web page.
11. A board of advisors and/or directors with excellent community visibility.
12. Endorsements from well-recognized and respected individuals.

You may have noticed that some items in the list above are quite inexpensive, whereas others are both time consuming and expensive. We suggest that all new businesses develop a plan to establish and continually enhance their legitimacy. While you may not choose to do them all, and appearances are not everything, the business's legitimacy is critical at the outset of the business.[6] Thus, every reasonable way to improve the firm's legitimacy should be taken.

LO12-5

Explain the importance of production management in start-up ventures.

The Importance of Production Management in Start-Up Ventures

Another important element in the success of a new business is the establishment of a production management system.[7] A *production management system* defines the steps that are involved in moving from your product or service offering to the point where you actually receive money. This importance is exaggerated in the early stages of a new business, as the firm has only limited resources, as well as strong time pressures to perform well at the outset. To illustrate, many years ago when inkjet printers were fairly new, we worked with a small group of individuals' rather simple but interesting plan to refurbish printer cartridges. This was targeted at college students. Their original plan had them handling the vast variety of cartridges on an individual basis. They would simply deal with each cartridge as it came in and depend upon their individual knowledge and experience to punch the hole in the cartridge, refill the ink, plug the hole, and finally seal up the cartridge for resale. They accepted the fact that they would develop procedures for each type of cartridge but thought that this would develop over time. The process of discovery would allow them to handle a wide variety of cartridges early in the life of the company.

We pointed out to the entrepreneurs that their projections depended upon their handling more than 10,000 cartridges a month by the sixth month of operation, and that an ad hoc system being handled directly by the owners would likely not lead to success. The time wasted as each cartridge was treated as a unique order would simply be unwieldy in a very short time period. As a result, they employed a mechanical engineer who developed a very simple set of procedures with fixed equipment to handle the most common types of cartridges. For these stations with fixed equipment, they employed individuals to process the most common cartridges. For all other cartridges they maintained a job shop section to develop procedures and process those cartridges. Over the next eight months, they developed a production management system and methodology that allowed them to dramatically cut costs. On more than one occasion the entrepreneurs have commented to us that more time spent prior to start-up in developing a process would have resulted in enormous financial dividends to the owners. The production system developed post-hoc was expensive and resulted in many lost opportunities.

It is important to emphasize that all businesses have production systems, whether or not they are codified. All service and Internet businesses have preferred ways of dealing with items such as customers, paperwork, orders, and services. These constitute the foundation of a production system. Putting together a production management system to handle the most common and expected routines will ensure consistent handling and enable the employees to focus their energy on the other, unusual aspects of the job.

While this topic is quite complex and is its own field of study, we discuss the two most important elements to production management as they relate to entrepreneurial business. These are production charting and quality.

LO12-6

Explain how production charting is accomplished.

How Production Charting Is Accomplished

There are many established software programs available for new business owners to help them establish the production processes they will use in their firms. To emphasize the importance of such methods, entrepreneurs need only look to franchises. The text will discuss franchises in greater detail in Chapter 14. Here we simply point out that one of the reasons that franchises are so successful is that they have well-established methods of operation. The franchisors have prepared these methods for the franchisees in a plan detailing each step that occurs in the production process and when each step is to occur. This type of exercise is enormously helpful for all new entrepreneurial businesses.

This level of detailed understanding about a firm's production typically comes from a **production chart**. You will recall that at the beginning of this chapter, we discussed a critical path chart. A production chart is similar; however, rather than focusing on the founding of the business, this chart details each step that must occur within the production process. It takes the reader step by step through the processes necessary to provide the customer with the finished product. It starts with the order being received and finishes with the final delivery to the customer. The production chart is similar to the critical path chart in that some steps in the production process can occur simultaneously while others must occur concurrently. In presenting this chart, we have chosen a slightly different format from the traditional one used in most textbooks. Most textbooks focus on established company production processes and have many items occurring concurrently; however, we have found that new firms have limited personnel and the processes are more sequential. The process detailed in the production chart in Figure 12.2 is very simple: production of a plaque from a trophy shop.

production chart
A chart that provides a detailed understanding of a firm's production process.

Even for early-stage ventures, the production chart can become complex quite quickly. Imagine the difficulty in producing meals from a menu that may have 25 different entrées with different vegetable selections. How does the restaurant assure that all of the items are produced so that those that take longer are started sooner, those that take less time are started later, and all items are finalized at approximately the same time and are delivered to the table when they are at their peak? Now add in complexities such as appearance, appetizers, salads, and drinks. The production chart for a business that appears quite simple can, in fact, be quite complex.

As noted, all businesses have a production process. It is easy to recognize such a process in a manufacturing setting. To illustrate, even a retail firm has a production process. Goods come into the store and then are counted, tagged, stocked, sold, detagged, and bagged, or if not sold moved to the discount area. If firms do not have a detailed understanding of the methods needed for these basic processes, it is quite easy to end up creating bottlenecks and procedures that negatively impact both customers and employees. One business that we got to know was in a tourist area and it catered to the tourist trade. To save money the owner decided to use a dial-up telephone line for credit card transactions. As compared to a dedicated high-speed line, this choice meant an additional 45 seconds per transaction, and dialing delays and busy signals were a common problem. Complaints continued to rise, and the owner noticed more and more people either walking out of the store or deciding, upon looking at the checkout line, to go elsewhere. As a result, the entrepreneur chose to move to a dedicated line for credit card transactions. At the same time, he changed his required procedure that each item purchased be recorded in a ledger by the cash register, as that process was slow and cumbersome. At some expense he moved to a bar code system to improve the throughput of customers. The dedicated high-speed Internet line and the bar code system were both more expensive, but once the owner realized the negative impact on his production

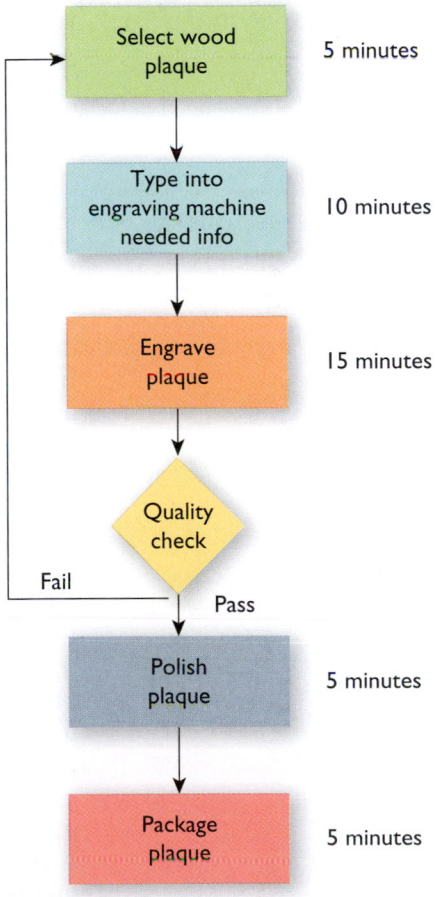

Figure 12.2
Production Chart

process of not having them, the rationale for each became quite obvious. If the entrepreneur had thought through their retailing business as a production process, they likely could have avoided the problems. They would have been able to put in place the changes as they built the stores, since they would have seen the impact on time and sales more clearly early.

In a similar vein, we once dealt with a clothing retailer who did not have a clear understanding of the store's current process, nor what processes should be in place. The owner would bring all goods in at cost and continue to carry all unsold items in inventory at their original cost. The predictable result was an ever-growing percentage of the store being consumed by obsolete stock, and this eventually led to failure, as the firm ended up with a storeroom and retail space full of goods that appeared on paper to be quite valuable, but were in fact items that had little or no market value. The firm's bank eventually figured out the ever growing stock of valueless materials and employed the clauses in the line of credit that allowed the bank to cut the credit line of the firm to virtually nothing. This cash crunch resulted in an inability to place orders for goods the store needed in the upcoming year, and the store eventually closed. There is no universally "correct" way to deal with the issue of obsolete stock; however, it is necessary to establish a procedure for handling such stock. The procedure should be aggressive and recognize that there is little to no value in holding onto obsolete inventory, even if its cost was significant.

There are many established production management systems that operate on any computer available to new business owners. If you are starting a business that is part of an established industry, then you should talk to others in the industry regarding the popular packages for the management of your business processes. Starting one from scratch is a waste of time and money. A little effort investigating the industry should provide tremendous positives for the organization.

LO12-7

Describe the importance of quality as a competitive tool.

The Importance of Quality as a Competitive Tool

Another important consideration in all aspects of a business venture is the investment in quality. In the recent past, designing quality into your product or service was a means to differentiate an entrepreneurial business from the larger mass-market businesses. Increasingly, however, quality is an assumed standard whether the entrepreneurial business is in manufacturing or is a service business. Individuals have to look no farther than fast-food restaurants. For illustration purposes, look at a franchise such as McDonald's. It sells a number of products for $1.00, has playgrounds for kids, maintains clean tables and restrooms, and even puts a toy in a meal for children. The playgrounds are expansive and expensive, while the food quality is guaranteed across the spectrum of all McDonald's restaurants. It is a tremendous value for a very small price, and each store opens with the full complement of offerings. If a new business is to compete against McDonald's, it will have to have a similar quality and quantity of offerings to be successful. Therefore, new businesses need to be clear about the expectations for quality in whatever business they pursue.

One of the keys to successfully delivering quality is the monitoring and measuring systems put into place by the founders. Dr. W. Edwards Deming is considered the father of the quality movement in the United States. One of his arguments is that quality needs to be constantly and consistently improved. Thus, there needs to be a continuous set of measures for each of the various processes of the organization. Without recorded data, it is impossible to judge the performance of the processes that have been put in place by the owners.

Deming went much further and argued that while the organization should set goals for quality in the organization, these goals are not to drive every action. If a firm focuses only on those goals, the firm might make short-term decisions that were detrimental to the overall direction of the company. To illustrate, a firm may have a target for on-time delivery that it is striving to improve upon. Although this is an admirable goal, and perhaps even a point of differentiation in the industry, if the firm gets so wrapped up in on-time delivery that this becomes the only focus of the organization, the firm can easily miss other critical issues, such as delivering the correct item. Delivering the wrong item on time would result in great statistical success (concerning timing, at least) but would destroy value in the firm.[8]

Deming strongly suggests that the firm be guided by what he calls the "scientific method." In this method, rather than changing lots of things at the same time, the firm should change only one thing at a time, measuring the impact of that change. It is through this systematic method that a firm knows if it is moving in the right direction and also knows the true impact of each change.

Additionally, Deming suggests that rather than focusing strictly on obtaining the lowest prices for supplies, firms should focus on the quality of the inputs. He argues that without quality inputs, the output has no chance to be high quality. To illustrate, there was a large privately held, relatively large bakery in Oklahoma that used 12 different types of flour. The owners shopped by price, so there were actually as many as 15 different suppliers they used at different points in time. The result was that the firm would use inputs that met the formal requirements for the flour, but each had slight differences in their characteristics, such as moisture content. These differences were very small, but they still led inexorably to differences in the baking processes. Thus, each time a new supplier's product was employed, the owner of the firm found that her workers had to test and adjust the production process. After years of handling this situation, the owner followed the advice of a close friend who simply recommended that the bakery employ one supplier who would guarantee the quality standard. Saving the constant testing and product waste would more than make up for any additional expense. It is this type of realization that has moved firms to focus on forming **strategic alliances**, where firms join together to form long-term, mutually beneficial relationships. Firms, both large and small, now seek to establish a reasonable price for their inputs and then seek out a long-term relationship with a supplier that can meet that price and supply a consistent, high-quality product. A consistent input helps the firm produce a consistent output.

strategic alliances
The joining together of firms to form long-term, mutually beneficial relationships.

The Type and Condition of Equipment Needed at Start-Up

LO12-8

Discuss the type and condition of equipment needed at start-up.

Acquiring the initial equipment for a business can be a daunting task. The basic equipment can easily be one of the most expensive elements for a new business. Clearly, a small manufacturer that needs to purchase specialized equipment will have a higher initial outlay when compared to a service business. Yet even an entrepreneurial business such as an Internet business can incur significant expenses for equipment as computers and related items are purchased. Businesses with even greater equipment needs, such as a restaurant, need to accurately evaluate the equipment needs while at the same time recognize that there is a wide flexibility in the types, ages, methods of acquisition, and availability of all equipment obtained for the new organization. Purchasing new equipment may guarantee that it is the most current available and that it will be delivered directly to the new business; however, it is usually the most expensive method, and delays may be significant if the items are not in stock. Purchasing older equipment has its own risks with quality and availability but should always be investigated. It is relatively common for new equipment to depreciate 50 percent or more in the first year. Similarly, it is possible to lease equipment. The ability to lease the equipment is particularly attractive to new firms as it has the lowest initial costs. However, over the long run, such leasing can prove expensive.

Therefore, the new business owner needs to clearly understand what equipment is needed, how long it will be before it will need to be replaced, and what are the long-term impacts of the decision. This understanding should also include both what equipment is needed to begin operations and how quickly the company might need more or even bigger equipment. The new business owner should then prepare a chart comparing the price and the positives and negatives of buying new, buying used, or leasing that equipment. The positives and negatives should include not only the immediate cost and the ability to overcome the cash flow crunch that impacts all new businesses, but also the impact on the firm's quality, and the long-term impact if the entrepreneurial business grows.

FLOW RIGHT BREWERY & BAR: A FAMILY AFFAIR

In the early days of the business development, Chris wanted to show his potential customers and suppliers that he was serious about the business and that he expected to be there for a long period of time—to establish his legitimacy. He knew from his conversations with other bar and restaurant owners that the first six months were critical to his success. However, he also knew that since that first six months would decide if he would survive, many suppliers would not provide goods at favorable terms, and would not trust him until they were sure he would be in business for a long period of time.

Chris was well established with the local home brewers, but he had virtually no relationships with the suppliers in the industry. This situation was even more critical because he was going into a location in which previous restaurants had regularly failed. Thus, his suppliers might fear he would follow the same path. Chris knew he would still need to buy several hundred thousand dollars' worth of equipment if he bought it new. He had the benefit of having some used equipment, which he could buy cheaply, but there was still the issue of beer brewing equipment, supplies, and food suppliers. Chris estimated he would need more than $100,000 to obtain the necessary equipment and supplies for the first month of operation. If he could get favorable terms rather than pay cash up front on the equipment, then his initial capital requirements would be significantly different and help him with his cash flow.

Chris decided to seek out his personal and family friends that could perhaps help him build relationships with his key suppliers. He found in his home brewing club that one of his friend's brother was a senior executive in a U.S.-based brewing equipment company that he had hoped to use. He could have sought out far cheaper Chinese-made brewing equipment, but he wanted the higher-quality equipment. The introduction of the brother to the firm was just what Chris needed. Interestingly, the brewing equipment company was looking to expand more aggressively; knowing that Chris was a serious prospect led them to make him a great deal on the equipment. Chris then tried the same approach with his food suppliers. This time he found a family friend who worked for a large regional food supplier. The food supplier was not as willing to arrange as much credit as the brewing company had been, but Chris thought it was manageable. Thus, Chris's effort to build legitimacy with the key suppliers was largely successful.

1. If Chris had not been able to connect to the supplier, what else could he have done to cut his costs of operation start-up?
2. Chris had equipment in the kitchen from the prior business. Should he have tried to replace that?
3. In your business can you think of ways to cut your start-up operational costs?

How Timing Is a Competitive Advantage

LO12-9

Explain how timing is a competitive advantage.

It is interesting to note that choosing when to start a business is an important operational element. The temptation for most new businesses is to start their operations as soon as possible. This is rarely an effective strategy. Instead, the potential entrepreneur should select the time to enter the market based on when it provides the greatest competitive advantage.[9] The timing of your start is a function of several factors: (1) the general environment, (2) competitor moves, (3) cycles in purchasing/supply patterns, and (4) lifestyle issues.

The general economy moves in cycles of boom, slowdown, recession (or the many other terms that are used as euphemisms for this term), growth, and boom. Although the general rule might be that you should open your business during or at the beginning of a boom, the reality is that different businesses depend on different conditions. A foreclosure business depends on poor economic times, and storage facilities do best when the economy is heading downward, among others.

Competitor moves may also dictate the opening of a new business. If your business plan is dependent on having no direct competitors within a specified radius of your operation, a move by another business may accelerate or dramatically alter your plans. Alternatively, the failure of several similar businesses may suggest an alteration of your opening or strategic positioning prior to your actually opening the business.

Some (we might suggest most) businesses have cycles for their purchasing. Some suppliers have production runs that are scheduled a year or more in advance. Your ability to obtain critical supplies may dictate your lead time and opening time. It can be difficult, for example, to obtain significant Christmas inventory in September. The shipping time for these goods and other factors typically requires that a retailer make decisions much earlier.

An entrepreneur that we advised some years ago had a significant issue with the supply of wooden tubes that were needed for its production. The sole supplier of this particular size and quality of wooden tubes had a production run of eight weeks in March/April of each year for that particular product. All orders had to be in place by January. This new business reoriented its entire opening and operation around the acquisition of these wooden tubes. The owners placed an order in January, took delivery in three batches between April and June (storing all of the tubes in a warehouse that they leased), and began production of their product in November. Their first sale was in February of the following year, by which time they had placed yet another order for the following year. The ability of the new business to understand these timing issues required extensive planning and forecasting, without which it would have failed.

The Issues Related to Time Management in the Starting of a New Business

LO12-10

Recognize the issues related to time management in the starting of a new business.

The last item is one that is meant to help the new business owners as they seek to manage this wide variety of operations. It is clear from the discussion provided here that the business owners will need to manage their own time efficiently if they are to be successful.[10] There are several steps that are helpful in this process.

1. Write down what has to be accomplished in all parts of the business formation.

2. Prioritize which tasks are critical and which would be helpful. Those that are critical must be done and should be the priority.
3. Segment items in terms of the time frame they need to be accomplished—short term and long term. The short-term items that are critical have to take priority. The fires that are burning have to be put out before the longer-term issues approach.
4. Allocate time that is strictly for dealing with operational issues. The more you become involved in establishing the business and its operations, the more individuals will wish to visit with you about the business. Even though some of these individuals will be helpful, many simply wish to sell you something you do not need or to find out what you are doing. As your agenda becomes filled you must ensure that your attention is not diverted to nonproductive activities. This does not mean you should not be flexible when opportunities arise, but it does mean that you must have a clear vision of your work goals.
5. Write tasks down and mark them off when you accomplish them. As your agenda becomes more complex, you will gain satisfaction from seeing things being removed from it. However, this method also ensures that you will not forget key items (there should be a strong tie back to your critical path chart). In writing these things down, it is best if you can do this in a systematic, organized manner. Keep a notebook or use a PDA every day to see what you must accomplish and take notes about it. This approach can also be a valuable resource for keeping notes about meetings, issues that hit you as you think about the business, and issues that others raise with you. From these items and other information, you can keep track of issues to do today, this week, this month, and so forth.

SUMMARY

There is a wide variety of operational issues that must be considered as the new business begins operations. These include (1) developing a critical path chart; (2) establishing a location; (3) financing considerations; (4) legitimacy; (5) production management; (6) production charting; (7) quality; (8) equipment; (9) timing; and finally, (10) time management. Each is important to the start-up of a new business, and with proper planning and implementation, these various activities can substantially improve the opportunity for success.

KEY TERMS

anchor stores 222
critical path chart 220
legitimacy 224
production chart 227
strategic alliances 229
strip shopping center 222

REVIEW QUESTIONS

1. Why is a critical path chart useful to potential investors?
2. Are all locations equal?
3. What elements should be considered when leasing a new business location?
4. What would you recommend that a new business do to improve its acceptance and legitimacy in the market?
5. Why is a detailed chart of how business operations are conducted important to the new business?
6. How can quality be built into any product or service?
7. Should all new companies open as soon as they are physically ready? Why or why not?
8. Explain some key time management techniques that will benefit any new entrepreneur.

BUSINESS PLAN DEVELOPMENT QUESTIONS

1. What elements would you include in a critical path chart for your proposed business? How would you ensure that your estimates were accurate?
2. What is the potential locations for your business? Evaluate the different locations and pick one that is the most attractive.
3. What criteria are critical for the location decision of your new business?
4. What are the specific ways you plan to build legitimacy for your business?

INDIVIDUAL EXERCISES

1. What are the "lease or buy" equipment issues you will face in your business?
2. Can you employ used, or will you need new equipment in your business?
3. What is the difference in price of new and used equipment in your proposed business?
4. What are the critical timing issues involved in your business?

GROUP EXERCISES

1. Establish a plan to address each of the critical issues related to the starting of operations for a new organization.
2. Imagine that your team has decided to franchise the business idea. Develop a set of processes/procedures that would allow a third party to become a franchise of your operation.
3. Present your operational plan to the class and ask for feedback.

ENDNOTES

1. A. Gunasekaran, L. Forker, and B. Kobu, "Improving Operations Performance in a Small Company: A Case Study," *International Journal of Operations & Production Management* 20, no. 3/4 (2000), pp. 316–36.
2. F. Levy, G. Thompson, and J. Weist, "The ABCs of the Critical Path Method," *Harvard Business Review* 41, no. 5 (1963) pp. 98–109.
3. K. Jensen and G. Pompelli, "Manufacturing Site Location Preference of Small Agribusiness Firms," *Journal of Small Business Management* 40 (2002), pp. 204–19.
4. A. Bouma, C. Durham, and L. Meunier-Goddik, "Start-Up and Operating Costs for Artisan Cheese Companies," *Journal of Dairy Science* 97 (2014), pp. 3964–72.
5. D. Shepard and A. Zacharakis, "A New Venture's Cognitive Legitimacy: An Assessment by Customers," *Journal of Small Business Management* 41 (2003), pp. 148–68.
6. B. Nagy, J. Pollack, M. Rutherford, and F. Lohrke, "The Influence of Entrepreneurs Credentials and Impression Management Behaviors on Perceptions of New Venture Legitimacy," *Entrepreneurship Theory & Practice* 36 (2012), pp. 941–55.
7. K. Papke-Shields, M. Malhotra, and V. Grover, "Strategic Manufacturing Planning Systems and Their Linkage to Planning System Success," *Decision Sciences* 33 (2002), pp. 1–30.
8. W. Deming, *Out of the Crisis* (Cambridge, MA: Massachusetts Institute of Technology, 1992).
9. K. Brouther and G. Nakos, "SME Entry Mode Choice and Performance: A Transaction Cost Perspective," *Entrepreneurship Theory & Practice* 28 (2004), pp. 229–48; J. Liao and W. Gartner, "The Effects of Pre-Venture Plan Timing and Perceived Environmental Uncertainty on the Persistence of Emerging Firms," *Small Business Economics* 27 (2006), pp. 23–40.
10. S. Covey, A. Merrill, and R. Merrill, *First Things First* (New York: Simon & Schuster, 1994).

CREDITS

Opener: Francesco Corticchia/E+/Getty Images RF; p. 215: IndigoIT.com; p. 221: blue jean images/Getty Images RF; p. 222: © Len Holsborg/Alamy.

part 5

chapter 13

learning objectives

After studying this chapter, you will be able to:

LO13-1 Explain the need for developing an exit or harvest plan and ideal timing for that plan.

LO13-2 Outline the steps for selling a business.

LO13-3 Discuss the concept of turnaround and business in decline.

LO13-4 Recognize the implications and issues involved in closing a business.

Exit/Harvest/ Turnaround

TEALUXE

Bruce Fernie opened Tealuxe in 1996 in Harvard Square, Cambridge, Massachusetts, to bring "Tea for All" to the masses in the same way that Starbucks brought specialty coffee to the world. Carrying more than 100 types of tea, he opened storefronts in trendy, urban, college campus areas. Tea, however, is not the same business as coffee is in the United States. Although tea is the second most popular beverage in the world after water, it is not very popular as a daily drink in the United States. Starbucks provided a premium product that a majority of Americans already drank on a daily basis: coffee. However, it was not clear that there was a demand for a wide range of teas beyond those Starbucks already offered.

Tealuxe stores were attractive and nicely placed, and some began doing a significant business. However, Bruce Fernie had no interest in actively managing the storefronts, or for that matter, the operational side of the business. He considered himself a big-vision person and did not enjoy the daily operations. With no consistency in operational management, the company made numerous missteps. For example, he once opened a storefront in the New York City Atrium at a rental rate that all but guaranteed failure. He closed that operation within six months.

Having to repeatedly put expansion plans on hold kept distracting the management from the business of running the stores. In July 2001, Tealuxe cut back to four stores from seven and filed for Chapter 11 bankruptcy. "Chairman and Co-Founder Bruce Fernie, who himself expressed no interest in running the business day to day, blames the management that was hired to implement his ideas and the abysmal real estate deals and store-level control they implemented."

A private equity firm purchased Tealuxe out of bankruptcy and attempted to grow the business. In 2010 the Tealuxe store in Cambridge was named one of the top five tea houses in New England. Despite positive reviews as of 2014, the company has been cut back to just two store locations. The company is looking to franchise as a means to grow. The chain's Internet business has become much more important to the firm, a fact that is highlighted on the firm's Web page (www.tealuxe.com/).

Businesses fail for many reasons, but for an entrepreneurial business, a hands-on approach and a complete understanding of the competitive advantage model for the business is essential to survival.

Questions

1. Given that Starbucks has purchased Teavana and is planning to grow that effort, what do you see as the future for Tealuxe?
2. Why has Tealuxe not grown beyond two stores despite the investment of capital?
3. What would you do to turn around the business?

Sources: J. Sloane, "Bruce Fernie Wants to Do for Tea What Howard Schultz Did for Coffee . . . Is He Kidding?" *Fortune Small Business* 11, no. 3 (April 2001); J. Sloane, "Tealuxe Puts Its Plans on Ice," *Fortune Small Business* 11, no. 8 (October 2001); K. Municheillo, "Best 5 New England Teahouses," *Yankee Magazine*, March/April 2010, www.yankeemagazine.com/article/travel/teahouses-me-ma-ct-ri; Tealuxe Web page, http://www.tealuxe.com/.

Eventually there will come a time when the founder(s) needs to, or wants to, exit business. This decision may be based on a variety of factors. One may be that the business has done very well and the founder(s) has decided to cash out of the venture. On paper the founder(s) may appear to be very wealthy, but if all of the assets are in the business, then the individual's assets are not liquid and are subject to rapid changes in wealth as the value of the business changes. Selling the business turns some of the hard earned sweat equity into cash. The ability to turn some or all of the business value into cash at some point allows the business owners a flexibility in their choice of actions and businesses as they go forward.

Alternatively, it may be that things have not gone well and the founder(s) needs to either turn the venture around or close down the business. A wide set of issues must be addressed in all of these cases, including such issues as a plan for establishing the value of the business, attracting buyers, negotiating a sale, meeting all of the legal requirements for the sale, consummating the deal, and paying off the investors. These issues can become even more complex if you have to look at turning a business around that has started badly. While difficult, the ability to turn a business around is a valuable skill. This chapter will explore these areas.

LO13-1

Explain the need for developing an exit or harvest plan and ideal timing for that plan.

Need for Developing an Exit or Harvest Plan and Ideal Timing for That Plan

The entrepreneurs benefit from considering several dimensions of what is required to sell the business, both at the founding and when they begin the selling process.

Why Consider Exit or Harvest Now?

It may appear odd to consider the topic of exit and harvest while you are only beginning the process of getting the new business up and running. However, early stage entrepreneurs must consider a well-defined exit plan before personality clashes arise. A business is an investment of both time and money. In addition, developing a practical exit plan can provide some peace of mind to the family and the investors so they know what to expect if things do not go as planned. The key starting point for any decision to exit or harvest the firm is establishing the valuation of the firm. Developing an accurate valuation as the firm begins to have cash flow helps:

1. Provide insight for the founders as to the amount of future capital and labor that they should invest in the effort.
2. The business obtain loans (either direct or working capital) by demonstrating the value of the firm to potential creditors.
3. Convince outside equity investors of the potential long-term returns associated with the harvesting of the business.
4. The owners field potential offers to buy out the business (a relatively common occurrence in the life of a business).
5. Benchmark the growth of the firm by establishing a true starting point.

Why Consider Exit or Harvest Later?

Having laid at least some initial groundwork will help the entrepreneurs if they later decide to exit the business. As discussed in Chapter 2, the entrepreneur must determine what he wants to accomplish in the business.

FRIENDS' HOME HEALTH

Although the founders of Friends' had never even considered selling their business, they were caught completely off guard when a hospital approached them about buying the entire operation. In the surprise call, the hospital president let Betty and Joan know that he would buy them outright now for $400,000, and furthermore, he wanted the founders to stay on with the business. The hospital would provide the founders a guaranteed two-year management contract at $90,000 per year per person, plus 15 percent of the yearly profits during those two years. The hospital president presented this deal to the founders of Friends' claiming that the total package was worth approximately $800,000 (assuming that profits grew respectably), which he claimed was the value of the business right now. The resulting conversation among the two partners focused on three critical issues. First, should they even consider selling the business at this point? Second, if they did consider selling, what would be a reasonable price for the business? Third, what were their personal long-term goals, and did this offer get them closer to those goals?

To consider these questions, Betty and Joan had to figure out how much the business was worth. For advice, they approached a friend who had worked in mergers and acquisitions (M&As) as a consultant to manufacturers, and he suggested that the real value of a business was simply the market value of the assets of the firm plus a premium (which he referred to as goodwill), which represented the future value of the firm. He suggested that many M&A deals pay a 20 percent premium above the market value of an established public business. Using this calculation, the founders estimated that the business was worth $180,000 ($150,000 in equity capital and equipment plus 20 percent). However, this number did not seem to account for the potential of the business, and in any case, was substantially less than what the hospital had offered.

The founders contacted two members of their board of advisors and asked for their advice. They quickly discounted the friend's advice regarding M&As as not applicable to a services business. They told the founders to forecast net cash flow for the next five years (five years was chosen as a reasonable return period) and then discount that number back to the present time using a reasonable discount rate for risky newer ventures (say, 20 percent). So, the founders estimated net cash flow for the next five years as follows:

Year 1 $94,296	5-Year Total Earnings $322,159
Year 2 $15,075	Discount Rate @ 20% 2.488
Year 3 $102,305	322,159/2.488 = $129,485
Year 4 $132,066	
Year 5 $167,009	

QUESTIONS

1. What do you think is a fair value for this firm?
2. Assuming that a fair value can be calculated, should the founders sell the firm at this point? Why or why not?
3. What does your answer to question 2 say about your risk propensity?

If the business is very successful but is no longer interesting or enjoyable, it is probably a good time to exit. A business takes too much time and personal commitment to be something that is not enjoyable. Similarly, there may be other opportunities available. The entrepreneur may not have time to run the existing business and pursue these new opportunities at the same time, so it becomes necessary to exit the first business. Alternatively, the founder may sense that whereas the business is strong now, the future does not hold the same potential for similar success, so it might be a good time to exit.

One example is an entrepreneur we knew who set up a number of sports shoe stores. Several years after founding, the owner began to realize that there were major chains entering the market, which was leading to market saturation in his area. He would have to completely reset the strategy of the business in order to compete in the future. This individual decided to harvest the venture and sell it to someone else. He reaped the value of the business that he had grown without having to go through the painful process of resetting the strategic position of the firm.

LO13-2

Outline the steps for selling a business.

Steps for Selling a Business

When a business owner decides to sell or harvest the business, there is a series of steps that need to occur. The first is to develop some sense of the true value of the business. The second is to prepare the business to be sold. The last step is the negotiation and actual selling of the business.

Valuation

There are several standard valuation models and rules of thumb for established, publicly traded businesses. For example, public companies have an established market capitalization that is technically the value of the business as it exists at the present time. Following the standard on Wall Street, this market capitalization already accounts for future earnings and all future prospects of the business that are known today. If you wished to acquire one of these organizations, the general assumption would be that the market capitalization is the floor from which all negotiations begin. Calculating the premium that will be offered above the market capitalization is more a matter of art than one of science.* Issues such as how much cash will be paid versus stock transferred and the future investment in the newly combined organization are a matter of negotiation, not to mention the overwhelming concern regarding what will happen to the executives of the acquired firm. These issues are substantially different when we consider the valuation and acquisition of a privately held venture.

Virtually all new businesses are private firms that do not report their earnings to the public. In addition, new businesses often adjust their annual company "earnings" with the payment of large year-end bonuses to the founders in order to limit the profit and therefore the taxes on the business. The new business may also have creative company **perquisites** ("perks") for the owners to minimize the tax owed by the organization. The owners of a new business may also have other individual personal expenses paid for by the firm. The result is that the firm pays fewer taxes, but the firm also may appear to be worth less than it is really worth to the entrepreneur.

perquisites

Benefits paid for by the company. Examples include vacations, vehicles, loans, gifts, financial contributions to retirement plans, and so on.

For example, a firm such as Friends' Home Health that is owned by two individuals allows the founders to use "profits" for the benefit of the firm as well as themselves in a perfectly legal and ethical manner. If sales were particularly good in one year, the founders may decide to provide luxury cars as a perk for themselves. This expense dramatically reduces the "profit" of the venture, whereas the reality is that the business is quite profitable. Similar expenses also occur in public companies; however, they are required to disclose such items in an audited annual report, whereas a new business venture rarely goes to the expense of having audited financial records. Thus, it should be clear that different methods of valuation are needed when considering the purchase of a private company.

There are a large number of unique systems used for the valuation of a private business. Most accounting groups and many private companies

*There are a number of other quick methods for calculating a purchase price, including a multiple of sales, discounted future earnings, discounted projected free cash flow, and so on. We provide all of this by way of comparison.

provide business valuation services. We would suggest that you work with these organizations when you are really ready to sell the business. They will use commonly accepted practices to refine the value of the ongoing business. However, in general, we encourage the entrepreneur to use only a few of the most common methods to get a rough estimate of the value of the business as the business begins and grows. Valuing a business is as much art as it is science. Ultimately, the true "value" of the business is the amount of money that a willing seller and a willing buyer agree upon for the sale of the business. Thus, you want to be well prepared for the range of prices that may be offered and understand why you might agree or not agree with those prices. An investor, lender, or potential purchaser may take issue with several of the assumptions in your projections, or might want to reduce the numbers more severely than the founders believe is realistic. To maximize the selling price of the firm, the founders must intimately understand the numbers to be able to discuss such issues intelligently with those individuals. These methods include (1) discounted future net cash flow; (2) price/earnings valuation; (3) asset-based valuation; (4) capitalization of earnings valuation; and (5) market estimation valuation.

Discounted Future Net Cash Flow. By far the most widely accepted method of valuation, and the most insightful, involves some form of discounting the estimated future net cash flows of the business. As you might recall from Chapter 6, cash flow tracks the actual cash inflows and outflows of the business. For estimation purposes, a potential buyer can subtract any perks that have affected the net cash position of the venture. The detail available in a well-designed cash flow statement and the understanding that it is not profit, but free cash flow that is the key to entrepreneurial success makes this the ideal document to use in the valuation of a business.

The cash flow method of valuation requires that the net cash flow of the business be projected for some period of time into the future. Our experience has suggested that estimating cash flows five years into the future and adding a salvage value for the firm is a good ballpark floor valuation for a business. For an Internet business, the cash flow method works very well although there is typically no salvage value for any of the assets since even used computers normally have minimal value. The information for this example appears in Figure 13.1.

In this example, the net cash flow for each year is as follows:

Year 1 $101,885

Year 2 $30,575

Year 3 $143,725

Year 4 $161,000

Year 5 $446,100

Those most interested in a good estimation of firm value (potential buyers, lenders, equity investors, and founders) will recognize that these numbers are simply estimates that are based on a set of assumptions. To understand and accept the cash flow predictions, it is important that each interested party accept the underlying assumptions. Therefore, a critical addition to any business plan, and certainly a necessity for any valuation analysis, is a complete set of assumptions used by the founders. An example from a group of entrepreneurs that were proposing a specialty transport company appears in Figure 13.2 and Figure 13.3. This company would transport people to sports events related to local colleges. The business would start focused on a single school and ultimately expand to other schools. The plan was to sell alcohol and limited food

RECEIPTS:	YEAR 1, $	YEAR 2, $	YEAR 3, $	YEAR 4, $	YEAR 5, $	TOTALS, $
Sales	$ 25,000	$325,000	$ 675,000	$880,000	$1,560,000	$3,465,000
Consulting	20,000	20,000	60,000	80,000	100,000	280,000
Total Receipts	45,000	345,000	735,000	960,000	1,660,000	3,745,000
Disbursements:						
Salaries	$ 45,000	$ 95,000	$ 210,000	$305,000	$ 450,000	$ 1,105,000
Travel	4,050	31,050	66,150	86,400	149,400	337,050
Car Leases	4,000	6,000	7,500	11,000	13,800	42,300
Rent	900	6,900	14,700	19,200	33,200	74,900
Payroll Taxes	2,700	5,700	12,600	18,300	27,000	66,300
Insurance	5,500	6,000	7,500	9,000	13,000	41,000
Fuel/Maint.	960	4,500	8,000	13,000	21,000	47,460
Executive Comp.	64,000	72,000	78,000	84,000	89,000	387,000
Benefits	13,500	28,500	63,000	91,500	135,000	331,500
Advertising	2,000	26,000	54,000	70,400	124,800	277,200
Supplies	225	1,725	3,675	4,800	8,300	18,725
Utilities	3,150	24,150	51,450	67,200	116,200	262,150
Misc.	900	6,900	14,700	19,200	33,200	74,900
Total Disbursements	$ 146,885	$ 314,425	$ 591,275	$ 799,000	$ 1,213,900	$ 3,065,485
Beginning Balance	0	98,115	128,690	272,415	433,415	
Equity Investment	200,000					
Net Cash Flow	**($ 101,885)**	**$ 30,575**	**$ 143,725**	**$ 161,000**	**$ 446,100**	**$ 679,515**
Ending Balance	$ 98,115	$ 128,690	$ 272,415	$ 433,415	$ 879,515	$ 1,812,150

Figure 13.1
Example Cash Flow Statement

on the bus. We will use this firm as an example to evaluate the different valuations that the firm could expect.

Discounting the Cash Flow. The example above illustrates that to understand a cash flow statement, an entrepreneur needs to have an in-depth knowledge of the assumptions that went into the statement. Given the nature of predictions and assumptions in general, there is a need for these values to be discounted by some rate that not only represents the return expected by an investor, but also accounts for the riskiness of the venture. We have seen discount rates range from a ridiculously low 10 percent to an almost absurd 90 percent. However, a rule of thumb for new businesses being operated by owner-managers is to use 30 percent as a discount factor. This should not only account for a generous annualized rate of return but also build in a reasonable factor for risk. While we are in favor of simplicity in these calculations, we recognize that some interested parties prefer to separate return from risk. There are a variety of sophisticated financial models available to those who wish to be more precise in their analysis.

Cash Flow categories will vary with the type of business being analyzed.

Figure 13.2
General Cash Flow Assumptions for Specialty Bus Company

Recall we are employing a specialty bus company under different valuation lenses. The assumptions that go into the cash flow, which allow us to make the valuation, include the following:

- Liquor sales are not included in the cash flow statement and are determined on a per trip basis, depending on how much alcohol the group orders. We will charge a 10 percent markup rate for each order.
- We applied an 8 percent payroll tax to salaries.
- Championship games for football are not accounted for in the cash flow statement. There will be a price markup that will be determined based on factors such as how big and how important the game is, who they are playing, and so on.
- We assume that the men's and women's basketball teams play a total of 6 out of 12 possible games in the tournament.
- We are assuming that the base school makes it to a bowl game.
- Pricing on the competitive map is based on football season rates.
- We plan to fill the buses during various alumni events during the summer. The base school currently has five major events on its annual calendar. We assume we can fill all four buses for each event because of their importance. This is accounted for in the cash flow statement. We assume there will be other events, which we can cater, whether through alumni associations or directly through the base school. We did not account for these numbers on the cash flow statement because estimating how many events we will book and how big each will be is difficult at this point, but we will stay in close contact with the school and alumni groups and work on making reservations. We are confident our summer sales will be higher.
- Gas costs were based on an assumption that the price is $3.60 per gallon for diesel fuel. According to the Energy Information Administration, this has been the average price for the last two years in the Midwest region.
- We assume there will be no significant economic recessions within the next five years.
- We have researched laws pertaining to continuous operation for a commercial driver and will assure that all itineraries are planned accordingly.

Using this rule of thumb, the entrepreneur should take the net cash flow figure generated for each year and discount that cash flow back to today's dollars. The discount rate remains the same, while the factor increases as you move farther away from today. Thus, in year 2, the discount rate is squared (1.3 * 1.3), in year 3 it is cubed (1.3 * 1.3 * 1.3), and so on. To illustrate with our previous example, we calculate the present value of the net cash flow below.

Illustration of Present Value of the Net Cash Flow. Using the information in Figure 13.1 and assuming a 30 percent discount rate, we can calculate the present value of the net cash flows as follows:

$$(101{,}885)/1.3 + 30{,}575/1.3^2 + 143{,}725/1.3^3 + 161{,}000/1.3^4 + 446{,}100/1.3^5 = \text{PV(NCF)}$$

$$(101{,}885)/1.3 + 30{,}575/1.69 + 143{,}725/2.19 + 161{,}000/2.85 + 446{,}100/3.71 = \text{PV(NCF)}$$

$$(78{,}373) + 18{,}091 + 65{,}959 + 56{,}372 + 120{,}145 = \mathbf{\$182{,}194}$$

Without accounting for the sale price of the business, this calculation would suggest that the current value of the business is approximately $180,000.

Figure 13.3
Example of Specific Cash Flow Assumptions

Although there are general assumptions that go into the cash flow calculation, an individual will also need to make assumptions for the very specific firm setting before the cash flow can be discounted. The specific cash flow assumptions we make include the following:

- Sales tax for each state and the surrounding municipality is 7 percent, applicable to the rental price.
- Income will be consistent throughout all of the centers in the different states. This is because we have hand-picked each school and have taken great efforts to make sure that they are all similar in population, athletic activity, demographic makeup, and geographic locations.
- Maintenance overhaul will occur in the first quarter for each bus at a cost of $1,000 per bus.
- All acquisitions and expansions will be financed internally; there will be no need for second- and third-round financing.
- Salaries are set at $30,000 for each officer, with an increase to $35,000 in year 3.
- Insurance is a once-a-year payment, including $10,000 for base coverage with each additional bus adding $1,000 plus tax, stamping, and processing fees.
- Waste removal is billed by volume plus service fees, estimating $75 to $100 per visit.
- Credit card charges account for 30 percent of all sales with a processing fee of 2.1 percent.
- Transportation costs are associated with moving buses within the state, either to their home stations or to meet customers.
- Accounting/legal fees will occur periodically throughout the year, with a concentration of accounting fees during tax season and legal fees during periods of expansion or acquisition.
- Fees and permits include registration costs, inspection fees, and other associated costs with each bus, as well as the costs of providing commercial drivers' licenses (CDL) and training to officers at the inception of the company.

price/earnings (P/E) ratio
A value derived from public companies that divides the current earnings per share into the price per share.

Price/Earnings Valuation. Another method of estimating the value of a business is to use the industry **price/earnings (P/E) ratio**. This is a relatively straightforward system that uses the industry in which the start-up operates. The founder should locate the P/E ratio for public companies in the same industry via the many sources of this information (the Internet, *The Wall Street Journal,* the library, etc.). That average should be multiplied by the net cash flow for year 5 and discounted back as a potential sales price in year 6 of the venture. Therefore, for our specialty bus company we employ 1 + the discount rate raised to the 6th power. In our example that would be 1.3^6 (4.826).

Illustration of P/E Ratio Valuation. This example illustrates how to calculate your P/E ratio valuation:

P/E for Industry	10 (obtained from industry sources)
Net Cash Flow for Year 5	$446,100
Discount Rate	30%
Sale/Residual Value	446,100 * 10 = $4,460,000
	$4,460,000/1.3^6$ = Discounted Sales Price
	4,460,000/4.826 = $ 924,005

Using these calculations, we would suggest that the value of the firm today would be the addition of the present value of the future cash flows plus the discounted sales price of the firm. For this example, that would be the following:

Discounted Cash Flow + Discounted Sales Price = Current Value

$182,194 + $924,005 = **$1,106,199**

There are two other relatively popular methods for valuing a business: asset-based valuation and earnings valuation.

Asset-Based Valuation. **Asset valuation** involves accounting for all of the hard assets of the organization: buildings (if owned), equipment (if owned), furniture, cash, and marketable securities held in the name of the company, as well as (in most cases) the value of any signed and executable contracts. Once all of the assets of the organization are tallied, the value of the business is typically calculated by taking that total number and adding an acquisition, or goodwill, value to it. This acquisition/goodwill value is determined by examining similar companies that have been acquired, or more often by simply looking at the percentage premium being offered in general on all new public acquisitions. If the business were performing poorly, there would be virtually no goodwill value. Asset valuation is typically the lowest business valuation number that you will calculate, unless you are an asset-intensive business. This valuation method works best for firms with hard assets and not an Internet business.

asset valuation
A method of business valuation that simply totals all of the hard assets of the organization and adds in a goodwill value.

Illustration of Asset Valuation. Following is an illustration of asset valuation for a restaurant rather than our bus company since it allows a richer set of assets. The bus company leased its buses, so there were very limited assets. In a case such as that for the bus company, asset valuation method is of limited use:

Building (Market Value Minus Mortgage)		=	$108,755
Equipment			
1.	1 grill	=	$ 8,450
2.	3 cook counters	=	$ 950
3.	2 fryers	=	$ 1,300
4.	1 walk-in freezer	=	$ 1,850
5.	3 refrigerators	=	$ 4,600
6.	2 computers/accessories	=	$ 1,300
7.	Various cooking utensils	=	$ 3,904
8.	Bar equipment	=	$ 3,700
			$ 26,054
Furniture			
1.	41 (2-top) tables	=	$ 10,900
2.	17 (4-top) tables	=	$ 6,050
3.	6 (6-top) tables	=	$ 2,800
4.	197 chairs	=	$ 13,902
5.	4 counters	=	$ 980
6.	1 complete bar	=	$ 3,700
			$ 38,332
	Cash/marketable securities	=	$ 26,800
	Total asset value	=	$ 199,941

Total Asset Value * Acquisition Premium = Value of the Business

$199,941 * 4.3 = $859,746

In this particular instance, a quick analysis of the industry revealed that an average asset-acquisition premium for this particular industry was running at approximately 4.3 times assets. Each industry will be unique and the appropriate multiple will vary over time with changing market conditions and industry M&A activity. Therefore, the business as it currently stands (via this method) would be worth approximately $860,000. This method tends to depress the true future value of a growing business, so some investors and lenders will factor in a growth premium to "bulk up" the total valuation. "Art" intrudes once again.

capitalization of earnings valuation

A method of valuation achieved by taking the earnings (net profit) of the organization; subtracting or adding any unusual items that the lender or investor feels are not customary, normal, or usual items; and dividing that figure by a capitalization rate.

Capitalization of Earnings Valuation. Very similar to asset valuation, **capitalization of earnings valuation** is performed by taking the earnings (net profit) of the organization; subtracting or adding any unusual items that the lender or investor believes are not customary, normal, or usual items; and dividing that figure by a capitalization rate. The capitalization rate is determined (rather loosely) by the nature of business, including longevity, business risk, consistency of earning, quality of management, and general economic conditions. The capitalization rate is generally an agreed upon number rather than something that can be "looked up."

Illustration of Capitalization of Earnings Valuation. This illustrates capitalization of earnings valuation using our example of a specialty bus firm:

Net Profit (Earnings) of the Company	=	$32,900
Capitalization Rate	=	0.2

$32,900/0.2 = $164,500

Using this system involves much more than simply accepting a final net profit figure. As was stated in Chapter 6, the net profit of a new business is an easily manipulated figure that is wholly dependent on the needs and desires of the founders. Therefore, lenders and investors adjust this figure to account for the individual actions of the founders. Would-be buyers readjust the net profit of the company to account for these nuances of a new business and then apply a capitalization rate that is a combination of the buyers' risk propensity and the current situation in the business acquisition marketplace.

market estimation

A method of business valuation that involves taking the earnings of the business and multiplying that figure by the market premium of companies in its industry.

Market Estimation Valuation. A valuation via **market estimation** is by far the simplest of the techniques. Fundamentally, it involves taking the earnings (or projected earnings) of the business and multiplying that figure by the market premium of companies in their industry. A popular method is to take the EBITDA (earnings before interest, taxes, depreciation, and amortization), reworking the figure based on an analysis of the cash flow statement, and multiplying the remaining figure by a market multiple. An examination of the NASDAQ or NYSE provides a group of companies in virtually every industry classification. Taking the group as a whole or attempting to find companies that are similar to your business yields an estimated market premium, also called an industry multiple, that can be used to calculate the value of the business. Once again, lenders and investors will attempt to adjust the earnings of the organization to reflect a more balanced picture.

Market Estimation Illustration. The following illustrates market estimation valuation using our sample specialty bus firm:

Net Profit (Earnings) of the Company	=	$32,900
Industry Multiple	=	13

$32,900 * 13 = $427,700

Valuation Overview. As can be seen, there are wide variations in the potential valuations of this business, from several hundred thousand dollars to one and a half million dollars. Every company has unique features that provide it with some type of competitive advantage. In Chapter 5, we developed a strong argument for the development of a sustainable competitive advantage that enabled the new business to gain true economic rents relative to the competition. These "art" characteristics of an organization are important considerations in the valuation of a business and should be part of the equation when determining the true value of your business.

EXERCISE 1

1. Using your projected cash flow statement, develop a business valuation for your proposed company. This will mean forecasting cash flow five years into the future.
2. Use your annual net cash flow as an estimate of earnings. Use the earnings valuation method and the market valuation method to estimate the value of your organization 5 years from now. Assume that the P/E for your industry is 7 and the acquisition premium is (P/E ratio plus 3).
3. Using the same cash flow statement, estimate your total assets and compute an asset-based valuation for the business.
4. Looking at the range of figures that you have just developed, explain why one particular figure is more representative of the value of the business.

Preparing the Business for Sale

When the determination has been made to sell the business, the entrepreneur must begin a process that is somewhat akin to selling a home. There is a need for the entrepreneur to make sure the business looks its best in order to obtain the highest premium possible.

One of the key issues for the survival of the business after the sale is the change in leadership that will occur. Consider for a moment a business we knew that sold equipment to research laboratories. The founder of the business had all the key contacts for the business. When he first tried to sell the business, there were very few individuals interested in the firm. This was despite the firm's having received the Outstanding Small Business of the Year award from the local government the prior year. The key problem was that there was little value in the business beyond the founder himself. Buyers bought the company's products because of the founder's reputation and his unique ability to install the products. Potential buyers did not want to buy a firm whose contacts and relationships walked out the door when the founder sold the business. This story raises important questions for any seller. How will the business run after the founder leaves? How do you transfer the founder's contacts and reputation to the new owners? There should be a transition plan in place for this transfer in order for any purchase to be viable.

This difficulty is compounded by the reality that most entrepreneurial businesses run a very tight operation where every individual has specific functions and there is little slack available for cross-training. The company founder might handle all of the marketing and sales for the organization. This may include meeting clients, handling contract negotiations, and being the point person for each customer, while the company has another individual handle all of the operational details. Replacing this personal contact person would require that the founder begin to incorporate others in the handling of customers and/or include a new individual to join her in the process of client meetings. All of this requires a significant investment in the future without obvious payoffs in the present. Most entrepreneurs find this quite difficult. These and other types of human resource issues unique to an entrepreneurial business were covered in Chapter 10.

The firm also needs to examine its operations to ensure that the procedures of the business are codified and simplified for easy handover to a new owner. It is a reality in entrepreneurial businesses that the operational procedures develop as the business grows. The effort to put these procedures in writing will go a long way toward making for a more seamless transition. Another operational issue is the accounting of the firm. A system where the founder keeps the books herself is perfectly acceptable and perhaps

ETHICAL CHALLENGE

In the process of preparing his firm to be sold, one entrepreneur sought to make the business look as attractive as possible to prospective buyers. He had the opportunity to make a large sale right before the business would be inspected, which would make his financials look much better. However, the entrepreneur was well aware that the buyer was in bankruptcy proceedings and that he might or might not actually be paid for the large sell. The entrepreneur also had a large manufacturing equipment base that could be made to look better, so they would be valued more with some minor cleaning. This was necessary since the maintenance records for this equipment were sketchy at best, so the value of the equipment might lie in its appearance.

QUESTIONS

1. What are the entrepreneur's legal requirements in presenting the business to a buyer?
2. Do the ethical requirements differ from the legal requirements in what must be presented? Isn't it simply "buyer beware"?
3. How do you as a business owner make sure that the firm looks attractive to purchase but at the same time provide realistic information?

even desirable when starting up and running the new business. However, a potential buyer wants to assure himself of the accuracy of the financial information. Our advice for ventures considering a sale is to contract with a CPA firm to have it do the following when looking to exit the firm:

1. Audit last year's financial statements.
2. Put all of the statements into a standardized format.
3. Develop procedures for the accounting of all activities.
4. Provide an audit of this year's financial statements and render an accounting opinion.

This effort provides a level of legitimacy to the business and assures the buyer of the accuracy of the financial statements of the organization.

Maintaining an estimate of the value of a business as it grows and develops is the responsibility of the business owner. However, the entrepreneur should obtain a professional valuation of the business before attempting to actually sell the business. The valuation may turn out to be much less than the owner feels that the firm is worth, and therefore there would be little need to pursue the attempt to sell the firm.

Specialization within a business, like hospital auditing, can make the process of selling a business more complicated. What are some things to consider?

The methods that will be used by the professional valuation experts will likely be very similar to those detailed earlier in this chapter. The entrepreneur would be well served to conduct one's own estimate and then compare that to what the professional advises. The entrepreneur should actively challenge the analysis and discuss it with the valuation professional. The knowledge that the entrepreneur develops regarding the valuation of the business will help as they negotiate the sale of the business.

Another important aspect in preparing the business for sale is the recording of all the informal practices of the organization. Policies and procedures developed in the life of a new venture should be recorded and available to a new buyer. Issues such as when to order certain supplies, what time to begin closing each day, the process of closing each day, the methods for dealing with customers, payment practices, human resource benefits and policies, and the like, must all be codified. Anyone who wants to purchase an entire company should have all of these practices in writing—both for ease of analysis and for clarity of understanding that this provides regarding the inner working of the business.

The business founders also need to plan for the type of sale that will maximize their returns. The best method to use to actually exit the firm will very much depend on the type of business. Businesses that have moved well beyond the founder's personality will be simpler to sell than those that are intimately tied to the active participation of the founder. Although there are literally thousands of possible ways to construct a sales agreement, it might take some careful forethought and years of preparation work to make the business valuable to an outside investor.

One of the authors recently worked with an established accounting business where the two founders were both in their early 70s. Although they were looking to exit the business, they really wanted a continuing revenue stream. One of the founder's sons was also an accountant who wanted to take over the company. Unfortunately, neither partner believed the son had the ability to carry on the work of the business in a managing role. Therefore, the two partners began to ponder how they would sell the firm. In the accounting business, as in many other companies, relationships are critical to the success of the business. Rather than make a quick sale that would lead to both founders leaving the firm immediately, they envisioned an opportunity in which they would leave gradually. They also had a specialized customer base that consisted primarily of hospitals. Hospital audits are usually completed on a schedule that differs from that of traditional corporate audits, which could allow a larger accounting business to better rationalize its accounting work flow. At a conference during the prior year, a larger firm had expressed an interest in an association with the partners' smaller firm. The two partners later approached the head of the larger firm and worked out a deal that included the following:

1. A small up-front cash payment
2. A five-year management agreement with the two founding partners
3. A gradual handover to executives from the larger firm
4. An annuity payment to the founders for 10 years, based upon bookings

The result was a smooth sale of the business in which both the acquiring and the acquired firms' owners were pleased with the results.

Actually Seeking to Sell the Business

Once the decision has been made to sell the business to an outside party, a number of choices are available to the entrepreneur. The most common is to sell the business intact to a third party with the aid of a broker or lawyer. A second very common option is to sell the business to a competitor or to a larger business interested in your location, your position in the market, your product, and so on. A third option is to divest portions of the business that will maximize the value of the business. It is not uncommon for the total value of the firm to be higher if the business is split into separate entities especially if there is real estate owned by the firm or the firm has become highly diversified over time. A fourth option, which is rarely used but is certainly the option most idealized by the business press, is an **initial public offering (IPO)**. The reality is that only a very small number of start-up businesses that end up being very high growth actually seek to conduct an IPO. In fact, for the entrepreneur, an IPO may not be the most profitable means to exit the business. Given the rarity of this type of event, we only mention the possibility of an IPO.

initial public offering (IPO)
The initial listing of a firm as a public entity in the public equities market.

Not surprisingly, actually putting a business up for sale is a bit more art than it is science. The process of getting the word out that a business is for sale can occur through a variety of avenues:

1. Hiring a business broker who will market the business for a percentage of the sale price
2. Contacting competitors or businesses that have expressed an interest in your business
3. Letting your accountant and your lawyer know that you are interested in selling your business. Individuals in both of these professions have numerous business contacts and may be aware of individuals seeking to buy a business
4. Contacting your suppliers and perhaps (if appropriate) your significant clients to let them know about your interest in selling the business

Negotiation Strategies

Although it may be obvious to state this, negotiating a sale is the art of trying to reach an agreed price between a willing buyer and a willing seller. Thus, a sale is based in the needs and wants of both parties. For example, if the buyer has other similar businesses in the city and the acquisition of your firm will provide coverage in the final section of the city where they currently are not located or will provide the buyer an outlet in the fastest-growing part of the city, then perhaps a higher price will be offered. Similarly, if the buyer is only interested in the business if he can get a bargain, he might try to pay less. The entrepreneur should not believe there is some absolute price that the buyer will not go above or below. Negotiating to sell the business is a process that the entrepreneur must actively engage in if she is to be successful.

Negotiation is a completely separate field of study, and texts exist for understanding the nuances and techniques that are available. Several important points to keep in mind regarding the negotiation of a sale include the following:

1. Use a professional mediator for anything but the most basic level of discussions. Your lawyer can play this role provided she has the experience. As we discussed in Chapter 9 (the legal aspects of the business), you will want all issues to be clear and specific. Do not make assumptions. Your lawyer can make sure that what you think the contract says is what is actually put in writing.
2. Know the buyer. Ask for as much information about the company that is making an inquiry as they ask from you, or more. If they agree to pay you over a period of years but they default after a year, the result may be that you have a failed business returned to you, with only part of the former value of the firm having actually been paid to you.
3. Retain your own advisors. It is very tempting to save money at this point and allow the buyer to provide the services; however, you are well served by having your own independent advisors.
4. Recognize that there are a myriad of options for selling the business. You may sell the company as a whole, or you can break up the business for maximum value. For example, you can sell the equipment to one company, the location to another, the name to yet another, among other scenarios. The goal upon exit is to maximize your own value.
5. Get cash for the firm. Frequently buyers may want to combine your firm with their firm to create a new business. As a result, the purchasing firm will offer you part cash and part stock in the new venture. If you take stock in the new venture, you are dependent on their success, and your liquidity is often reduced.

FLOW RIGHT BREWERY & BAR: A FAMILY AFFAIR

Chris had not been in business six months before his former boss in the mortgage processing unit at the bank approached him early one morning with a question that shocked Chris. Would Chris be interested in selling the business and continuing to run it as the manager? His former boss was impressed by the setup that Chris had achieved and by the rapid increase in his business. Chris had hired a full-time brewmaster, a bar manager, and a significant staff of servers, cooks, and bartenders, only one of whom was a family member. His sister had graduated from the career school she attended and was doing a magnificent job, not only with the books but in handling the whole back-room operation. She had an amazing ability to carry on a conversation with various staff members while completing her work as fast as the work came in.

Flabbergasted at the offer, Chris asked his former boss how much he thought the business was worth. He answered Chris that he didn't know right then, but he knew a good operation when he saw one. He wanted to have a chance to go over the books, and he asked Chris to think about a few things in the meantime. How much did he think the business was worth? Would he want to maintain an ownership interest in the business? How long might he be willing to commit to running the business if his former boss purchased it from him? Would he sign a noncompete agreement, and if so, how long did Chris think was a reasonable period of time?

Chris quickly got his bearings and told his former boss that before he could see any of the books or even say anything about this, Chris wanted some time to think, and he needed to talk with his family, who had an ownership interest in the place. Chris told him that he would get back to him within a week.

QUESTIONS

1. What would you recommend that Chris do during the next week? Why?
2. The business is so new, why would Chris even consider an offer at this point?
3. What would you advise him to do to determine the value of the business right now?

6. Look to the details. For example, new owners frequently want a noncompete agreement from you once you sell. This will prevent you from directly competing with the new owners for *X* number of years. However, if your buyout is not substantial, how will you make a living? Be sure you know all the details and ramifications of the negotiations.

Turnaround and Business in Decline

LO13-3

Discuss the concept of turnaround and business in decline.

Another related issue that faces entrepreneurial businesses is turning around a firm that is in a decline. It is possible that you have developed a solid business that prospered for a number of years. However, after some time and for a variety of factors, both internal and external to the firm, the business starts a period of decline. The effort to reverse that decline is referred to as **turnaround**.[1]

turnaround
The effort to reverse the decline of a business.

It is very difficult to turn around an entrepreneurial business successfully once it starts into a decline. The fact that these businesses have limited slack* or excess resources results in the businesses' having a very small leeway to respond to a decline. This is in contrast to large firms with massive resources, which the firms can rely on for years in the face of poor performance.

*"Slack" in this case includes the time available per individual that is not dedicated to day-to-day work.

Remodeling is just one way to help turnaround. What are some other options?

The firm must first seek to retrench.[2] This activity is analogous to medical situations where doctors must quickly seek to stabilize the patient before they can do more substantive actions. If they do not stabilize the patient first, the patient might die and there will be no value in trying other activities. For an entrepreneurial business, such retrenchment efforts focus on the firm's gaining control of its cash flow quickly, regardless of the impact to the long-term effort. This can be accomplished by bringing in accounts receivable more quickly, delaying the payment of accounts payable, renegotiating with suppliers so that supplies do not have to be paid for in cash, eliminating staff, and working with employees to cut costs. Once the bleeding of cash flow has been slowed, the firm can move on to more substantive actions.

While it is obvious that a huge environmental shift in the economy can cause a serious decline in virtually all businesses, the root internal causes of decline are usually based in either operating or strategic problems. To place it in straightforward terms, operating problems relate to either not selling enough of the product or not being sufficiently efficient in producing the product. Strategic problems are most often related to poor positioning choices. Strategic problems often include diversifying into unrelated domains and not being able to successfully manage the business.

Unfortunately, businesspeople tend to focus on the easiest problems to solve first. These are most often simply symptoms that take significant time to correct and yield very little in overall business results. Therefore, we advise businesspeople to pick the one key reason that the business is suffering. Identify it as either operating or strategic and dedicate the resources of the firm to solving that one immediately.

If it is an operating problem, then the solution should be an operating solution. These solutions include increasing marketing or marketing effectiveness to sell more products if the problem is that sales are down. Alternatively, if the problem is production inefficiency, then the focus should be oriented toward reengineering, simplifying, and measuring. Recall that we discussed quality management in Chapter 12. This is most often the focus of operating solutions and is certainly one of the best places to start the effort to turn around the business.

Strategic solutions rely on exiting those poor strategic choices that have been made over the years. We watched a wonderfully successful firm that installed in-ground pools diversify into backyard furniture and toys (such as swing sets). The business had solid positive cash flow and was looking to find a positive outlet for all the cash it was generating. Within a year the owners realized that not only were they losing money on their new business, but they were also installing fewer swimming pools because their corporate officers were distracted by trying to get the new business up and running. They quickly exited the non–pool installation businesses and redoubled their efforts on their core operations. It took almost two years to return the firm to the point where it had been before the foray into the seemingly related business. Recall that we discussed in Chapter 2 the need for entrepreneurs to evaluate the skills they personally possess before going into a business. In this situation, the entrepreneurs may be quite good at managing a pool installation business, but that does not mean that they will be successful with businesses that appear on the surface to be related. The key to success is not seeking to learn the backyard furniture business (one that involves a wide inventory with no need for installation), but instead, focusing exclusively on the pool installation business. When bad strategic choices are made, exit them quickly.

The business press suggests for a large, established business that the CEO of the organization and its top management team be changed in a turnaround situation. The argument suggests that these individuals have paradigms, or ways they view the world, that created the decline in the first place. It is therefore supposed to be difficult for such individuals to see the problems and be creative in developing solutions to solve those problems. Entrepreneurial businesses do not have this option since the entrepreneur is running the business. We have found few business founders that are looking to fire themselves. Therefore, it is necessary that the entrepreneur in a decline situation actively seek creative solutions. While not easy to do, this means that they must question themselves and others to a much greater extent than they have done before.[3] A well-developed board of advisors, which we have discussed previously, can be a critical aid in this regard. A board of advisors that will provide honest and insightful advice that challenges the entrepreneur can be very helpful in viewing new ways to compete and new ways to overcome the problems faced by the firm.

EXERCISE 2

1. Imagine Chris had not been as successful in the bar/brewery business as he actually has. What do you think he should do to determine the turnaround actions he should follow?
2. What is the greatest barrier such a small service firm faces in such a turnaround?

Implications and Issues Involved in Closing a Business

LO13-4

Recognize the implications and issues involved in closing a business.

It is unfortunate, but bankruptcy may need to be filed by the entrepreneur if the turnaround effort does not succeed quickly enough. The processes/procedures for bankruptcy are arduous and have lasting impact upon the founder(s), and yet there are circumstances where this is the only viable route. There are several types of bankruptcy that can be filed.[4]

Chapter 11 bankruptcy allows the firm to be reorganized. When you file a Chapter 11 bankruptcy, the firm receives immediate protection against all lawsuits and other efforts to collect from the firm. At this stage the firm has 90 days to propose a reorganization plan. This plan needs to show how the business will pay off its past-due debts and stay current with its other debts. The company's banker and other creditors will commonly refer to your account as a "workout." They will be willing to meet with you and seek a resolution regarding the money that is owed to them. Most creditors will be willing to take less than their full payment with the hope that the strength of the firm will return in the future and they will then be in a position to receive more of their debt repayment. If they do not work with the failing business, they face the potential of the business simply liquidating and the lender receiving only a small percentage of the proceeds from the sale of the assets. This reduction in the amount of money that the creditors ultimately accept is referred to as a "haircut."

If the firm's debts are less than $2 million, there is a fast-track version of Chapter 11 that gives creditors far less control than in a larger organization Chapter 11 filing. The fast-track plan must show how back taxes will be brought current over a five-year period. It must also show how those creditors who have pledged collateral behind their debt will be brought current. The unsecured creditors are those who do not have collateral pledged behind their debt, and their debt is the lowest priority. It is generally not necessary to show how unsecured creditors will be paid in this type of Chapter 11 reorganization. During the reorganization process it is possible to terminate leases, contracts, and union agreements that are too burdensome. The bankruptcy judge has the ability to force creditors to accept a plan for reorganization if it appears equitable and fair but the creditors are still unwilling to accept it.

Unfortunately, there are instances where the business must simply be closed. In this case, a Chapter 7 bankruptcy is invoked. In these cases, selling the business consists of selling the "assets" of the business. The assets of the organization include all of the physical assets (equipment, signs, furniture, fixtures, etc.) as well as any valuable intangibles, such as the corporate name or patents held. The process is similar to that of selling the business, but the owner can add a liquidator to the scenario, as well as the possibility of an auction, as a quick means to clear out of the business.

Two other types of bankruptcy are Chapter 12, used by family farming businesses, and Chapter 13, which is used by sole proprietorships. In each of these cases, the individual files for bankruptcy and includes the firm in his or her personal assets and liabilities. Chapter 13 is intended for entrepreneurial firms with limited debts and assets. The effect of a Chapter 13 filing is similar to that of a Chapter 11. However, since it is for a smaller firm, the process is even easier. For example, the time to approval is typically quicker, and no creditor committee is required.

A final point to be made regarding the turnaround or closing of a business is the protection of personal assets. As was discussed in Chapter 9 (legal), the form of business chosen has many impacts upon the operation of the business as well as the ending of the business. One of those is the extent to which the individuals involved in founding a firm are personally liable for its debts. Incorporating a business (using the Subchapter S, Subchapter C, or LLC forms that were discussed in Chapter 9) goes a long way toward providing limited liability to the entrepreneur. However, many entrepreneurs personally guarantee loans that are made to the company. Doing this negates the limited liability nature of a corporation and exposes the entrepreneur to a major loss of personal assets. While no one starts a business with the intent of failure, the reality is that many do fail. Effectively preparing for that possibility at the beginning of the venture can be a great blessing in the event that the business does not develop as the founder(s) had hoped.

SUMMARY

This chapter focused on the exit, harvest, turnaround, and closing of the entrepreneurial business. These are tough but important issues that should be considered when designing a new business. What should be clear is that these activities are as much art as science. Even something that appears as straightforward as business valuation is actually a process that leads to a set of results as opposed to a unique answer. The entrepreneur who chooses to pursue starting a new venture is well advised to develop a plan for harvesting a business as well as handling situations that might require a major turnaround or closure.

KEY TERMS

asset valuation 243

capitalization of earnings valuation 244

initial public offering (IPO) 247

market estimation 244

perquisites 238

price/earnings (P/E) ratio 242

turnaround 249

REVIEW QUESTIONS

1. Why would an entrepreneur seek to exit a business?
2. How can an entrepreneur be a millionaire on paper yet have no money in the bank?
3. What are the steps in valuing a business?
4. Explain the difference in the following valuation methods.
   a. Present value discounted cash flow.
   b. Price/earnings ratio.
   c. Asset value.
   d. Capitalization of earnings.
   e. Market estimation.
5. What steps should a business owner go through to prepare the business to be sold?
6. What four options does a business owner have to sell the business?
7. Which of these is the least likely to be pursued by the business owner?
8. What are six things a business owner should keep in mind as he enters negotiations to sell a business?
9. What is a turnaround?
10. What are the different types of bankruptcy and when are they each appropriate?

BUSINESS PLAN DEVELOPMENT QUESTIONS

1. As you think about your potential business, what would be the most likely valuation method you can use?
2. Thinking toward the future, if you ever had to turn around your business, what would likely be the key issue that drives that problem? Is there some means to ensure that you address that problem before your business is up and running?

INDIVIDUAL EXERCISES

1. Develop a harvest plan for your planned business. Have several fellow classmates review the plan for completeness.
2. What are the two or three things that you would want most out of a sale or succession negotiation?
3. Imagine a worst-case scenario. Explain how you have protected your personal assets.

GROUP EXERCISES

Form into groups in the class. Go to your favorite search engine and put in the term "small business for sale" and your city name.

1. What website did you identify with firms for sale in your area?
2. How many firms are listed?
3. Pick one business. What is the asking price for that business?
4. What is the basis for that asking price? Can you see one method that they appeared to use from the types of valuation methods discussed in this chapter?
5. Tell your group about your evaluation of the business that is for sale and whether you think it is a good business opportunity or not.

ENDNOTES

1. Ndofor, Hermann Achidi; Vanevenhoven, Jeff; Barker, Vincent L. *Strategic Management Journal*, 34, no. 9, (September 2013), pp. 1123–33.
2. Schmitt, Achim; Raisch, Sebastian. *Journal of Management Studies*, 50, no. 7, (November 2013), pp. 1216–44.
3. R. Quinn, *Deep Change: Discovering the Leader Within* (San Francisco, CA: Jossey-Bass Publishers, 1996).
4. R. A. Anderson, I. Fox, and D. P. Twomey, *Business Law: Principles, Cases, Legal Environment* (Cincinnati, OH: South-Western Publishing, 1999).

CREDITS

Opener: Diana Parkhouse/Flickr/CC-BY-2; p. 235: © Pixtal/SuperStock RF; p. 240: Richard Eriksson/Flickr/CC-BY-2; p. 246: Phronimoi/CC-BY-2; p. 250: Royalty-Free/Corbis.

chapter

14

learning objectives

After studying this chapter, you will be able to:

LO14-1 Describe the elements of franchising.

LO14-2 Explain the process of buying a franchise.

LO14-3 Discuss the process for buying an existing business.

Franchising and Purchasing an Existing Business

LA MADELEINÉ AND PATRICK LEON ESQUERRÉ

In 1965, Patrick Leon Esquerré earned his MBA from a leading business school in France and went to work for an international accounting and consulting firm. Over the years, although not trained as a chef, he had an increasing number of opportunities to work with people in the food industry, including those who planned the food-related stages of the pope's visit to Paris. In the early 1980s he met an American who wanted to bring a variety of American-themed concepts, such as a rodeo and a honky-tonk made to look like the famous Billy Bob's, to Europe. Ultimately, however, the pair decided instead to bring French food to the United States. Unfortunately for Patrick his American partner went bankrupt before he could fully start the business. The result was Patrick had to back the venture with his own money: $100,000.

Ultimately Patrick was able to find other investors to join him. Key among them was Stanley Marcus, who had founded the chain of Neiman Marcus department stores. Marcus became both an advisor to and key supporter of Patrick. This relationship opened many doors for the business. For example, when Patrick tried to establish their first location near Southern Methodist University in Dallas, the real estate agent wanted $21 a square foot in rent with a three-year minimum lease, first year's rent in advance, and would offer no improvements to the property. After a call from Stanley Marcus, the rent became $14 a square foot with a nine-year lease, one month's rent in advance, and $50,000 from the landlord for improvements. The first café opened in 1983.

Today, 30 years later, La Madeleiné includes franchises in its operations and has over 60 restaurants. Patrick is no longer the sole owner, instead capturing much of his sweat equity by selling the chain to Group Le Duff; however, Patrick is still involved in the business as an advisor.

Questions

1. What do you believe would be involved in creating a franchise operation for your business?
2. How long do you believe that Patrick should have run his business before he was ready to start franchising? Why?
3. We have discussed establishing legitimacy of a new business as critical. Do you believe that is the role Mr. Marcus played in this firm? Do you have similar individuals that could help establish the legitimacy of your business?

Sources: E. Elan, *Restaurant News* 39, no. 5 (January 1, 2005), pp. 116–18; D. Eng, "Even Texans Can Love Quiche," *Fortune* 158, no. 4 (2013), pp. 27–30; La Madeleiné web page http://lamadeleine.com/history/

FRIENDS' HOME HEALTH CARE

Friends' HOME HEALTH

Cheryl Williams

A good friend of Betty and Joan's, the founders of Friends' Home Health Care, was Cheryl Williams. She observed the hard work and risk that the two founders of Friends' Home Health had taken on. Even though she was impressed with her friends, she decided to take a different path. In thinking through what she would do, she knew her inclination for risk taking was less than that of the Friends' Home Health founders. In addition, she did not have the same sets of skills that were readily applicable to a business in home health care. She also knew that organization was not one of her strong assets. In fact, she really needed to gain some discipline for her own success.

The resulting path seemed to take advantage of Cheryl's strengths and yet compensate for her shortcomings. Specifically, she decided to find a franchise to purchase. The opportunity for success is much higher with a franchise than it is with an untested start-up, if for no other reason than that the business model has been tested and refined prior to a new acquisition of the franchise. In addition, there is some level of support (although it can vary considerably) from the business that sells the franchise. Thus, franchising seemed to offer a calculated risk she could tolerate. She also knew that franchises typically came with operational systems already in place. These preexisting operational systems would help Cheryl to overcome her shortcomings in organization.

However, the realization that a franchise might offer the best opportunity for her was just the first step in her business start-up process. Which franchise should Cheryl choose? An initial investigation found that there were thousands of franchisors, with wide variations in the availability, price, resource requirements, level of support, and success rate of those various franchises. Cheryl knew that she wanted to be in a service industry with lots of customer contact, and while her experience in sales was deep, it was not very broad (she had been with the same company since she graduated high school 10 years earlier).

She therefore began looking for holes in the services provided by businesses in the city in which she lived. Two specific opportunities came to light. The first was in fast food; specifically, there was no sandwich shop in her part of town. Although there were hamburger joints, pizzerias, sit-down establishments, and ethnic restaurants, there were no sandwich shops. The second opportunity seemed to be with companies that provided extra storage for people. Cheryl lived in a fast-growing section of town where people were constantly moving but did not always have a place to store their goods. Cheryl felt that there were strong opportunities for both types of franchises and therefore began to investigate each in more depth.

Cheryl next looked into the specific firms in these two industries that offered franchising in her area. For the storage industry, the first was a storage facility with a fixed location close by where people lived, while the second was a box arrangement in which people filled a large container at their home that was then shipped and stored in locations that were more remote. Each type of franchise was relatively expensive. Even without buying the land where things were stored, the costs could easily run over a $1 million dollars. The franchisors seemed to provide start-up support and strong management, which was attractive. However, this was far more than she could afford even if she mortgaged all of her personal assets. Therefore, she ruled this idea out and began to focus on the possibility of a sandwich shop.

In her initial screening, she found that the cost of a variety of franchised sandwich shops was dramatically less. The cost could be as low as $50,000 and rarely would exceed $250,000. In each of the franchises she investigated, she would not have to own the building but could lease her space, which would significantly lower her costs. However, the range of services offered by the franchisor to the franchisee also varied greatly. She began a more detailed examination of the franchises available. Ultimately, she narrowed it down to three franchises. Each of these had an initial cost of approximately $150,000, had very strong operational plans, and had well-developed support services. For example, each of these franchises helped the franchisee locate the store in the best location available and had managers on staff that worked onsite during the pre-start-up and start-up phases of the business. Furthermore, although it would be a stretch financially, she and her husband believed they could put together sufficient funds to begin this type of operation.

After initial conversations with each of the three potential franchisors, Cheryl contacted several franchisees from each of the franchisors. She chose the franchisees by looking in phone books in different cities. The sample she selected may not have been ideal since it was not a random selection, but it avoided using the franchisors' lists, which she figured might provide one-sided information.

(continued)

Interestingly, even within her limited sample, Cheryl found that franchisees for two of the companies had significant complaints about support and value for their dollar. Only one franchisor had no franchisees that were unhappy. Looking at the success statistics (profit levels, sales growth, number of franchisees that go out of business, and increasing sales price of franchisees wishing to sell), Cheryl found that this one franchisor ranked the highest in the industry. This franchisor offered a relatively unique concept for a sandwich operation, utilizing a wrap that was somewhat like a tortilla. Further, the franchisor used a seven-mile radius as its competitive density, meaning that no other franchisee of that particular brand would be allowed to open a shop within seven miles of Cheryl's. Thus, the strategy of the firm, its product, and its operations all seemed to be a good fit with Cheryl's skills and needs, and with the opportunity that Cheryl saw in the area. She proceeded to start negotiations to buy a franchise from this franchisor.

QUESTIONS

1. What are the questions and concerns Cheryl Williams should have focused on as she began her investigation of franchises?
2. Franchisors do not sell a franchise to anyone that wants one. What could Cheryl do to become an attractive candidate as a franchisee for the franchisor?

This book has focused principally on the process of starting a new entrepreneurial business from scratch. Two other common options exist for individuals interested in starting their own businesses. The first is purchasing a franchise. The other is purchasing an existing business. Both of these activities have opportunities and drawbacks in comparison to starting a new business and we will examine these, beginning with the opportunities and drawbacks with franchising.

The Elements of Franchising

LO14-1

Describe the elements of franchising.

The purchase of a well-honed, thoughtfully positioned franchise can dramatically decrease the downside risk inherent in the process of starting a business. Franchising can be viewed as the new business entrepreneur's creation of a business from a well-established formula. Thus, the franchise is essentially a prepackaged business, where there are policies, procedures, and buying patterns in place prior to beginning operations.

The **franchisor** is the firm that originates the idea for the business and develops the operational methods. The entrepreneur is the franchisee. The **franchisee** pays a fee to obtain a franchise from the franchisor. This fee entitles the franchisee the right to open a branch of the business in a given area, use the franchisor's name, and operate a business within the guidelines of the agreement. The franchisee also receives operational advice on how to run the business and typically some level of marketing support to promote the firm. Responsibility for the business location, establishment of the business, and build-out is the franchisee's, and must usually be fulfilled in accordance with the specifications of the franchisor.

franchisor
The firm that originates the idea for the business and develops the operational methods, then sells them to franchisees.

franchisee
The entrepreneur who buys the franchise from the franchisor.

franchise agreement
The basic contract generated by the franchisor for all franchisees; it usually contains clauses requiring the purchase of supplies, the displaying of marketing material, and the payment of fees that are based upon the sales of the branch operation.

The franchisor, in turn, establishes minimum standards regarding the operation of the business. For example, the **franchise agreement** is the basic contract generated by the franchisor for all franchisees and it usually contains clauses requiring the purchase of supplies, the displaying of marketing material, and the payment of fees that are based upon the sales of the branch operation. The requirements, however, may be more extensive. For example, McDonald's requires that its franchisees clean not only their own property but also the territory that borders their franchise unit.

The International Franchise Association reports that in 2007 (the latest data available at the time of publication) that franchises made up almost 900,000 establishments in the United States, providing almost 18 million jobs.[1] The range of franchises you use every day would likely surprise you. For example, most hotels, most restaurants, and many daily service providers are locally owned franchise operations.

In part, the reason franchising is so widespread is that the franchisor can offer a standard, well-known product, that is produced by a consistent, well-tested process. The group purchasing power for supplies, supported with specific regional and perhaps more generic brand-building national advertising, furthers the success of the franchise. The franchisor will also continue research and development on the products and processes that a small single business simply could not afford to pursue. This all occurs with the entrepreneur spending less of her resources than if she had had to found such a firm by herself. The franchisor benefits by enabling a rapid expansion while minimizing the funds invested in that expansion.[2]

Going into business with a Sonic franchise, for instance, allows you the freedom of ownership while also providing built-in support. How might ownership differ for franchisees versus traditional business owners?

The success of franchising is dependent on the hard work of the franchisee and the value added by the franchisor.[3] You will recall that we discussed agency theory in Chapter 2. There are factors that mitigate alignment of goals between a manager and an owner. In a franchise operation, businesspeople work for themselves, not for some large corporation and, as a result, all the decisions that the entrepreneur makes are to maximize the value of their own business. The success of franchising is also a result of the fact that the franchisee will act in ways to maximize the profit of the business where a corporate employee might not do so, a prediction consistent with agency theory.[4]

The franchisor makes money in a variety of ways, including these: (1) selling the franchise to the franchisee; (2) selling supplies to the franchisee; (3) collecting a percentage of sales; and (4) in some cases, providing company-specific training courses/materials. For example, a very successful franchisor such as Sonic, which sells hamburgers and related items using a drive-in format in more than 40 states, charges a fee to obtain a franchise, but the significant income comes from royalties and being able to sell the franchisee items that range from Sonic-labeled hamburger wrappers to the peppermints that come with the food. The franchisor typically argues that it can obtain the supplies cheaper through its bulk buying; plus, it wants to ensure that the output continues to be a consistently high-quality, name-enhancing experience, since it is sold under the Sonic brand. A franchisee that has inconsistent quality or service not only hurts her own business, but impacts the brand image of all franchisees.

The continuing revenue stream to the franchisor from royalties and selling of inputs to the franchisee is a more important revenue source than the initial fees for selling the franchise. Thus, the franchisor and the franchisee are successful by helping each other. The franchisor makes money when the franchisee stays in business, needs lots of inputs, and pays continuing royalties. On the other hand, the franchisee is successful if the franchisor puts a program in place for all of the franchisees to be successful, such as high-quality marketing, good site selection, high-quality products, and continuous research into both product/process development and brand management.

The Process of Buying a Franchise

LO14-2

Explain the process of buying a franchise.

As we have emphasized throughout this text, the entrepreneur that is best prepared will be the most likely to succeed, whether her focus is starting a business from scratch, buying a franchise, or purchasing an existing business. Thus, many of the issues in choosing a franchise are similar to the issues already examined in this text.

General Franchise Questions

Some issues can be viewed as broad, generic issues rather than issues specific to that particular franchisor. These general issues include the following:

1. The potential franchisee should carefully evaluate her individual interests and skills to determine a potential fit with running a franchise and to identify an industry or multiple industries in which she wishes to attempt to purchase a franchise.
2. When determining the industry to enter, each potential franchisee should examine that industry, the potential competitors in the industry, and their position relative to other new franchisees that are entering the industry.
3. The potential franchisee should carefully examine the competitive strength of various franchises in the industry. For instance, what are the various sustainable competitive advantages in the market?
4. The individual looking to buy a franchise should identify a franchisor that is the best potential match for him or her in terms of support, history, expansion plans, and so on.
5. The person considering a franchise should examine that franchisor as though the potential franchisee were buying the whole business. This includes contacting other franchisees to discuss their experience as well as comparing the franchisor to other franchise opportunities.

Specific Franchise Questions

Each franchisor will have a different package it will try to sell a franchisee. The franchisee needs to examine the exact package that is offered and balance the cost and the benefits offered. The issues to consider in examining which franchise to purchase include these: what a franchise includes; franchisor and franchisee obligations, as stipulated in the United Franchise Offering Circular (UFOC); and steps in the process of obtaining a franchise.

Each of the issues to consider in purchasing a specific franchise will be examined in turn.

What Does a Franchise Include? An extraordinary range of support can be provided by a franchisor to the franchisee. This ranges from simply buying into a name and general plan for operation to what almost amounts to a full partner for your business. There is no universal standard regarding what is provided by a franchisor; instead, as in any market system, different franchisors offer distinct sets of supports at varying prices. The entrepreneur must choose which package of benefits she wishes to pursue, at what price, and with what level of control by the franchisor. The discussion below lists some of the issues that a new businessperson buying a franchise should consider to ensure the franchise has the right mix of supports and costs for him.

Both the franchisor and the franchisee have an alignment of interest in their mutual desire to produce a quality product and successfully expand the business. However, they can have honest disagreements about what is best for the organization. Franchisors make decisions based on what is best for the total business; franchisees want to have the ability to cater to their local market. Thus, can you as a local franchisee of a sandwich shop in Texas add hot peppers to the standard sandwich—or if you are in Wisconsin, can you add sauerkraut to the same sandwich? The franchisor may want uniformity and thus consistency, but the franchisee will want the flexibility to meet local needs. The individual buying a franchise needs to examine if the franchise will have the level of flexibility she feels is necessary for success.

When you purchase a franchise, you typically are buying some consistent items, although the specifics of what you are buying in each individual case should be examined. These include the right to:

1. An established name, branded products, and service.
2. Operate under that name for a period of time. The time period is usually some standard, such as 5, 10, or 20 years.
3. A single store or the right to have multiple units.[5]
4. A commitment from the franchisor to limit the number of franchises within a specific radius of the new franchise. This is one of the most important issues involved in the purchase. One of the key competitive advantages is having the name-brand operation without having to compete against fellow franchisees. In the best situations, franchisees work with each other in local geographic areas.

The franchisor typically provides both the operational systems and the monitoring techniques to run the business in a manner that matches the rest of the organization. The specificity of this operational information varies widely from franchisor to franchisor. You will recall from Chapter 12 that an in-depth understanding of operations is necessary to be successful in an entrepreneurial business. Although most of the operational management systems will have been designed by the experience of the franchisor, the franchisee must intimately understand both why and how these systems work. To illustrate, if you purchase a franchise for a shop that makes photocopies, the franchisor will have established procedures for the design of the internal layout of the shop, plus the look and feel of the physical storefront. It will have established processes for virtually every type of service that could be requested by a customer. If you do not have at least a minimal understanding of copy shops, it will be difficult to judge the operating system the franchisor is providing. Buying a franchise does not eliminate the need for the entrepreneur to have a deep understanding of the business. If you do not have that understanding you cannot judge the quality of the operational support provided by the franchisor.

True understanding of those processes comes from experience. In many cases, potential franchisees are required to work in an established operation of the business for some period of time prior to their being allowed to purchase a franchise. This time period allows the potential franchisee the opportunity to learn the business from the ground up, learning the procedures not from a manual, but from experience with an established operation. This fact is particularly important since some franchisors have very specific limits on how many changes you can make to their operational systems. The franchisor wants a franchisee in Oklahoma City, Oklahoma, and another in Utica, New York, to operate in essentially the same manner in order to develop and preserve the brand. A careful examination of the amount of regional or local customization available can be an important part of the business acquisition process.

A number of specific support areas that the potential franchisee should use to evaluate the franchisor's operations include the following:

1. *Accounting Support.* As part of the operational aspects of the business, the franchisor will often provide an accounting system that is custom tailored to the dual needs of the franchisor and the franchisee.

2. *Marketing Support.* This is a broad area that encompasses such things as brochures, signs, logos, television advertisements, newspaper advertisements, sales techniques, and internal business design. The quality, quantity, and overall value of each of these items can vary widely from franchisor to franchisor. There are also some significant downside risks to this apparent positive. First of all, advertising support comes at a price. Most franchisors charge each franchisee a fee that becomes part of a larger common advertising budget. The franchisor develops the advertising and buys the spots or spaces in the newspapers. Doing this centrally allows for volume discounts as well as expertise in ad development and placement. Second, if you are the only franchisee in Colorado while most of the other franchisees are in Minnesota, Iowa, and Wisconsin, you are likely to see a smaller relative share of the advertising budget being targeted to your area. Thus, you would want to know what the franchisor's marketing plans are if you are the isolated franchise in Colorado.
3. *Training.* Franchisors offer a variety of training opportunities for the new franchisee and their employees. These include classroom training, training at other locations, having an experienced manager work at your location for a period of time, or, as we have mentioned, working at a current establishment. The more that is offered as part of the franchise fee the better it is for the franchisee. In addition, the availability of continued training opportunities should be an important criterion to help ensure franchisee success.
4. *Real Estate Services.* Some franchisors operate a large and profitable real estate brokering service. Others offer a more basic site selection service, or nothing at all. The assistance in real estate selection, acquisition, building construction, and the like, can be invaluable if done professionally.
5. *Other Services.* Human resources support to develop performance management programs; quality control methods; forecasting; and purchasing of equipment are all very valuable services that act as guidelines rather than mandates in deciding on a franchise.

As this discussion indicates, there is a wide range of potential activities that the franchisor may provide to the franchisee. The range of those activities, the quality of those activities, and the cost should be judged by the entrepreneur.

EXERCISE 1

1. Rather than starting a business from scratch, you have decided to look into franchises. What industry and what franchise opportunities might you consider?
2. What special skills do you bring to the franchise?
3. What market conditions exist that suggest to you that this franchise might be successful?

Government Requirements for the Franchisor-Franchisee Relationship. The principal governing mechanism of the franchisor–franchisee relationship is the **Uniform Franchise Offering Circular (UFOC)**. As with many business domains, at one time there were excessive abuses in the industry. Individuals thinking they were buying a franchise that gave them an opportunity for success found that they had paid for what amounted to little more than a name, which often had a terrible reputation. The result was the passage of the UFOC, which specifies what information must be provided to the franchisee prior to her investment.

Uniform Franchise Offering Circular (UFOC)
The principal governing mechanism of the franchisor/franchisee.

This document must be provided to the franchisee early in the process of her buying a franchise. In effect, the UFOC is a franchisor disclosure document with 23 specified items:

1. **The Franchisor, Its Predecessors, and Affiliates.** Full disclosure on any predecessors to the current business and other businesses affiliated with the business must be disclosed.

2. **Business Experience.** The background of the principals must be detailed. Issues such as how long they have been in the business and their experience in the industry must also be detailed. You want to make sure those running the franchisor have experience in the industry.
3. **Litigation.** Any pending litigation must be noted. Such litigation can destroy the value of your franchise if it concerns issues such as who developed the idea for the product and your franchisor loses.
4. **Bankruptcy.** Any prior or current filings by firm or key management must be disclosed.
5. **Initial Franchise Fee.** Under items 5 and 6, the franchisor must disclose all fees that are charged.
6. **Other Fees.** The "other fees" category is an area that entrepreneurs should clearly understand. The cost of the initial purchase of the franchise may appear low, but if there are extensive fees that the franchisor can charge the franchisee for services that are offered, the value of the franchise may be very different than initially thought. The supports provided may appear to be desirable; however, there may be separate costs for those supports that are independent of the initiation fee to buy the franchise.
7. **Initial Investment.** This is more than the initial fee paid by the franchisee; it includes a reasonable estimate of the total investment needed to begin operations.
8. **Restrictions on Sources of Products and Services.** This is one of the critical parts of the document, where franchisor sourcing is detailed. The potential franchisee needs to be clear about what must be purchased directly from the franchisor and what may be sourced independently.
9. **Franchisee's Obligations.** Specific obligations must be listed. For example, the franchisor may require that the product be produced by certain equipment and that equipment be replaced on a certain time schedule. These restrictions can extend into domains that the entrepreneur may not initially consider to be the purview of the franchisor. Thus, once again questions such as what flexibility the entrepreneur will have in operating the franchise need to be examined. For example, upon opening, you as the franchisee may be happy with some balloons, having the local mayor cut a ribbon, and a story that goes into the local paper. But the franchisor may have an extensive program that it requires of all new franchise openings. The franchisee may be required to fund these activities through various fees, whether or not he agrees with the program.
10. **Financing.** Many franchisors make significant financing available to potential franchisees. The financing available and terms are outlined in this section of the document.
11. **Franchisor's Obligations.** In this section, all of the ancillary services are detailed. As outlined above, this may include site selection, training, placing experienced managers on-site for a period of time, and so on.
12. **Territory.** This section details the amount of exclusivity your franchise will have relative to other operations of the franchisor.
13. **Trademarks.** Items 13 and 14 detail the exact status of all trademarks, patents, copyrights, and trade secrets that are part of the business.
14. **Patents, Copyrights, and Proprietary Information.**

15. **Obligation to Participate in the Actual Operation of the Franchise Business.** The franchisee can be required to take an active role in the daily management of the business, as opposed to simply hiring managers.
16. **Restrictions on What the Franchisee May Sell.** This section lists limits placed on the franchisee by the franchisor. The franchisor may put extensive restrictions on the franchisee as to what she can do with the product and its production.
17. **Renewal, Termination, Transfer, and Dispute Resolution.** The exact method of dispute resolution is detailed, along with which party will have the financial responsibility.
18. **Public Figures.** This details any public figures or celebrities involved in the business and what they are paid.
19. **Earnings Claims.** This section contains a description along with some specific detail regarding the financial performance of typical franchisees.
20. **List of Outlets.**
21. **Financial Statements.**
22. **Contracts.** This section contains sample contracts you will be asked to sign later.
23. **Receipt.** You will be asked to sign a page to acknowledge that you received this information.

The entrepreneur is well served to study the document carefully to understand all of the details of the business arrangement. It is a long document, and should be read through several times and reviewed with an attorney prior to agreeing to the stipulations. A clear understanding of the document now will prevent significant problems in the future.

Franchise Process. The founding of a franchise is quite similar in form and method to creating a new business from scratch. A significant up-front cash payment is necessary, and the ability to leave the venture if the entrepreneur does not enjoy the business is severely limited. Similarly, an assessment of the skills of the individual should be a mandatory beginning of any new business investigation. If the individual has no skills in styling hair and he buys a hairstyling franchise, the odds of success are not particularly good, regardless of what supports are present in the franchise.

A successful franchisee has taken steps to understand the new market, such as location, longevity of demand, and skills needed.

Depending on the franchisor for market analysis is a poor move under any circumstances. The market must also be thoroughly and independently understood by the potential franchisee. As we pointed out earlier, sometimes there is a very good reason that no similar businesses are in a particular area. We knew an individual who was searching out a franchise to buy. She hit upon the idea of buying a franchise that supplies temporary employees to local businesses. Unfortunately, all of the local businesses (and there were only a few) used only full-time employees. The market for temporary workers was severely constrained. We would also caution against purchasing a franchise that is part of a fad. Pet rocks were a lot of fun for a while, but owning a pet rock or Pog franchise was a disaster for the franchisees. Fads died as quickly as they were born, but the franchise agreements lasted anywhere from 5 to 20 years. It does little good to invest money in a franchise that will see demand for the product disappear quickly. In the case of a fad, we have very simple advice. Get in, make as much money as you can as an independent, and GET OUT!

The International Franchise Association is a good source for quickly locating potential franchisor firms; its Web page can be found at www.franchise.org. Each of the franchisor firms typically has a Web page where you can request information from that firm. They will gladly send you a packet of information that details the firm's operations, its business, and the costs of the franchise. At this stage, there will be a very short application form that the entrepreneur must fill out. With this information the franchisor will call the entrepreneur and have a phone interview to ensure that the individual is at least a potential match for the firm. The entrepreneur needs to note that it is a mutual selection process. The franchisee can select among one of the 10,000 or more franchise opportunities. The franchisor also gets to decide to whom it will sell a franchise. Given the geographic restrictions imposed by many franchisors and encouraged by the franchisees, it is in the best interest of the franchisor to pursue only the most motivated, best capitalized, and most skilled individuals. A poorly performing or disruptive franchisee detracts from the overall operation as well as taking time and effort of the franchisor away from the business of growing the brand. Because of this, it is simply easier to make sure that there is a match between the two parties from the beginning.

Once the potential franchisee has been vetted (a credit and personal background check has been completed), the entrepreneur will be sent the complete UFOC and asked to fill out a more complete application. A series of meetings ensues between the franchisor and other franchisees in the area, between the franchisor and the potential franchisee, and between the potential franchisee and the other franchisees in the area. The ability to meet other franchisees is critical in the evaluation process. Although the UFOC does not require that specific information on profitability of individual franchises be provided, it is quite simple to back into such information by calculating the total profits of the group and then dividing by the total number of franchises. Unfortunately, there may be a bimodal distribution, with some great performers and some that perform poorly. The ability to interact with franchisees in your geographic area, with similar profiles to what you can expect from your operation, helps provide great insights into the reality of the franchise life. You will gain tremendous insights from these individuals regarding their relationship with the franchisor. The relationship between franchisor and franchisee is somewhat like a marriage; they are both dependent on each other for success. If the relationship is an unhappy one, there can be nothing quite as miserable. Existing franchisees can also provide insight regarding the value of the franchisor's staff. Many of the services that the franchisor provides are dependent on the quality of the people providing the service. Marketing advice is a qualitative area that can be either very helpful or of limited value, depending on who is developing and delivering the research.

Assuming that both parties are pleased with their findings, negotiating the deal is the next step. Although the franchise fee tends to be set in stone, most franchisors are willing to negotiate on a wide range of items. For example, if there are few franchises in an area, the franchisor may be willing to finance a greater portion of the start-up expenses, provide additional marketing support, or even pick up some of the initial expenses of a franchise in order to get a foothold in a new geographic area. Similarly, if you have had prior success in business and the franchisor is new, it might negotiate a completely different deal with you in order to get started with a self-sufficient operator. Also, very high-profile individuals frequently can negotiate unique deals. For example, in a region of the country where there is a professional athletic team, high-profile players on that team often obtain preferential opportunities. This allows the franchisor to publicize that that person is one of its franchisees. The entrepreneur

ETHICAL CHALLENGE

Over the past few weeks you have been reviewing the franchise agreement for a new concept in fruit, which is made to look like a flower design. You have met with several current franchisees and talked with the franchisor on more than a few occasions. You have had the opportunity to see them in operation and to look at the books. After all this effort, you have concluded that you don't need the franchisor to run a business like this one. You've decided to open up your own fruit into flower design and delivery shop and plan to run it virtually the exact same way as is done by the franchisees.

You have made a significant effort to make some of the operations different, but you also like most of what you saw. What you didn't like was the up-front fees, which were estimated to be over $500,000, and the fact that you would have to pay the franchisor 8 percent of sales.

QUESTIONS

1. Do you have any ethical obligations to the original franchisor?
2. No one is required to buy a franchise; therefore, isn't their opening all the books simply their means of trying to make a sale?
3. Does a firm have any obligation other than to make money?

should explore what aspects of the contract are negotiable by making a list of wants and desires.

Some areas that such negotiations should explore include up-front capital requirements, financing arrangements, and continuing fees. Does the ability exist to purchase other franchises or build out the existing franchise? The time frame of the franchise (5, 10, 20 years) may be negotiable, as well as a first right to renew your franchise. An important consideration is not only the territory of the initial franchise, but also first rights on adjacent or fast-growing territories. Some franchisors will have performance quotas to maintain the franchise; if your business faces performance requirements be sure to ask what those quotas are and what percentage of franchisees meet the quota. If you fail at those quotas, or some other aspects of the franchise, can you negotiate the remedies to solve that problem? Does the franchisor require a personal guarantee? The personal guarantee is something many successful entrepreneurs seek to avoid, because it places their personal assets at risk. Are there operational constraints that you feel would put you at a disadvantage relative to your competition that you wish to have the franchisor waive? The entrepreneur is well served to take the time to work with a lawyer and develop a solid contract that meets the needs of the franchisor and still gives the franchisee the best opportunity for success.

EXERCISE 2

1. What specific concerns do you have regarding a potential franchise?
2. Put together a list of three items that you must have in place prior to accepting a contract to purchase a franchise.
3. Do you believe that franchises are more or less risky as compared to beginning a new business from scratch?

The Process for Buying an Existing Business

LO14-3

Discuss the process for buying an existing business.

We covered the process of obtaining a franchise first because this process is well defined and well regulated, and there is a wealth of information available to anyone who would like assistance. Another very popular means of going into business for oneself is the purchase of an existing business. To illustrate the concept and some of the difficulties in buying an existing business, consider the friend of the Flow Right Brewery & Bar founder, named Jack Chen.

FLOW RIGHT BREWERY & BAR: A FAMILY AFFAIR

JACK CHEN

Jack Chen was a good friend of Chris's and as Jack observed Flow Right prosper he became more convinced he should follow his desire to go into business for himself. He had a good job working for an engineering firm where he was able to use his computer and technology skills, but he felt that his prospects for rising any further in the organization were limited. He was increasingly concerned with the strategic direction that the firm was pursuing and believed that the advice of longtime employees was being routinely ignored. This led Jack to begin to investigate new business opportunities.

Jack knew he wanted to do something that took advantage of his computer and technological skills. Therefore Jack began to look at new businesses tied to the Internet. He knew that phone apps were a market that was exploding in size; however, he also knew that getting noticed among all of the apps out there was very hard to do. Jack also knew that social networking was a high-growth area for technology. One recent study found that those with mobile devices spend over 30 percent of their time on social networks. Outside of the biggest players in each market the rest of the field tended to be very fragmented.

In each area, the issue came down to how to structure his venture so that it was unique in the marketplace and attracted sufficient attention to make a business. He thought of potentially focusing on some specific niche, such as a sport or a given activity, but soon found that there were already extensive numbers of such activities; there was even one for scrap bookers.

Next Jack explored virtual data rooms. He knew that increasingly, firms were moving out paper copies from their offices to load documents on "the cloud." One aspect of this transition is that firms would need secure locations to place documents for their far-flung teams when conducting sensitive activities, such as due diligence for a merger and acquisition. The result is the creation of virtual data rooms, which hold the data securely. It is expected that the virtual data room industry will double between 2014 and 2017 to over $1.7 trillion dollars.[6] However, it takes a large staff to do such work, so the initial investment appeared to be approximately $500,000 by the time start-up costs were considered. While the two largest firms have relatively small market shares, Jack was still concerned that these firms would be very aggressive in their pricing and hard to beat.

This led Jack to look at Internet-based franchises. He found that these franchises could cost from $99 to $25,000. He believed the actual costs would be double or triple the cost of the franchise by the time he included other start-up costs. However, with total costs at less than $100,000, Jack thought these franchises were potentially a great option.

QUESTIONS

1. What factors should Jack focus on when evaluating an Internet-related franchise?
2. The key success factors of franchises typically are the operating systems they provide the entrepreneur, which help the entrepreneur ensure that he can run the business effectively from day one. Would such a benefit also be present in an Internet franchise?

How to Buy an Existing Business

Similar to a franchise, an existing business has the benefit of having an established set of processes; although unlike a franchise, a continuing business has an established cash flow that you are purchasing. As such, the operation has a higher likelihood of success when compared to starting a business from scratch, and yet as Jack Chen's experience illustrates, that does not mean that buying a business does not take as much planning and thought as starting a business from scratch. There are still significant risks involved in buying a business.[7]

Because a business you may buy is an ongoing entity, there is a greater premium attached to the business than if you started it from scratch. The primary exception to this is if you buy a troubled business at a discount. If that is the case, you will need to quickly restructure that business. Turnaround is a special topic and requires very specific skills for you to be able to act quickly to reverse that decline.[8] Our typical advice to entrepreneurs is to not attempt such activities unless they have specific skills and a plan to turn around a business that is in significant decline.

For the purchase of a reasonably stable or healthy firm, all of the same processes that have been discussed in this text should be the foundation of your effort. Therefore, you first need to understand your own skills and abilities and the nature of the current market. Assuming that you have completed all of the preliminary analysis effort, there are still several unique aspects to purchasing an existing business. These include (1) locating a business to purchase; (2) developing a plan for the business; (3) negotiating a deal to acquire exactly what you want from the operation; and (4) organizing the process of change within the organization.

Locating a Business to Purchase. Locating a business for sale is a job that takes lots of patience and effort. There are **business brokers** in virtually every city in the United States that specialize in selling businesses. Additionally, businesses are listed for sale in newspapers, in local magazines, and on websites. All of these are fine places to start your search process; however, we recommend several other means for finding a business that meets your needs:

business brokers
Businesses that specialize in selling businesses.

1. Attorney and CPA firms may have clients who have expressed their desire to sell their business. Contacting local firms and asking about businesses they might know that are for sale usually yields some interesting possibilities.
2. Our personal favorite way to find a business to buy is to identify a particular business that you believe is not maximizing its opportunity, one to which you believe you could bring unique skills and advantages that could propel the business. We recommend that you put together a short letter to the owner indicating your interest in the business and follow that up with a request to take the owner to lunch to discuss the opportunity. Most (if not all) owners of an ongoing business are willing to listen to an offer to buy their business.
3. The trade association for an industry usually maintains a listing of all member companies and is a wealth of information regarding the status of various organizations within the industry.
4. The local Small Business Administration Office and/or the Small Business Development Center in your area has significant contact with businesspeople and both are geared toward supporting and encouraging the growth of entrepreneurial business.
5. Another favorite of ours is to look at the bankruptcy filings in your local community. Many companies file for bankruptcy due to lack of financial resources or poor management practices. The opportunity to contact these individuals and buy the operation before the bankruptcy procedure is completed can be the source of a business at a bargain price. However, remember that this effort would be a turnaround project that would require unique skills and abilities.

Plan of Operation. Once you have located a business for sale, but prior to beginning the negotiations to purchase the business, you as the potential entrepreneur should develop a plan of operation for the business. The cost of the business should include any premium for its current performance. What will you do differently from what is currently being done? If you are paying a premium for a business but have no plans to change the business operations, then how do you hope to achieve success?

Will you bring a new mission to the business? Will you position the firm or its product differently? Do you have some unique talent or skill that will make the business that you are considering buying a success, or make it more successful? An understanding of what you have to offer and what the current business is missing will provide the basis for your negotiations. What is important to the current owner may or may not be important to the potential owner, given the new direction for the company. Adding value to a business is a critical step in the process of deciding to purchase a business. We would recommend that the entrepreneur take the same approach as was outlined in Chapter 5 to develop a new mission for the organization. What are the resource-based advantages of the new organization under the new leadership?

Having developed a new plan for the business, the potential entrepreneur is prepared to negotiate the deal. In Chapter 13 we outlined procedures that a seller should use to put her business in the best position for sale, as well as negotiation strategies. We would recommend that a potential buyer do the same and demand this from any seller.

Finally, there is the complex issue of organizing the process of change from the former business to the new business. Although there are a number of ways in which this can be accomplished, the tasks are relatively the same. We must point out that there is a lot of nuance and "art" in the handling of these processes. Once negotiations are complete and all contracts are signed, there will be a transition period that should be spelled out in the contract for sale. During that transition time period, a number of tasks should be completed. The new owner should accomplish the following:

1. Meet and discuss the transition with every member of the current staff. If there is a layoff plan, then that should be enacted immediately.
2. Spend significant time being visible in the new operation, talking with employees, making suggestions, and doing some of the more menial work.
3. Make all significant changes in one day so as to alleviate any lingering concerns by the employees.
4. Implement new metrics and standards as soon as possible.
5. Ask the former owner(s) not to be at the business for several weeks while the transition is taking place. Loyalties and work processes get confused when the former owner is around every day.
6. If appropriate for the type of business that has been purchased, send out a letter or e-mail to every customer and supplier informing each one of the ownership change. Ideally this letter should be signed by both the former owner and the new owner.

SUMMARY

This chapter examined two common methods for becoming an entrepreneur. Both techniques fundamentally rely upon all of the same analysis and development techniques that have been developed in this text. Franchises are a well-developed and expansively available method for starting a business. There are more than 750,000 franchises in the United States, and franchises are rapidly expanding in many parts of the world.[9] Franchise operations run the gamut from those that are fully developed complete partners in business to others that are little more than a name. Franchises significantly improve the chance of survival for an entrepreneur but do not eliminate the potential for failure.[10] We reviewed the UFOC as well as those areas that are unique to a franchise operation. We finished the chapter with a discussion of the unique considerations involved in buying an existing business.

KEY TERMS

business brokers 267
franchise agreement 257
franchisee 257
franchisor 257
Uniform Franchise Offering Circular (UFOC) 261

REVIEW QUESTIONS

1. How does a franchise work?
2. How do the franchisee and the franchisor differ?
3. What is the benefit of buying a franchise versus starting your own business? Are there any drawbacks?
4. What are the questions a person should ask herself before she starts a franchise?
5. What is typically included in a franchise?
6. What is the UFOC? What are its major provisions?
7. Why would someone buy an existing business?
8. How do you locate a business that you would like to purchase?
9. Once you actually buy the business, how do you make sure that you are successful?

INDIVIDUAL EXERCISES

1. Starting with the Independent Franchise Association Web page, www.franchise.org, put together a plan for purchasing a franchise.
2. For the industry that you chose in Exercise 1 of this chapter, how many franchise opportunities exist?
3. What resources exist to help you in your effort to acquire a franchise?

GROUP EXERCISES

1. Form small groups in the class. As a class, pick one industry, such as retail restaurants. Have every team then select a franchise to buy in that industry independently.
   a. What is the range of franchises picked?
   b. What is the range of costs and services offered?
   c. Why did each team pick the franchise that it did? List your top five reasons for picking that franchise.
   d. Each team should make a five-minute presentation on the franchise it picked as if it were selling the idea to an investor.
   e. Then vote as a class for the best franchise idea.

ENDNOTES

1. International Franchise Association, "Building Local Businesses one Franchise at a Time," http://buildingopportunity.franchise.org/
2. R. Dant and P. Kaufmann, "Structural and Strategic Dynamics in Franchising," *Journal of Retailing* 79 (2003), pp. 63–76.
3. M. Grunhagen and M. Dorsch, "Does the Franchisor Provide Value to the Franchisee? Past, Current, and Future Value Assessments of Two Franchisee Types," *Journal of Small Business Management* 41(2003), pp. 366–85.
4. J. Combs and D. Ketchen, Jr., "Why Do Firms Use Franchising as an Entrepreneurial Strategy? A Meta Analysis," *Journal of Management* 29 (2003), pp. 443–66.
5. J. Bercovitz, "The Option to Expand: The Use of Multi-Unit Opportunities to Support Self-Enforcing Agreements in Franchise Relationships," *Academy of Management Proceedings*, 2002, pp. Y1–Y7.
6. J. Quittner, "Thinking of Starting a Business? Lock Down Profits in Virtual Data Rooms," 2013, www.inc.com/best-industries-2013/jeremy-quittner/virtual-data-rooms.html
7. S. Kaufman, "Before You Buy, Be Careful," *Nation's Business* 84, no. 3 (1996), pp. 46–48.
8. R. Doyle and H. Desai, "Turnaround Strategies for Small Firms," *Journal of Small Business Management* 29, no. 3 (1991), pp. 33–43.
9. M. Haller, "Slow Steady Growth to Continue for Franchises in 2013," *International Franchise Association*, 2013, www.franchise.org/Franchise-News-Detail.aspx?id=58916
10. S. Holmberg and K. Morgan, "Franchise Turnover and Failure: New Research and Perspective," *Journal of Business Venturing* 18 (2003), pp. 403–19.

CREDITS

Opener: Anthony92931/CC-BY-2; p. 255: Ron Heflin/AP Images; p. 258: Mike Mozart/Flickr/CC-BY-2: p. 263: jakerome/Flickr/CC-BY-2.

part 6

MiniCases

MiniCase 1
Thinking Critically: Beau Davis—The Varsity

MiniCase 2
Thinking Critically: Steve Clary—Steve's Barber Chair

MiniCase 3
Thinking Critically: Cassmer Ward—The Clear Collar

MiniCase 4
Thinking Critically: Charles Kezengwa—Hannington Massage

MiniCase 5
Thinking Critically: Greg Adams—OCJ Apparel

MiniCase 6
Thinking Critically: Charlie Gasmire—Cofounder and Director of Marketing at Vendevor (vendevor.com)

MiniCase 7
Thinking Critically: Ashley Murphree—Founder of Carpe Diem Private Preschool (www.carpediempreschool.com)

MiniCase 8
Thinking Critically: Paul Solitario—International ThermoDyne

MiniCase 9
Thinking Critically: Nick Barber—Sigma Relocation Group, LLC (www.umovefree.com)

MiniCase 10
Thinking Critically: Joy Shivar (www.JustAJoy.com)

MiniCase 11
Thinking Critically: Andrew Hooks—Cornelius Pet Care (www.corneliuspetcare.com)

MiniCase 12
Thinking Critically: Jeff Barry—RavioliOli

MiniCase 13
Thinking Critically: Alton Updike—Alton's Kitchen & Cocktails (www.altonskitchen.com)

MiniCase 14
Thinking Critically: Jennie and Gary Grassia—Trifork Enterprises, LLC

MiniCase 1

THINKING CRITICALLY

Beau Davis—The Varsity

At almost every college and university in America there are stores that sell every product imaginable labeled with the school name or mascot. Beau Davis recognized this fact but as a student at Texas Christian University (TCU), he also recognized that the products for sale with the TCU emblem did not match the nature and desires of the student body. Beau has a strong family history with TCU. The school is like many in the southern United States that were started after the Civil War, a time at which a large number of private schools were started in the South by churches. Most of these church affiliations today are more historical than representative of a strong control of the school by a given denomination.

Beau knew that the student population at the private university (where annual expenses exceed $50,000 a year to go to school) wanted high-quality clothes, but the local bookstores and other retailers were selling low-quality and cheap school-related clothing. The stores were simply following a time-tested model that worked well at the big state schools where the student body is more representative of a broad range of society, and often with much lower incomes. The existing retailers were pursuing a strategy that was not tailored to the local market they were trying to serve.

Beau used this inconsistency in desire and offering to establish the Varsity, a store that sells higher-end clothing items. The brands offered are typically some of the higher-end clothing brands any store might offer such as Polo, Ralph Lauren, Columbia, and Ping Golf. The result of this higher quality is that the average price for a shirt is $60 in the Varsity while shirts would be $30 and of lower quality in other local stores. All things in the Varsity relate to TCU. The store is approximately 1,000 square feet in size, and has been open for four years. The key selling season for the store is during the football season.

To fund the store, Beau brought in eight investors who committed $300,000. The investors included some family and friends but more broadly were people associated with the university in some manner. Beau and his partner committed their intellectual and physical efforts to the business as they had no significant capital at that point in their lives. The two partners provided the investors with a seven-page business plan and a twenty-page offering describing the business. The base for the business plan came from talking to other retailers. Beau discovered that if the other retailers did not see him as a direct competitor, then they would be very helpful overall. The Varsity typically maintains about $180,000 to $200,000 of merchandise in inventory.

Beau sought to save as much money as he could when starting the business by doing such things as living in an apartment behind the store location and using his extra bedroom in the apartment for business storage. However, while seeking to save money, Beau also made some key mistakes. One mistake was rather than investing in a solid point-of-sale system that would allow him to better use the Internet, he went with a cheaper system. The cheaper system was unable to support all of the activities he wanted to do with e-commerce. Today he has largely had to shut down his e-commerce efforts and seek to rebuild them in a whole new manner. He is currently seeking to use Square to establish a presence on the Web; this product is used by many small businesses to gain a place on the Web. Beau wishes he had raised $400,000 rather than $300,000 to have been able to obtain a better point-of-sale support system. The idea for the business is so attractive and reasonable that he now believes he could have raised that much money with relative ease. Underestimating his ability to obtain the initial funds at the time led him to target too low, which then set in motion problems such as not being able to aggressively pursue e-commerce options for the firm.

An interesting aspect that Beau highlights for a firm like his that targets a differentiated product is that most typical advertising methods do not work. Even advertising in specialty outlets such as the campus newspaper largely leads to very limited results. Instead, the best forms of advertising are through social media including Facebook and working with a blog specifically around TCU athletics. The social media connect specifically to individuals who are interested in the products and understand the positioning of the firm.

Epilogue

In the summer of 2014, the Varsity shut down as the lull in the summer was too great—the cash flow simply could not cover the existing costs. This situation was aggravated in part because the owners anticipated that the fall football season for TCU would be one of its best and had laid in extensive inventory. In hindsight, the owners also began to realize that many retailers such as the campus bookstore had learned from the Varsity and were now also handling high-end retail goods, which competed directly with the Varsity. At its closing, the Varsity was able to get out of its lease at no cost since there was another tenant who wanted the space. The inventory was sold for 30 cents on the dollar.

QUESTIONS

1. The Varsity's largest number of sales occur from September to December, because of football season. The sales then drop dramatically. What would be your advice to the firm about how to build up sales other times of the year without losing their TCU focus?
2. Think of private schools in your area or state. Would a business like this work in those areas?
3. What other niche businesses can you think of that serve a higher-end market, but which big national firms are not now serving?

MiniCase 2

THINKING CRITICALLY

Steve Clary—Steve's Barber Chair

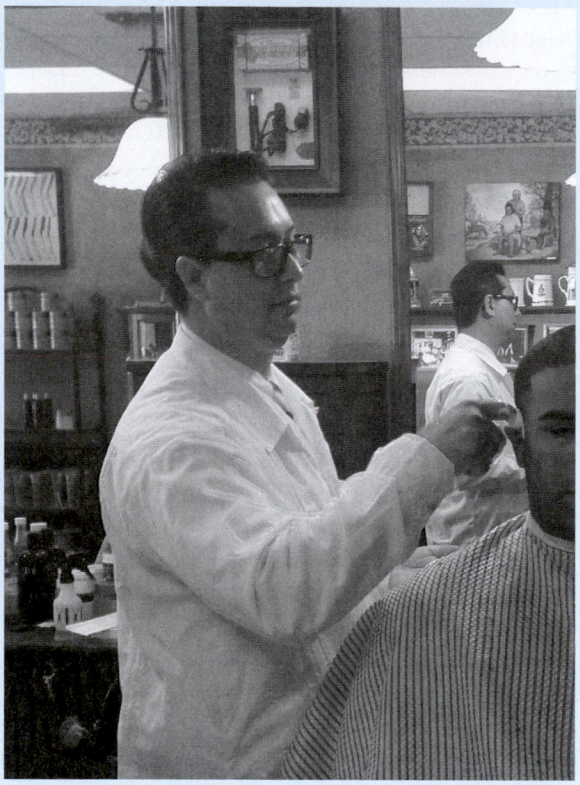

Since his childhood, Steve Clary knew he wanted to be an entrepreneur. This drive led him to try many different businesses, including selling insurance, prearranged funerals, and upholstery. However he found his calling as the owner of a barbershop.

Once he had decided to become a barber, it took Steve nine months to complete barber school; such schools cost from $11,000 to $18,000, depending on the specific school chosen. After Steve had passed the state licensing test, it took another $700 to buy supplies, such as clippers, to actually cut hair. Initially he worked for other barbers, keeping a percentage of the sales. The demand for barbers is quite high; there is a big difference between a barber and a stylist. Barbers are licensed separately and only a barber can cut beards with a straight razor. The result is that there are only a small number of barbers relative to the number of stylists.

Today Steve owns his own three-chair barbershop with all the income and responsibility falling to him for the shop. Steve serves an average of 60 people per week at an average of $25 per cut. He also does hot-towel shaves and facials for which he charges extra.

To make the jump from working for others as a barber to owning his own shop, Steve had to consider many factors, including the following:

- Would his regular customers follow him to his own shop?
- How would he decide where to locate his new shop?
- Did he have sufficient savings to cover the period of operation before he would reach breakeven in his new shop?

Locating a place was not an easy job. He had to balance the issue of the cost to operate with the potential traffic flow. While Steve believed that most of his customers would follow him, he also knew that he could not expect these loyal customers to travel too far. Thus, he looked for a location that was within a five-mile radius from where he originally had been operating, and that was within his budget. Steve knew he could not afford to buy a shop at that point in time, so he looked for places to rent. In calculating his rent he also knew that he would need to be able to afford both the rent, all the internal changes/additions that would be needed, utilities, and his commercial general liability insurance. Steve ultimately found a good location in the former pharmacy of large grocery store focused on the Hispanic market. While Steve is Hispanic, he did not expect to get much walk-in traffic from the store since his services were relatively expensive at $25 a haircut. Fortunately, the location would take only minimal changes in setup since those would be Steve's expense, and he planned to do all the remodeling himself. The utilities in this location would not be extra since the store had no way to allocate any costs to just this small part of the store. The monthly cost for the rent was approximately $1,100.

One key thing Steve had learned in his other business efforts was that advertising is key to success, but that an entrepreneur has to be clear on what really works. Specifically he found that most printed advertising did not work well. Similarly, although he has a website, he has found that only people who already knew him used it. He could not get through the mass of websites to reach potential new customers. Instead, he found that he needed to target specific customers—those homeowners whose homes are valued at over $150,000. He identifies neighborhoods through the Internet that meet that criteria within five miles of his shop and places a door hanging at each house with a coupon for a discount on a haircut. Steve does the door hanging himself to save costs and to ensure that it is done right. He typically does this several hours each week before he comes into the shop to cut hair. He has also been successful with customers rating him very highly on Web-based services such as Yelp.

The new shop has been a fulfillment of a life calling to be an entrepreneur. In the future, Steve is setting plans in motion to buy his own building. While he has three chairs in his shop, to date he has not been able to find the right people to work those chairs. His hope is to find individuals much like himself when he was starting out, who will work the chairs for a percentage of the revenue they bring into the shop.

QUESTIONS

1. Steve's wife had a good position with health insurance benefits, which allowed Steve to pursue his efforts to start a business. What are the additional issues that an entrepreneur has to consider if he or she doesn't have this type of support?
2. Steve says a key mistake he made in earlier entrepreneurial efforts was not having enough savings to allow him to overcome the hard times. How much savings is enough? If you were Steve, how much savings do you think he would have needed to start his own shop?

MiniCase 3

THINKING CRITICALLY

Cassmer Ward—The Clear Collar

Cassmer Ward had been in an entrepreneurial situation before he helped found The ClearCollar (www.theclearcollar.com). For example, he joined a struggling engineering firm as the CEO. The engineering firm was losing money on revenues of less than $1 million. Over the next six years Cassmer was able to move the firm to profitability with revenues in excess of $25 million. In 2008, Cassmer found an opportunity that was too obvious and too good to ignore.

Cassmer was in one of our EMBA Entrepreneurship courses and pitched an idea that had been crafted by his father-in-law years before but never developed into a business. In the early 1990s, Alan Donaldson who was an emergency-room nurse with more than 20 years of experience was frustrated with the classic cervical collar that must be repeatedly removed from a person's neck to be checked following a neck injury. The new product was clear, allowing the emergency-service professional the ability to continuously assess the patient's neck without having to frequently remove the collar.

One evening, using everyday household plastics, Alan created the prototype of what would become the world's first fully transparent cervical immobilization collar. A man ahead of his time, he found that the technology and process to manufacture a comfortable, transparent cervical collar simply didn't exist.

In 2008, Cassmer formed a team of EMBA students and, with the blessing of Alan Donaldson, they developed a business plan that won the EMBA Business Plan Competition. The team then decided to turn the plan into a real business. Cassmer said, "It ended up being a perfect storm for success, the technology in TPE (plastic) technology was there, survey research indicating that the market was eager for this kind of product was there, and, of course, the patent was there. Now all we needed were start-up funds."

Cassmer and two other classmates dedicated themselves full-time to the effort for the next twelve months. The new ClearCollar team promoted the concept to angel groups, medical professionals, and medical investors across the nation. The new company formed a board of directors and a board of advisors. The group felt that they needed at least $1.2 million to bring the idea to life. The founding team contributed $50,000 to get things started and went out and raised the rest of the capital over the course of a year. They ultimately raised $2 million.

For the ClearCollar team, getting molds cast, lining up manufacturers, working with distributors, and fighting an entrenched powerful set of competitors all proved to be substantial barriers to success.

The biggest impediment to early success, however, was the ability to make the product accessible. While the company had built a sales model based on sales representative-based distributors, they found that those distributors were very slow to react. The distributors wanted to see customers asking for the ClearCollar. Once customers asked about the ClearCollar, then the distributor became interested. This created an issue, as the company had to market to both direct consumers and to the distributors.

Another issue was the adoption time lag for a new technology in the emergency rooms. No one wanted to be an early adopter from the purchasing side. Although all of the direct users loved the ClearCollar, they didn't make the purchasing decisions. The purchasing decisions were made by a number of different sources (e.g., the municipality, the hospital, a third-party owner) This made it an uphill battle. Even with some of what became Cassmer's biggest accounts, it took 12 to 18 months to close the deal.

The ClearCollar team never planned on the sales cycle taking that long and did not have the resources to deal with this issue. At the same time, response/capacity from the manufacturing partner created issues. New versions with improvements were delayed, and shipping to customers on time became a big issue. This all became a huge demotivating factor for the sales team.

The result was, despite early strong interest in the product, the firm now has only one employee and is basically an order fulfillment company. The board is in the decision-making process deciding whether to sell the company now (which would be at a low valuation), bring in more capital (ditto), or selling/licensing all of the intellectual property (IP).

What Advice Does Cassmer Have for New Entrepreneurs?

1. You need to have great internal operations to fulfill orders, support sales/customers, and manage inventory. You will get offers from a lot of people/partners who can help or have advice on how to do so effectively. Be cautious. Be sure to listen, but only do what is best for your business model, not what makes sense for them.
2. Everyone thinks sales come from a good marketing plan. Wrong. It is from an excellent sales plan. What does this mean? Not only know how to make your product accessible, but what are the hoops you need to jump through to make it accessible? Who does the purchasing? What is most important to the decision maker? Is the decision maker the user? If not, whom does the product benefit and how can that benefit the decision maker? Understand what it takes (and how long) to complete the sale. The decision-making process when you buy a pack of gum is completely different from when you buy a car. What type of decision-making process is used when buying your product?
3. Make sure you are accountable and/or hold any vendors, partners, suppliers to the terms and conditions of your business. As a business owner, you want to provide your product as easily as possible to your customer. In order to do so, you are responsible for all factors from raw materials to delivery. Whomever you partner with to assist in the sales cycle must be a party that buys into and delivers the same message/service that is representative of your company.

QUESTIONS

1. Why hasn't the ClearCollar simply dominated this industry if the product is so attractive?
2. If an investor promises to invest an additional $2 million in this company, what would you recommend that the board do with that investment to improve the sales of the company?
3. How would you differentiate marketing from sales?

MiniCase 4

THINKING CRITICALLY

Charles Kezengwa—Hannington Massage

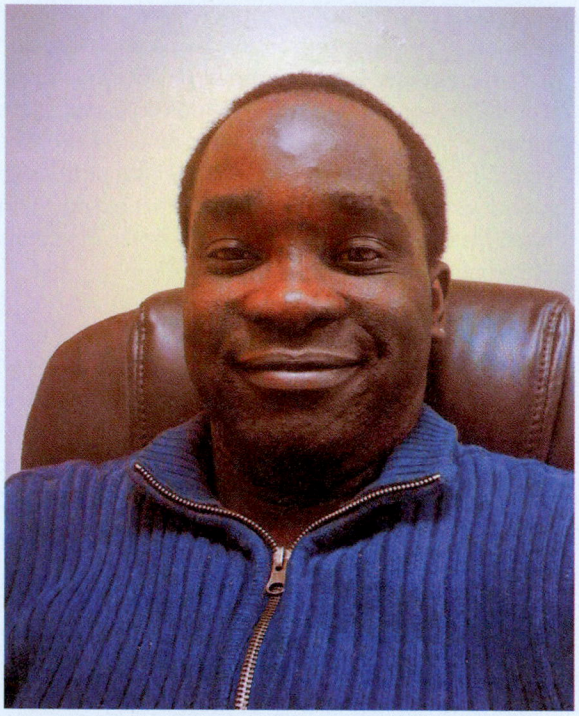

Charles Kezengwa is an immigrant from Kenya who in 2007 went to massage school to learn a skill that would allow him to earn a good living, control his life, and also have rich interaction with people. Massage school costs from $10,000 up to $50,000 and typically takes 9 to 12 months. The difference in price depends mostly on whether the school is a public community college or a private school. Passing a state exam is required to be licensed to be a massage therapist.

Immediately after graduating from massage school, Charles sought to open a massage salon. He and a friend from the massage school raised $15,000 and rented a nice facility on a major road. The facility had four massage rooms. Two other associates of Charles's initial partner asked to join their effort. Although these associates could not bring capital to the venture, they agreed to do the marketing for the new business. Almost immediately, however, the two new partners argued they should get 60 percent of the profits of the new business because they were bringing in the new customers. Charles refused, and the business, as a general partnership with no agreements on how to handle such disagreements, closed. The capital was lost, and Charles then began to work for another massage salon.

While disappointed that the business failed, as Charles gained experience by working for someone else, he learned more about massage therapy and people's health. The goal for the masseuse is not only to make the person feel better, but also to help improve their health. The view of the industry is that by massaging an individual's body, the masseuse is connecting to the client's digestive, nervous, and immunity systems. Over the next three years Charles's skills and abilities improved. Although minor issues in the firm existed, Charles believed the salon was a good setting for him. In October 2011, Charles and all the other employees of the relatively large massage salon were called together and told that the business was immediately closing. In hindsight, Charles could see that the business had not been well managed. It was expensive in terms of rent for the facility and the amenities offered were not well thought out. In addition, the business did not have a good marketing program.

At this stage Charles decided to again start his own massage salon, but on his own this time, with no partners. He knew he did not have the capital he really needed to start a business but saw no other options. Thus, with less than $150 in hand, he started Hannington Massage. The key issue that Charles focused on in his business was marketing. A massage is a true discretionary expenditure for the client. Costing an average of $70 an hour, individuals will buy a massage only when all other expenses in their lives are paid for. A side result of the discretionary nature of the massage business is a large number of cancellations.

To market his business, Charles relies on a wide range of media such as Facebook, Living Social, Groupon, and Twitter. Discount services such as Groupon and Living Social require that a firm offer their product for a 50 percent discount when they list with the service, 50 percent of which is then given to the discount service. The result for Charles is that a discount coupon is a loss leader. A key issue that became clear to Charles from his first effort with the discount service is that many people would buy his service via the coupon but then not become permanent customers. If the person does not become a permanent customer, then the service sold represents a loss to Charles. Licensed massage therapists can only actually give massages for about 30 hours a week. Long term, it is too physically destructive for the masseuse to work more hours than that. Additionally, the reality of running a business takes about an hour of office work including accounting, marketing, and record keeping for each hour-and-a-half massage that is given. Thus, each person who does not become a long-term client is not only a financial loss but he or she is taking a time slot that cannot be sold to a long-term customer. In addition, only long-term clients are likely to tip him, which can run up to 20 percent of the cost of the massage.

The result is that in Charles's first online marketing discount effort, more than 145,000 e-mails went out, 20,000 people opened the e-mail, and 6,000 people then clicked to see the offer. He sold approximately 600 coupons, of which 450 were redeemed, but very few led to long-term customers. Thus, while this marketing effort appeared to generate over $16,000 in revenue, he actually considered it a loss. One way Charles has overcome this low retention rate is to be far more specific in his requirements for the discount sold. Now he requires the person who buys the coupon to use it—no gifting. He reasons that the customer who does not buy the coupon is not likely to return as a long-term customer. In addition, he sets a shorter time frame for using the coupon. Again, he reasons, if a person does not come in quickly he or she is less likely to become a long-term client. He also does not allow individuals to split a coupon (some individuals had purchased a coupon and come in asking for 30 minutes for themselves and 30 minutes for someone else). Only new customers can use the coupon. The result of these restrictions is that Charles has reduced the number of coupons purchased through the discount services to several hundred, but he now gets 10 percent who may become long-term clients. Thus, to recover from the normal attrition of customers, once a year, he will now run such a discount promotion offer.

Today Charles has a full and rich practice. He has a full schedule giving approximately 30 hours of massage a week and another 15 hours of office-related work. His average massage revenue is approximately $50 an hour because of discounts given through services such as Living Social but also because clients who prepay for large packages of multiple massages also get a discount. Approximately 50 percent of Charles's customers are long term, with each averaging a massage a month. The remaining customers are usually shorter-term people with a given physical need.

What Advice Does Charles Have for New Entrepreneurs?

Charles suggests that key issues for entrepreneurs is to have a clear vision of your customers as you enter the business. If you have the skills in the business you want to do and connect to the right customers, an individual will be successful. However, if the right customer is not reached, then the entrepreneur can waste a significant amount of time. Charles also encourages entrepreneurs to not view the competition as bad. Instead, he suggests you work with others, including your competitors. The goal to growing the business is to offer the best product—not to seek to underprice or out-advertise your competition. If entrepreneurs focus on providing the best product possible, the competition becomes less of a threat. The positive outlook on your work that results also generates positive outcome on your business.

QUESTIONS

1. How would a service such as Hannington Massage keep long-term customers coming back? Are there special things that can be done in a service like this?
2. If you were advising Charles, would you suggest he hire other licensed massage therapists? Why or why not?

MiniCase 5

THINKING CRITICALLY

Greg Adams—OCJ Apparel

As an entrepreneurship major at Texas Christian University, Greg Adams had many chances to develop business ideas. One of the ideas that came about from this effort was OCJ Apparel (www.ocjapparel.com). OCJ is a firm that focuses on making college-branded jeans and other clothing items for more than 50 major universities around the nation. The firm started with jeans that had each university's logo on the back pocket and has since expanded the line to T-shirts, shorts, and other related products for both men and women.

Greg graduated from college in 2009. He noted that while there were a vast number of goods with logos attached to them, most could not be worn to nicer settings such as a party after a game. After he noted the gap in the market, he wanted to do some research on how to fill this niche. As a result, he designed a set of jeans with the University of Kansas logo (a school where his sister was enrolled). He hired one woman from each sorority on campus to wear the jeans following a game. Each of the women took notes on how many people noticed the jeans and if they liked them. The response was overwhelmingly favorable. They had people literally walk up to them and ask where to buy the jeans. In exchange for a free pair of jeans and a little bit of money, the company got an initial indication that there was a market for the product.

Even though Greg did not have background in apparel, he was able to learn quickly about the industry and begin to develop designs. Almost all university logos go through one of two clearinghouses that must approve the use of the logo. The clearinghouse often does the entire process for the university, although there are other times when the local school will want final approval of a product. The clearinghouse approval can be long as the applicant has to both be approved as a vendor and then be approved for each product the vendor wants to sell. Greg was able to obtain the clearinghouse's approval for his products, which gave him access to 95 percent of the schools he wanted.

In 2010 Greg was also able to source his key input, which was a denim manufacturer; a key limitation in this industry is that there are limited suppliers and manufacturers of denim that are of sufficient quality level for the United States. When Greg was able to secure his inputs and manufacturer, he considered it a major success. The access to the manufacturer was through a key advisor to Greg and his firm. After further testing of products in 2010, he was able to launch his product line in 2011 with six key universities across the nation.

The success of 2011 allowed OCJ Apparel to obtain licensing for 26 schools in 2012 and more than 55 in 2013. Today they are at 61 universities with an ultimate goal of 70. Greg believes that schools must be of a certain size, alumni base, game day attendance, and other specific characteristics to ensure successful demand for his products. Thus, he is clear that he is not targeting the entire set of universities in the United States.

The firm was on track to be at breakeven by fall of 2014. There are five full-time employees at the firm and three design interns. The firm has raised approximately $1 million dollars from friends and family. The plan for the firm after it reaches breakeven is to explore the potential outside investors if the firm wishes to expand more rapidly. The total units the firm will sell is estimated at 10,000 for 2014. The design of OCJ jeans has been so good that they have been asked to develop a line of jeans for Niemen Marcus—one of America's leading high-end retailers. The hope for the future is to have more of their own brand of products in other high-end retailers. The firm is clear that they market a product not for a mass market such as Walmart, but for a higher quality and higher margin outlet that can be either a specialty line or a university.

What Advice Does Greg Have for New Entrepreneurs?

1. The lead time in the business is always twice as long as you predict. Being on the retailer shelf August 1 when students return is key to his business. The approvals from all the sources took longer than he expected,

so he initially did not make that key deadline. Thus, he recommends that entrepreneurs create realistic time lines and deadlines, and then stick to them. If one retailer or school is still missing from the plan, move on without them.

2. Incentives for people who work for you goes beyond money. In OCJ Apparel's new building, Greg is giving the best office to the salesperson who sells the most over a given period. The activity builds a team effort around sales but still creates a low-cost reward for the person doing the best.

QUESTIONS

1. What are the key deadlines in your planned business? What will happen to your business if any one deadline is not met?
2. Do you have any critical supplier issues that must be addressed before the business can be developed?
3. How would you grow this business?

MiniCase 6

THINKING CRITICALLY

Charlie Gasmire—Cofounder and Director of Marketing at Vendevor (vendevor.com)

Vendevor is a company that allows a small business to start selling its products online almost instantly from its existing website, Facebook page, or blog. A firm that intends to sell online generally has had to hire a tech team to help shape the individual Web page to process sales and accept payments. Vendevor has tools that can allow the firm to almost instantly start selling online by accepting credit cards for payment; Vendevor transfers those sales almost instantly to the firm's bank account. An additional benefit that is particularly attractive is that it allows a firm to bypass third-party sources such as PayPal or other typical merchant accounts and payment gateways that have monthly fees and transaction fees that begin to add up. The attraction of these benefits is that Vendevor has been experiencing exponential growth.

The three founders of the firm all came from Baylor University. Two of the founders were students and one was an instructor. The instructor and one of the students had a class together where the student had to develop a business plan. The initial business plan was to be a wedding-related business. The student in the class (Charlie) was already in a small business with a fellow student who was an amazing programmer. The investigation of the wedding business and Charlie's other small ventures led to the recognition of a core need for businesses to sell their products on the Internet and to ensure they got payment without having to use sources such as PayPal, which did not look professional on their website. The plan for the wedding business that originated in class was dropped in favor of Vendevor.

The three entrepreneurs initially raised $40,000, which allowed them six months to develop the initial product and gain five customers. Today the firm has raised approximately $500,000 and is approaching breakeven with more than 9,000 clients who have signed up with Vendevor. The firm has five full-time and several part-time employees. The expectation is that number will increase significantly over the next year with one new salesperson per month being added. The firm will be very well positioned in this new area if it is ever approached by a strategic buyer (a large wealthy firm looking to enter the niche). While the team works very well together, they set up the firm with well-defined documents on how the process would work if one of the founders wanted to leave or somehow did not fulfill his share of the work.

The firm has a seven-member advisory board that is very supportive of the firm. The benefit of a strong advisory board can be seen in the firm's ability to accept credit cards on behalf of their clients. One board member put the founders in touch with a bank looking to expand into the Internet space. The bank partnered with Vendevor so that the bank and Vendevor both grew in expertise. The bank knew from their analysis of Vendevor's model that there was a real opportunity for high growth. Vendevor saw an opportunity to partner with a bank that would set the processing fee very competitively. The bank's staff supports Vendevor by doing background checks on each of the firms that signs up to ensure each is legitimate and has bank fraud tracking experts. The result has been a win-win that has benefited both the firm and the bank. Even though some of the advisory board members are family friends, they all bring expertise to the firm. For example, the CEO for one of the largest application makers for cell phones in the United States serves on the board. The board members meet virtually and always remain actively interested in the entrepreneurial venture.

What Advice Does Charlie Have for New Entrepreneurs?

1. Build a team with members who have different skills. Vendevor has to have solid programming, but it also needs employees who can interact with the businesses it is serving and relay back their needs to the programmers for product iterations and new features. It took the skill sets from all the founders to bring the business together.
2. Laser-focus on your exact customer and deeply understand these customer needs. Charlie believes that successfully handling all the things an entrepreneur has to take care of—such as HR—will not matter without customers and sales. Vendevor has grown without massive venture capital backing. It has done so by proving its products to the customers who are willing to pay for the service, thus gaining their financing from their customers as they pay for products.
3. Learn from competitors. You do not have to reinvent the wheel each time. Your competitors often have already done the hard part of figuring out how to succeed. Thus, as they looked to build the compensation for their salespeople, they learned from others and then designed a system that worked for them.
4. The key on the Internet application like Vendevor is to become sticky. That is, you want as many services and connections to the customer as you can so that if they change to another competitor they have to make many changes that make leaving difficult. Thus, helping the customer to develop new uses for your services is key. Such an approach not only makes Vendevor sticky, but it also helps the customer grow, which is a win-win.
5. One thing Charlie would do differently relates to the online advertising that the firm initially placed with outlets such as Facebook. The cost of customer acquisition is a key success factor in an Internet business. Although some of their competitors use online advertising, these firms have far deeper pockets, so when they waste money it does not hurt as much. Vendevor, however, was hurt by these efforts as they did not have as much money to waste. Charlie would have been more disciplined and focused more clearly on cost and exact financial benefit of each advertisement.

QUESTIONS

1. As you consider your business, how will it be sticky so that customers cannot leave?
2. What are the skills you need in your business? Does your team provide all of the skills you need?

MiniCase 7

THINKING CRITICALLY

Ashley Murphree—Founder of Carpe Diem Private Preschool (www.carpediempreschool.com)

Ashley Murphree's life started as a refugee from Vietnam. She and her family became what was commonly referred to at that time as "boat people" by fleeing Vietnam in a boat after the nation fell to the North Vietnamese Army. On their way to Malaysia and hopefully freedom, Ashley and her family were attacked by pirates, who took their boat and threw the family into the sea, where they eventually floated onto an island that was part of Indonesia. The island was largely isolated from the world, but the family survived there for a year until they were discovered and the Red Cross sought to help. Ashley and her family were eventually moved to Malaysia and ultimately to the United States by UNICEF. From that very difficult beginning, Ashley has now built a very successful preschool system, Carpe Diem Preschool, with four different locations. The preschool is unique in that it pursues a highly differentiated strategy: All teachers have four-year college degrees, the student–teacher ratio is low (there are 130 staff in her schools for approximately 600 students), daily music classes are taught by trained musicians, and a high level of security is provided for the students.

The idea for the preschool came from Ashley's own life. After graduating college in 1995 with a degree in business, she worked for several firms in human resource roles. However, as she started her own family, she wanted to continue to work but needed quality care for her children. She was not satisfied with the options that she found, particularly with the instructors' level of education and experience. Therefore, in 1999 she decided to learn about setting up a child care center and two years later she opened her first unit. The start-up capital for the venture ($400,000) came from Ashley's own 401(k) and from her family. Her family funding included her mother's retirement funds, which she cashed out for her daughter's start-up.

To be able to open the preschool, Ashley extensively planned for the venture including visiting over 30 different preschool facilities. She even worked at a competing preschool to get firsthand knowledge. However, despite the best-laid plans, when her preschool opened in 2001 the telecommunications and wireless industry in her region crashed, which meant that many of the parents Ashley was counting on as customers were now financially strained. The business therefore took longer to reach breakeven than Ashley had planned. A key element that helped Ashley break through and start her strong financial progress forward was connecting with a public relations person. This person was able to have Ashley featured in a number of newspaper and magazine articles. The free publicity drew in new clients. The nature of the business is that when a family has one child who does well, they later place more children in the school. The publicity about Ashley and her Carpe Diem Private Preschool plus the increasing presence of siblings resulted in far greater demand than she could meet.

The outcome of the strong demand led Ashley to open her second preschool in 2005. It took approximately two years for the preschool to open, including the search process for a location, obtaining the land, and obtaining all licenses. The second preschool broke even in one year. The third day care opened in 2009. However, the fourth day care was a slightly different arrangement.

The demand for the day care had been so strong that a friend of Ashley's asked to join in the process. Although the result is still a Carpe Diem Private Preschool, Ashley has used this venture to explore the potential of franchising the concept. She has developed extensive systems and manuals that she has used with her friend. She helped him identify the location and navigate the process to establish the school. In addition, she advised him on setting the school up and in training the staff. However, rather than directly control the school, she has set it up to take a percentage of revenue. Any changes she makes in her school she passes on to the newest school. Thus far, the new school has been a great success.

The new school has allowed Ashley to see the potential for expanding her method of preschool to a wide range of other areas. Her target market is high-income areas with young families. She consistently gets calls from developers asking her to locate a preschool in their new developments—a preschool of this caliber is seen as a key attraction to young parents in the same way being close to a leading private school is an attraction. Ashley believes the key benefit to being a successful entrepreneur is controlling your own life. Today, Ashley generally visits her schools weekly, and she is always available on phone. The core outcome of her success is that she has the freedom to do what she wants, not what others want.

What Advice Does Ashley Have for New Entrepreneurs?

1. Double at a minimum the time and money you think it will take to start your business. Everything takes longer and is more costly than you expect. Don't run out of time or money just as your idea starts to take hold.
2. Get good people you trust. You want the business to be able to run without you. If it cannot run without you, then you can never sell it or never be away from it for any period of time.

QUESTIONS

1. Would a day care based on the same principles as Carpe Diem Private Preschool be viable in your area?
2. How does Ashley protect her competitive advantage as she goes forward?
3. What lessons from Ashley's experience will help you start your business?

MiniCase 8

THINKING CRITICALLY

Paul Solitario—International ThermoDyne

For many entrepreneurs, their entrepreneurial process is not a single venture, but many different ventures, until one of them leads to great success. This was the case for Paul Solitario. Paul graduated from the College of William and Mary in Williamsburg, Virginia, with a degree in economics and an emphasis in international banking. Over the next 19 years he worked in banking, always taking the lead as the banking industry exploded in its scope.

It's important to understand that the various elements of banking were highly restricted by the 1932 Glass–Steagall Act. During the 1980s and 1990s, banks pushed the bounds of the Act in order to take advantage of both technology and expertise. The entire Glass–Steagall Act was dismantled by Congress in 1999.

Paul was on the forefront of the evolution of the banking industry as part of the team that created Private Banking with First Union (now Wells Fargo) back in 1987. Back then, Private Banking was focused on leveraging the net worth of wealthy individuals and Paul's industry focus was on the health care industry. In 1990 First Union began to realize that Private Banking was probably more of an investment management business than a bank, and they chose to leverage their recent investment into the discount brokerage industry. Paul became the first person in the bank to obtain a Series 7 license. The Series 7 is a license to trade securities in the United States and is required of all stockbrokers.

However, in early 2001, First Union downsized their operations and Paul was offered a different position or a year's pay if he left the firm. He took the pay and began to work part time as the interim treasurer for a health care company. It was at this time he embraced his first entrepreneurial opportunity when he was asked to lead a new business with partial ownership in the firm.

PPN Wireless was a technology firm that wanted to place wireless Palm 7 PDAs in the hands of doctors for free. In exchange, pharmaceutical companies that contracted with PPN would send these doctors short abstracts from research papers. The pharmaceutical companies then asked the doctors to fill out surveys through the phone. Whereas the typical response rate by doctors to surveys from pharmaceutical companies was in the single digits, PPN Wireless achieved response rates between 85 and 100 percent. In addition, the number of prescriptions being written by these doctors for the products covered in the research papers rose substantially.

With Paul as the president, PPN Wireless was growing steadily and profitably until the attacks of 9/11. At that time the pharmaceutical industry pulled back their marketing efforts and left PPN Wireless with significantly reduced income. After realizing that the company could no longer afford Paul's salary, Paul sold his shares in the business back to his investors and returned to banking as a senior vice president in wealth management at First Citizens Bank. For the next three years he held this position, although he still wanted to have his own business.

In 2005 he joined with another investment banker and they started their own middle-market investment firm, which was quite successful. Looking to really focus his talents in what he saw as the sweet spot in the industry, Paul went out on his own in 2010 and formed Cerium Capital. There Paul sought out businesses with current sales between $10 and $150 million that were either looking to complete a merger and acquisition transaction or raise either debt or equity capital. After a short period of time, Paul added management consulting to the practice and invited a former senior McKinsey consultant to become his partner to help deliver the joint investment banking/management consulting services.

It was in that capacity that Paul was introduced to a professor at Wake Forest University in Winston-Salem, North Carolina, who had patented a method to convert both thermal (heat) and kinetic (motion) energy into electricity via a flexible, thin, clothlike, organic material. Paul, along with two other team members, convinced the professor that their team had the expertise to exploit the product's incredible market potential. The result was the founding of International ThermoDyne (www.itlthermodyne.com). Under the leadership of the new management team, the company opened a second lab, where they created the working prototypes of the material that they refer to as PowerFelt. As part of the launching of International ThermoDyne, the team quickly closed their first significant capital raise.

For PowerFelt, the business applications for the product are simply astounding. A few examples include:

1. Housing. A house wrapped in PowerFelt (much like they are wrapped today in plastic materials) would have the ability to not only power itself, but to sell excess power to the grid.
2. Automobiles. Cars with PowerFelt-lined seats, hoods, roofs, tires, and brakes could provide electricity to improve gas mileage and extend battery life.
3. Clothing. PowerFelt-lined clothes could generate enough electricity to charge cell phones or power wearable electronic devices.
4. Military. The uses are enormous from putting on tents, to power equipment, to reducing the numbers of batteries soldiers must carry in the field.

What Advice Does Paul Have for New Entrepreneurs?

1. It takes a team to be truly successful. No one person has the ability to be really good at sales, manufacturing/development, and finance.
2. Whatever you're offering, make sure you understand what your customer's pain points are and make sure that your product's value proposition addresses those issues.
3. Try to get to a minimally viable product as soon as possible. Not only does it help cash flow but it also helps focus the effort around the customer's needs. No amount of surveys, questionnaires, or encouraging words from mentors can substitute for a customer's willingness to pay for your product or service.

QUESTIONS

1. The path to entrepreneurial success can be a rocky one. What are your plans if your first venture fails?
2. How will you leverage your knowledge from prior work or ventures such that it is an asset for a new business idea?

MiniCase 9

THINKING CRITICALLY

Nick Barber—Sigma Relocation Group, LLC (www.umovefree.com)

Nick Barber graduated from college in 2004. He knew then he wanted to be an entrepreneur like his father, but he was not sure what he wanted to do. He had worked in college for a large multifamily management firm whose work included marketing apartments. The nature of the apartment industry is that the developer would build the complex and then hire a management and marketing firm to reach some given occupancy rate, at which time the firm would be able to market the project for sale. Thus, Nick initially looked at the apartment industry for his first business.

One factor that Nick noted in the apartment industry was that the apartment's occupancy occurred in two ways: (1) renters either found the apartment via the apartment's own marketing activities, or (2) apartments would engage third-party marketing services to advertise the apartments for a fee. Apartment locating services were one such third-party option. These apartment locators would sometimes be all a real estate firm did, and at other times it was part of a larger real estate operation. In either case, if a renter signed a contract with the apartment complex, the real estate company received a referral fee, typically half of one month's rent. Most of the smaller apartment-locating firms tended to be small and typically located in a strip center with a few desks and chairs.

The process of locating an apartment in early 2000 was still low technology with individuals having to fill in paperwork and be driven to the apartment by the apartment locator. The advent of technology had not been implemented effectively in the industry. Nick realized that if he could bring technology to the industry he could have an opportunity to improve the customer's experience and revolutionize the industry. However, Nick also realized that bringing technology to the apartment-locating industry would not totally replace knowledgeable sales agents. A complete technology process would result in individuals being able to review lots of listings, but would fail to provide personalized customer service and might not mean the firm would get paid for the referral. There would be no effective way to know when a customer signed up for the apartment since there would be no way to know which apartments they ultimately visited and leased.

That said, technology could bring a number of relatively obvious efficiencies to the process, including providing profiles of apartments, to maintaining a customer database to track new and repeat clients and save a real estate agent's time. The use of technology also meant that a salesperson did not actually have to accompany a client to an apartment complex but instead could work from a central location and provide the client apartment information over the phone, fax, or e-mail. The whole process would still need a salesperson to work with clients to help them identify apartments that meet their needs, provide needed information to clients, follow up with them during the process, and also help secure the apartment and any discounts that may be offered. Technology could be used to streamline the sales process and automate the time-wasting manual processes that had plagued traditional apartment-locating firms.

The outcome was a new approach to apartment locating. The firm developed into the brand name UMoveFree. The salespeople never meet the clients face to face, but they are still able to serve their needs via the Internet and phone. Nick's firm has grown to be one of the largest apartment locators in the United States in terms of apartment leasing with over 2,000 apartment leases signed each month. His database of clients numbers over 2 million renters. To be able to collect their fee from the apartment complex, they must ensure that the customer notes they were referred by UMoveFree. Nick's salespeople encourage their customers to remember this critical step by offering a free moving service or a $200 rebate for customers who find their apartment using UMoveFree's service. The free move or rebate offer is also used as a value proposition when marketing the service to prospective renters. While this is a great incentive, Nick sees his 100 plus experienced apartment agents as the key advantage to the firm. Good people who are highly motivated to do a good job provide the service to the clients that is key to success.

While Nick's firm is one of the largest apartment locators in the United States, it operates only in Texas, meaning the opportunity for growth is substantial. The firm works with over 95 percent of apartments in the Texas cities that UMoveFree operates in. Another option for future growth is the ability to leverage the firm's strong relationship with its clients to also offer complementary products and services such as home purchase assistance, renter's insurance, or other services that renters may need before or after they move into an apartment.

What Advice Does Nick Have for New Entrepreneurs?

One of the key insights Nick has for potential entrepreneurs is that it does not take massive cash to start a business. UMoveFree's initial investment was less than $25,000. Nick worked at his other job with the apartment management firm as he and his business partner developed the business and saved the money for their start-up. Even today most of the cash he makes is plowed back into the business. Nick says that funding the company's growth through profit may have taken longer, but he has a business that is largely debt free, and his ownership is not diluted by outside investors. The result is that the business is completely owned by himself and his partner.

QUESTIONS

1. As you consider financing, would it be possible for you to start your business in a similar fashion?
2. As you consider technology, do you see general rules for when technology should totally replace people and when it is appropriate to differentiate your people in the process?

MiniCase 10

THINKING CRITICALLY

Joy Shivar (www.JustAJoy.com)

Joy Shivar was raised in Boonesboro, Kentucky, in a house whose core was built only three years after the original Fort Boonesboro was founded. Her mother was in the antiques business and, while Joy attended lots of shows growing up, she was not inspired to be an antiques dealer. That all changed in 1996 when she was attending a show and discovered Civil War antiques. She loved the story behind each item and how close the whole event was to today's generations. She was hooked on a passion that led to her successful entrepreneurial venture.

Joy started collecting Civil War antiques and selling some of those to dealers. Her original idea was to develop a nice collection at no cost by selling just enough to fund all the rest. At antiques shows, individuals line up hours in advance seeking to be the first person in line. In fact it is possible to pay to be that person in the hope of gaining the best goods. However, Joy found that even when she paid to be the first person in line, the items she really wanted were already sold. She found out that dealers would buy and sell to each other while they were setting up their exhibits the night before. She decided at that moment to become a dealer.

Joy has set up and run booths at antiques shows throughout the southeastern United States. She is well known in the antiques community. As her collection and skills in Civil War antiques developed, she learned that anything that could be tied to a particular person was worth substantially more money. Furthermore, those items had particular interest and value to the descendants of the person with whom that item was associated. While there are many websites selling antiques and there are thousands of genealogy websites, there was nothing available that allowed for the tracking and buying of antiques tied to specific people. With that, the JustaJoy.com Family Heirlooms Exchange was born.

Joy worked for six years to develop a site that was rich in content before she ever released the site to users. She spent part of every day loading items into the site as the programmer was developing it. The site went live in May 2011 and caters to all types of antiques, not just those from the Civil War, but the key differentiator is that the items are connected to specific people. Individuals who pay a membership fee are able to search the site by surname or by a general search. Members can post as many items as they wish to sell. E-mail alerts are automatically generated to other members who care about the surnames associated with newly posted items. The interested member then contacts the member with the item and the details are negotiated. Joy does not, at present, charge commissions on sales or charge a buyer's premium on purchases, nor does she limit searches or antiques postings. The key income for the website comes from the $20 per year membership fee.

Joy sees the business as a cross between a named antiques sales site for dealers and an information exchange for anyone seeking items from their family's past. Joy likes to think of the business as a place where history and heritage meet. The site has roughly 5,000 items available at most times. These items are associated with nearly 60,000 surnames as a single item often has more than one surname association. Antiques available on the site have run the gamut from *A Book of Concord* (c. 1580), which is part of the historic doctrine of the Lutheran Church, to WANTED posters, to a Civil War Confederate coat that is for sale for $95,000.

While the site is doing well, it provides insufficient income for Joy to give up her work as an antiques dealer working trade shows. She would like to develop the site into something more akin to eBay, where dealers pay for placement and pay a percentage of their sales. Unfortunately, however, she is limited by the fact that most dealers have their own websites. Although those sites do not provide a central depository that is searchable by surname, most of the dealers do not seem to be interested in enhancing their web sales. Joy's goal is to ultimately focus all her efforts on the website. In the classic chicken-or-egg conundrum, in order to draw in the dealers as paying customers, she is trying to develop the site into a content-rich location that people seeking named antiques go to first.

What Advice Does Joy Have for New Entrepreneurs of Online Businesses?

1. Developing the content side of the business still takes personal selling. Until you hit a point where the business reaches a tipping point, it is important to sell people on the value.
2. Spend lots of time designing the website idea before you ever employ a programmer. It is very expensive to have to keep redesigning the website unless you are an expert.
3. While outside investment in the business was offered by many people, control of the business was one of the big reasons that Joy developed it herself. If you really know what you want, then try to do it without outside investors.

QUESTIONS

1. Are there other businesses similar to antiques tied to specific families that could be developed?
2. What special skills would be required to create such a business? For instance, is knowledge of antiques a prerequisite?
3. How would you connect the online business with the business of antiques shows?
4. How would you incorporate personal selling with the online business?
5. How would you overcome the objections of other antiques dealers to the idea of paying for postings on Justajoy.com?

MiniCase 11

THINKING CRITICALLY

Andrew Hooks—Cornelius Pet Care (www.corneliuspetcare.com)

Andrew Hooks's path to his entrepreneurial venture took some rough roads and he needed a powerful drive to change his life. For the first 10 years after high school, Andrew worked as a ceramic tile installer and construction laborer. He found himself increasingly relying on alcohol and seeing his life slipping away from him. Then in a moment of clarity three and a half years ago, he decided to stop drinking and develop some real discipline his life. He has not had a drink since. He decided to pursue fitness and became a personal trainer. He competed in the 2013 Gold's Classic Competition for which he followed an extremely strict workout and diet plan. That experience showed him that he could do anything he set his mind to and to this day he works out at the gym at least twice per day.

Having found a focus in his life, Andrew wanted to pursue his own business but did not have an idea of what to do. His mother came up with the idea. She kept seeing cars go by that had advertising wrapped all around the vehicle. One of the advertisements that caught her eye was about pet sitting and pet care. Andrew had always been around animals, and his personality allowed him to be comfortable with virtually everyone. His mom knew that in the relatively wealthy area of Cornelius, North Carolina, there had to be plenty of people who needed pet care services. Cornelius is a suburb of Charlotte, North Carolina, at Lake Norman just north of the city.

Andrew looked into the business and found that there were a wide variety of pet services already in the area. If he was going to pursue this, then he needed to stand out from the crowd. Interestingly, the pet-sitting business is mostly made up of independent contractors driving to people's houses or established locations where people bring their pets for boarding (hourly or daily). There are only a few large chains in the industry.

Andrew felt that the key success factor and the way he would have to differentiate himself was through his advertising. However, Andrew also knew that traditional print media was no longer the right answer. Andrew's father is in the Internet marketing field and Andrew had developed a good skill set in Web design. Leaning on that ability, he decided to focus his efforts on the Web page. After doing research, Andrew found that 90 percent of customers go online to locate and learn about a service provider.

In September 2013, Cornelius Pet Care (www.corneliuspetcare.com) was born. The website was the differentiator and Andrew carefully crafted a state-of-the-art mobile-compatible website complete with a shopping cart so that it would be the number-one listing on Google whenever anyone looked for pet care, pet sitting, pet sitter, or a whole host of other related search terms in the Cornelius area. Andrew would say that it is hands down one of the nicest local pet care services websites in the country. He understood how the Google algorithms work, which take into consideration all kinds of factors including site age, page load speeds, back links, social media activity, domain authority, and many other aspects. Andrew then set out on a SEO (search engine optimization) campaign, which took him hundreds of hours and is continued to this day, writing and creating blogs to maintain a social media presence that is tied to the website. Through his understanding of Google algorithms and hard work, Andrew was able to get his site to number one just three months after its launch, out-ranking several other local pet sitter's websites that have been in place for years.

The business is still in its very early stages of life. He gets 100 percent of new business from his Web page, even though he is trying to expand the message around town in more visible ways with shirts and notices. As the business has grown, he has taken on a partner who has invested cash and time. When asked about how the business will handle future growth, Andrew shared that he is planning to use contract employees whom he has personally trained in his processes and approaches. His plan is to attend the first meeting with every new client and the pet care provider who will be handling the account.

What Advice Does Andrew Have for New Entrepreneurs?

1. Get all of the business licensing and standard operations of the company completed before you start making sales. An accounting package, procedures for operation, and a plan for managing the business is crucial.
2. Develop a sophisticated Web page. Today most customers use the Web to decide which company they will use. These customers are virtually sold before they ever contact you. Don't scrimp here.
3. Getting repeat customers is all about exceeding their expectations.

QUESTIONS

1. With the business you are contemplating, how much of the sales pitch and process could be completed online?
2. How will you market the business at the outset?
3. What processes should be in place before you make your first sale?

MiniCase 12

THINKING CRITICALLY

Jeff Barry—RavioliOli

There are new businesses that do everything correctly, pivot well as the environment changes, have great customer value, and yet still fail to achieve breakeven. Jeff Barry had been serving friends and family his grandmother's ravioli recipes for 20 years. During all that time, he worked in specialized parts of banking, including asset-based financing and equipment leasing. Jeff was essentially a numbers guy who had a passion to start an entrepreneurial venture centered around his specialty approach to ravioli.

Jeff finally decided to get serious about the effort during the recession of 2009. Noticing that the fast casual dining market seemed immune to the recession and was growing like no other part of the market, he felt the time was right for him to start a restaurant based on that ravioli concept. RavioliOli was to be a fast-casual dining restaurant where fresh handmade specialty ravioli were delivered to your table within five minutes of ordering. The location was going to be slightly upscale and the décor was going to be warm, comforting, and comfortable.

Jeff did a complete competitive analysis using himself and his family to learn all they could about competing restaurants. The family would go to various fast-casual concept restaurants and record how many people dined there during lunch and dinner. He tracked average meal ticket prices and looked for locations that had great road access and parking. Building on his understanding of the competition, Jeff then took six months to develop a full business plan that was ready to pitch to investors.

Jeff started his search for investors with a friend who had money to invest. After securing that investment, he was referred to one investor after another and he was able to quickly raise the capital that he believed he needed to start the company. This included $175,000 of his own money. Securing the location took far longer. He looked at close to a hundred sites with various realtors. Finally, in early 2011, Jeff found the perfect location in Oak Brook, Illinois, just west of Chicago. Jeff really loved the location because of its access to major roads, great parking, visibility, and access to the corporate lunch crowd. Although the real estate market was still reeling, the cost of the lease was substantial (although well within Jeff's business plan projections). After extensive negotiation, Jeff signed a lease for 2,200 square feet and began to generate specific plans for the space. Working with designers and architects, they developed a great space. There is an old adage that says a new business will cost twice as much as you expect and take twice as long. Jeff had heard this and felt like he was prepared when it did happen. However, in the approval process with the landlord and building inspectors, Jeff was surprised to find out that his kitchen was going to require special ductwork that had not been accounted for in the plans. Several other smaller items were also required for unexpected changes, all of which ended up costing an additional $110,000.

As a part of his original business plan Jeff had set aside $220,000 in working capital to take care of contingencies and provide the business with a cash buffer. He decided to have all the small items and the new ductwork installed. RavioliOli opened for business in late February 2012.

Everything was going well at first. There were opening parties, Groupon offers, and lots of press about the new business. However, the working capital fund was rapidly depleting as revenue did not cover expenses. It is not unusual for a new restaurant to take 18 to 24 months to achieve monthly breakeven. In the case of RavioliOli, however, the reserves had been spent early on the ductwork and other items, so Jeff took out an equity line loan on his house for $75,000 and met with the investors who pitched in an additional $110,000. Neither Jeff nor the investors took any additional equity with this infusion. As Jeff ran the numbers with the new capital he realized the business needed to have sales of $2,000 every day of the week to achieve breakeven. When you have a Sunday that brings in only $700, you have to make that up on other days. Jeff thought he could do it, but realized it would be hard.

In the meantime, other negative things were happening in the business. Personnel turnover became a critical issue. A key success factor for a restaurant are its cooks. Jeff needed people who could efficiently make the ravioli the desired way. Unfortunately, two cooks left in March and the head chef and store manager left within the first three months. Jeff ended up working at the store 18 plus hours a day trying to ensure it succeeded. As the pressure on the business grew, it increasingly became a family affair as everyone pitched in to serve customers. Sales continued to grow but were not close to breakeven. At the big July 4th festival in Oak Brook, RavioliOli sold 4,000 plus toasted raviolis and then ran out (much to the dismay of the dozens still standing in line). There seemed to be great demand for the company offering.

After nearly driving himself into the ground, Jeff hired an experienced restaurant manager who quickly put procedures in place and relieved Jeff of having to do everything himself at the restaurant. Jeff and the new manager were able to drive costs down some, but the issue remained that they were not hitting $2,000 day ($60,000 month) in revenue. Jeff spent countless hours trying to renegotiate the lease to no avail. He cut back staff as far as he could and still reasonably serve customers.

Jeff met with everyone who would meet with him about the business to get advice on how to turn things around. He learned from experienced restaurateurs that he was right in line with his costs, procedures, and approaches. He was also told it would just take time to develop.

In December 2012, Jeff met with his investors again to secure more funds. The business was out of money and was still losing money each month. The investors had put in all the money they wanted to invest and recommended that Jeff close down the business. Unwilling to take this step just yet, Jeff dipped into his 401(k) retirement fund for $100,000 while not getting any additional share of the business for his new investment. With the ability to keep going with his own investment, Jeff obtained the blessing of his current investors to obtain a new major investor in the business even if their equity was diluted. He was meeting with several potential investors every month seeking fresh capital.

While sales continued at a very slow and yet steady rise, the business was out of money again by February 2013. Jeff met again with his investors. He shared with them that he had an investor who was ready to put in $150,000 and Jeff needed everyone to pitch in another $7,000 to $8,000 ($40,000 total), so the business could stay afloat until April when the new money would come in. All of the investors and Jeff pitched in the money. Unfortunately, however, by April the new investor's circumstances had changed and he decided not to invest in the business.

RavioliOli was simply out of money. The business was now approaching $50,000 in revenue a month. Jeff made the decision to pull the plug on his beloved restaurant 14 months after it had opened.

What Advice Does Jeff Have for New Entrepreneurs?

1. Go with your gut. If it feels right, do your homework and go for it. There are no guarantees in any venture, or even more so, in any job. To the extent that you can, pinch pennies and keep fixed cost as low as possible.
2. Anticipate, Anticipate, Anticipate! Whatever the venture, do things right; you'll know when you break that rule. Start early in your life. . . part of my issue was that I was approaching 50 years old, and had three kids in college, one in high school, and tuition became a huge overhead in the grand scheme of things. I loved running the business, but I hated losing money. Having said that, a very good friend of mine who knows me quite well and saw me sweating out the losses reminded me that money is indeed a renewable commodity and somehow, someway, we always figure out a way to get it back.
3. Although I made many mistakes, I don't regret a single minute. We created memories of a lifetime through our ravioli-making parties, birthday events, family gatherings, catering jobs, special events, and captivating our younger patrons' bright-eyed amazement as we rolled out the Ravs. We built something very cool, very different, very original, and something for which I am very proud.

QUESTIONS

1. Can your business survive a long lead time to break-even? How long do you project?
2. Other than have more money, what could Jeff have done to save the business?

MiniCase 13

THINKING CRITICALLY

Alton Updike—Alton's Kitchen & Cocktails (www.altonskitchen.com)

Alton "Al" Updike started in the restaurant industry as a 15-year-old busboy at a country club in Deltona, Florida. He worked at several different restaurants and cafés through the rest of high school and his first foray into college. Al started at the University of Florida but decided to drop out of school in his sophomore year. For the next year he worked a series of jobs shucking oysters, cooking at Macaroni Grill, and finally culminating in a job running a backhoe digging graves. He listened to other members of the grave-digging team talk about how long they had been doing that work, and he decided to go back to school and pursue what he really enjoyed—the restaurant business.

Al went to school at the University of Central Florida and graduated with a bachelor's degree in business administration. While he was there he took every course that he could in the tourism management program. He graduated in 1997 and even though he was offered a management position at Macaroni Grill, he decided to pursue a job with Houston's Restaurants. Houston's is an upscale restaurant chain with about 40 locations in 10 states that is well known in the industry for its rigorous management training program. Over a six-month period, trainees work every aspect of the business. Al was not hired into the training program directly. He started as a line cook and joined the management program within three months. Al worked for Houston's for the next seven years at locations in Orlando, Miami, Atlanta, Houston, and Dallas.

A former Houston's manager contacted Al in 2004 and asked him to join his new restaurant near Charlotte, North Carolina. They were crafting a restaurant where all the food would be fresh (no freezers) with an upbeat elegant style. They wanted to institute the process-oriented approach that was the hallmark of Houston's. Al and his wife moved to Charlotte and he started as the kitchen manager and then general manager of the first location. After two years the owners decided to open a second location and asked Al to set it up and run it. Over the next two years Al opened up and ran two new locations before asking to move back and run the original restaurant.

When Al returned to Charlotte he found that while he had been away starting up new restaurants, the original restaurant that had started the chain had slipped substantially. Over the next year he worked to bring it back up to the level it had been before. The whole effort reinforced something that he and his wife had been contemplating for a long time. He felt he was ready to open his own restaurant. He was being paid very well and enjoyed the business, but he was ready to work for himself.

In early 2010, Al signed a lease to open Alton's Kitchen & Cocktails. Al put up $20,000, a partner put up another $20,000, and a third partner put up $10,000. They invested the $50,000 in a three-year CD and then used that asset to take out a loan to start the business.

The location they leased had been two different restaurants over an eight-year period of time and had each closed because the owners had decided to get extravagant with their spending. The restaurant space was quite large (much larger than Al really wanted), but much of the basic needs of a restaurant were in place. They renovated the building and were ready to open within four weeks. Al could have opened for Valentine's Day 2010 (a traditionally fantastic day for restaurants), but felt that his staff was not ready. Alton's opened for business officially on February 15, 2010.

As is typical in the industry, business for the two months was brisk as customers tried out the new place. However, sales plummeted starting in mid-April and stayed down into the summer. Al tried every marketing idea he could think of to increase sales. He found that Groupon was helpful in getting new customers, but he had to agree to provide $50 worth of food for a $25 Groupon, and Groupon kept half of the $25. Thus, Al received only $12.50 for every $50 in food and drink he provided. He liked the volume increase but lost significant money for every coupon that was used. His first partner dropped out of the business within three months of its opening and his other partner dropped out in November. Being a big believer in good karma, Al promised both partners that once the loan was paid off that he would return their invested capital and this he did.

Sales did not start picking up until September 2010. What Al realized was that there was a "Lake Season," which drove the sales pattern at the area restaurants. Alton's Kitchen & Cocktails is located very near Lake Norman just north of Charlotte. It is a very popular lake with thousands of houses and dozens of parks situated on its 520 miles of shoreline. Once Lake Season started, most of the regular customers were out on the lake rather than eating in restaurants. Al had a banner winter season that year and was far more prepared for the big sales drop-off that occurred just as expected in mid-April 2011.

Al also began taking advantage of boot-strapping marketing efforts. For example, Al took part in Charlotte Restaurant Week. The event, which is actually two weeks in length, showcases restaurants in the area. All the participating restaurants create special three-course menus that sell for $30. The inclusion brought (and continues to bring) in lots of new customers.

Al also realized that he would need to adapt his operations as he moved forward with the restaurant. One adaptation was to add lunch, something that most other restaurants in the area offered. He also noticed that few places in the area had brunch menus and even fewer had creative brunch menus. One of his successful efforts was his Saturday and Sunday brunches. Today, he uses a wide variety of social media and is a big believer in the classic "sign on the road" as a means of drawing in new customers and staying relevant to regulars.

What Advice Does Alton Have for New Entrepreneurs?

1. Make sure that if you venture out on your own, with or without partners, that you have a strong support team and/or family around you. Both of my partners believed in what we were doing, but their wives/family didn't embrace the financial and workload responsibility that is required to be an owner. They were both out within 10 months.
2. Change will occur very often when you are trying to create your own culture from scratch. It's important to communicate these changes constantly to all levels of the workforce.
3. I believe in karma! My industry is based on integrity, trust, and accountability. On a daily basis my employees ask themselves "What would Al do?"

QUESTIONS

1. What kind of company culture do you want to create at your new business?
2. How have your life experiences prepared you for your new business?
3. From your perspective, what are the pros and cons of partners?

MiniCase 14

THINKING CRITICALLY

Jennie and Gary Grassia—Trifork Enterprises, LLC

Gary and Jennie Grassia have been happily married for 17 years. During that time they have built both a family and a business. For many years, Jennie's parents owned a franchise called "Little Gym" that provided athletic activity and developmental education for young children. Jennie and Gary started working at the gym in high school and college, respectively, eventually becoming managers of the two facilities in the franchise, and then partners. In the fall of 2008 the opportunity to start a new franchise by themselves became available: Simply Fondue.

Simply Fondue is a restaurant franchise operation that is based on fondue cooking. A fondue restaurant is one where the raw food is cooked at the table by the customer. The food arrives at the table cut into bite-sized segments and is then cooked to taste by the customers using long forks. Fondue is generally thought of by Americans as dipping food in cheese and chocolate—which is certainly part of the experience. However, "fondue" comes from a French word "to melt." So in addition to the cheese and chocolate fondues, there is also hot oil or broth, which can be used to cook a variety of items, including beef, chicken, shrimp, and mushrooms. The restaurant has a real competitive advantage in comparison to other restaurant operations because it does not require a large kitchen staff to cook the food; only preparation is needed. For this particular Simply Fondue's market, the typical ticket for an individual plate at the restaurant will average approximately $45. Thus, the restaurant is thought of as a high-quality (because you can see your food being cooked), higher-priced meal experience.

The Grassias had become familiar with the Simply Fondue franchise 12 years before by frequenting a nearby Simply Fondue. They had known for a while they wanted to start another business, so they had been doing a wide-range examination of different types of franchises available. They were drawn to the restaurant business, since there always seemed to be demand and there were many well-established franchisors. They were drawn to fondue franchises, since it seemed like a unique niche, but one with growing demand. There are two major franchise chains that offer such food. Gary visited with both major franchise groups, but the leadership of the Simply Fondue franchise operation really impressed him. He was convinced that this would be the most supportive franchisor. One critical key issue that became clear for Gary and Jennie when they were involved with the child development franchise was the importance of strong support by the franchisor. Franchisors promise support in return for the monthly royalty payments that the franchisee must pay. However, the follow-through and willingness to help the franchisee succeed is often less than promised. Thus, one of the key issues that Gary focused on when making his evaluation of the two franchise systems was which one was actually going to be the most helpful to them. He found that the total costs of the franchise purchased from either group would be the same, and the nature of what was promised was largely the same. Thus, the judgment of which franchise to buy would be based on which one of the franchisors would actually follow through on what it promised.

They began to look at locations for a restaurant in the large southwestern city in which they lived. However, by early 2008 they realized that the corporate franchisor was also looking to open a corporate store in their city. In fact, the franchisor had already begun lease negotiations to open a store in a very popular downtown area. Using the contacts that he had developed in his research on the businesses, Gary contacted the president of the franchisor company. During the next few conversations it became clear that the franchisor president wanted either a company, or privately owned franchise in this downtown location, but it was too good a location to not have something in place soon. The Grassias were able to arrange to buy the franchise and take over the lease negotiations. The funding for the purchase of the franchise, the preparation of the restaurant, and other initial costs came from a Small Business Administration loan.

The preparation of the site took longer than expected: nine months. The space had been a storage location prior to their purchase and lacked everything needed for the restaurant. However, they did not have to pay rent during the construction phase, so even though it took a long time, it was not nearly as costly as it might have been. In most retail operations, the key ingredient for success is often said to be location, location, location, but the Grassias' experience highlights the fact that while that is true, another variable is the cost of that location. Their location is much cheaper than many in the same downtown area because, although they have a street-front entrance, their restaurant is actually downstairs in a basement.

The restaurant is open and is performing well. The success of the business has led the Grassias to start the process of opening another restaurant. The learning associated with the Simply Fondue restaurant has given the couple the confidence to believe they now have the rich skills necessary to do the next restaurant by themselves without a franchise. The royalty fees that are paid to the franchisor can be up to 4 percent of the revenue of the business. Retaining that fee can be a critical factor in profitability. The success of the business has also allowed Gary to go into the business only two days a week. Those two days are the busiest in the restaurant, Friday and Saturday, so he spends 15 hours both days working, but it does now allow him to spend more time at home. There is still plenty of work done from home, but the Grassias find the greatest benefit of being an entrepreneur is the ability to spend more time with the family.

Running a successful franchise has allowed the Grassias to refine their management skills. Today the family uses five key elements in that management. One is Open Table, in which individuals can reserve a table electronically. The Grassias have found 80 percent of their customers use this system. The restaurant is open only for dinner due to the cooking time for the food at the tables. The fact such a high percentage of reservations come through this system means each morning they can tell what the night's business will be. If the level of reservations does not appear to be at the level they desire for the evening, they can work either through Facebook or via their own e-mail list of customers to offer a one-night special. The result is that they can almost exactly predict what their customer activity will be in a day. They also have employed Groupon effectively, especially during the slower summer months to generate cash flow. However, they have found they have to provide very specific limitations on their Groupon coupon to prevent abuse. They limit an offer to two coupons per table and they also ensure that the coupon is not for the entire cost of a meal. Failure to do so means that two to three people could come in and share a single meal among themselves.

What Advice Do the Grassias Have for New Entrepreneurs?

1. Work with people. It does not pay in the long run to yell and make unreasonable demands. The restaurant was in a historical building and putting up the signage they really wanted was a problem. However, by working with the owners of the building they were eventually able to achieve a positive setup.
2. Keep lines of communication open with your partner and those with whom you have to deal on a regular basis, such as lenders, leaseholders, and so on. They all want you to be successful as that is how they will get paid. These relationships are mutually beneficial, and a solid relationship is the key to their success.
3. Run your franchise in the manner that the franchisors suggest. Why pay for a franchise if you are not going to do what they suggest? They have systems that are proven. Take full advantage of that. Beyond that, if you do not do as they suggest and something goes wrong, you cannot go back to the franchisors for support.

QUESTIONS

1. What other restaurants that are franchises are you familiar with?
2. Would a fondue franchise work in your city or section of the city?
3. Is a franchise approach to your first business a good way to develop skills needed to run your own business?

CREDITS

p. 272: © Garry D. Bruton; p. 274: © Travis Black. p. 276: © Portrait Innovations; p. 278: © Charles Kezengwa; p. 280: © Garry D. Bruton; p. 282: © Baylor University Marketing & Communications; p. 284 © Ray Perenia; p. 286: © Paul Solitario; p. 288: © Garry D. Bruton; p. 290: © Charles E. Bamford; p. 292: © Charles E. Bamford; p. 296: © Charles E. Bamford; p 298: © Jennie and Gary Grassia.

Building a Business Plan

Developing a business plan is central to preparing to launch a new business. The key is not the document itself as much as forcing the entrepreneur to think through the multiple dimensions of the business to make sure they line up. Too often new ventures appear to be great ideas but fail because of details that the entrepreneurs did not realize they needed to address. The business plan helps the entrepreneur ensure as few unpleasant surprises occur as possible. It is the discipline and the thought process that occur in writing the business plan that makes the effort so valuable.

There are as many formats for a business plan as there are people to design one. Nevertheless, most business plans have some elements in common. The list below is a comprehensive list of potential elements in a business plan; we would not expect every plan to incorporate all of these elements. The entrepreneur must exercise considerable discretion to determine which elements are important to his or her particular business plan. For example, developing a new restaurant will drive the plan to deal extensively with operational issues since these will be particularly critical to its success. On the other hand, a new bookstore will push the business plan to focus more extensively on marketing as an especially critical factor of success. If the business is an Internet business, then the marketing—particularly how to get through the mass of clutter on the Internet and be one of the top firms that comes up when someone uses a search engine like Google—becomes critical.

We will briefly describe the major areas in a business plan and highlight particularly critical elements that entrepreneurs should include in their plans. Then we will present a plan that was developed by students while they were taking a course using the first edition of this text. It is not an example of a "perfect plan"; rather, it is an example of what might be reasonably accomplished.

Key Parts of the Business Plan

Executive Summary

- Brief Description of the Company
- Mission Statement/Value Proposition
- The Product and/or Services Being Offered
- Competitive Advantages
- Brief Financial Forecast
- Management Team
- Current Advisors
- Financing Requirements and Return Expected

You can conceive of this particularly critical section of the plan as the "hook" that encourages the reader to examine the entire plan. The executive summary is very useful in ensuring that you, the entrepreneur, remain focused in your analysis. If you cannot briefly explain your complete business concept in one to two pages, then you have not thoughtfully and thoroughly analyzed the potential business. You should be clear about how you will provide value to the customers, what the value proposition is for the business, what your competitive advantage is, and how your background has prepared you for this business.

History and Position of the Business to Date

- The Company's Mission
- Company History from Business Conception to This Point
- Management Team and Key Personnel
- Business Structure

This is the section of a business plan, which many entrepreneurs choose not to include. If you have created other businesses and your new business is somehow dependent on those businesses for success, then such information is important. However, for most entrepreneurial businesses, the issues highlighted here simply provide context to potential investors, clients, and/or suppliers.

Market Research

- Target Markets
- Geographic Area Within Which the Business Will Operate
- Competitive Environment and Opportunity Space
- Competitor Analysis
- Position of the Firm
- Market Description
- The Desired Customer
- Market Growth Opportunities

Market research codifies and describes the specific market space that you hope your new business will occupy. The preparation of this section helps assure that there is a group of customers available for your business and that the business will be in a position to acquire these customers.

Business Strategy

- Mission of the Small Business
- Strategy
- Value Proposition
- Evaluation of Competitive Advantage
- Length of Time Before Imitation
- Comparison to Substitutes

You need to specify how the firm will compete in its targeted market. The firm's strategy details not only how you expect it to compete, but it also begins the process of exploring the expected outcomes of that strategy and the potential dangers to the firm from its competitors. The issue of imitation is a continuing one for all organizations as they try to achieve and maintain what is unorthodox about their businesses.

Financial Analysis

- Cash Flow Projections and Analysis
- Ratio Analysis
- Break-Even Analysis
- Expected Gross and Operating Margins

Financial analysis is a major concern for all new businesses. This section in your plan will focus on a discussion of the various financial concerns related to the start-up and running of your business. Tables with your actual data should appear as support for this discussion at the end of your plan. A key part of financial analysis is the funds use. The topics covered here include:

- Funds Required and Timing
- Use of Funds
- Funding Sources
- Valuation
- Distribution of Control

Ultimately you will need money from others and/or will need to be clear about how you will spend the money if you are self-funding the business. Therefore, your business plan needs to specify those numbers. The greater the detail provided, the more help the plan will provide you in establishing benchmarks that can be evaluated to judge your new firm's progress.

Operations

- Location
- Accounting Systems
- Quality Control
- Build Out
- Hours of Operation
- Processes
- Equipment
- Staffing Schedule
- Critical Path Analysis to Start the Business

Operations include the details about how you will operate your business, and these details will differ widely depending on the type of business you are launching. If it is a manufacturing business, then the operations section will be central to your plan. For example, your equipment may be part of the competitive advantage of your manufacturing firm and as such you will want to spend considerable time on that aspect of the business. On the other hand, if your new business is a restaurant then the equipment is typically generic and not a major factor in the firm's success, so your business plan will minimize its discussion. The location of your restaurant would be an important element of its success, however, so you should elaborate on that aspect of your business.

A particularly important part of the business plan is the marketing. Sometimes it will be a separate section. It addresses issues that include:

- Target Customer
- Sales Forecast
- Pricing
- Methods of Promotion
- Promotion Scheduling and Placement

The marketing plan specifies how your firm will reach the target customer. Particularly critical here is the specification of the customers and the details of how you actually will price and promote the product to those customers. One of the most difficult areas for any new business is how to actually reach the customers in a way that they will want to buy your product or service. Getting customers to change to your firm from another is very hard to accomplish.

Risk Analysis

- Discussion of Systems Risks and Controls
- Discussion of Business Risks and Controls

There are risks in every business. You do not need to spend extensive effort detailing the risks, although you want to acknowledge them. For example, we mentioned that young people starting a business may not have extensive prior experience in business. In this section you may wish to acknowledge those risks and illustrate what actions you are taking to ensure the success of the business. For example, if you have obtained a board of advisors consisting of successful business people who will work with you to reduce your risk, then this is an important point to illustrate.

Summary

The next section contains a sample business plan. As you read the plan, remember that we have noted both positives and negatives. As with all plans there are items that need additional research as well as items that are simply not researchable. Entrepreneurs need to gather as much information as they can and present that information as clearly and as concisely as possible. Although there is always other information that they would like to include, ultimately all potential entrepreneurs must make decisions with less than complete information.

Note that many of the sections of this plan do not match the exact order of our key areas list at the start of this appendix. A business plan is not a formula within which the entrepreneur can plug various pieces of information. Instead it is a document that should be read easily and be very understandable. The information should appear where it ultimately makes the most sense as well as where it best supports the entrepreneur's arguments about the new business.

Fraudian Slip

Confidential Business Plan

DRAFT
This is NOT an offering

AUTHOR NOTE
The Fraudian Slip was a plan created in Dr. Chuck Bamford's Executive MBA elective class in Entrepreneurship at the University of Notre Dame. This course is time-compressed, so it is not possible for the students to continue to refine the plan. Although generally well developed, the plan has flaws (as all do) and is not intended as a perfect example. Instead it is an effective vehicle for discussing the issues developed in this text and demonstrating their application. The format, detail, and approach are expressed quite well. The authors wish to thank the students responsible for this plan: Anthony Baerlocher, Cathy Bush, Mike Frey, Chris Kuhlmann, Nate Lazenga, Natalie Reynolds, Jason Speckman, and Nick Talarico.

Table of Contents

Executive Summary	3
Cash Flow Statement	5
Advisor and Team	7
Strategy	8
Business Model Design	10
Marketing	12
Milestones	13
Exit Strategy	15

Executive Summary

The Fraudian Slip is a dime-sized GPS tracking device intelligently mounted in high-value packages prior to shipping. The disposable device enables continuous, real-time tracking of high-value items, which reduces the number of claims insurance companies must pay out for lost packages or fraudulent claims.

It is estimated that insurance companies pay out over $12 billion annually for fraudulent loss claims (Source: FM Global website). Items sent via shipping companies and couriers can be tracked at various points in time, but the rudimentary scanning and RF trackers most prevalently used can be easily circumvented and fraud is common. Fraudian Slip's device and service provides constant monitoring of packages by providing the location of the package, and it also monitors temperature, humidity, and notifies when a package is opened.

The Fraudian Slip's initial target market is companies that sell shipping insurance (third-party shipping insurers, postal companies, and courier companies). This industry is estimated to be a $4.29 billion industry (Source: IBISWorld 2014).

Ideal customers are insurance companies insuring the shipment of high-value items to reduce claims. Examples include high-value art collections being transferred from a private collection or museum to another museum for an exhibition and expensive prototypes of new products.

Fraudian Slip will train insurance companies to require this value-added service for all customers who ship insurable items that meet a certain value threshold. By requiring the insured party to pay for Fraudian Slip, the insurance company will be able to maintain continuous monitoring of the shipped item(s) at no additional cost. Insurance companies will also be trained to offer the Fraudian Slip as an option for individuals or companies who are shipping items that do not have a high enough value to warrant the insurance company to require the Slip. For example, if a company is shipping an artifact from the company's founder that holds little cash value, but much sentimental value, the company could elect to purchase the Slip to maintain a constant awareness of the location and status of the item during the shipping process.

Competitors include: (1) Companies that target businesses (Agheera, Spark Nano, Global Tracking Group, Self-Insuring Shipping Cos.) and (2) Wholly owned subsidiaries (FedEx's SenseAware).

Insurance companies spend huge amounts of time and money processing and paying claims for items lost or damaged during shipping. Currently there are companies that will customize shipment tracking and monitoring systems for special shipments. However, no company exists that focuses exclusively on catering to the needs of insurance companies. The Fraudian Slip will tailor the delivery of the product and service to the unique demands of insurance companies, offering them a way to reduce fraud payouts and increase customer confidence in the safe passage of their items and the certainty of knowing that their claim will be less likely to be delayed for fraud evaluation.

Current package tracking software focuses on identifying where a package is in the shipping process at given points in time with an aim for providing peace of mind to senders. The Fraudian Slip puts technology in the hands of insurance companies allowing them to continuously monitor an item throughout the shipping process. Insurers can identify where a package has been and what it's been through allowing them to better identify fraud and reduce the cost of reviewing and paying claims.

The Fraudian Slip requests an initial investment of $880,000, which is expected to be adequate to complete the testing phases and initial sales efforts and to fund the company until sales are adequate to produce regular profits, which we anticipate to be 18 months. In exchange for an initial investment of $880,000, Fraudian Slip is offering a 35% equity position with a first right to buy back the equity position.

AUTHOR NOTE

Before completing the Executive Summary we would recommend that the plan list out very specifically who is contributing money, how much they are investing, and what percentage of the company they will receive for this investment. These details are important to potential investors.

Investors are interested in the projected returns of their investment.

Below you will see that the Pro Forma Cash Flows have been presented immediately after the Executive Summary. Without the context of the plan, these are difficult to evaluate at this point. We would recommend that the Pro Forma Cash Flows be placed at the end of the plan.

The business plan is trying to hook an individual's interest. If the investor is interested he or she will go to the appendix.

Cash Flow

THE FRAUDIAN SLIP, LLC CASH FLOW FY2014

	February	March	April	May	June	July	August	September	October	November	December	January
Receipts												
Subscriptions	$ 0.00	$ 0.00	$ 0.00	$ 0.00	$ 0.00	$ 0.00	$ 0.00	$ 0.00	$ 20,000.00	$ 25,000.00	$ 40,000.00	$40,000.00
Policy Receipts	0.00	0.00	0.00	0.00	0.00	0.00	0.00	0.00	0.00	5,000.00	12,000.00	20,000.00
Other	0.00	0.00	0.00	0.00	0.00	0.00	0.00	0.00	0.00	0.00	0.00	0.00
Total	$ 0.00	$ 0.00	$ 0.00	$ 0.00	$ 0.00	$ 0.00	$ 0.00	$ 0.00	$ 20,000.00	$ 30,000.00	$ 52,000.00	$60,000.00
Disbursements												
Maint./Repair	$ 0.00	$ 0.00	$ 0.00	$ 0.00	$ 0.00	$ 0.00	$ 200.00	$ 200.00	$ 200.00	$ 400.00	$ 400.00	$ 400.00
Acquisition	0.00	0.00	0.00	5,000.00	0.00	0.00	0.00	0.00	2,500.00	6,000.00	10,000.00	12,000.00
Lease/Mort.	2,850.00	2,850.00	2,850.00	2,850.00	2,850.00	2,850.00	2,850.00	2,850.00	2,850.00	2,850.00	2,850.00	2,850.00
Utilities	250.00	250.00	250.00	250.00	250.00	250.00	250.00	250.00	250.00	250.00	250.00	250.00
Salaries	23,000.00	23,000.00	23,000.00	35,000.00	35,000.00	35,000.00	35,000.00	35,000.00	35,000.00	35,000.00	35,000.00	35,000.00
Hourly Labor	0.00	0.00	0.00	0.00	0.00	0.00	0.00	3,333.33	5,000.00	8,333.33	8,333.33	10,000.00
Payroll Tax	1,840.00	1,840.00	1,840.00	2,800.00	2,800.00	2,800.00	2,800.00	3,066.67	3,200.00	3,466.67	3,466.67	3,600.00
Sales Tax	0.00	0.00	0.00	0.00	0.00	0.00	0.00	0.00	1,40.00	2,10.00	3,640.00	4,20.00
Insurance	5,500.00	0.00	0.00	0.00	0.00	0.00	0.00	0.00	0.00	0.00	0.00	0.00
General Cleaning	100.00	100.00	100.00	100.00	100.00	100.00	100.00	100.00	100.00	100.00	100.00	100.00
Advertising	0.00	0.00	0.00	0.00	0.00	0.00	0.00	5,000.00	2,000.00	2,000.00	2,000.00	2,000.00
Employee Benefits	7,590.00	7,590.00	7,590.00	11,550.00	11,550.00	11,550.00	11,550.00	11,550.00	11,550.00	11,550.00	11,550.00	11,550.00
Fees/Permits	50.00	0.00	0.00	0.00	0.00	0.00	0.00	0.00	0.00	0.00	0.00	0.00
Credit Card Charges	0.00	0.00	0.00	0.00	0.00	0.00	0.00	0.00	0.00	400.00	960.00	1,600.00
Office Supplies	100.00	100.00	100.00	100.00	100.00	100.00	100.00	100.00	250.00	250.00	250.00	250.00
Accounting/Legal	5,000.00	0.00	0.00	0.00	0.00	0.00	0.00	0.00	0.00	0.00	500.00	0.00
Furniture	3,000.00	0.00	0.00	2,000.00	0.00	0.00	0.00	0.00	0.00	0.00	0.00	0.00
Computers/software	2,500.00	0.00	0.00	2,000.00	0.00	0.00	0.00	0.00	0.00	0.00	0.00	1,200.00
Travel	0.00	4,000.00	2,000.00	0.00	0.00	0.00	2,500.00	2,500.00	4,000.00	4,000.00	4,000.00	4,000.00
Communication	1,500.00	1,250.00	1,250.00	1,250.00	1,250.00	1,250.00	1,250.00	1,250.00	1,250.00	1,250.00	1,250.00	1,250.00
Total	$ 53,280.00	$ 40,980.00	$ 38,980.00	$ 62,900.00	$ 53,900.00	$ 53,900.00	$ 56,600.00	$ 65,200.00	$ 69,550.00	$ 77,950.00	$ 84,550.00	$ 90,250.00
Net Cash Flow	($ 53,280.00)	($ 40,980.00)	($ 38,980.00)	($ 62,900.00)	($ 53,900.00)	($ 53,900.00)	($ 56,600.00)	($ 65,200.00)	($ 49,550.00)	($ 47,950.00)	($ 32,550.00)	($ 30,250.00)
Cash on Hand												
Opening Balance	$ 0.00	$826,720.00	$785,740.00	$ 746,760.00	$683,860.00	$ 629,960.00	$576,060.00	$ 519,460.00	$454,260.00	$404,710.00	$356,760.00	$ 324,210.00
Investment	880,000.00	0.00	0.00	0.00	0.00	0.00	0.00	0.00	0.00	0.00	0.00	0.00
Receipts	0.00	0.00	0.00	0.00	0.00	0.00	0.00	0.00	20,000.00	30,000.00	52,000.00	60,000.00
Disbursement	53,280.00	40,980.00	38,980.00	62,900.00	53,900.00	53,900.00	56,600.00	65,200.00	69,550.00	77,950.00	84,550.00	90,250.00
Balance	$826,720.00	$785,740.00	$746,760.00	$683,860.00	$629,960.00	$576,060.00	$ 519,460.00	$454,260.00	$ 404,710.00	$356,760.00	$ 324,210.00	$293,960.00

THE FRAUDIAN SLIP, LLC CASH FLOW YEARS 2-5

	Year 2 Q1	Year 2 Q2	Year 2 Q3	Year 2 Q4	Year 3 Q1	Year 3 Q2	Year 3 Q3	Year 3 Q4	Year 4	Year 5
Receipts										
Subscriptions	$ 150,000.00	$ 150,000.00	$ 180,000.00	$ 200,000.00	$ 200,000.00	$ 210,000.00	$ 220,000.00	$ 230,000.00	$ 940,000.00	$ 960,000.00
Policy Receipts	80,000.00	120,000.00	160,000.00	200,000.00	240,000.00	265,000.00	290,000.00	315,000.00	1,340,000.00	1,420,000.00
Other	80,000.00	85,000.00	90,000.00	100,000.00	110,000.00	115,000.00	120,000.00	125,000.00	505,000.00	510,000.00
Total	**$310,000.00**	**$355,000.00**	**$430,000.00**	**$500,000.00**	**$550,000.00**	**$590,000.00**	**$630,000.00**	**$670,000.00**	**$2,785,000.00**	**$2,890,000.00**
Disbursements										
Maint./Repair	$ 1,200.00	$ 1,500.00	$ 1,800.00	$ 2,000.00	$ 2,100.00	$ 2,200.00	$ 2,200.00	$ 2,200.00	$ 8,800.00	$ 8,800.00
Acquisition	36,000.00	30,000.00	30,000.00	30,000.00	30,000.00	30,000.00	30,000.00	30,000.00	120,000.00	120,000.00
Lease/Mort.	8,550.00	8,550.00	8,550.00	8,550.00	8,550.00	8,550.00	8,550.00	8,550.00	34,200.00	34,200.00
Utilities	750.00	750.00	750.00	750.00	750.00	750.00	750.00	750.00	3,000.00	3,000.00
Salaries	105,000.00	150,000.00	150,000.00	150,000.00	200,000.00	200,000.00	200,000.00	200,000.00	800,000.00	800,000.00
Hourly Labor	30,000.00	30,000.00	30,000.00	30,000.00	60,000.00	60,000.00	60,000.00	60,000.00	240,000.00	240,000.00
Payroll Tax	10,800.00	14,400.00	14,400.00	14,400.00	20,800.00	20,800.00	20,800.00	20,800.00	83,200.00	83,200.00
Sales Tax	21,700.00	24,850.00	30,100.00	35,000.00	38,500.00	41,300.00	44,100.00	46,900.00	194,950.00	202,300.00
Insurance	5,500.00	0.00	0.00	0.00	5,500.00	0.00	0.00	0.00	5,500.00	5,500.00
General Cleaning	300.00	300.00	300.00	300.00	300.00	300.00	300.00	300.00	1,200.00	1,200.00
Advertising	6,000.00	6,000.00	6,000.00	6,000.00	4,000.00	4,000.00	4,000.00	4,000.00	16,000.00	16,000.00
Employee Benefits	34,650.00	49,500.00	49,500.00	49,500.00	66,000.00	66,000.00	66,000.00	66,000.00	264,000.00	264,000.00
Fees/Permits	0.00	0.00	0.00	0.00	0.00	0.00	0.00	0.00	0.00	0.00
Credit Card Charges	4,800.00	4,320.00	3,600.00	3,600.00	3,600.00	3,600.00	3,600.00	3,600.00	14,400.00	14,400.00
Office Supplies	750.00	750.00	750.00	750.00	1,000.00	1,000.00	1,000.00	1,000.00	4,000.00	4,000.00
Accounting/Legal	10,000.00	0.00	0.00	0.00	20,000.00	0.00	0.00	0.00	20,000.00	20,000.00
Furniture	3,000.00	0.00	0.00	0.00	3,000.00	0.00	0.00	0.00	3,000.00	3,000.00
Computers/software	3,600.00	2,000.00	0.00	0.00	10,000.00	0.00	0.00	0.00	15,000.00	15,000.00
Travel	12,000.00	12,000.00	12,000.00	12,000.00	20,000.00	20,000.00	20,000.00	20,000.00	80,000.00	80,000.00
Communication	3,750.00	3,000.00	3,000.00	3,000.00	3,000.00	3,000.00	3,000.00	3,000.00	12,000.00	12,000.00
Total	**$298,350.00**	**$ 337,920.00**	**$340,750.00**	**$ 345,850.00**	**$ 497,100.00**	**$ 461,500.00**	**$464,300.00**	**$ 467,100.00**	**$ 1,919,250.00**	**$ 1,926,600.00**
Net Cash Flow	11,650.00	17,080.00	89,250.00	154,150.00	52,900.00	128,500.00	165,700.00	202,900.00	865,750.00	963,400.00
Cash on Hand										
Opening Balance	$ 293,960.00	$ 305,610.00	$ 322,690.00	$ 411,940.00	$ 566,090.00	$ 618,990.00	$ 747,490.00	$ 913,190.00	$ 1,116,090.00	$ 1,981,840.00
Investment	0.00	0.00	0.00	0.00	0.00	0.00	0.00	0.00	0.00	0.00
Receipts	310,000.00	335,000.00	430,000.00	500,000.00	550,000.00	590,000.00	630,000.00	670,000.00	2,785,000.00	2,890,000.00
Disbursement	298,350.00	337,920.00	340,750.00	345,850.00	497,100.00	461,500.00	464,300.00	467,100.00	1,919,250.00	1,926,600.00
Balance	$ 305,610.00	$ 322,690.00	$ 411,940.00	$ 566,090.00	$ 618,990.00	$ 747,490.00	$ 913,190.00	$ 1,116,090.00	$ 1,981,840.00	$ 2,945,240.00

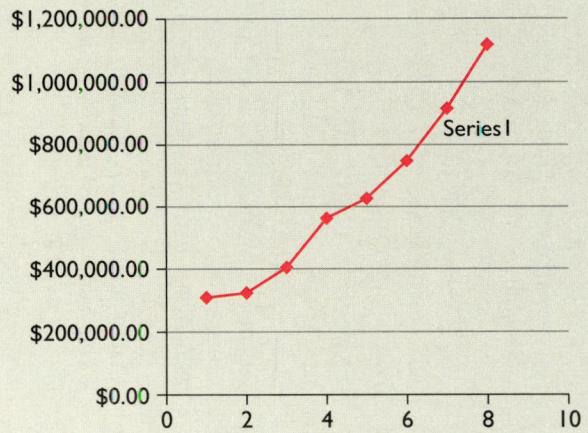

Anthony Baerlocher, MBA
Executive Director of Advanced Game Design, WMS Gaming

Expertise: Intellectual property development and strategy, game design and development, product creation, legal consulting for the gaming industry, math modeling, and development team leader. Entrepreneur.

Cathy Bush, MBA
Bush & Co. Advertising

Expertise: Strategic planning and implementation, marketing, advertising, and public relations. Building teams that increase market share, brand recognition, profitability, and quality performance. Entrepreneur: service firm and manufacturing company.

Mike Frey, MBA
Director of Sales and Marketing, Harlo Corporation

Expertise: Building and leading sales and marketing teams focused to increase market share, brand recognition, profitability, and quality performance. Strategic planning and implementation, product/service development and planning. Entrepreneur: small-business owner.

Chris Kuhlmann, CHFP, MBA
COO and CFO of Lakeland Community Hospital Watervliet

Expertise: Strategic planning, financial operations, and enterprise turnarounds. Revenue cycle streamlining, labor productivity and process improvement, and national wholesale distribution of tools and equipment.

Nate Lazenga, MBA
Design Engineer at Manufacturing Technology, Inc.

Expertise: Design engineer responsible for creating technical execution plans, concepting, designing, detailing, and troubleshooting equipment and tooling. Entrepreneur: founder of a sports organization.

Natalie Reynolds, MBA
Assistant VP, Certus Bank

Expertise: Client operations and management, employee management and motivation, analyzing and achieving operational efficiencies, coordinating multiple departments internally and externally.

Jason Speckman, MBA
Senior VP – Industrial Advisory Services, Cushman & Wakefield

Expertise: Industrial leasing representation and acquisition/disposition services. Underwriting investment real estate, creating and executing extensive marketing campaigns, managing long-term capital transactions.

Nick Talarico, CPA, CIA, MBA
Manager of Internal Audit, Do It Best Corp.

Expertise: Internal auditor with fraud investigation background has audited industries including manufacturing, construction cooperatives, and retail. Creates audit methodology to ensure risks are analyzed during the audit plan process. Audits performed: financial, operational, safety and compliance.

AUTHOR NOTE

Including bios is a crucial part of a business plan. Investors invest in the people that are going to run the business. However, note that the desire for bios can vary widely among investors. Some investors are looking for full-page bios about each founder. Other investors are only interested in the bios if they directly relate to the proposed business. Still other investors want something short about each founder. The plan should be tailored to the specific desires of the investor. In part this is why many business plans put them at the end of the plan.

Strategy

The real value of the Fraudian Slip is to the insurance company in being able to reduce paid claims for lost, damaged, or stolen shipments that are insured by customers. While it might make sense to employ awareness campaigns to customers, ultimately the path will be a push strategy.

AUTHOR NOTE

Deciding who the real customer is for a business is crucial. While some believe that the customer is the one who actually pays the business, others believe it is the consumer who must choose the final product/service. There is probably no right answer here; however, the choice made will dramatically affect the organization, operation, and success of the new venture.

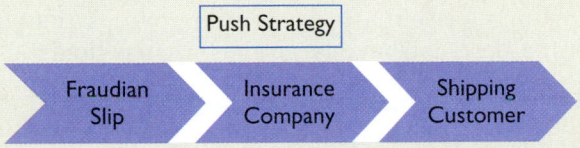

Fraudian Slip will "push" the value proposition to the insurance companies by offering the GPS device as a means to real-time tracking of insured shipments. This device will be free of charge to the insurance company, as it becomes a pass-through expense to the end customer. In essence, the insurance companies will have to sell this to their customers as a value-enhanced feature. Fraudian Slip will assist its customers in selling this service through three very important steps.

AUTHOR NOTE

The labeling of this device as a GPS device seems simplistic and probably not what the authors intended here. It appears from the description that it is a whole set of capabilities and would suggest that those be listed out very carefully early in the plan.

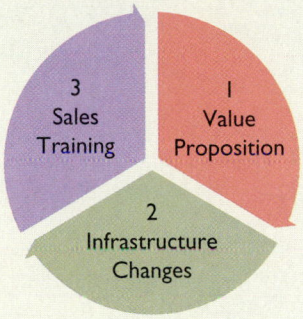

2. **Value Proposition** – Fraudian Slip has to do an effective job selling the value proposition to insurance companies. None of the components of the marketing strategy matter if insurance companies are not convinced there are real and tangible savings from lost, damaged, or stolen shipments. Part of this value proposition is to create a marketing strategy so that the insurance company can increase its business with this unique offering.
2. **Infrastructure Changes** – Fraudian Slip will assist the insurance companies in modifying all of their forms, applications, website inquiries, and so on so that the device/service is an available option to all customers who are insuring their shipments.
3. **Sales Training** – Lastly, Fraudian Slip will train the insurance company personnel on how to effectively promote and sell this option to its customers. This will include information on the device, how it works, and the advantages of real-time tracking. It has been proven that salespeople will more often sell what they know rather than what gives them the biggest commission. Fraudian Slip's job is to make sure they are intimately familiar with all aspects of this service.

AUTHOR NOTE

Repetition is one of the traditional problems in most plans. The Value Proposition has already been clearly and effectively articulated. There is no value in repeating information in a plan. This would have been cleaned up in the revision process if there had been time to do so. We left this in here as an example of what happens so easily in the development of a plan. Focus on being concise.

Competition

There are several companies who are attempting to provide real-time GPS tracking, but none that focus primarily on the insurance companies who insure worldwide package delivery. In fact, GPS shipment tracking products/systems seem to fall into one of two customer segments: (1) Retail: Products such as the Spark Nano are sold on eBay.com, Amazon.com, and other retail sites meant for use by the end user and (2) Wholesale/Industry: A common target is either shipping companies that move products globally or companies that have large fleets where logistics are essential for efficient deployment of trucks. Below are some examples.

	FRAUDIAN	AGHEERA	SPARK NANO	GLOBAL TRACKING GROUP	SUBSIDIARY CORPS. I.E. FEDEX "SENSEAWARE"
True Real-Time GPS Tracking	√	√	√	√	×
Monitors Speed	√	×	×	√	√
Monitors Temperature	√	×	×	×	√
Monitors Humidity	√	×	×	×	√
Notifies Upon Opening	√	×	×	×	×
Primary Customer	Insurance Cos	Shipping Cos	Retail/Industry	Retail/Industry	Shipping Cos
Retail Availability	√	√	√	√	×
Fee Structure	Per Use	Per Use	Per Unit	Per Unit/Rental	Per Use

Business Model Design

Currently the shipping industry experiences exposure to risk when a parcel owner ships high-value items. Figure 1 shows the current setup of the shipping industry. If the package does not reach the intended user either because the product is lost or because the package is fraudulently rerouted, the insurance company must pay out claims. Paying out claims is a real concern for any insurance company. If the insurance company can track packages and review the route of the package from start to finish, it can reduce the number of claims it must pay by finding lost packages and more successfully identifying instances of fraud.

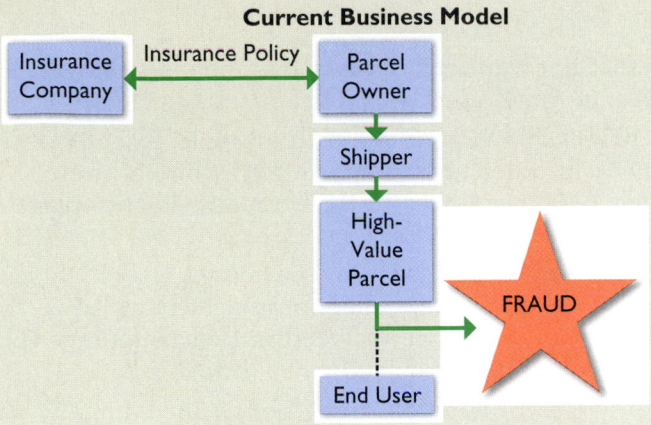

Figure 1

AUTHOR NOTE

An effective diagram like this one makes the whole process visual and takes the place of hundreds of words. We recommend the use of pictures, diagrams, and charts as much as possible.

The Fraudian Slip is a total solution that helps insurance companies reduce their exposure to claims by reducing their risk through tracking via the Fraudian Slip device. This device is an extremely small and portable electronic transmitter for real-time tracking of insurable items that easily slips into parcels. Fraudian Slip manages the entire process for the insurance companies. When a policy is sold, Fraudian Slip is notified, which sends a device to the shipper, monitors its progress, and reports back to the insurance underwriter when the package is delivered or tampered with. Figure 2 shows the new business model after the Fraudian Slip enters the marketplace.

AUTHOR NOTE

Here is a prime example of where a picture or drawing is absolutely needed. The reader has no ability to visualize the actual look of the product. As the plan is discussing the product, a whole group of questions now become relevant:

1. How does this one small device do all these amazing things?
2. How will this small, inexpensive device have sufficient battery power?
3. It appears that the device must transmit. How will it accomplish this in a steel container aboard a ship?

Putting yourself in the chair of the reader allows you to effectively address questions as they would logically arise in the reading of the plan.

There may be very effective answers to these questions.

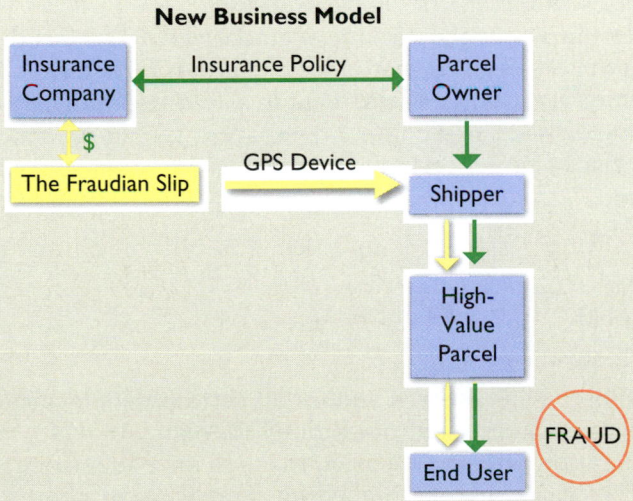

Figure 2

Revenue Generation

The Fraudian Slip's value to insurance companies allows four different forms of revenue generation.

1. Every parcel that is considered "high replacement value" must have the device in order to be shipped. Every one of these shipments will yield $100 per policy to the company. High replacement value is anything over $20,000.
2. Parcels that are considered with high sentimental value, regardless of replacement value, may have the device included in their shipping. These will also yield $100 per policy.
3. In addition to the policy, the company will charge a 1% premium based on the value of the product being shipped.
4. Client account subscription fees will generate $5,000 per year.

AUTHOR NOTE
This picks up on one of the most important elements of a plan. That is the BUSINESS MODEL. There are millions of great ideas out there; it is those that can be turned into a profitable model that will be funded and developed. Here the authors need to develop how the full business model will work.

Example:

$20,000 Rolex shipped within the United States.
Common insurance premium for jewelry: $3.00 per $100* in value + $100 Fraudian Slip coverage
$20,000/100 = $200
$200* 3 = $600
$600 + $100 = $700
Fraudian Slip Premium:
$20,000 *.01 = $200
Total premium insure charges $900
*(P.A.F. Insurance posted rates)

AUTHOR NOTE
This is an excellent section that is too wordy. This needs to be turned into a graph/chart/picture that achieves the same result.

Marketing

Sales Cycle/Customer Acquisition: Cargo-related crime is estimated to cost the United States economy more than $12 billion annually in merchandise losses (Source: FM Global website).

The target market is the 15 largest underwriters of freight insurance. These underwriters provide insurance to FedEx, UPS, as well as International Intermodal cargo carriers. This is a relatively concentrated industry, which means very few companies share a very large risk.

A partial list of target customers includes:

- Parcel Insurance Plan: UPS and FedEx
- Catlin Group: Capacity is up to US $30 million on any one shipment
- FM Global
- P.A.F. Insurance

Our sales force will research and target certain people within the insurance providers, including but not limited to, policy makers, risk analysts, and risk mitigation officers. Decision makers, once identified, will be contacted. Our service will be compelling, and we will acquire customers because:

- Fraudian Slip will reduce the dollar amount underwriters will pay out thus increasing their profitability and lowering their risk exposure.

- Tiered packages will offer varying levels of service, and offerings can be tailored to the needs of the individual customer.

A graphic representation of this process is below:

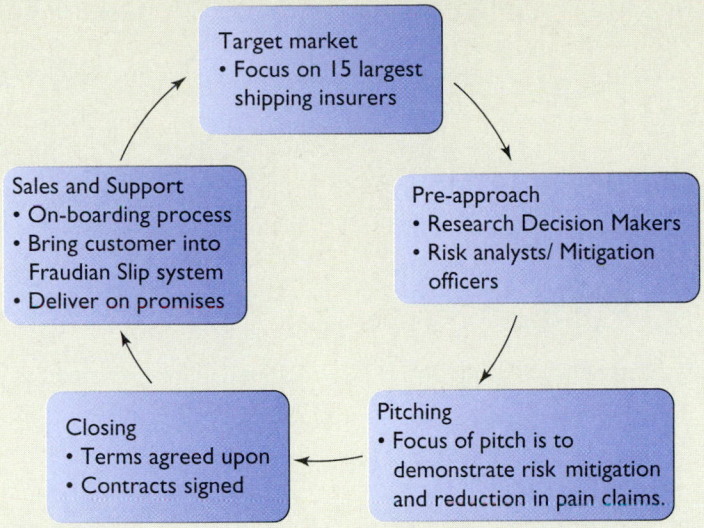

Milestones

Fraudian Slip, currently in the pre-seed stage, is looking to partner with a venture capital firm to launch the start-up phase of the risk reduction technology company.

The funding will allow us to:

- Develop a viable technology device.
- Build the products and online service for initial beta testing with customers.
- Develop a marketing and sales plan for the launch.

Initial development will take nine months, followed by product testing with customers for approximately five months, then a full launch. This short time is due to sourcing the devices and not fully developing them. Many of the foundations for this technology, such as multisensor and real-time GPS devices, are already available and are used in global supply chains. We will license the current technology and incorporate it into our design while developing the online application. The online application will allow users to view real-time data such as location, temperature, and light exposure to determine if a package has been opened while in transit. The following is a high-level schedule of some significant milestones for this initiative:

AUTHOR NOTE

There is a rule of thumb we have already discussed in the text. That is, all plans take twice as long as you expect and cost twice as much. The authors need to detail out the steps with a timeline and cost column for each of the bigger elements they list below in their Milestone chart.

MILESTONE	MILESTONE GOAL
Complete Design Specifications—Tracking Device	The architectural design satisfies all product requirements, is FAA, DOT, UL, and FCC approved, and is suitable for input into the detailed design process.
Complete Prototype	Design implemented, approved, and is suitable for device development.
Complete Online Application	Design implemented, approved, and is suitable for input into the development of code.
Sales and Marketing to Acquire Customers	Approved sales and marketing plan implemented.
Testable Version of Device and Online Application—Beta	Preidentified initial customers will conduct beta testing.
Ship Final Version to Customers	With testing completed, final version ready for shipping to customers.

Upon investment of capital for Fraudian Slip, a detailed schedule will be created by the assigned project team to include all tasks and deliverables.

Exit Strategy

Exit Timing

- Anticipate an exit in approximately 5 years of receiving funding. However, the optimal time to harvest will be assessed on an ongoing basis by monitoring current EBITDA and the median EV/EBITDA multiple within the Commercial and Professional Services industry.

Mode of Exit

- Mode of exit will likely be a disposition to an established investment firm or a firm that is attracted to the relationship with shipping and/or the insurance industries—two industries that will never disappear.
- No intention to merge with another company based on existing goals of ownership individuals. However, ownership will consider a merger if it is determined to be in the best interest of the shareholders.
- Do not anticipate that an IPO will be the optimal exit strategy because of the requirement to disclose certain information that competitors can access and to avoid difficulties with vendors.

Estimated Reversionary Value Range

- Anticipated median EV/EBITDA multiple range for Commercial and Professional Services industry in year 5 is 9.0–10.0 times EBITDA.
- Projected EBITDA in year 5 is $963,400.

AUTHOR NOTE

This is a crucial section for an investor. This needs to be fully developed.

1. Who might be interested in acquiring this company?
2. What is the company worth? Need to do a valuation analysis.
3. Need to reference the Pro Forma Cash Flow chart (another reason to put it at the end) and explain how these numbers work.
4. Where did the EBITA number come from for the industry? How did the authors calculate it for the Fraudian Slip?

Harvest is a tough issue. Some investors don't like to see anything about harvesting because they want the founders committed to success. Most investors want to look at this potential in great detail before they consider investing and would require far greater financial information.

This plan is a great foundation for that effort and could easily be extended.

glossary

A

activity ratios Ratios that measure the efficiency with which you are handling the resources of the business.

ADA Americans with Disabilities Act.

agency theory A managerial theory that argues that individuals act to maximize their own benefit. Thus, in settings where there is a split between ownership and control (most publicly traded corporations), the agents (managers) must be monitored, or they will act to maximize their own benefit, not necessarily that of those who own the firm (the shareholders).

anchor stores Major retail stores, such as department stores in a mall. They serve as the anchor for the retail establishment.

asset-based lending A loan provided for the purchase of a necessary asset for the business.

asset lease A form of lease tied to a particular asset used by a business to conserve cash and maintain the latest versions of whatever equipment is available.

asset valuation A method of business valuation that simply totals all of the hard assets of the organization and adds in a goodwill value.

B

balance sheet Summary of the assets and liabilities of the small business.

benchmarking Working with and learning from a company outside of your industry that has a particular skill that is potentially critical to your operation.

board of advisors Individuals outside the small business that advise the firm; formed at the discretion of the founders (regardless of the legal form chosen).

bonus A reward offered to the employees based on their performance; similar to profit sharing. Typically, bonus systems are not as well defined as profit sharing; instead, the level of reward is left more to the discretion of the small business owner.

bootstrap marketing Marketing efforts that require little capital.

bounded rationality Rational decision making that is constrained by the background and history of the person making the decision.

brainstorming A creative process whereby a group of individuals are brought together and asked to generate ideas with little or no effort made to evaluate the potential for each idea.

break-even analysis Tool for the analysis of when the firm will reach breakeven.

break-even point The level where revenue coming into the firm is sufficient to cover expenses. When starting a business, it will take time for the business to reach this level.

budget Projection of all the costs that will be incurred by the organization over, say, the next year, and allocation of that expense evenly over the relevant time period.

business angels High-net-worth individuals that invest in businesses; a business angel does so not as a business, but as an individual.

business brokers Businesses that specialize in selling businesses.

C

capabilities Resources that combine to allow the firm to perform functions.

capitalization of earnings valuation A method of valuation achieved by taking the earnings (net profit) of the organization, subtracting out or adding back to it any unusual items that the lender or investor feels are not customary, normal, or usual items, and dividing that figure by a capitalization rate.

cash flow Total dollar inflow minus total dollar outflow of the business.

commission Some percentage of sales, paid by the small business owner and typically associated with the compensation of sales representatives.

competitive advantage Those things that your business does better than anyone else in your industry.

competitive map An analytical tool used to organize information about direct competitors on all points of competition.

contract An agreement between two parties to perform certain activities for some consideration.

contract sales force Independent salespeople with a wide variety of experiences and contacts, provided by companies on a contract basis.

copyright Ownership of creative materials the copyright holder has generated, such as books, magazines, advertising copy, music, artwork, or virtually any other creative product, whether published or unpublished.

cost-plus pricing The price of a product or service, obtained by the small-business person's initial determination of the cost structure, followed by the owner's determination of the desired profit margin, and finally, the addition of that profit to the cost.

credit card Card entitling the owner to use of revolving credit that is not tied to any particular asset, does not have a set repayment schedule, and is usually tied to a much higher relative interest rate.

critical path chart Chart that demonstrates how the activities necessary to start the firm fit together and build on each other. This chart allows you to understand which activities can occur concurrently and which must already be in place before the next activity can occur.

crowdfunding Funds received by a business by soliciting a large number of very small investors usually via the Internet.

current assets Assets such as cash or those assets that can easily be converted to cash, such as accounts receivable and notes receivable.

current liabilities Liabilities or debts that the small business has to pay within one year. These include accounts payable, notes payable (such as bank notes), and accrued payroll.

D

debt A generic term to describe any type of non-equity funding tied to the business.

deviation analysis Analysis of the differences between the predicted and the actual performance.

discrimination Hiring, dismissal, level of pay, or promotions based on the basis of race, color, gender, religious beliefs, or national origin of the employee. Such actions are prohibited by federal and state laws.

draw A distribution of funds from the business. It is usually in the form of a cash dispersion in advance of salary, a bonus, an expected year-end distribution, and the like.

E

economic rent Financial gains garnered from an asset or capability that are in excess of the ordinary returns in that particular industry.

economies of scale A condition that allows the long-run average cost to continue downward as production increases. It leads (in its most extreme case) to a condition where a single firm producing 100 percent of the production is the most efficient. In reality this condition is moderated by the ability of management to control the size.

elasticity of demand Consumers' response to price changes. For example, as the price of luxury items increase, the demand usually declines as these goods are not essential and their purchase can be delayed. This would be called elastic demand. However, items such as cancer drugs typically have inelastic demand as you will not stop using them as price increases.

entrepreneurial breakeven When a new venture's net cash flows exceed the initial investment plus the time value of the money invested.

equity Investment in the small business by the owners of the firm.

equity investment Funds received by the business in exchange for a percentage ownership of the business.

equity theory The theory that we all judge how we are treated relative to how we see others being treated.

exit barrier Barriers, such as investment in capital assets, that keep a firm from leaving that industry.

F

factoring The practice of selling accounts receivable at a discount to another company in order to receive immediate cash.

Fair Labor Standards Act (FSLA) The act that established a minimum wage for workers.

family business A business that is run by and for a particular family.

first-mover advantage The phenomenon whereby the first firm to a market obtains the loyalty of the customers.

fixed assets Assets that have a physical presence; they include land, buildings, office equipment, machinery, and vehicles.

fixed costs Costs that must be paid no matter how many goods are sold, such as rent for the building.

float The difference between when the money goes out and when it comes in. For example, if you deposit a check today in payment for some good, typically you do not receive cash when you deposit it. Instead, there is a period of float before it is credited to your account.

followers: Firms that enter a market after the first mover.

Fortune 500 The list published annually by Fortune magazine listing the 500 largest corporations (by sales) in the United States.

fragmented markets Markets in which no one competitor has a substantial share of the market and the means of competition varies widely within the same market space.

franchise agreement The basic contract generated by the franchisor for all franchisees; it usually contains clauses requiring the purchase of supplies, the displaying of marketing material, and the payment of fees that are based upon the sales of the branch operation.

franchisee The entrepreneur that buys the franchise from the franchisor.

franchisor The firm that originates the idea for the business and develops the operational methods, all of which are then sold to franchisees.

G

gap analysis A relatively simple process of systematically examining the difference between what was expected and what occurred. Thus, there is an examination as part of opportunity analysis of opportunities in the marketplace and the individual firm's ability to address those gaps with its accumulated skills, history, and so on.

general partner In an LLP, the individual considered the manager of the firm, who, as such, has unlimited liability for any debts or judgments against the firm.

grants Special funds, neither equity or debt, designed to aid businesses in specific areas.

H

harvest plan A plan to exit the small business. This typically means sell the business to another firm or take it to an IPO.

hourly wage The amount paid per hour for work performed.

human resources Defined in economics as the quantity and quality of human effort directed toward producing goods and services.

hybrid compensation system A system employed by a small business where there is a salary along with the commission.

income statement Revenue of the firm minus expenses.

incubator Facilities that house new businesses, providing many critical services for these new businesses.

independent representatives Representative for a variety of products for a number of companies in that given domain who tries to sell those products.

industry Those direct competitors selling similar products/services within a specified geographic radius that is consistent with a customer's willingness to travel to purchase the product/service.

initial public offering (IPO) The initial listing of a firm as a public entity in the public equities market.

intangible assets Resources and capabilities in a business that are not physical but are just as critical to success, such as relationships with a key supplier.

job description Description of the duties involved in a job that is to be filled.

legitimacy The acceptance by key stakeholders, such as customers and suppliers, that you are a genuine business that will still be in operation next year.

leverage ratios Financial calculations used to examine the relative level of indebtedness of the small business.

liquidity ratios Financial calculations that measure the short-term ability of the firm to meet its obligations.

LLC A limited liability corporation.

LLP A limited liability partnership.

loan A contractual agreement whereby the firm receives some amount of money that must be repaid over a specified period of time at a specified interest rate.

long-term liabilities Liabilities that are owed by the business and are ultimately due more than a year from the current date. These include mortgages payable; owners' equity; and stockholders' equity, which is the investment by these individuals in the business.

loss leader A product sold by a business at a non-operating loss (i.e., the price accounts for only the actual cost of the product) to simply get customers in the store.

market estimation A method of business valuation that involves taking the earnings of the small business and multiplying that figure by the market premium of companies in its industry.

marketing plan The plan developed by the small business to specify who the customers are and how they will be attracted to the company.

metric A measure to evaluate whether a person or firm is meeting its goals.

mission statement A brief statement that summarizes how and where the firm will compete.

mixed-model promotions Promotions that have a cost but also have an element of community support.

normal or ordinary competitive factor Describing those areas of a business that are simply standard practice in the industry and are necessary for the business to be a player.

organizational slack Excess resources in an organization; typically found in large organizations rather than small businesses.

OSHA The Occupational Safety and Health Administration, which is charged with protecting the health of workers.

partnership A category of business formation that includes both general and limited types.

patent A claim of intellectual property that covers a specific innovation.

performance review A review by the small business owner of an employee's goals and the outcomes on those goals over some given time period.

perquisites Benefits paid for by the company. Examples include vacations, vehicles, loans, gifts, and financial contributions to retirement plans.

price/earnings (P/E) ratio A value derived from public companies that divides the current earnings per share into the price per share.

pricing floor The break-even point, or the lowest amount that can be charged.

production chart A chart that provides a detailed understanding of a firm's production process.

profit and loss statement (P&L statement) A financial statement that summarizes the revenues, costs, and expenses incurred during a specific period of time.

profit sharing A firm's offer to share a percentage of the profits at the end of the year or some other period of time with the employees. This is used, for example, in a hybrid system, in which the firm may set some relatively low level for salary.

profitability ratios Financial calculations that evaluate the performance of the firm and its ability to make economic rents over and above its costs.

pro forma Method by which a business owner estimates what the balance sheets and income statements will look like at some point in the future.

promotion The means by which a small business advances its product or service.

pure promotions Promotions that are strictly a financial arrangement in which you pay for some output, such as a radio advertisement.

ratio analysis A series of ratios along four areas of company performance (liquidity, activity, leverage, profitability) that provides a picture of the health of the company.

resource-based analysis A methodology and theoretical approach that examines the functioning of the business in terms of whether a product or service simultaneously meets the criteria of being rare, durable, nonsubstitutable and valuable.

S

salary A set amount of compensation for a given time period.

sales management The method, means, and individuals that produce the relationship with the customer.

sensitivity analysis An examination of the best- and worst-case cash flow scenarios.

shrinkage The difference between what is sold and what was brought into the business.

Small Business Assistance Centers Centers funded by the Small Business Administration that advise individuals wishing to start new businesses.

sole proprietorship The simplest form of business organization, characterized by the fact that the person who owns the business and the business itself are treated as the same entity.

stakeholders Individuals or other organizations that impact the success of the business.

strategic alliances Firms joined together to form long-term, mutually complementary relationships.

strategy The broad approaches the small business will use to accomplish its mission.

strip shopping center A small retail center located typically along a major road. The center has only small businesses, and the center itself occupies only a small strip of land along the major street.

Subchapter C Corporation An organizational form that treats the firm as a unique entity responsible for its own taxes. There are no limitations to shareholder participation and the "owners" are protected beyond their equity investment.

Subchapter S Corporation An organizational form that treats the firm as an entity separate from the individuals. This allows the owner(s) to treat the income as they would if the firm were a sole proprietorship or a partnership. It has limitations in the number and type of shareholders.

substitute A product that performs a similar function or achieves the same result, but is not a precise imitation.

supplier credit Another form of non-equity funding that is available. Suppliers often will provide credit on both physical assets (refrigerators, molding equipment, etc.) and the actual supplies provided.

sustainable competitive advantage An advantage that others cannot immediately copy.

synergy The connection between the entrepreneur's skills, understanding of an industry, and the ability to create a competitive advantage such that the sum of the parts of the new business is greater than the individual parts alone.

T

tangible assets Hard assets, such as equipment or a location.

threats to operational financing Specific threats to the new venture in financing its growth, including high development costs, rapid expansion plans, high inventory needs, and/or an entrepreneurial team with a low asset base.

threats to profit margin The threats created to the success of a new venture related to its ability to establish and maintain a high-margin product or service.

threats to sales generation schemes Threats created to a new venture regarding its opportunity to sell to many customers and to obtain repeat business.

time value of money The calculation of the value of your investment in time and money if you did not do the proposed venture, based on the realization that there are other uses of your investment dollars and your raw time.

trademark Claim of intellectual property that is associated with a specific business. This may be the name of the firm, a symbol representing the firm, or its products.

turnaround The effort to reverse the decline of a business.

U

unemployment compensation The provision of financial assistance for some period of time to those people who lose their jobs through no fault of their own; every state has a law providing such assistance.

Uniform Franchise Offering Circular (UFOC) The principal governing mechanism of the franchisor/franchisee relationship.

United States Small Business Administration (SBA; www.sba.gov) The agency officially organized in 1953 as a part of the Small Business Act of July 30, 1953, to "aid, counsel, assist and protect, insofar as is possible, the interests of small business concerns." It is a wealth of information and assistance at all levels of organizational development and management.

unusual or unique competitive factor Describing those areas of a business that are unique or unusual when compared to the standard practices of the industry, and that provide the opportunity for the business to gain value over and above the ordinary returns in the industry.

V

variable costs Expenses that vary according to how many goods are sold or produced.

venture capital fund A fund that is organized to make significant equity investments in high-growth new ventures.

virtually free promotions Promotions that have a very limited financial cost but have a time-commitment requirement from someone in the firm.

W

workers' compensation The provision by law of some type of compensation to employees who are disabled or injured while on the job.

case index

A

Adams, Greg, 280–281
Alton's Kitchen & Cocktails, 296–297

B

Barber, Nick, 288–289
Barry, Jeff, 294–295

C

Carpe Diem Private Preschool, 284–285
Case studies
- Adams, Greg, 280–281
- Barber, Nick, 288–289
- Barry, Jeff, 294–295
- Clary, Steve, 274–275
- Davis, Beau, 272–273
- Gasmire, Charlie, 282–283
- Grassia, Gary, 298–299
- Grassia, Jennie, 298–299
- Hooks, Andrew, 292–293
- Kezengwa, Charles, 278–279
- Murphree, Ashley, 284–285
- Shivar, Joy, 290–291
- Solitario, Paul, 286–287
- Updike, Alton, 296–297
- Ward, Cassmer, 276–277

Clary, Steve, 274–275
Cornelius Pet Care, 292–293

D

Davis, Beau, 272–273

G

Gasmire, Charlie, 282–283
Grassia, Gary, 298–299
Grassia, Jennie, 298–299

H

Hannington Massage, 278–279
Hooks, Andrew, 292–293

I

International ThermoDyne, 286–287

K

Kezengwa, Charles, 278–279

M

Murphree, Ashley, 284–285

O

OCJ Apparel, 280–281

R

RavioliOli, 294–295

S

Shivar, Joy, 290–291
Sigma Relocation Group, LLC, 288–289
Solitario, Paul, 286–287
Steve's Barber Chair, 274–275

T

TheClearCollar, 276–277
The Varsity, 272–273
Trifork Enterprises, LLC, 298–299

U

Updike, Alton, 296–297

V

Vendevor, 282–283

W

Ward, Cassmer, 276–277
www.JustAJoy.com, 290–291

subject index

Page numbers followed by n refer to notes.

A

Accounting
  accounts payable, 132
  chart of accounts, 130
  check register, 131
  expense accounts, 131
  in franchises, 260
  inventory account, 131
  managing data flow, 133–134
  payroll, 132–133
  petty cash register, 131
  preparing business for sale and, 245–247
  Profit and Loss Statement (P&L Statement), 132–133
  software for, 133
Account receivable turnover, 144
Accounts payable, 132
Accrual-basis accounting system, 129
Acid test, 143
Activity ratios, 143–145
  account receivable turnover, 144
  calculating, 144–145
  defined, 143
  inventory turnover, 144
  total/fixed asset turnover, 144
ADA. *See* Americans with Disabilities Act (ADA)
Adler, Alan, 119
Advertising, 201, 204. *See also* Marketing; Promotion
  newspaper, 200, 205
Advertising agency, 205
AeroPress, 119
Agency theory, 22
Amazon.com, 4, 211
Americans with Disabilities Act (ADA), 170, 192
Anchor stores, 222
Angel investors. *See* Business angels
Apple computers, 4
Asset-based lending, 123
Asset lease, 127
Assets
  activity ratios and, 144
  balance sheets and, 111–112, 140
  current assets, 111–112, 140
  debt-to-assets ratio, 145
  extraordinary assets, 85–86
  fixed assets, 111–112, 140
  return on assets (ROA), 146
  tangible/intangible, 85
  valuation, 243–244

B

Balance sheets, 111–112, 140
  defined, 111
  pro forma, 111
Bank of America, 137
Bankruptcy, 251–252, 262, 267
  franchise process and, 262, 267
Banks, 123, 224
Bed Bath & Beyond, 11
Benchmarking, 69–70
Benefits, employee, 187–189
Best Buy, 5, 78
Big Five Test, 26–27
Bing, 205
Bloomberg Businessweek, 197
Bloostein, Oren, 3
Board of advisors, 173–174
Board of directors, 173–174
Bonding, 172
Bonding insurance, 172. *See also* Insurance
Bonus system, 187
Bootstrap marketing, 207
Bounded rationality, 25
Bowen, Adam, 197
Brainstorming, 45
Branson, Richard, 4
Breakeven, 115–116
Break-even analysis, 114–116
Break-even point, 24
  defined, 24
  in entrepreneurial ventures, 115–116
  in pricing, 202
Briggs, Katherine, 26
Budget
  versus cash flow statements, 101–106
  defined, 101
  developing cash flow statements and, 106–109
  example of, 101–102
Business angels, 12, 127
Business brokers, 267
Business exit, 234–253
  avenues for sale of business, 247–248
  closing the business, 251–252
  ease of, 69
  harvest plan, 12, 236–238
  negotiation strategies, 248–249
  preparing business for sale, 245–247
  recording informal practices and, 246–247
  steps in selling a business, 238–249
  timing of, 236–238
  valuation, 238–245
Business ideas, 39–44
  additional skills, 42–44
  choosing a business, 46–53
  deficit analysis, 53
  education, 41
  family experiences, 42
  generating, 39–44
  hobbies and activities, 40–41
  initial analysis, 46–47
  opportunity identification, 44–45
  skills analysis, 40
  work experience, 41–42
Business incubators, 32, 225
Business mission. *See* Mission statements
Business plans
  building, 300–303
  business purchase and, 267
  business strategy, 301
  executive summary, 300–301
  financial analysis, 302
  history and position of the business to date, 301
  key parts of, 300–303
  market research, 301
  operations, 302–303
  risk analysis, 303
  small *versus* entrepreneurial firms, 11–12
Business purchase, 267
Business risk, 50
Business strategy, 301. *See* Strategy
Business threats. *See* Threats to business success
Business turnaround, 249–251
BusinessWeek, 137
By-laws of the organization, 166

C

Camp, Garret, 37
Canace, T. G., 98n
Capabilities
  defined, 80
  developing list of, 85
  durability of, 88
  ease of substitution of, 88
  evaluating competitiveness of, 87–89
  rareness of, 88
  value of, 88–89
Capitalization of earnings valuation, 244
Caribou, 3
Carnegie, Andrew, 6
Carter, Jimmy, 7
Case studies. *See also* Flow Right Brewery & Bar; Friend's Home Health
  AeroPress, 119
  Guayakí Sustainable Rainforest Products, Inc., 57
  Indigo IT, 215
  La Madeleiné, 255
  Numi Organic Tea, 97
  Oren's Daily Roast, 3
  Philly Pretzel, 19
  Ploom, 197
  Tealuxe, 235
  UberCab, 37
  USA Gypsum, 177
  VaVaVroomonline.com, 137
  Weedmaps, 157
  Zane's Cycles, 77
Cash-basis accounting system, 129
Cash flow, 96–117
  analysis, 100–106
  balance sheet and, 111–112
  break-even analysis and, 114–116
  versus budgets, 101–106
  defined, 98
  deviation analysis and, 104–106
  float, 101
  income statement and, 112–114
  initial funding and, 128
  versus profit, 98
  sensitivity analysis and, 108
  understanding, 98
  valuation and, 239–242
Cash flow statements
  versus budget, 101–106
  developing, 106–110

deviation analysis and, 104–106
examples of, 102–105, 240
expenses and, 107–108
projected, 150, 151, 152
revenues and, 107–108
sensitivity analysis and, 108, 149–150
Cash inflows, 107
Chapter 7 bankruptcy, 252
Chapter 11 bankruptcy, 251–252
Chapter 12 bankruptcy, 252
Chapter 13 bankruptcy, 252
Chart of accounts, 130
Check register, 131
Cheers, 208
Chrome, 205
Circuit City, 78
Circumstance motivators, 28
Cisco, 126
Civil Rights Act, 182
Clinton Foundation Global Initiative, 57
Coca-Cola Company, 171
Coffin, Charles, 4
Commission, 186
Community support, 32, 206
Compensation, 185–187
bonus system, 187
commission, 186
equity theory and, 185–186
hourly wage, 186
hybrid compensation system, 186
legal issues with, 187
profit sharing, 186–187
salary, 186
unemployment compensation, 192
workers' compensation, 172, 191–192
Competitive advantage, 70–73. *See also* Sustainable competitive advantage
defined, 70
location used as, 221–223
resource-based analysis and, 71–73
sources of, 71–73
timing in starting new business and, 231
Competitive map
criteria list for, 66
defined, 65
development of, 65–68
example of, 67
Competitors, 51
competitive map development and, 65–68
defining, 63–65
developing information about, 62–65
ethics and, 69
industry definition and, 60–62
industry trends and, 70
as threat to business success, 51–53
timing in starting new business and, 231
Contracts
defined, 166
items to include in, 167
leases, 167
Contract sales force, 210–211
Copyrights, 171–172
Corporate name, 165
Corporations, 164–166
limited liability corporation (LLC), 166
Subchapter C corporation, 165–166
Subchapter S corporation, 164–165
Cost/benefit analysis, 32–33
Cost of goods sold, 144
Cost-plus pricing, 203
Costs, fixed/variable, 115
Craig, Rob, 215
Credit cards, 124
Credit sales, 144
Critical path chart, 218–221
defined, 220
examples of, 219
software for, 220
Crowdfunder.com, 30
Current assets, 111–112, 140
Current liabilities, 111–112, 140
Current ratio, 143
Customers
customer lists from former employers, 27
defining, 60–62
elasticity of demand and, 68
target customers, 65, 200–202

D

Danko, William, 8
Debt, 123
credit cards, 124
loans, 123–124
supplier credit, 124
Debt-to-assets ratio, 145
Debt-to-equity ratio, 145–146
Deming, W. Edwards, 228–229
Deviation analysis
cash flow and, 104–106
financial analysis and, 148–149
Discounted future net cash flow, in valuation, 239–240
Discrimination, 182
Distribution channels, 210–212
contract sales force, 210–211
independent sales agents, 210
mail-order catalogs, 211–212
Web pages as, 211
DiZio, Dan, 19
Draws, 162
Drug testing, 184–185
Drywall, 177
Due diligence, 53

E

E-cigarettes, 197
Economic Gardening, 9
Economic rents, 87
Economies of scale, 5, 22
Edison, Thomas, 4
Education, 41
Elasticity of demand, 68
"Elevator pitches," 47
Employee benefits, 187–189
Employee firing, 190
Employee hiring, 179–185
discrimination, 182
establishing operations and, 224
interviews, 182–184
job advertising, 181–182
job description, 180–181
job offer, 185
references, 181, 183–184
testing, 184–185
Employee probation, 190
Employee retention
benefits, 187–189
compensation, 185–187
performance reviews, 189–190
Employer Identification Number, 169
Enneagram personality test, 26
Entrepreneurial breakeven, 115–116
Entrepreneurs
circumstance motivations of, 28
enjoying business, 33–34
evaluating entrepreneurial orientation of, 23–27
personality of, 25–27
personal motivation of, 28
prior experience of, 24–25
risk tolerance of, 23–24
skills and experience of, 41–42
small business success and, 20
supports of, 29–33
training for, 44
triggers for starting a business, 27–28
Entry barrier, 69
Equal Pay Act, 187
Equipment, 229–230
Equity
debt-to-equity ratio, 145–146
defined, 100
initial funding and, 128
return on equity (ROE), 146, 147
Equity funding. *See also* Equity investments
business angels, 127
businesses as equity investors, 126
crowdfunding, 127
venture capital fund, 126–127
Equity investments. *See also* Equity funding
business angels, 12, 127
businesses making, 126
crowdfunding, 127
defined, 122
venture capital fund, 12, 126–127
Equity theory, 185–186
Esquerré, Patrick Leon, 255
Ethics
business goals and, 10
competitor information and, 69
competitors and, 87, 154
customer lists from former employers and, 27
investors and, 129
legal issues and, 167, 246
mission statements and, 87
risk analysis with family finances and, 51
in sales, 206
European Union, 12
Executive summary, of business plan, 300–301
Exit barrier, 69
Expense accounts, 131
Expenses, 107–108
External analysis, 57–73
benchmarking, 69–70
competitive advantage, 70–73
competitive map development, 65–68
competitor information, 62–65
defining your customers, 60–62
defining your industry, 58–60
ease of entry or exit, 69
elasticity of demand, 68
industry trends, 70
overview, 58
substitutes and, 68
External environment examination, 58
Extraordinary assets, 85–86

F

Facebook, 4, 8
Factoring, 128
Fair Labor Standards Act (FLSA), 187
Family businesses, 20, 29–30, 192–193. *See also* Flow Right Brewery & Bar
Family history, in skills analysis, 40
Farrah, Ron Brilland Pat, 4

Fast Company magazine, 197
FDA. *See* Food and Drug Administration (FDA)
Fernie, Bruce, 235
Financial analysis, 137–155, 302
  deviation analysis, 148–149
  financial foundation, 138
  measurement focus, 153–154
  measuring the firm, 138–141
  ratio analysis, 141–148
  sensitivity analysis, 149–150
  short surveys, 150–153
Financial cushion, 122
Financial tools
  balance sheets, 111–112, 140
  break-even analysis, 114–116
  income statements, 112–114, 141
Financing, 119–135
  accounting, 129–134
  establishing operations and, 223–224
  for franchises, 262
  funding, 122–129
  identifying key issues, 120–122
  support for start-up, 32–33, 48–49
  threats to operational financing, 50–51
Firefox, 205
First mover advantage, 86
Five Guys, 4
Fixed assets, 111–112, 140
Fixed costs, 115
Float, 101
Flow, Chris, 31
Flow Right Brewery & Bar
  business exit, 249
  business idea generation, 43
  cash flow statement development, 110
  establishing operations, 230
  external analysis, 65
  financial analysis, 149
  financing and accounting, 133
  franchising a business, 266
  human resources, 191
  licensing, 173
  marketing, 208
  mission statement, 93
  start-up, 31
FLSA. *See* Fair Labor Standards Act (FLSA)
Flyers, 205
Followers, 86
Food and Drug Administration (FDA), 197
Ford, Henry, 4
Ford Motor Company, 4
Forms of business
  corporations, 164–166
  partnerships, 161–164
  sole proprietorship, 160–161
Fortune 500 companies
  break-even analysis and, 115
  defined, 4
  financial analysis and, 143
  financing and, 224
401(k) program, 189
Fragmented markets, 64
Franchise agreement, 257
Franchisee
  defined, 257
  obligations of, 262
  restrictions on, 263
  training for, 261
  vetting of, 264
Franchising, 254–269
  buying a franchise, 259–265
  buying an existing business, 265–268
  elements of, 257–258
  examples of, 257–258, 264–265
  franchise process, 263–265
  government requirements for, 261–263
  production charting and, 227
  supports for, 260–261
Franchisor
  defined, 257
  ethics and, 265
  money making by, 258
  obligations of, 262
Franklin, Ben, 177
Freud, Sigmund, 26
Friedman, Milton, 10
Friend's Home Health
  business exit, 237
  business idea generation, 38–39
  cash flow statement, 99
  customer definition for, 61
  establishing operations, 217–218
  financial analysis, 139
  financing and accounting, 121–122
  franchising a business, 256–257
  human resources, 178
  industry definition, 61
  legal issues, 159
  marketing, 199
  mission statement, 80
  start-up, 21
Funding, 122–129
  asset leasing, 127–128
  equity investments, 124–127
  factoring, 128
  initial funding, 128–129
  non-equity funding, 122–124

G

Gap analysis, 44, 47–53
  business threats, 50–53
  competitors and, 51–53
  finances and, 48–49
  nonfinancial resources and, 49
  overview, 47
  risk in, 49–50
  time and, 49
General Accounting Office, 9
General Electric, 4
General Motors, 7, 22, 188
General partner, 126, 163
General partnership, 161–163
Geographic market, 200
Glamajama, 11
GlamaLIFE.com, 11
"Glass ceiling," 10, 28
Google, 14, 205
GQ magazine, 197
Grants, 124
Great Depression, 6
Gross profit margin, 146, 147
Group Le Duff, 255
Guayakí Sustainable Rainforest Products, Inc., 57
Guinness Book of World Records, 119

H

Hartfield, Justin, 157
Harvest plan, 12, 236–238. *See also* Business exit
Health insurance, 188
Hewlett, Bill, 8
Hewlett-Packard (HP), 8
High-growth business, 127
Hobbies and activities, 40–41
Hoerling, Keith, 157
Home Depot, 4
Hourly wage, 186
Human resource management, 176–195
  Americans with Disabilities Act (ADA) and, 192
  compensation, 185–187
  elements of, 179
  employee hiring, 179–185
  employee probation and firing, 190
  employee retention, 185–190
  family businesses and, 192–193
  for franchises, 261
  human resources, defined, 179
  Occupational Safety and Health Administration (OSHA) and, 192
  unemployment compensation law and, 192
  workers' compensation laws and, 191–192
Hybrid compensation system, 186

I

IBM Credit LLC, 124
Inc. magazine, 77
Income statements, 112–114, 141
Incubators, 32, 225
Independent representatives, 210
Indigo IT, 215
Industry
  defined, 60
  defining, in external analysis, 58–60
  economic rents and, 87
  NAICS codes for, 59
  research of, 62–63
  trends in, 70
Industry, defined, 60
Industry associations, 58
Initial public offering (IPO), 12, 247
Insurance, 172, 188–189
  bonding, 172
  health, 165
  liability, 168, 172
  property, 172
  workers' compensation, 172
Intangible assets, 85
Intel, 126
Interest, 145–146
International Franchise Association, 258, 264
Internet. *See* Web pages
Interviews, 182–184
Inventory
  in financial analysis, 143–145
  inventory account, 131
  inventory turnover, 144
  just-in-time (JIT) inventory, 133
  shrinkage, 131

J

J.C. Penney, 11
Job advertising, 181–182
Job description, 180–181
Job interviews, 182–184
Jobs, Steve, 4, 8
JTI, 197
Jung, Carl, 26
Just-in-time (JIT) inventory, 133

K

Kalanick, Travis, 37
Karr, Steve, 57
Kelleher, Herb, 25
Kickstarter.com, 30
Knievel, Evel, 24
Kroger, Barney, 4

L

LaSalle Bank, 137
Lauder, Estee, 4
Lauren, Ralph, 4

Layoffs, 28
Leases
asset leasing, 127–128
as contract, 167
real estate agents and, 223
Legal issues, 156–175
board of advisors and/or board of directors, 173–174
with compensation, 187
contracts, 166–167
copyrights/trademarks/patents, 171–172
ethics and, 167
forms of business, 160–166
franchises and, 265
insurance, 172
laws, rules, and regulations, 169–171
leases, 167–169
licensing, 170–171
overview, 158–160
Legitimacy, 224–225
Leverage ratios, 142, 145–146
calculating, 145–146
debt-to-assets ratio, 145
debt-to-equity ratio, 145
defined, 145
times interest earned, 145
Liabilities
balance sheets and, 111–112, 140
current/long-term liabilities, 111, 140
in partnerships, 163–164
of sole proprietorship, 160–161
Liability insurance, 168, 172
Licensing, 170–171
Limited liability corporation (LLC), 166
Limited liability partnership (LLP), 163
LinkedIn, 13
Liquidity ratios, 141–143
calculating, 143
current ratio, 143
defined, 141
quick (acid) ratio, 143
Liquor licenses, 170
LLC. *See* Limited liability corporation (LLC)
LLP. *See* Limited liability partnership (LLP)
Loans, 123–124
Location
competitive advantage and, 86
mission statement and, 83
as nonfinancial resource, 49
operations and, 221–223
as tangible asset, 85
Long-term liabilities, 111
Lorillard, 197
Loss leader, 202

Mail-order catalogs, 211–212
Maple, Denise, 137
Marcus, Stanley, 255
Marijuana, 157
Marijuana Enforcement Division, in Colorado, 157
Market
fragmented market, 64
geographic market, 200
market estimation, 244
target customer and, 60, 200–202
Market estimation valuation, 244
Marketing, 196–213
bootstrap marketing, 207
distribution channels, 210–212
in franchises, 261
identifying market, 198–200
marketing plan, 198–202
pricing, 202–204
promotion, 204–207
sales management, 207–212
target customer and, 60–62, 200–202
Market research, 62–63, 301. *See also* External analysis
McDonald's, 228, 257
Medical insurance, 188. *See also* Health insurance
Metrics, 82–83
Microsoft, 126
Millionaire Next Door, The (Stanley and Danko), 8, 13
Minority Enterprise Development Program, 32
Mission statements, 78–83. *See also* Strategy
defined, 78
design of, 80–83
effective *versus* ineffective, 80
ethics and, 87
impact of, 83
metrics and, 82–83
overview of, 78–80
Mixed-model promotions, 204
Monsees, James, 197
Myers, Isabel, 26
Myers-Briggs, 26
Myers-Briggs personality test, 26

NAICS. *See* North American Industry Classification System (NAICS)
NAICS (North American Industry Classification System) code, 59
National Venture Capital Association, 127n
Negotiation
in acquiring franchise, 267–268
in sale of business, 248–249
Neiman Marcus department stores, 255
Net profit margin, 146, 147
Net sales, 146
Newspaper advertising, 200, 205
Noncompete agreement, 162–163, 190. *See also* Secrecy agreement
selling a business and, 249
Non-equity funding, 122–124
credit cards, 124
debt, 123
grants, 124
loans, 123–124
supplier credit, 124
Nonfinancial resources, 49
Nordstrom, 11
NORML (lobbying group), 157
North American Industry Classification System (NAICS), 59
Numi Organic Tea, 97

Occupational Safety and Health Administration (OSHA), 170, 192
Operating income, 145, 146
Operating profit margin, 146, 147
Operations, 214–233
critical path chart, 218–221
equipment, 229–230
financing considerations, 223–224
initial actions for, 216–218
legitimacy, 224–225
location lease/purchase, 221–223
production charting, 226–228
production management, 226
quality, investment in, 228–229
threats to operational financing, 50–51
time management and, 231–232
time taken to establish, 231
timing in starting, 231
Operations and business plan, 302–303
Opportunity analysis, 44
Opportunity identification, 44–45, 58
potential businesses, 44
Oren's Daily Roast, 3
Organizational slack, 20, 249, 249n
OSHA. *See* Occupational Safety and Health Administration (OSHA)

Packard, Dave, 8
Partnerships, 161–164
Patents, 171
PAX, 197
Payroll, 132–133
Perdue, Frank, 5
Performance reviews, 189–190
Perquisites, 238
Personality tests, 25–26
Personal motivations, 28
Personal risk, 50
Petty cash register, 131
Pirates of the Caribbean, 81
Ploom, 197
Porter, Michael, 88, 89
Price/earnings (P/E) ratio, in valuation, 242–243
Pricing, 202–204
cost-plus, 203
loss leader and, 202
pricing floor, 202
of services, 203
Pricing floor, 202
Production chart, 227
Production charting, 226–228
Production management, 226
Profit, *versus* cash flow, 98
Profitability ratios, 142, 146–147
calculating, 147
gross profit margin, 146, 147
net profit margin, 146, 147
operating profit margin, 146, 147
return on assets (ROA), 146, 147
return on equity (ROE), 146, 147
Profit and Loss Statement (P&L Statement), 132–133
Profit margin
gross profit margin, 146, 147
net profit margin, 146, 147
operating profit margin, 146, 147
threats to, 50
Profit sharing, 186–187
Pro forma, 111
Promotion, 204–207
defined, 204
mixed-model promotions, 204, 206
pure promotions, 204–206
virtually free promotions, 204, 207
Property insurance, 172. *See also* Insurance
Pryor, Alex, 57
Pure promotions, 204–206
flyers, 205
newspaper advertisement, 205
radio/television advertisement, 205–206
signs, 204
trade shows, 206
Web page and Internet promotion, 205

Quality, investment in, 228–229
Quantity discount, 204
Quick (acid) ratio, 143

Radio advertising, 205–206
Rahim, Ahmed, 97
Rahim, Reem, 97
Ratio analysis, 141–148
  activity ratios, 143–145
  commonly used ratios, 142
  defined, 141
  leverage ratios, 145–146
  liquidity ratios, 141–143
  profitability ratios, 146–147
  summary of ratios, 147–148
Real estate
  leases and, 223
  services for franchises, 261
References, 181, 183–184
Regulations, benefiting new businesses, 169–171
Reinventing the Wheel: The Science of Creating Lifetime Customers (Zane), 77
Resource-based analysis, 72–73
Return on assets (ROA), 146, 147
Return on equity (ROE), 146, 147
Revenues, 107–108
Revised Uniform Partnership Act, 163
Risk, 49–50
  business, 50
  gap analysis and, 49–50
  personal, 50
  ratio analysis and, 142–143
  risk tolerance, 23–24
Risk analysis, 303
Risk Management Association, 143
ROA. *See* Return on assets (ROA)
Roberts, Peter, 167
ROE. *See* Return on equity (ROE)
Rotary Club, 30
Roth 401(k) program, 189

Salary, 186
Sale, of existing business. *See* Business purchase
Sale of business. *See* Business exit
Sales, in ratio analysis, 149–151
Sales management, 207–212
  defined, 207
  distribution channels, 210–212
  ethics and, 206
  forecasting sales, 209–210
  overview, 207–209
  threats to sales generation schemes, 50
SBA. *See* United States Small Business Administration (SBA)
Schedule 1 narcotics, 157
Schuck, Heather, 10–11
Schulze, Richard M., 4–5
SCORE. *See* Service Corps of Retired Executives (SCORE)
Sears, Roebuck and Company, 167
Secrecy agreement, 190. *See also* Non compete agreement
Sensitivity analysis, 108, 149–150
Service Corps of Retired Executives (SCORE), 32
Shrinkage, 131
Signs, 173, 204
Skills analysis, 40
Small business
  around the world, 11
  buying an existing business, 255–269
  choosing a business, 46–53
  cost/benefit analysis, 32–33
  defined, 12
  enjoyment of, 33–34
  versus entrepreneurial business, 11–13, 22–23, 143
  high-growth, 12, 127
  history of, 6–7
  incubators, 32, 225
  owners today, 8
  reasons for starting, 4–6
  society benefits from, 8–11
  start-ups, 4, 11
  supports for, 29–33
  triggers for starting, 27–28
  types of, 12–13
  women as owners, 10–11, 28
Small Business Act of 1953, 4
Small Business Assistance Centers, 32, 93, 110, 124, 170
Small Business Development Centers, 267
Small-to-medium-sized enterprises/businesses (SMEs/SMBs), 12
Social networks, 30–31
Sole proprietorship, 160–161
Sonic, 258
Southern Methodist University, 255
Southwest Airlines, 25
Stakeholders, 8
Stanford University, 119
Stanley, Thomas, 8
Starbucks, 3, 4, 235
Strategic alliances, 229
Strategy, 89–93
  application of, 91–92
  defined, 89
  differentiation approach, 90–91
  low-cost strategy, 89
  steps in developing, 90–91
Strip shopping center, 222
Subchapter C corporations, 165–166
Subchapter S corporations, 164–165
Substitutes, 68, 88
Succession, 193
Super Aerobie flying disc, 119
Supplier credit, 124
Supports for small business, 29–33
  community supports, 32
  family, 29–30, 42
  financial support, 32–33
  social networks, 30–31
Survey, in financial analysis, 150–153
Sustainable competitive advantage. *See also* Competitive advantage
  assets and capabilities, 85
  defined, 84
  first mover advantage, 86
  followers, 86
  identifying, 84–85
Synergy, 40

Tangible assets, 85
Target, 11
Target customer, 60, 200–202
Task chart, 220
Tealuxe, 235
Technological skills, 41
Technology
  accounting software, 133
  production charting software, 226
  project management software, 220
Television advertising, 205–206
Threats to business success
  competitors, 51–53
  due diligence and, 53
  threats to operational financing, 50–51
  threats to profit margin, 50
  threats to sales generation schemes, 50
Threats to operational financing, 50–51
Threats to profit margin, 50
Threats to sales generation schemes, 50
Tiffany's, 59
Time
  critical path chart and, 218–220
  start-up and, 49
  time management, 231–232
  time value of money, 115–116
Times interest earned, 145–146
Timing
  for exiting a business, 236–238
  for starting new business, 231
Title VII of the Civil Rights Act, 182
Tocqueville, Alexis de, 6
Total/fixed asset turnover, 144
Toyota, 188
Trademarks, 171
Trade shows, 206
Training
  of entrepreneurs, 52
  for franchisees, 261
  staff, establishing operations, 224
Triggers, for starting a business, 27–28
Turnaround, 249–251
2/10, Net 30 policy, 121

UberCab, 37
UFOC. *See* Uniform Franchise Offering Circular (UFOC)
Unemployment compensation, 192
Uniform Commercial Code, 159
Uniform Franchise Offering Circular (UFOC), 261
  contents of, 261–263
  defined, 261
Uniform Partnership Act, 163
United States Patent and Trademark Office, 171
United States Small Business Administration (SBA), 4, 32, 57, 170, 267
USA Gypsum, 177

Valuation, 238–245
  asset-based valuation, 243–244
  capitalization of earnings valuation, 244
  discounted future net cash flow method of, 239–242
  market estimation valuation, 244
  overview, 245
  price/earnings (P/E) ratio and, 242–243
Van Wyngaardt, Shane, 215
Van Wynsgaardt, Denise, 215
Variable costs, 115
VaVaVroomonline.com, 137
Venture capital-backed firms, 12
Venture capital fund, 12, 126–127
Venture capital startups, 12
Virgin, 4
Virtually free promotions, 204, 207

W

Walmart, 4, 5
Walton, Sam, 4
Washington, George, 177
Weaver, Terry, 177
Web pages
  as distribution channel, 211
  for promotion, 205
  small business start-up and, 51
Weedmaps, 157
Wilkerson, J. E., 98n
Wilson, Charles, 7
Winfrey, Oprah, 4
Women, 10–11, 28
Workers' compensation, 172, 191–192
Workers' compensation insurance, 172. *See also* Insurance
Work experience, 41–42
Working Mom Manifesto: How to Stop Hoping for Happiness and Start Creating It, The (Schuck), 11
World Bank, 11
Wozniak, Steve, 8

Y

Yahoo!, 205

Z

Zane, Chris, 77
Zuckerberg, Mark, 8